THE FORGOTTEN MEMOIR OF JOHN KNOX

THE FORGOTTEN
MEMOIR
OF JOHN KNOX

A Year in the Life of a Supreme Court Clerk
in FDR's Washington

EDITED AND WITH A FOREWORD
AND AFTERWORD BY
DENNIS J. HUTCHINSON AND
DAVID J. GARROW

THE UNIVERSITY OF CHICAGO PRESS
CHICAGO AND LONDON

JOHN FRUSH KNOX (1907–1997) served as private secretary and law clerk to Supreme Court Justice James C. McReynolds during the October 1936 term. After working at various law firms, he took over the family mail-order business and then worked as an insurance adjuster.

DENNIS J. HUTCHINSON is the William Rainey Harper Professor in the College and Senior Lecturer in Law at the University of Chicago. He is the author of *The Man Who Once Was Whizzer White,* a *New York Times* Notable Book.

DAVID J. GARROW is Presidential Distinguished Professor at the Emory University School of Law and the author of several books, including the Pulitzer Prize–winning *Bearing the Cross.*

The University of Chicago Press, Chicago, 60637
The University of Chicago Press, Ltd., London
© 2002 by Dennis J. Hutchinson and David J. Garrow
All rights reserved. Published 2002
Printed in the United States of America

11 10 09 08 07 06 05 04 03 02   1 2 3 4 5

ISBN: 0-226-44862-2

Library of Congress Cataloging-in-Publication Data
Knox, John, 1907–1997.
    The forgotten memoir of John Knox : a year in the life of a Supreme Court clerk in FDR's Washington / edited and with a foreword and afterword by Dennis J. Hutchinson and David J. Garrow.
        p.   cm.
    Includes bibliographical references and index.
    ISBN 0-226-44862-2 (cloth : alk. paper)
    1. Knox, John, 1907–1997.   2. United States. Supreme Court—Employees—Biography. 3. United States. Supreme Court—History.   4. Law clerks—United States—Biography. I. Hutchinson, Dennis J.   II. Garrow, David J., 1953–   III. Title.
KF373.K (Knox) A3 2002
347.73'2636—dc21
[B]   2002017354

Foreword

THE DOCUMENT you hold is, as its author proudly but anxiously noted, the first of its kind—the personal memoir of a law clerk to a member of the Supreme Court of the United States. John Frush Knox (1907–1997) served as private secretary and law clerk to Justice James C. McReynolds during the October 1936 term of the Court, the year in which President Franklin D. Roosevelt introduced legislation that his critics correctly pointed out was designed to "pack the Court" with justices who would ratify the constitutionality of his New Deal programs. During the previous two terms, the Court had invalidated several legislative components of the New Deal. After his landslide reelection in 1936, Roosevelt introduced a plan which he disingenuously claimed would improve the Court's efficiency by expanding its number by one justice for every one then seventy or older; if enacted the plan would have increased the Court from nine to fifteen members and assured Roosevelt a friendly majority on most constitutional issues raised by the New Deal. McReynolds, age seventy-five, was one of the prime targets of the plan.

Knox kept a daily diary during the term, the extension of a practice he began as a lonely high school student before attending the University of Chicago (1926–1930, Ph.B.) and the law schools of Northwestern University (1931–1934, LL.B.) and Harvard (1934–1936, LL.M.). His experience with McReynolds seemed alternately to fascinate and terrorize Knox. McReynolds died in 1946, and Knox finally resolved his ambivalence over recounting his experience in early 1952 when he began to convert his diary into a memoir.[1] For the

---

1. In a draft introduction to the memoir, Knox revealed that the work began as a thirty-page paper to be read at a regular meeting of the Chicago Literary Club, but "once the door of memory

next eleven years, he rehearsed his recollections of the tumultuous term until by the summer of 1963 he had 978 pages of double-spaced typescript. He revised portions of the manuscript twice, in 1976–1977 and in 1981. The resulting document was part transcription, part recollection, part social commentary, and part scrapbook. He detailed conversations, meticulously noted social engagements, and extensively quoted from opinions of the Court, from popular press accounts of the term, and from books and magazine articles touching on the justices, the president, and the controversies of the day.

The memoir had obviously become an end in itself as well as a labor of love for Knox, a private chronicle of public figures that mirrored his own diary account of his private world. But what to do with the document now that it was complete? Shortly after beginning the memoir, Knox sent sample chapters to carefully selected friends, including an old law school chum and a retired personal secretary at the Supreme Court whose discretion he trusted implicitly. The lawyer, Gerald P. Rosen, congratulated Knox on his achievement but added a note that must have haunted Knox and helped to keep the enterprise underground: "I suppose you realize that your account leaves you as naked as it does McReynolds. I also suppose that, like all other writers, you have no objection to self-revelation." [2]

The project remained a private conceit until 1978 when Knox, at age seventy-one and retired for four years, decided to make portions of the document public. He did so with the care and ambivalence that marked his sovereignty over the manuscript for the final two decades of his life. On the one hand, he decided to send portions of the manuscript to several libraries—the University of Chicago Law School, Northwestern University, Harvard, the University of Virginia (where the McReynolds Papers are lodged), and the Library of the Supreme Court of the United States. On the other hand, only the Supreme Court Library received a copy of the entire manuscript, and even then with provisions that precluded anyone photocopying the material; the other libraries *initially* received four or five chapters, although Harvard now has all but two of the fourteen chapters. From 1976 to 1981, he formally

---

was opened, it was a book, not a sketch, that emerged." Introduction (1976) at ii–iii, D'Angelo Law Library, University of Chicago Law School (cited hereafter as "Chicago Collection").

2. Gerald P. Rosen to John Knox, May 27, 1954, Box 1, Knox Papers, Harvard Law School Library (cited hereafter as "Harvard Collection"). A quarter-century later, Knox conceded the point in a letter to a law clerk to retired Justice William O. Douglas: "My manuscript . . . covers exactly what happened to me while I was law clerk. Not a word was changed or altered. When I was stupid, and that was very often, I admitted it. It is easy for me to look back now with hindsight and wonder why I didn't do something differently." Knox to Monte J. Povda, Feb. 4, 1978, Chicago Collection.

registered copyright claims to most of the manuscript, but on a chapter-by-chapter, or group-of-chapters, basis. There is no apparent design to the distribution pattern, and none of the libraries retains transmittal information that explains why or when it received the particular chapters it did.

Scholars have been able to study the memoir since 1978, and indeed from then until shortly before his death Knox corresponded with researchers, granted interviews, and allowed his personal copies of the manuscript to be read. Yet only James E. Bond, McReynolds' latest biographer, cites the work, and even then only in passing.[3] None of the many recent studies of the Court-packing plan refers to Knox's magnum opus. The work, so long in genesis and distributed so hesitantly, has been neglected to the point of being forgotten.

One of the reasons Knox may have decided to "release" his work, however stingily, may have been the changing historiographical climate respecting the Supreme Court. Knox's expressed anxieties to Gerald Rosen in 1954 over the propriety of publishing his memoir,[4] must have been mitigated over time by the publication of books that reported internal deliberations at the Court. Biographies of Harlan Fiske Stone[5] in 1956 and of Louis D. Brandeis[6] in 1957 reported conversations and quoted documents hitherto thought forever secret and beyond even the call of history. Knox's own manuscript, reflecting the historic custom, pointedly emphasized that no secret votes would be revealed. Yet Knox does quote McReynolds' table talk—his views on law and politics, including his nakedly racist assumptions about blacks and Jews. Perhaps encouraged by the success of the Stone book, Knox tried to sell his manuscript to at least two New York publishers, but the size and idiosyncratic style of the manuscript defeated his ambitions. And in 1974, J. Harvie Wilkinson III published a chaste account of his clerkship with Justice Lewis F. Powell, Jr., 1972–1973,[7] so at least as a formal matter Knox's artifact was no longer unprecedented.

3. James E. Bond, *I Dissent: The Legacy of Chief [sic] Justice James Clark McReynolds* (Fairfax, Va.: George Mason University Press, 1992). Bond cites the memoir only a few times (pp. 8, 80, 101, 102, and 135).

4. [Knox memorandum re Rosen correspondence], May 27, 1975, Box 1, Harvard Collection.

5. Alpheus T. Mason, *Harlan Fiske Stone: Pillar of the Law* (New York: Viking Press, 1956).

6. Alexander M. Bickel, *The Unpublished Opinions of Mr. Justice Brandeis* (Cambridge, Mass.: Harvard University Press, Belknap Press, 1957).

7. J. Harvie Wilkinson III, *Serving Justice: A Supreme Court Clerk's View* (New York: Charterhouse, 1974). See a review by Benjamin W. Heineman, Jr., 88 Harv. L. Rev. 678 (1975). See

Today the work thus lacks the unique status that Knox proudly proclaims for it at various points in the manuscript. Its value lies both in what it reveals about the operation of the Supreme Court and in its depiction of a social culture now long gone—Washington, D.C., in the interwar years. In its depiction of one aspect of both worlds—the supporting staff of the Court during that period—Knox's memoir remains unique. No other work captures the tightly knit relationship between a justice and his tiny staff: secretary cum law clerk, "messenger" (driver, valet, general factotum), and cook. Although the new Supreme Court building had been open for one year by the time Knox joined McReynolds' staff, most of the justices retained their old habits of working at home in studies equipped with full law libraries (only Chief Justice Charles Evans Hughes and Justice Owen J. Roberts regularly worked in the new building). The working environment was thus intensely personal, more ducal than bureaucratic, and Knox makes that lost world vivid.

As Knox soon discovered, his duties included not only stenography and legal research, but also negotiating the elaborate rituals of Washington society. He would be called upon to represent the justice at social events, to handle invitations quickly and diplomatically, and to observe the complicated protocols associated with personal calling cards (printed and engraved, flat and "turned up," official and private, and so on). For Knox, who had never used a calling card despite an active social life in college and two law schools, the extra-judicial duties were at first bewildering. He was guided through his new world by the justice's two permanent staff, Mrs. Mary Diggs, the cook, and Harry N. Parker, the "messenger." Parker was a member of a now unrecognized and underappreciated community in Washington, black employees who performed personal services for government officials, often for life, and frequently from generation to generation. Parker's mother, Emma, supervised state dinners at the White House during the McKinley and Taft administrations. Harry Parker, who was born in 1879, became messenger to Justice McReynolds in 1919 and served him until the justice retired in 1941; he then worked for Justice Robert H. Jackson until shortly before his death in 1953 at age seventy-four. Two of Parker's sons also worked at the Supreme Court: the older, Emerson R. Parker, was messenger to Justice Frank Murphy, later replaced his father with Justice Jackson, and eventually worked for Justice John Marshall Harlan.

---

generally David J. Garrow, "'The Lowest Form of Animal Life'? Supreme Court Clerks and Supreme Court History," 84 Cornell L. Rev. 855 (1999).

Harry Parker emerges in Knox's memoir as the balance wheel of the Mc-Reynolds household. In addition to his nominal duties of delivering messages and draft opinions to other members of the court, Parker serves as McReynolds' driver on occasion, makes all purchases for the household, organizes dinners and brunches, and prepares the justice's lunch (he was, noted his obituary, "known as an excellent caterer,"[8] and his eggnog recipe was featured in the local press).[9] His most important function in the McReynolds household was to smooth relations between the chronically irascible justice and his other staff members. Parker also headed off unpleasant encounters between the justice and the public, soothed the justice's lady friends, and generally kept the household on an even keel. According to one of the justice's closest social companions, Mrs. Katherine Ogden Savage, "For years Harry did almost everything but breathe for the Justice."[10]

Beyond the portrayal of the day-to-day household, Knox captures, sometimes with a tin ear but always earnestly, the racial stratification of the McReynolds household. Trying to get off to a good start, Knox routinely engages Parker in small talk; McReynolds remonstrates Knox for being too familiar with the staff, on what are clearly both social and racial grounds. When Parker and Mrs. Diggs invite Knox to stay for lunch while the justice is away from the apartment and thus unaware of the fraternization, the servants instinctively sit at a separate table from Knox in the tiny kitchen—an awkward moment that Knox takes the initiative to repair.[11] Most of the racial code was beyond Knox's capacity to address, of course. The most demeaning note, as Knox recounts, was McReynolds' expectation that Parker would act as a

8. "H. N. Parker, Runner at Supreme Court," *Washington Evening Star,* Nov. 4, 1953, p. A16. In an ironic twist which Knox's memoir notes only inferentially, no member of the Supreme Court attended Justice McReynolds' funeral, but Chief Justice Warren and five of his colleagues attended the requiem mass for Parker. "Warren, 5 Associates at Court Aide's Rites," *New York Times,* Nov. 6, 1953, p. 27.

9. Harlan Fiske Stone popularized the recipe during his Chief Justiceship. See "To the Bag," 2 Green Bag 2d 199 (1999).

10. Excerpt of letter to Knox, n.d., Box 3, Georgetown University Library (cited hereafter as "Georgetown Collection"). Mrs. Savage was the widow of the president of the Riggs Bank in Washington, a friend of McReynolds' from 1917 until his death in 1946, and a fellow resident of 2400 Sixteenth Street, N.W.

11. When the manuscript of his memoir later languished without a publisher, Knox excerpted the vignette into a first-person story, "A Tale of Racial Equality," which he tried unsuccessfully to sell to the *Atlantic Monthly* and the *Reader's Digest.* Box 2, Georgetown Collection.

human bird dog on duck hunting trips to the Maryland Eastern Shore—wading through icy water to retrieve the justice's kill.

The highly personalized culture of the justices' households changed not long after the term Knox details. After World War II, all members of the Court worked in the building, with professional secretaries and separate legal assistants who were recent graduates of elite law schools. Justice Lewis F. Powell, Jr., later analogized his chambers and those of his colleagues as "nine little law firms,"[12] an image that never would have occurred to his predecessors in the late 1930s.

The opening of the new Supreme Court building in October 1935 began the transition from a highly personal to a more bureaucratic institution. *Upstairs, Downstairs* was yielding to modern management. Much more important, of course, was the political upheaval of the day. The term that Knox lived through, and relived again and again, was a turning point in American constitutional history. The depression that began in 1929 triggered a variety of legislative responses at the state and federal level, and initially the Supreme Court seemed willing to certify their constitutionality. But beginning in 1935 the Court began handing President Franklin D. Roosevelt one constitutional defeat after another: finding that Congress delegated away legislative power or exceeded its power over interstate commerce, the Court invalidated the Railroad Retirement Act of 1934,[13] parts of the National Industrial Recovery Act,[14] the Agricultural Adjustment Act,[15] and the Bituminous Coal Conservation Act of 1935,[16] among others. The decisions increasingly came by one-vote margins. Then in June of 1936, the Court held in *Morehead v. New York ex rel. Tipaldo*[17] that a state minimum-wage law for women and children violated the Due Process Clause of the Fourteenth Amendment. The vote was again

---

12. Richard L. Williams, "Justices Run 'Nine Little Law Firms' at Supreme Court," *Smithsonian*, February 1977, p. 84. See also Lewis F. Powell, Jr., "Address to the American Bar Association Annual Meetings," 62 A.B.A. J. 1454 (1976). Justice Potter Stewart claimed that Justice John Marshall Harlan (II) originated the image. Stewart, "Reflections on the Supreme Court," 8 Litigation 8, 12 (1982).

13. *Railroad Retirement Board v. Alton Railroad*, 295 U.S. 330 (1935).

14. *Schechter Poultry Corp. v. United States*, 295 U.S. 495 (1935).

15. *United States v. Butler*, 297 U.S. 1 (1936).

16. *Carter v. Carter Coal Co.*, 298 U.S. 238 (1936).

17. 298 U.S. 587 (1936).

5 to 4, with Justice Owen J. Roberts joining what had come to be known as the Four Horsemen of the Apocalypse—Justices Willis Van Devanter, McReynolds, George Sutherland, and Pierce Butler—whose hostility to the New Deal and state economic regulation was implacable and sometimes acidly declared. Justice Harlan F. Stone's provocative dissent accused the majority of deciding the case based on their "personal economic predilections."[18] The decision was roundly condemned, and the question became whether the Court would continue to buck the forces of economic recovery, and also whether the Court would become an issue in Roosevelt's reelection campaign in the autumn.

Knox's memoir recaptures the uncertainty that common knowledge now makes hard to imagine: would Roosevelt win reelection, or would the electorate follow the Court and reject the constitutional shortcuts and their chief promoter? Here and there, both Knox and McReynolds draw comfort from polls by the *Literary Digest* predicting a close race. When Roosevelt is reelected by the largest margin in American history, the *Literary Digest* disappears from the McReynolds household; when the Court-packing plan is announced, a pall settles over the household, as Knox wrote to a friend not long after the fact: "[A]fter Roosevelt launched his amazing attack on the Court much of the enjoyment of being with the Court vanished. The Js. went into a chilling retirement from then on."[19] In fact, Knox suspected "something" was going on even before the plan was announced: "The justice has been tipped off to something, but I don't know yet what it is. He is either fearing inflation or being forced to resign. He has had me go through his records back to 1903 [when he first came to Washington as an assistant attorney general], he has been calling up his stock brokers, etc. A millionaire from Wall Street came down to advise him to ship part of his money to Canada and England."[20] A few days after the plan was made public, McReynolds regained his composure, and panic apparently was replaced by personal resolve, as Knox wrote to his parents: "It is definite that McR. is not going to resign voluntarily. This is the inside dope, but don't tell anybody!! He said so himself. However, he seems to think the bill may go through."[21]

18. Id. at 633.

19. Knox to Alice Clement, May 14, 1938, Chicago Collection.

20. Knox to Folks, n.d. [between Jan. 31 and Feb. 4, 1937], Chicago Collection.

21. Knox to Folks, Feb. 21, 1937, Chicago Collection.

The fate of the president's plan was only part of the drama left to unfold during the remainder of the term. The Court had already heard arguments, and in fact had cast secret tentative votes, on a case that raised the *Morehead v. Tipaldo* issue again. Also looming on the docket were cases questioning the constitutionality of the new Wagner Act regulating labor relations, and, necessarily, the scope of congressional power over interstate commerce. Inside the McReynolds household, the drama was cast in more personal terms—whether the pressure on the Court would cause McReynolds to lash out even more at his personal staff, especially his anxious law clerk, who was risking his job more frequently by being absent from the apartment when McReynolds expected him there and, worse, by developing social connections with the justice's frequent companion, Mrs. Savage.

John Knox is a natural memoirist if not a gifted writer (his exclamation points are so numerous that they quickly pass from annoying to meaningless). But how accurate is his account? From high school until midway through World War II, he kept a daily diary, either handwritten notes in a pocket date book or, often in addition to those notes, a more detailed typewritten version. By the time he was midway through law school, his single-spaced, typed diary had reached 750 pages, and he declared: "My name will survive as long as man survives, because I am writing the greatest diary that has ever been written. I intend to surpass Pepys as a diarist." [22] The diary eventually reached more than two thousand pages, although large portions of it have now been lost.[23] In addition, Knox kept carbon copies of thousands of letters he wrote from the time he was in high school. He was a meticulous, even fussy, record-keeper, although he implies at one point in the memoir that only some of the quoted dialogue is actually verbatim.[24] None of the surviving diary material or letters contradicts the details of the memoir, and some of the letters provide contemporaneous support (and probably the basis) for the manuscript.

22. Knox diary, July 28, 1931, Chicago Collection.

23. The Chicago Collection contains extremely incomplete typewritten diaries from 1929 through the outbreak of World War II in 1939, when Knox appears to have suspended the entries. The Georgetown Collection, Box 20, contains fragments of typewritten diary notes for 1936–1937, scraps of handwritten notes for the year and subsequent years, copies of typewritten diary entries for 1940–1941 (which include detailed reflections on the October term 1936) and 1962–1963 (details of career), and scraps of other notes, journals, and stenographic records. A small collection of Knox Papers at the University of Virginia contains copies of the 1940–1941 diary entries.

24. See chapter 1, note 3.

Who was this self-styled Boswell? John F. Knox was an extremely thin, painfully shy teenage boy who grew up in suburban Chicago during the Roaring Twenties. As a senior at Oak Park High School, he was so lonely that he began a daily diary to record his misery and to provide his own solace. He also developed an infatuation with war, not so much with guns and armor, but with the romance of valor and sacrifice. One grandfather was a Civil War veteran (on the Confederate side), so Knox began corresponding with other veterans. Their stirring accounts spurred interest in survivors of other wars, including the Mexican War, the Crimean War, and the recent World War. From veterans he moved to collecting the autographs of celebrities, including Helen Keller, Admiral Richard Byrd, William Howard Taft, and Kaiser Wilhelm II (whose provision of a signed hand-tinted lithograph portrait earned Knox a picture and story in local newspapers).

During college and law school, Knox expanded his private circle to include justices of the Supreme Court of the United States, first Oliver Wendell Holmes (a Civil War veteran who was wounded three times), then Van Devanter (who had relatives who fought for the Confederacy), and finally Benjamin N. Cardozo, whose professional reputation apparently exempted him from the prerequisite of martial affiliation. Knox was seventeen when he first wrote Holmes; the other justices came later, after Knox began law school. Not only did Knox correspond with many of the justices (including sending birthday cards regularly to Justice Cardozo, among others), but he invited himself to Washington for audiences with several of them: he met his first "live" Justice (Holmes) in 1930,[25] then added McReynolds in 1931 and Stone in 1932. Others followed shortly thereafter. Knox established such familiar terms with Justice Cardozo that by March of 1935, when Holmes died, Knox telegraphed Cardozo and begged for a seat at the funeral service, which Cardozo arranged and confirmed by return cable.[26] Elated by the news, Knox took several days off from his graduate legal studies at Harvard and sped to Washington. Before attending the services, Knox spent a half-hour at the home of Justice Van Devanter.

25. For his account of the meeting, a lunch at Holmes' summer home in Beverly Farms, Massachusetts, see "A Luncheon with Justice Oliver Wendell Holmes, Jr., and Alger Hiss," 71 *The Brief: Phi Delta Phi Quarterly* 96 (Winter 1975–1976). Knox took several photographs of Holmes, both individually and with his law clerk, Hiss.

26. Knox prepared a two-page, single-spaced account of the funeral in 1981. Knox Papers, April 7, 1981, Box 1, Georgetown Collection. Knox also attended the burial service, which he photographed.

Although Knox felt most warmly toward Cardozo, his most sustained correspondence was with Justice Van Devanter. Knox first wrote Van Devanter,
who had been appointed to the Supreme Court in 1911, in 1932, when Van Devanter was seventy-three and Knox, twenty-five, was beginning his second
year of law school. Within a year, Knox had invited himself to Washington to
visit Van Devanter, and the justice—either beguiled or bored—volunteered
to show him Arlington National Cemetery and Mount Vernon. As Knox finished his law degree at Northwestern, he would write Van Devanter from time
to time, notifying him of his academic progress, asking for advice on beginning a career, and even seeking views on social questions (whether it was
rude to refuse alcohol at dinner parties, whether delaying marriage helped or
harmed a career, and so on).

Dissatisfied with his opportunities in Chicago, Knox decided to pursue a
graduate law degree at Harvard Law School. He was admitted and awarded
modest financial aid, the Robert Darrah Jenks Scholarship, which he supple-
mented with odd jobs on campus, mostly secretarial work for the Harvard
Lampoon or part-time chauffeuring for Professor Joseph Beale. On the way to
Harvard, he pressed his advantage with Van Devanter and asked him for an
introduction to anyone in the Boston legal community. Van Devanter had
written lengthy letters about the bar and his early career in Wyoming, which
both charmed Knox and fueled his correspondence, but the request prompted
the justice gently to put his foot down: "My mail brings many letters from
[numberless young men and older ones]—some whom I do not know, some
whose fathers I have known, some who have known members of my family,
and some who know mutual friends, etc. Some of the letters are pathetic, some
indifferent and some reflect real judgment and character in the writer. Some
are from persons who are seeking clerkships, or almost any place commanding compensation in the Executive Departments here. Women write on behalf
of their husbands, sons, and nephews."[27] Knox wrote back, anxiously hoping
that he did not "exceed the bounds of propriety"[28] with his request.

Harvard turned out to be the happiest period of Knox's life: "My first
glimpse of the Yard," he wrote in his diary when he returned to visit in 1940,
"makes my eyes fill with tears. How lovely were my days at Harvard—each

27. Van Devanter to Knox, April 5, 1934, Box 18, Book 48, Willis Van Devanter Papers, Manuscript
Division, Library of Congress (cited hereafter as "Van Devanter Papers").

28. Knox to Van Devanter, April 17, 1934, Box 37, Van Devanter Papers.

one like some rare jewel." [29] He was able to join the "right" club (Lincoln's Inn), he enjoyed an active social life, and he finally developed some direction to his career. He set his sights—indeed, fixated as time passed—on securing a position with Ropes, Gray, Boyden & Perkins, which he viewed as the best firm in Boston. Forgetting his apology eighteen months previously, Knox even contemplated asking Justices Van Devanter and Cardozo for letters of reference to the firm. He evidently thought better of it, but not before dropping their names in a familiar tone during correspondence with the hiring partner at Ropes & Gray.[30] Knox estimated that it would take him eighteen months to secure the position; in the meantime he planned to work in Washington, D.C., as either a secretary or a legal assistant. In November of 1935, he wrote personal letters to all ninety-six members of the United States Senate. The letter mentioned his qualifications (type 114 words per minutes, take 200 words dictation per minute on a stenotype machine), and, "to identify myself better," he shamelessly enclosed with each letter "a picture taken with the late Mr. Justice Oliver Wendell Holmes at his summer home. I am sorry he is dead now, for he would have been glad to recommend me." [31]

At about the same time, Knox detailed his plans to Van Devanter and asked him to put him in touch with anyone in Washington needing secretarial help in the fall of 1936. Van Devanter passed on the letter to Justice McReynolds and informed Knox of what he had done. Knox responded immediately and, as ever, transparently: "A term, however short, as a Supreme Court secretary would enhance my chances with Ropes & Gray to an unusual degree, of course. But aside from that consideration I would be very enthusiastic about such a position and would put my whole heart and soul into the work." [32] The possibility of achieving "the rarest opportunity which very few ever obtain" [33]—as Knox described the job to Van Devanter—must have seemed like manna from heaven, and at a very welcome time. The first year at Harvard, whatever its extracurricular delights, had been rocky academically.

29. Knox diary, July 24, 1940, Box 20, Georgetown Collection.

30. Knox to John Richardson (Ropes & Gray), October 12, 1935, Chicago Collection.

31. Knox to, e.g., Sen. Theodore G. Bilbo, November 24, 1935; Sen. Hugo L. Black, November 25, 1935, Chicago Collection.

32. Knox to Van Devanter, November 16, 1935, Chicago Collection.

33. Ibid.

Knox made only the minimal passing grade in Professor Felix Frankfurter's Public Utilities course. Even though he made the top grade in Professor Manley Hudson's International Law course, Knox somehow put off Hudson personally, and as a result of Hudson's intervention (plus the near-failing grade from Frankfurter), the Jenks Scholarship was not renewed.

With his application to Ropes & Gray stalled, Knox reset his sights on Washington and picked up the pace of his pen-pal relationships with the members of the Supreme Court. Van Devanter put him off in January of 1936 ("rather premature to discuss the matter now"[34]). Six months later, shortly before Knox was to receive his LL.M. from Harvard, Van Devanter wrote again, this time very formally and at considerable length, in the service of a "Justice of our court [who] has been inquiring of me whether I know a young man who is qualified to be his secretary and who would like such a position."[35] Knox shot back a response to each of the questions posed by Van Devanter (age, health, education, marital status, tobacco use, etc.), but then heard nothing for a fortnight and assumed one more goal had failed. Then, on the day he took his degree, he was summoned to Washington by Justice McReynolds for an interview, as he recounts in chapter 1.

They had met once during one of Knox's self-invited trips to Washington to see Justice Van Devanter, but the meeting was brief and seems to have left no distinct impression on Knox, which is somewhat surprising. James Clark McReynolds cut a distinguished and memorable figure in Washington, first as assistant attorney general in the Theodore Roosevelt administration, later as attorney general for Woodrow Wilson, and finally, from 1914, as associate justice of the Supreme Court.[36] McReynolds was the product of a severe upbringing in a mountainous area near the Kentucky-Tennessee border of the

---

34. Van Devanter to Knox, January 23, 1936, Box 19, Book 51, Van Devanter Papers.

35. Van Devanter to Knox, June 3, 1936, Box 19, Book 52, Van Devanter Papers.

36. The only published monographic treatment of McReynolds' career is Bond, *I Dissent*. See also F. D. G. Ribble, "James Clark McReynolds," 32 U. Va. L. Rev. 909 (1946) (one-page memorial in issue dedicated to McReynolds); R. V. Fletcher, "Mr. Justice McReynolds: An Appreciation," 2 Vand. U. L. Rev. 35–46 (1948); Calvin P. Jones, "Kentucky's Irascible Conservative: Supreme Court Justice James Clark McReynolds," 57 Filson Club Historical Quarterly 20 (1983); and four unpublished doctoral dissertations: Barbara Barlin Schimmel, "The Judicial Policy of Mr. Justice McReynolds" (Yale University, 1964); Doris A. Blaisdell, "The Constitutional Law of Mr. Justice McReynolds" (University of Wisconsin, 1952); Stephen T. Early, "James Clark McReynolds and the Judicial Process" (University of Virginia, 1952), and J. B. McCraw, "James Clark McReynolds and the Supreme Court, 1914–1941" (University of Texas, 1951). S. Price Gilbert, "James Clark McReynolds, 1862–1946" (privately printed, 1946), is a brief appreciation.

Old South. His father was a doctor who was a member of the Campbellite wing of the Disciples of Christ, and he was known locally in Elkton, Kentucky, as the "pope," for the self-professed infallibility of his views. His son graduated as valedictorian from Vanderbilt University and swept through the law course at the University of Virginia in fourteen months. Like his father, he viewed public education and the virtue of the common man as humbugs, so he rejected ancestral partisan loyalties and William Jennings Bryan to become a Gold Democrat. That political twist and his demonstrated legal ability helped to bring him to Washington as a trust-buster under Theodore Roosevelt in 1903. One of his chief targets was the tobacco industry. In 1913, Wilson, who admired McReynolds' record of zeal in the antitrust field, made him attorney general, but soon discovered he was a disruptive cabinet member and was pleased to promote him to the Supreme Court.

McReynolds was tall, trim, and enjoyed the countenance and bearing of a Roman senator. He dressed impeccably and was equally home in polite society or in duck blinds and on golf courses. Yet he also was, in the view of many, the "rudest man in Washington," with unspeakable manners—sarcastic, peremptory, and antagonistic. A doyen of society, he was nonetheless known to leave a dinner party abruptly if seated below the salt, literally or figuratively. Most notoriously, for someone in his position, he was unashamedly anti-Semitic and racist. He detested Justices Brandeis and Cardozo. For example: there is no official photograph of the Court in 1924, because McReynolds would not sit next to Brandeis as protocol required; during the formal swearing-in of Cardozo in 1932, McReynolds was observed casually reading a newspaper on the bench; and he declined to sign the traditional letter of regret from the Court when Justice Brandeis retired in 1939. McReynolds' hostility was so unqualified that there was no fraternization between the staff of his household and those of the two Jewish justices. His racial views were unreconstructed products of his rural Kentucky youth—paternalistic and decidedly patronizing. McReynolds was dismissive of Harry Parker's desire to send his sons to college and made clear to Mary Diggs that with her intellectual ability she was lucky to have a job. During the term Knox served him, McReynolds was sharply criticized when he publicly defended his judicial equanimity by claiming that he tried to protect "the poorest darky in the Georgia backwoods as well as the man of wealth in a mansion on Fifth Avenue." [37]

37. McReynolds' remark received front-page coverage in both the *Washington Post* and the *New York Times* on March 17, 1937, although the *Times* primly changed "darky" to "backwoodsman." See also chapter 10, note 9.

In fact, McReynolds found little protection in the Constitution for black men and women, whether victims of Jim Crow justice in southern courts[38] or applicants to racially segregated state universities.[39] His Constitution vindicated property and states' rights in no uncertain terms and brooked no debate. The hallmark of his judicial work product was brevity, to the point of terseness.[40] His opinions were brisk, conclusory, and unencumbered by the finer points of precedent or detail. At the memorial service after his death, then-Attorney General Tom C. Clark politely captured McReynolds' intellectual mien: "[T]he salient points in his character and philosophy were a rigid righteousness, an unyielding determination, and unshakable stability. When he felt deeply on a question, his view absorbed him so completely that he had the greatest difficulty in moderating his expression, or in tolerating sustained argument by those who opposed him."[41] Justice Holmes, whom McReynolds viewed as an old fool, thought McReynolds an uninteresting lawyer but an "extraordinary personality—what matters most to him are personal relations, the affections. He is a *Naturmensch*—he has very tender affections and corresponding hates."[42] The hates extended to wrong-minded individuals and uncivilized behavior, an expansive category, including, for example, tobacco use (filthy), women wearing red nail polish (vulgar), and men wearing wristwatches (effeminate). Court lore of the day likened working for McReynolds to crossing a mine field on a daily basis.

John Knox had parlayed fascination with celebrity and a cheeky presumptuousness into a secretaryship, or clerkship, for a member of the Supreme

38. See, e.g., *Moore v. Dempsey*, 261 U.S. 86 (1923) (dissent); *Powell v. Alabama*, 287 U.S. 45 (1932) (dissent); cf. *Johnson v. Zerbst*, 304 U.S. 458 (1938) (dissent).

39. *Missouri ex rel. Gaines v. Canada*, 305 U.S. 337 (1938). Dissenting, McReynolds wrote that if the state were forced to accept a black into its all-white law school, the consequence, "as indicated by experience, would damnify both races." Id. at 353.

40. In one case which he viewed to be important, *United States v. Curtiss-Wright*, 299 U.S. 304 (1936), he abandoned writing a sustained dissent in favor of a one-sentence statement announcing his views and left for a weekend of duck hunting instead of producing an opinion explaining his viewpoint. See chapter 9.

41. 334 U.S. v, xvii (1948).

42. Melvin I. Urofsky, ed., "The Frankfurter-Brandeis Conversation," 1985 Sup. Ct. Rev. 299, 316 (conversation of July 3, 1923). Cf. Mark DeWolfe Howe, ed., *The Holmes-Laski Letters* 842 (Cambridge, Mass.: Harvard University Press, 1953): "Poor McReynolds is, I think, a man of feeling and more secret kindliness than he would get credit for. But as is so common with Southerners, his own personality governs him without much regard for others." (Holmes to Laski, June 4, 1926).

Court of the United States, but he scarcely had any idea what (or whom) he was in for. Although he acknowledged that the opportunity was "rare," it is important now to understand that the position did not carry the prestige or earmark for success that it enjoys today. Most of the justices in the mid-1930s used a permanent stenographer/legal secretary. The exceptions were Justices Brandeis, Cardozo, and Stone, who took their annual staff from Harvard, Harvard, and Columbia, respectively; Frankfurter was the gatekeeper for the appointments from Harvard,[43] as he had been for Justice Holmes since 1915. Justice McReynolds did not want new staff annually, but his temper and manners made appointments in his chambers of irregular duration, to say the least: of the eleven clerks who served McReynolds prior to Knox, six stayed for one year, three for two, one for three, and one, Maurice Mahoney, for seven (1927–1934).

In many respects the secretaryship was evolving during the mid-1930s into the full-time professional research assistantship that is now associated with the title "law clerk." As much as anyone, Frankfurter was responsible for making the position prestigious, short-term, and a springboard to influential positions in government. He insisted that his "lads" have a top academic rating and unquestioned discretion before placing them with justices such as Holmes, Brandeis, and Cardozo, whose reputations he was simultaneously burnishing with his own scholarship.[44] Justice Stone, the former dean of Columbia Law School, staffed his clerkship in a similar vein. There were thus two staff cultures at the Supreme Court in October term 1936 — the elite, "rotating" staffs from Harvard and Columbia, and the career secretaries used by the majority of justices. Chief Justice Hughes used the legal secretary that former Chief Justice William Howard Taft had hired in 1929, and the others all had men who had served them for six to nine years.

John Knox knew that he was an anomaly at the Supreme Court — a Harvard man who obtained his position without the endorsement, indeed without the knowledge, of Felix Frankfurter. Someone more mature would have found pride or irony in the fact, but for Knox it was one more factor stoking his chronic insecurity. Yet he always had his diary (now nearing two thousand

43. Knox discovered Frankfurter's role during one of his visits to Washington, D.C., during law school, and so, predictably, he wrote Frankfurter a lengthy letter reporting his visits with members of the Court and seeking his support for a clerkship upon graduation. Knox to Frankfurter, August 7, 1932, Box 1, Georgetown Collection. Frankfurter's response — if any — does not survive.

44. Cf. Scott Messinger, "The Judge as Mentor: Oliver Wendell Holmes, Jr., and His Law Clerks," 11 Yale J.L. & Human. 119 (1999).

single-spaced typed pages) to which he could retreat for comfort. The memoir that grew out of the diary—and the carbon copies, and clippings, and social invitations, and so on—would become his own ultimate triumph. When a lifetime of hesitancy about going public conspired with failing health and equally failing finances after he retired, the memoir became destined for posthumous publication, if any. Our edition is faithful to the text without belaboring the reader with every detail of Knox's social year in Washington or with extensive quotations from public documents, Court opinions, and newspaper reports. Most of his footnotes have been retained; footnotes to the text that have been supplied by the editors are so noted. Text that has been shortened or summarized is presented in brackets. The title is ours; Knox called his work, "Experiences as Law Clerk to Mr. Justice James C. McReynolds of the Supreme Court of the United States during the Year That President Franklin D. Roosevelt Attempted to 'Pack' the Court (October Term 1936)." We are grateful to the many librarians who assisted us in our research, and we thank the libraries of Georgetown University and Harvard Law School for permission to quote from their holdings. We are also very grateful to Mrs. Virginia B. Whitehill, cousin to John Knox and legatee of the literary rights to the manuscript, and to Mr. and Mrs. David Bliss, who helped Knox in his final years and stored duplicate copies of the manuscript and other papers left by Knox and not included in the estate. Ross Davies, Anne Ford, Katy Hutchinson, and David Roe provided valuable editorial advice; Pat Evans and David Painter facilitated difficult research tasks; and Jelena Pantel was instrumental in preparing the manuscript for publication.

DENNIS J. HUTCHINSON
DAVID J. GARROW

New Year's Day 2002

THE FORGOTTEN MEMOIR OF JOHN KNOX

1

THIS IS THE story of a bachelor
seventy-five years old, and of my experience with him and his negro maid and
butler. This bachelor's name was James Clark McReynolds, and he was an Associate Justice of the Supreme Court of the United States. I was once his secretary and law clerk, and the four of us shared the same apartment every day
for a year during one of the most crucial periods in the history of this country. During that year there was a devastating quarrel between the White House
and the Supreme Court. This quarrel was begun by the President of the United
States in an effort to gain control over the Justices of the Court. The President
failed, and he carried the imprint of this failure upon his character as long
as he lived. But the Justices also failed. Theirs was a Pyrrhic victory, which was
soon rendered meaningless by resignations and deaths among their ranks. But
in their brief hour of triumph, they knew real glory.

In the middle 1930s the Supreme Court of the United States was composed
of nine gentlemen who were soon destined to be referred to as the Nine Old
Men. At the head of the Court stood Chief Justice Charles Evans Hughes, who
had barely missed being elected President in 1916. Hughes wore a striking
white beard, had a magnificent voice, and some thought that he looked like
most any one of the twelve disciples. Associated with Hughes on the Court
were Justices Louis Dembitz Brandeis, Benjamin Nathan Cardozo, Harlan F.
Stone, Owen Josephus Roberts, Willis Van Devanter, James Clark McReynolds, Pierce Butler, and George Sutherland. In 1933, when Franklin D. Roosevelt moved into the White House, these nine Justices were at the peak of
their judicial careers, and each, in his own way, sought to preserve the dignity
and the prestige of the greatest tribunal of its kind in the world. It was not
long, however, before this tribunal began speeding toward a head-on collision

with the executive branch of the government as represented by President Roosevelt. When that collision took place in the year 1937, it was my privilege to be associated with the Court as a law clerk and confidential secretary to one of the nine Justices. My experiences while serving in such a capacity form the contents of this book.

Looking back from the [present], it is somewhat difficult to visualize the Washington of 1933. A man by the name of Hoover, who some thought was solely responsible for the Great Depression, had just left the White House, and the age of the wizards of reconstruction had commenced. With a New Deal at hand, the "wasteful spending" of President Hoover was to be reduced, along with the number of governmental bureaus—or so the new President had promised in his campaign speeches—and the insignia of the Blue Eagle was to be supreme throughout the land.[1]

Since the year 1860, the Supreme Court had been holding its sessions in the old Senate Chamber in the Capitol building. This was a comparatively small room with a somewhat intimate atmosphere, [where] Webster, Calhoun, Clay, and other statesmen had delivered great antebellum speeches. But after some seventy-five years, this dignified sanctuary had become too cramped, [so the Court moved] into a building of its own for the first time in its history. This structure was a colossal monument of white marble, exuding such a merciless glare in the summer sun that the guards outside would be forced to wear colored glasses. At the entrance to the building there were great bronze doors of enormous weight. Behind these doors was a vast corridor resembling the entrance to a tomb of the ancient pharaohs, and branching off from this corridor was the most modern equipment enjoyed by any court in the world. With such a temple of justice available to house its proceedings, the Supreme Court of the United States took on added strength, power, and prestige at almost the same moment that its battle with the New Deal began.

Little known to the public, but of great importance in carrying out the routine work of the Court, was the classification of employees known as Court secretaries. There were both legal secretaries, called law clerks, and non-legal secretaries. Each secretary was assigned to work for one of the nine Justices.

---

1. [Editors' note: A stylized blue eagle was the logotype for the National Recovery Administration—an agency designed to organize American business industry by industry—which was the cornerstone of the first New Deal. The agency's goal was to have each industry set wages and prices in order to prevent any more economic instability. The logo became a pervasive symbol of government intervention in private enterprise.]

Some secretaries were permanent employees and had served their Justices faithfully for many years. Others were hired for one year and left after their terms expired. Most Justices had just one secretary in those days, but a few retained two. One of the secretaries to the Chief Justice had ably served Chief Justice William Howard Taft for many years, and after Taft's death had been retained in service by Chief Justice Hughes.

After 1933 it became well known that Professor Felix Frankfurter of the Harvard Law School was recommending many graduates of that school for positions in Washington with the New Deal administration. While ostensibly doing little else but teaching classes at Cambridge, Frankfurter was busy placing friends or "disciples" of his in key positions in the government. The professor, born in Austria in 1882, was a nervous, jumpy little man. Possessed of rare talents in the law, together with great self-assurance and arrogance, Frankfurter had become a friend of many world figures, including Franklin D. Roosevelt. With [Roosevelt as President], the Harvard professor had access to the White House.

Each year Professor Frankfurter would also recommend to the Supreme Court two recent graduates to serve in Washington as law clerks for the ensuing year. These men were generally assigned to Justices Brandeis and Cardozo. In the past Frankfurter had also chosen the secretaries for the late Justice Oliver Wendell Holmes. Holmes, who was born in 1841, retired from the Supreme Court in 1932 but still took a new secretary each year from the Harvard Law School until his death in 1935. During 1929–1930 Holmes' secretary was a graduate by the name of Alger Hiss. A few years later his brother, Donald Hiss, also served as Holmes' secretary. Another Frankfurter appointee, Dean Acheson, was assigned for a year to Justice Brandeis. It was not until many years later that the names of some of these Supreme Court secretaries, or law clerks, took on added meaning.

During the early days of the New Deal, there were four Justices of the Supreme Court who were considered as conservatives: Van Devanter, McReynolds, Butler, and Sutherland. Many times the Court split 5 to 4 in deciding a case, and these four Justices usually constituted the minority. During 1935 Justice McReynolds told Justice Van Devanter that he (McReynolds) would need a new law clerk and secretary for the period from June 1936 until June 1937, but that he was puzzled as to whom to select. Justice Van Devanter offered to locate such a person who could be assigned to Justice McReynolds, and the latter happily accepted the offer. Perhaps the selection could be made from the 1936 graduating class of the Harvard Law School but without Professor

Frankfurter's knowledge. The new law clerk, of course, would have to meet certain requirements, such as being an acceptable "WASP" conservative who never smoked cigarettes, who knew how to type and take dictation, and who also met certain scholastic requirements.

One day in the fall of 1935, I [received a letter from Justice Van Devanter informing] me that I was being considered as law clerk to a Justice of the Supreme Court of the United States and that the year's appointment would pay about three thousand dollars, and he wondered if I could come to Washington during the Christmas vacation for an interview with him.

In the latter part of December 1935, I did go to Washington. I met Justice Van Devanter, and in the quiet of his study we talked for nearly an hour. During this time he puffed contentedly on a pipe and at intervals slowly filled it with more tobacco. He did at least nine-tenths of the talking during the interview. He discussed at some length his early days in Wyoming, and while he did so I noted that the Justice lived in a large apartment house and that his own quarters were tastefully but simply furnished. During our conversation I also learned that Justice Cardozo lived at the same address, but I was not asked to meet him, or Justice McReynolds, or in fact any other Justice. It appeared that Justice Van Devanter had no wife living, and apparently his sister resided with him.

At first I thought the Justice seemed a bit stern and forbidding, but after a while he became quite talkative as he sat staring rather absentmindedly out of the window. Again he mentioned early pioneer days in Wyoming, where he had practiced law as a young man. He became more and more friendly as the minutes passed, and somehow the conversation turned to Justice Holmes, [who had died earlier in the year]. I asked the Justice if he had known Mrs. Holmes. At once his manner changed, and he became very solemn. With his eyes flashing, and showing displeasure, he leaned across the desk and said, "I should say I did. But do you know that when she died her husband at first refused to hold a funeral for her! Yes, sir, Holmes said he was not going to permit any funeral—he was a Unitarian or something. Well, young man, do you know that several of the Justices and I had to go down to Holmes' house, and we didn't leave there until he had promised to hold a funeral for his wife. A funeral simply had to be held, of course, not only to pay respects to a fine woman but also to uphold the dignity of the Court!"

While talking with Van Devanter, I noticed that a framed silhouette of Chief Justice John Marshall was hanging on the wall. The Justice pointed to it with pride. He was a staunch admirer of Marshall, and he talked of him for some minutes. Van Devanter then gave evidence that it was time for us to end our conversation and for him to get back to work. I bade him a friendly good day and took the elevator downstairs to the lobby.[2]

Weeks went by, and I heard nothing more from Justice Van Devanter. Then in the spring a [handwritten] letter arrived, which he had mailed on April 22, 1936: "I write this merely to the end that you may know that you are being considered. It may not come to anything, but you should be prepared for a possible call." At that late date in the school year I still had not been asked to meet any other Justice but him. However, I decided to wait and not apply for a job in any law firm until the matter of the Supreme Court appointment was definitely settled one way or the other.

More weeks passed, and it was June of 1936. Harvard's great Tercentenary Celebration was in progress to mark the three hundredth anniversary of the founding of the University. I had heard nothing from Washington, so I planned to drive up to Quebec with my parents, who had come in from Chicago for my graduation. On the morning of the eighteenth, I was ready to walk over to the Yard [for the graduation ceremonies] when a special delivery letter arrived which had been mailed in Washington the day before, a letter written by hand on Supreme Court stationery and signed, "J. C. McReynolds." It read as follows:

Mr. Justice Van Devanter has given me an account of his correspondence with you and has expressed a favorable opinion of yr. qualifications for the position of Law Clerk.

He tells me that you are to graduate this week and can be here conveniently—next Monday June 22 for an interview.

My clerk is leaving July 1.

I want an all round man who can & will do everything possible to help me.

Apparently you measure up to the situation: but an interview is necessary in order that no mistake be made by either of us.

My present purpose is to be here on Monday the 22nd. If you can conveniently come at that time, I will be glad.

There is a possibility that I may go over to N.Y.—the University Club Cor 54 St. & 5th Ave.

---

2. There I noticed a man carrying a briefcase and walking briskly into the building. I recognized him from newspaper pictures as Senator Borah of Idaho, who had been representing his state in the United States Senate since 1907. [I realized] that Van Devanter, Cardozo and Borah all lived in the same apartment building.

If so, I will wire you on Saturday & see you there.

This is only a possibility however. In the absence of any other advice I will expect to see you on Monday at my apartment 2400—16th St. (N.W.) at 10 o'clock A.M.

Please send spl. delivery letter on receipt of this.

Faithfully Yours,

J. C. McReynolds

Jno. Knox

Even at this late date I recall that I wondered why each sentence in this letter was written as a separate paragraph. The way some of the words were abbreviated was also unusual, and this was the first time I had ever received a letter in which my first name was spelled "Jno." on both the envelope and the letter itself.

Upon returning to my room after the graduation exercises, I found a telegram from Justice McReynolds advising me to meet him for sure in Washington at ten o'clock on the following Monday as he had decided not to go to New York after all. My projected trip to Canada was therefore canceled, and my parents drove there alone the next day. Before leaving for Washington, however, I spent two more days in Boston and Cambridge reviewing old scenes for the last time. I also stopped in at the college library to look up an old issue of *Fortune* magazine, which contained a detailed write-up about each Supreme Court Justice. I regretted that the article was quite uncomplimentary in its references to McReynolds. "If he is going to be my Justice," I thought, "I hope he is not as bad as all that. Probably just an exaggeration after all."

As I boarded the train to Washington, the enormity of my ignorance of the Supreme Court of the United States can hardly be exaggerated. I was, of course, anticipating with interest my meeting with Justice McReynolds. I also looked upon the tribunal as one composed of nine calm, amiable gentlemen who lived near each other, who had much in common, who were all friendly with one another, and who met occasionally in a group—along with their secretaries—to discuss various legal cases. I assumed, of course, that I would become well acquainted with all the other law clerks and secretaries. I also assumed that I would often attend the Court sessions, hear great legal arguments, and watch famous trial lawyers in action.

As soon as I arrived in Washington that Monday morning, I hailed a taxicab at the Union Station and asked the driver to take me to 2400 Sixteenth Street, N.W.—the address Justice McReynolds had mentioned in his letter. At the time I did not realize that this was probably the most elaborate and exclusive apartment building in Washington and occupied by numerous people of prominence. [By way of] a private driveway in front of the building, I reached the front entrance, [where] a negro porter smilingly opened the door. I found myself in a cavernous hall, heavily carpeted, at the far end of which were some elevators.

In walking down the corridor on the fifth floor I thought to myself, "What a place!" I wouldn't have been surprised if a butler in red livery had opened the door when I rang. Arriving at apartment 507 I pressed a buzzer, and after a few moments I could hear someone walking rapidly across a bare floor. Suddenly the door opened in front of me and there stood, not a butler, but Justice McReynolds himself. He nodded and said, "Good morning, I have been expecting you. Come right this way." With that statement I was ushered into a hall bare of all carpeting and most furniture. "Some of the rugs and furniture have been stored for the summer as I am going out of town," said the Justice. "Please follow me."

I did not realize at the time that I was in an apartment containing two separate entrances from the hallway, ten rooms, three baths, and an outside balcony overlooking a portion of the city. The Justice walked rapidly to the far end of the apartment, and I found myself in a large study in which there were several chairs, two desks, and numerous books. McReynolds sat down at one desk, asked me to be seated, and methodically got out a pencil and pad and began to take notes of our conversation.

"Justice Van Devanter has told me about his correspondence with you, but of course there are a number of details to be discussed today." Then he noted down my age, education, where my parents lived, etc., and then asked abruptly, "Do you smoke?" Taken rather aback I said, "No, I don't," but in a tone of voice which meant, "No, I don't, but should I?" "Well, I'm glad you don't smoke," said the Justice. "There is no smoking here in this apartment. No secretary of mine can smoke."

His next words were, "And now may I see a sample of your handwriting?" With that he handed me a sheet of paper on which I signed my name and wrote a few words. The Justice then scrutinized my handwriting carefully but made no comment concerning it. "I assume, of course, that you know how to type," were the next words I heard. "Yes, I do know how to type," I replied. "In fact, I can type over one hundred words a minute, which is probably faster than you will require." The Justice also made no comment regarding this statement but went on to say, "And you take dictation, too? That will be necessary."

With these words I paused and then said rather hesitantly, "Well, I can operate a stenotype, and with that I can take dictation at about a hundred words a minute." The Justice's eyes narrowed. "What is a stenotype?" he asked. "Why, it's a machine type of shorthand—a little machine—you know—" and I rather awkwardly tried to explain what a stenotype looked like. But the Justice broke in and said, " I wouldn't have one around the house! What I want is a law clerk who can take dictation with a pencil, not with some machine you have to carry around with you." McReynolds was then silent for a few moments, during which he slowly opened and closed his left hand in a rather nervous fashion, looking at his fingernails very intently at the same time. I was later to learn that this was a characteristic gesture of his when concentrating. Then slowly and deliberately he said, "Well, I'm afraid you won't do. I want a law clerk who can type and take dictation with a pencil and not with any kind of machine!" And with that he gazed up at the ceiling as if to indicate the conversation had come to a conclusion.

At this moment my brain jelled. I could see the clerkship with a Justice of the Supreme Court of the United States suddenly being snatched away from me at the last moment because of some discussion about shorthand. This was an impossible last-minute disaster, entirely unexpected. I suddenly heard myself saying almost emphatically, "Well, if you are going out of town and don't need me for about six weeks, I can spend that time brushing up on my pencil shorthand so that I can take dictation as you require."

"Indeed," replied the Justice, "so you really had sense enough to learn the other kind of shorthand, too!" Then after some hesitation, and with more opening and closing of his left hand, he finally said, "Well, you really should be here in Washington while I am gone in order to read the petitions for certiorari that will be coming in during the summer. But, on the other hand, if you want to wait six weeks before reporting to work, I shall give my approval. Of course, you won't be paid any salary during those six weeks, you understand."

"That will be quite satisfactory," I said. At that stage of the proceedings I would have consented to work for the entire year at no salary rather than not to work at all.

"Your salary will be twenty-four hundred dollars for the year," the Justice said. "I shall also expect you to rent an apartment in this building, so that you will be available at all times in case I need you. There will be hundreds of petitions for certiorari coming in during the summer, and I want you to read each one. Then summarize each petition in one page of typing, single spaced. Give me the facts of each case, the question of law presented, the holding of the lower courts, and your own personal recommendation whether you think the petition should or should not be allowed."

"I shall do that," I said rather weakly.

"Well," concluded the Justice, "I'll let the Clerk of the Court know that I have appointed you as my law clerk; also Justice Van Devanter. There is a library and a typewriter here in the apartment. You will do no work at the new Court building. If you need any books, a messenger from the Court will bring them out to you in a truck." With that statement it was evident the interview was at an end.

Things had moved a little too rapidly for me to do anything more than note, in a rather cursory fashion, that the Justice was approximately six feet tall, very powerfully built, impeccably dressed, and with gleaming white, heavily starched shirt cuffs. He was in his middle seventies but remarkably active for his age. In his youth he must have been quite handsome, and he still retained a strong and good-looking face for an elderly man. Yet there was something about him that caused me to feel that here was a man who had very little sense of humor—at least toward secretaries. He had not "thawed out" during our conversation like Justice Van Devanter had done the Christmas before. McReynolds had retained his formality throughout the entire interview.

I looked up the manager of 2400, and after some lengthy negotiations I rented the smallest apartment that was available in the building. It contained a tiny hall, to the right of which was a full-sized bath but with no window. To the left of the hall was a small bedroom with one window opening onto a court. The bedroom was just big enough to accommodate a dresser, a small desk, one easy chair, and a narrow bed. For these accommodations I was to pay fifty dollars a month plus one dollar extra for the use of the telephone.

After renting the apartment, I strode down the long first-floor corridor once more and out of the building into the June sun. "You are a fool!" I said to myself. "You don't know a word of pencil shorthand and never did! How in the world are you ever going to learn shorthand in only six weeks? And after that how can you read and summarize all those petitions for certiorari in time for the opening of Court in the fall!"

I saw no taxi in sight, so with a rather heavy heart I began to walk. As I left the premises I gave little attention to the fact that the apartment I rented had no kitchen facilities in it, that there appeared to be no stores near 2400, and in fact I did not even know in which direction a shopping district lay. Nor would I have any car at my disposal if and when I lived in the building. "Maybe I am supposed to eat in the Justice's apartment," I thought to myself. How wrong I was I did not at the time realize.

My next stop was at the Supreme Court building itself, where I went directly to the office of the Clerk of the Court and asked to meet the Clerk personally. In those days the Clerk was a most charming and efficient gentleman by the name of Charles Elmore Cropley. He appeared to be in his middle forties but may have been older. Greeting me very cordially, he took me into his private office and there talked at considerable length. "Now first of all, Mr. Knox," he said, "you will need to know certain things, or you can never succeed even one month with the Justice. The most important point to realize is that your future success or failure lies in the hands of Harry Parker."

"Harry Parker?" I asked incredulously. "Who is he?"

"Well," said Mr. Cropley, "around the Supreme Court building, Harry is known as the one who really keeps the McReynolds household going. Harry is a colored messenger who has been working for the Justice since about 1913. But he is far more than just a messenger. He is also the Justice's cook, his confidant—in fact, his alter ego. Without Harry's complete confidence and trust in you, it will be impossible for you to think of being the Justice's law clerk."

In a few minutes I was introduced to Harry. For me it was an historic meeting, for I really took an instant liking to him. He exuded friendliness and was all smiles when introduced to me. "I've had a hard day so far," I told Harry. "Washington isn't just like I thought it would be. I have to learn shorthand in six weeks and then read hundreds of petitions for certiorari before the Court opens in the fall. What's the score here as regards this job I'm taking on?"

With a twinkle in his eye, Harry Parker suggested that he take me on a personally conducted tour of the entire Supreme Court building. This he did, and in a leisurely and entertaining way he explained every point of interest. We finally arrived at a door marked "Justice McReynolds," and upon opening it I was taken into a large and imposing suite of offices. It was, however, empty. There was also a room of equal size reserved for the Justice's secretary. Harry explained that there were nine suites like this in the building—one for each Justice—and that most of them were just standing empty. Justices McReynolds, Brandeis, Cardozo, Stone, Van Devanter, Butler, and Sutherland all preferred to work at home instead of at the Court. Chief Justice Hughes and Justice Roberts, however, were making use of their quarters at that time.

When Harry and I arrived at the beautiful Supreme Court library, I could not help but say, "This is all very impressive—much more beautiful than I had expected." By that time I was so thoroughly sold on the idea of being a

Supreme Court law clerk that I would have agreed to learn shorthand in two weeks instead of in six if that had been possible.

Before parting with Harry, I learned that his wife taught in the Washington schools, and that he had three sons whom he hoped to see through college. One of them worked part time in the Supreme Court cloakroom. Harry then asked me where I expected to live, and upon telling him that the Justice had requested me to reside at 2400, Harry asked, "What salary is he going to pay you?" When I told him the amount, Harry commented that it would not be enough. "I will see if I can talk with the Justice about getting you an increase," he said. "It is very expensive to live in Washington at that address."

I then told Harry that I was ready to go back to Chicago but would see him in about six weeks. "Just one last word of advice," Harry said. "You can't smoke or drink, and you can't have no dates with girlfriends during the year. If anybody is going to do any dating, it will be the Justice and nobody else. You will also be fired if the Justice ever calls up his apartment during the day and finds that you are not there. You cannot eat at the Justice's, and you will have to walk six or seven blocks to a restaurant at Eighteenth and Columbia Road. If you don't have no time to go out for breakfast, you can have a bottle of milk delivered to your door every morning. Remember, the Justice is a bachelor and has a number of prominent lady friends, and don't you get too friendly with any of them. That is, if you want to keep your job."

I began to suspect that he was exaggerating just to see how I would react. "Now Harry," I said, "if you don't mind me calling you Harry so soon, how can the Justice fire me if I am not in when he calls up during the day? I might be down the hall mailing some letters or downstairs picking up the mail at the desk. I could still be 'on the job' and yet not right inside his apartment when the telephone rang."

Harry shook his head back and forth. "That don't make no difference," he replied. "You just better be there when he calls." Harry had not had the advantages of a college education, but his English at times could be just as emphatic and descriptive as if he had gone to college, perhaps more so.

"One thing more," he said. "Someone else will be in the apartment, too. That's Mary Diggs, the maid. Mary, you, and I will be there working for the Justice. Mary keeps the place clean. I go to market, do the cooking, and do the messenger work for him. You will do the law work. When you get back from Chicago, there's lots more to learn, too."

I bade Harry a cordial farewell, and a few days later I was back in Chicago investigating the shorthand problem. I discovered at once that I could not learn either Gregg or Pitman shorthand in only six weeks. Nor did a system called "Speedwriting" seem to be practical for my purposes. Finally I found a shorthand teacher who said she could teach me in less than six weeks a virtually unknown kind of shorthand called the Dickinson method. [Because the Justice stayed longer than expected in Europe, I was able to delay my return to Washington until late August. By then]—and after a tremendous mental struggle—I actually could take dictation in Dickinson shorthand at ninety to one hundred words a minute. I felt that this speed would be sufficient, so on the afternoon of Friday, August 28, 1936, I took a train back to Washington.

I reached the apartment house of 2400 on a hot and humid Saturday morning. After leaving my luggage at my own small quarters on the fourth floor, I walked up one flight to the Justice's apartment. This time Harry answered the door in response to my ring. "Well, well, well, good morning, Mr. Knox," he said. "So you got back all right! Come here, Mary, and meet Mr. Knox, the new secretary." A smiling and friendly colored woman then entered the hallway of the Justice's apartment and said, "Hello." This was, of course, the first time I had seen Mary Diggs, but I also liked her from the very first. She proved to be one of the hardest working and most efficient employees I have ever met, and we soon became good friends.

"The Justice hasn't got back to town yet," said Harry. "He'll be here by next Wednesday. And now that you know shorthand, I better show you where you are going to work!" With that he pointed to a room at the end of the hall and laughed. I walked to the entrance of this room, looked in, and caught my breath. The floor of the entire room was literally filled to a depth of more than a foot with hundreds of statements of fact, briefs, answers, etc.—all comprising what seemed to be countless petitions for certiorari. There were at the time approximately five hundred petitions piled on the floor of that room. All of these would have to be read before the opening of Court in October, and a page referring to each petition would then have to be typed. I had five weeks and two days in which to do this work as the first Court session was scheduled for Monday, October 5, 1936.

"I think I better get to work. Don't you think so?" I said to Harry. To this Harry replied, "Oh, Mr. Knox, you're not going to do any work today—you're going to a funeral."

"A funeral? Are you serious?" I queried.

"Now don't tell me you don't know who's getting buried today. The Secretary of War just died. The Justice isn't here to go to the funeral, and so I'll give you his pass and you go and represent him."

I then remembered reading on the train that Secretary of War George Dern had indeed died. A few hours later I presented [Justice McReynolds' admission] card at the door of a Washington church and entered to attend the funeral of a man I had never known or even seen.

Though it was Saturday afternoon, Harry and Mary were still working at the Justice's apartment when I arrived back at 2400. After exchanging a few comments with them about the funeral, Harry then asked to see my calling card.

"My what?" I said.

"Why, your calling card, of course. If it doesn't look just right, you've got to have a new one printed."

I laughed and said, "I don't have any calling card. I never did have one. Where I used to live we just didn't seem to need calling cards, and when I got to Harvard I never bothered to have one made up."

"Lord Almighty!" gasped Harry. "How do you think you're going to get along in Washington without a calling card? Where do you come from, boy, anyway?"

I then explained again that my home was in Chicago, as he already knew, and that I still did not have a calling card even though I had attended as many as twenty Boston debuts in one season while I was at Harvard. It was probably a Middle Western oversight.

"Well, you've got to have an engraved card," said Harry, "and in the lower left-hand corner it must say that you are Secretary to Mr. Justice McReynolds. But first you'll have to have one printed while you're waiting for the engraved card to be made."

"I'll attend to it Monday," I said, "if you'll tell me which printer to go to. But I do want to start reading the petitions not later than Monday afternoon. As tomorrow may be my last free Sunday for some time, I think I'll go sightseeing." And with that comment I left apartment 507, having completed my first day as Secretary and Law Clerk to a Justice of the Supreme Court of the United States. The only trouble was that the Justice had not put in his appearance as yet.

He arrived in Washington, however, on the following Wednesday, September 2, 1936. Mary and I stayed at the apartment while Harry went down to the railroad station to meet him. They returned together, and as Harry opened the front door of the apartment I hastily walked out into the hall to greet the Justice. McReynolds entered slowly, carrying a cane, and he rather noisily dropped it in an umbrella stand near the door. Then Harry took the Justice's hat and coat, bowed slightly, smiled, and began making small talk.

After the Justice's hat and coat had been handed to Harry, I noticed with a hasty glance that McReynolds was impeccably dressed, and that he had a very erect military carriage. To my surprise he did not exhibit any enthusiasm whatever about returning home after traveling thousands of miles, nor was there any reference to where he had been. Not once in all the months to come did he ever mention Europe or having been there in the summer of 1936. Nor did he inquire about my shorthand, as I had expected him to. Surely Justice Van Devanter would have mentioned it, but not so Justice McReynolds. Instead McReynolds nodded in a rather formal fashion but did not smile. However, in a voice of considerable graciousness he said, "How do you do, Mr. Knox. I am glad to see you are back. There are some things I want to talk over with you."

I obediently followed the Justice into his large study, and as soon as he sat down, I sat down, too. Later on I was to be cautioned by Justice Van Devanter that I should always stand in Justice McReynolds' presence until asked to sit, and that I should use the word "Sir" when addressing him.

"I am going to raise your salary to $2,750," were the Justice's first words. "Harry has spoken to me about your expenses here in Washington, and after talking with him I have decided to pay you more than $2,400."

I thanked him sincerely, and I meant it. That amount had considerably more purchasing power in 1936 than it does today. However, when Harry later learned about the increase to $2,750, he was very unimpressed. He pointed out the fact that the Justice did not pay my salary in the first place, and that it was paid entirely by the government; also that the Justice could designate any amount from $2,400 to $3,600 for the year's work. "If he wants you to live in this apartment building, where you will have extra expenses, then he should pay you more. On that salary you won't be able to eat many of the fancy meals they serve in the dining room downstairs. You better eat all of your meals over at Eighteenth and Columbia Road," were Harry's final words about the matter.

After commenting about my raise in salary, the Justice opened his desk drawer and drew out an official looking document which almost resembled a college diploma. He signed it methodically and carefully—inserting my name and, as I recall now, the amount of my salary. This was my official confirmation as his law clerk. "Send this down to the Clerk's office," were his next words. "He will need it for his files."

"Now, will you please take a letter?" And with that the Justice began dictating to me for the first time—after I had the opportunity to walk hastily into my own office to pick up the stenographic notebook which I had brought with me. I fully expected him to inquire about my shorthand, but at no time did he ever mention the subject. He just assumed that I knew it perfectly. Later on I was to learn that the Justice always took for granted that his law clerk would, of course, be perfect in every particular—even to making a minute and correct forecast of tomorrow's weather.

To my great surprise, I found that McReynolds dictated in a slow and deliberate fashion. My fears that my shorthand speed would fail me at a crucial moment never materialized. A speed of eighty words per minute was more than ample for his needs, and as it turned out I never made a single mistake in dictation during the entire time that I was with the Justice. Many times he would ask me to read back my notes, but when working on a legal opinion we used to progress so slowly that often I would write out difficult phrases in English instead of in shorthand. Since he never asked to see my notes, he never knew what shorthand system I used or whether part of it was in English.

"In your work here," the Justice next said, "you will be both a secretary and a law clerk. I have no use for women secretaries and always prefer my law clerk to do secretarial work, too. I have had women working for me in the past and have always had to discharge them. They ultimately became very possessive and wished to run the whole show."

The Justice next explained the system of telephones in the apartment. There was a telephone on his desk and one on my desk. Our rooms were adjoining but separated by a short hallway. Conversation in his room could not be heard in my room, and vice versa, so I would have ample opportunity to concentrate on my work without any outside disturbance. The telephones on our respective desks were connected to a private line and had an unlisted number. Any call on this line would be of importance—either from another Justice of the Supreme Court or from a close friend of McReynolds'. If I answered an incoming call on the private line, I could signal the Justice in his office by pressing a buzzer if I wished him to take the call. He could also signal me by pressing a similar buzzer. At this late date I can still hear the sound of that buzzer, which would pounce upon the stillness of the room with a low hissing sound.

There was also another telephone in the apartment. It was the house phone and was connected with the downstairs switchboard. All calls from the public would come over this line. This telephone was placed at a considerable distance from both my office and the Justice's office. It was down the hall near the kitchen, and whenever the house phone rang it would invariably be answered by Harry—if he were in the apartment. A continuous ringing of the phone would indicate that Harry was not in the kitchen and that I should walk down the hall and take the call.

Before giving me his final instructions on this first day, the Justice also said that Harry would hand me a key to the apartment but that I was never to work later than 7:00 P.M. "And please do not come here after seven o'clock unless you telephone me first," he cautioned. "A dinner party might be in progress, and I would not want the noise of a typewriter to be heard at such a time. You will also begin work at nine each morning, and you can quit at five or six if you finish all your work for the day."

He then showed me a large closet in a nearby room, which was piled high with Supreme Court stationery, carbon paper, etc. In this closet there was also a filing cabinet filled with correspondence arranged alphabetically. From the closet I then obtained certain necessary supplies and began to transcribe my first letter for him. I had also brought with me to work on that day a typewriting eraser and a green eyeshade. As I went alone into my own office and sat down at the typewriter for the first time since the arrival of the Justice, I congratulated myself that McReynolds appeared to be so friendly. "He let me take all those weeks off to study shorthand," I said to myself, "and yet I should have been here all the time working on these petitions for certiorari. That was very kind of him, and now he has given me a raise in salary." So I adjusted the paper in the typewriter, put on my eyeshade, and went to work.

In the middle 1930s at Harvard it was customary for virtually every law student to wear a green eyeshade, which clamped over one's ears like a pair of glasses. Ultimately I grew so dependent upon this green eyeshade that it became a part of my very nature. I still remember walking by row after row of desks in the Law School Library reading room and seeing scores of students bent over their books and wearing this same kind of eyeshade. Such a shade kept outside distractions reduced to a minimum. I put [my shade] on at Justice McReynolds' without even giving it a thought. Before I had finished with my typing, however, the Justice had occasion to leave his room, walk down the long hall near my room and then on to the kitchen to see what Harry was cooking for dinner that evening. On his way back from the kitchen I heard his rapid, military steps stop suddenly in front of me. I looked up and said, "I shall have these letters ready in a moment. I'm now typing the last one." But the first words I heard were, "What in the world is that!" in a tone of voice which sounded both astonished and offended at the same time. For a few moments I did not even know what the Justice meant, and I looked around the desk to see what was wrong with it, or with the typewriter.

"No, no, I meant that thing you're wearing!" said the Justice.

"Oh!" I replied, "why, it's my eyeshade. We all wore eyeshades at school, and I brought this one down here with me."

"Take it off!" ordered the Justice. "It looks like hell. I don't ever want to see it again."[3] And with that he walked back to his own office.

I did take off the eyeshade at once and never used it again, but at the time I felt offended in some vague sort of way. I had just concluded that the Justice was going to be quite friendly when he had suddenly and unexpectedly displayed a fit of temperament. Later on I was to learn that each time McReynolds found himself becoming friendly or informal with anyone in his household, he would suddenly retreat behind a wall of formality and issue a pronouncement that would leave no doubt as to our lowly status in the scheme of things.

As soon as I had finished transcribing the dictation which the Justice had given me, I stopped long enough to count all the petitions for certiorari which were then on the floor of my office. I then calculated how many days it was before the opening of Court in October, and by this method I ascertained the exact number of petitions which I would read each day. I forget the figure arrived at, but it was truly a staggering one—and meant that I would have to read petitions for certiorari seven days a week and in the evenings, too. There was nothing to do but plan to work until seven o'clock each evening and then take a few petitions to my room to read after dinner. So that day I stayed until past the Justice's dinner hour. At six o'clock I heard Harry announce dinner, and the Justice walked into the dining room to eat.

The rooms in the apartment were so arranged that I could not help noticing a number of things. Instead of sitting at the large dining room table, the Justice sat in a corner of the room at a very small table which Harry had set. During the meal Harry stood at the entrance to the dining room, saying nothing unless spoken to and watching the Justice eat. As soon as one course was consumed, he would remove the dishes and bring on the next course. Now and then McReynolds would ask a question, and sometimes a rather lengthy conversation would ensue.

---

3. For some reason I remember vividly that these were the exact words which the justice used on this occasion. Many snatches of conversation have faded from memory in the passing years—but not this particular incident.

I was so near to the dining room that I could hear nearly everything that was said. I hesitated to type for fear that the noise of the machine would prove distasteful, so I busied myself reading one of the petitions. But as I glanced at the lines of print, I could hear the Justice ask, "Harry, what are you going to do with those sons of yours?"

"Well, sir," replied Harry, "I hope to send them to college."

"College! Do you mean to say *they* are going to college? Why don't you train them to be handymen like yourself? There's no need for them to go to college!"

"Oh yes there is!" replied a firm voice. "I want them to do better than I did. I didn't have no such advantages, but nowadays my boys needs to go to college."

"Humph—I don't see any sense to that," replied the Justice. "One of your sons has a good job in the Supreme Court cloakroom. Why doesn't he plan to stay there?"

As this colloquy was going on, I thought to myself, "I shouldn't eavesdrop like this! But how can I help hearing what's being said? I guess I better close up and leave." So after McReynolds had finished his dinner, had read the letters I had typed, and had signed them, I bade him good evening and walked into the kitchen preparatory to leaving the apartment. First, however, I made sure I had the front door key which Harry had given me a few days before. "You can drop those letters in the chute in the hall," Harry suggested. "Now that the Justice is back in town, be here promptly at nine in the morning, and a few minutes before nine you can pick up his morning mail at the desk downstairs. Personal letters are always to be handed to him without being opened."

"OK, Harry," I replied as I closed the kitchen door behind me.

I then walked over to Eighteenth and Columbia Road and went into a nearby restaurant. It happened to be Chinese. I had already purchased a New York paper at a newsstand across the street from the restaurant, and after I had ordered pork chops American style, I glanced at the paper for the first time. Governor Landon had just made another speech and was feeling quite confident of victory in November. While glancing at this news I could not help but wonder why the Justice did not want Harry's sons to go to college. "That was odd," I thought, "but maybe he assumed they wouldn't get through and that Harry would spend his money for nothing." I was still too naïve to realize that I had met for the first time in Washington the problem of advanced education for the colored people. At least one Justice of the Supreme Court of the United States was opposed to such an idea.

On Thursday, September 3, 1936, I started in earnest to read and brief the petitions for certiorari. I was already becoming considerably uneasy about the short time that remained before the opening of Court. However, the Justice never mentioned the petitions, and did not seem disturbed in any way about the passage of time. That morning he received a telephone call on his private extension phone. It was from a Mrs. Francis M. Savage, who was expecting to play golf with the Justice and some friends that day. Before long McReynolds left the apartment, to be gone for the rest of the day.

[Mrs. Savage] was a widow who occupied the apartment directly above the Justice's. Her late husband had been a prominent banker and philanthropist who had been a leader in building up the business portion of Gary, Indiana. Some weeks were to elapse before I was to meet Mrs. Savage for the first time. When she and several other friends went golfing with the Justice that day, I did not realize that she would prove to be a friend who would be of enormous help to me later on in the year.

As soon as the Justice had left to go golfing, Mary Diggs came out of the kitchen, greeted me with an infectious smile, and said, "Mr. Knox, I think I'll just clean this place plenty today and make it really shine. The Justice is not going to be back for a long time." And then, as I typed out page after page, Mary polished and scrubbed and rubbed and waxed.

It was late afternoon before McReynolds returned to the apartment. I hurried to finish typing the material I was working on, for I thought he might want to dictate some more letters. He walked past the door of my office without looking in and then went into his own office. Presently, however, I heard his footsteps again in the hall. He was asking me in a rather loud voice where Mary was. My first thought was that he had noticed how well she had cleaned the apartment during his absence, and that he was going to compliment her for it. When she arrived from the kitchen, however, I could not help overhearing the Justice say, "I thought you were supposed to be a maid who would keep this place clean!"

A bit thunderstruck I looked out from my room and glanced down the hall. There I noticed the Justice running his finger along the top of one of the bedroom doors, which was ajar. "Look at this dust!" he was saying. "When are you ever going to learn to be thorough in your work?"

I could see that poor Mary was crushed, but she said nothing. After a few moments she drifted rather helplessly back into the kitchen and disappeared behind the swinging door. The Justice then walked back to his office, and though I could not see him I gathered that he had settled himself at his desk for some work. In about ten minutes I walked silently off in the direction of the kitchen and rather hesitatingly peaked in.

Mary had been crying—that I could see. Her eyes were a bit red, and she gave a short sniffle and tweaked her nose with her right hand. Harry was in a corner of the kitchen fixing soft-shelled crabs for the evening meal—[something the Justice considered to be a great delicacy, as I would later learn]. "I'm sorry you were criticized, Mary," I said in a low voice. "You did work hard today."

Finally I ventured to ask why she worked for the Justice at all if he upset her like that. She looked at me and hesitated a moment before saying, "Why, I can't stop! I haven't got my two hundred dollars!"

"Does somebody owe you two hundred dollars?" I inquired.

"No, no, it ain't that," she replied. "I've been trying for years to save two hundred dollars, and I just can't do it, so I has to keep on working here."

"It's this way," Harry spoke up. "She needs two hundred dollars to pay her lodge, so she can get a good funeral when she dies."

At this point I relaxed a bit and smiled. "But Mary, you're not ready to die," I said. "Why, you've got lots of time to earn that two hundred dollars."

"That's what I keep telling her," said Harry, "and if she weren't colored, I'd be sure she was Justice McReynolds' sister."

"I ain't neither Justice McReynolds' sister and you know that, Harry Parker!" Mary rather indignantly replied.

"Of course, I knows it," countered Harry, "but you and the Justice are just alike—always worrying and stewing and getting upset about things that never happen. Why, you're going to live for years yet, and you don't need to worry now about not having no money for your funeral."

Even at this late date I can still see the three of us talking in subdued tones in that kitchen. Harry then lifted a wet hand out of a dishpan full of water, and pointing at me he said, "You better get out of here, Mr. Knox! If the Justice buzzes for you and finds you gone, it won't be so good for you."

Turning to go I replied, "I'm leaving, but I'm still right here in the apartment, and I could always tell him that I came in here to ask you for some advice."

"Asking me for legal advice, I suppose! Humph!" said Harry as he put his hands back in the dishpan.

While walking very quietly down the hall and back to my office, I suddenly caught myself thinking, "What has come over me anyway? I've been here only a few days, and I'm already planning on how to deceive the Justice by slipping in and out of the kitchen. Justice Van Devanter would not approve of this, I am sure!"

And so the days passed one by one. In a week I had a large and rather impressive pile of typed sheets ready for McReynolds to look over. Each page was a complete digest of one of the petitions for certiorari, with a recommendation at the bottom as to whether the petition should be allowed or denied. After a few more days I laid them all on his desk and then waited for the heavens to fall. To my great surprise, however, he finally emerged from his office holding a few sheets of paper in his hand, saying, "These are quite satisfactory, Mr. Knox. However, in this particular case you say, 'This petition is utterly without merit and should be denied.' Now, the word 'utterly' is unnecessary. Don't use it again. Otherwise, your analysis meets with my approval."

This was the first and last comment he ever made regarding the hundreds of pages that I was ultimately to type prior to the opening of Court in October. I gradually became almost like an automaton. I read a certain number of petitions each day in the week, and then I typed out comments regarding them. The pile of typed sheets grew ever higher. The apartment was silent as a tomb, and no noise could be heard except the clicking of my typewriter.

The next evening, however, when I was getting ready to leave for dinner, the Justice unexpectedly announced, "Tomorrow I shall be driving up to West Point, and I shall need you to come along with me. We will be gone for several days, so make your plans accordingly. I want to get a fairly early start to get ahead of the weekend traffic."

All I could think of was, "Oh! Oh! Now I'll never finish reading all of these petitions!" But instead I said, "Yes, sir, and I hope you will have room in your car for my satchel."

After this announcement, I left the apartment through the front door as the Justice happened to be standing in the hall. He was gazing at one of the numerous colored drawings of birds which were hung in his apartment. Once outside in the plush carpeted corridor, however, I took a few steps down the corridor and knocked quietly on the kitchen door. Harry opened this door, and as usual he was busily getting dinner. Looking at me rather surprised he said, "What's the matter? I thought I just heard you go out."

"I did go out," I replied, "but I just wanted to tell you that the Justice and I are enrolling in West Point and are driving up there tomorrow."

"Well, is that so?" Harry said in a tone of some surprise. "I'm certainly glad to hear that, and I hope both of you stay away a long time."

"What's the matter?" I queried as I closed the kitchen door behind me. "Here I've been slaving away for days, and now you want to get rid of me."

"Well, it's no joking matter," replied Harry. "All I means is that I hope the Justice gets all of the traveling bug out of his system on this trip so he won't want to go duck hunting this fall."

"Are you a duck hunter, too?" I said with a smile.

"Now listen, Mr. Knox," said Harry, "I can't stop fixing dinner to explain about ducks, but just let me tell you something. When the Justice goes duck hunting and shoots any ducks, they always fall in the wrong places. Then he wants me to wade into the water and fetch 'em out. I'm no hound dog, and I'm getting too old to do that. Why, every time we go hunting I think for sure I'll get pneumonia."

I looked at Harry incredulously and a broad smile crossed my face. "You mean to say you're a retriever, along with everything else, and that he doesn't take a hunting dog with him?"

"I suppose it sounds funny," replied Harry, drawing himself up in true seriousness, "but did you ever try wading into cold water up to your waist to fetch out some dead ducks, and then have no place to dry out or warm yourself for several hours? Man, oh, man, is that cold work!"

Thinking that the Justice might look through the swinging door and see me in the kitchen with Harry and Mary, I brought the conversation to a rapid conclusion, asking just one or two more questions. "Where does the Justice keep his car, Harry?"

"Why, in the garage in the basement here," I was told.

"And I suppose it's some kind of limousine? Am I going to drive it or will he drive?"

"It's a limousine, all right," said Harry, "but not the kind you think. Now let me see, I bet the Justice has at least a hundred thousand dollars saved up, but he can't yet afford no limousine. When he wants a limousine, he borrows Mrs. Loose's."

"Who's she?" I queried.

"Why, Mrs. Jacob Leander Loose, the Loose-Wiles biscuit woman—a very rich widow. You'll see her later on, no doubt." With that announcement I left, to sort over some clothes which I wanted to take with me on the auto trip.

The next day was Friday, September 11, and the Justice had expected to leave promptly at 8:00 A.M. However, I woke up just a bit too late to walk over to Eighteenth and Columbia Road in time to eat a good breakfast, which I thought I should do in view of the plans for the day, and get back to 2400 in time to meet the Justice. He was waiting for me and had been for some fifteen minutes. Yet he displayed no real impatience and told me to get my satchel and meet him in the front of the apartment building, as the car had been brought around to the Sixteenth Street entrance.

In a few minutes the elevator took me downstairs. Not seeing the Justice anywhere, I walked briskly down the corridor and out into the open. There standing near an automobile parked at the curb was the Justice. He was wearing long gauntlets of the type that motorists must have used around 1912. I also noticed that the car was a 1929 convertible six-cylinder Buick coupe.

While putting my satchel into the storage compartment, I noticed that the license on the car was number 62 — obviously a low number for the District of Columbia. Seeing my apparent interest in the license, McReynolds rather proudly volunteered the information that the Justices of the Supreme Court were allotted numbers from 50 to 75, and that any District policeman seeing number 62 would, or should, instantly know that it was a car belonging to the Court.

It soon became evident that the Justice had taken me along to serve as Master Mechanic and Tire Changer in case anything went wrong. A more inappropriate selection could hardly have been made. I not only lacked the remotest knowledge of the nuts and bolts making up a Buick coupe, but I would have been hard put even to change a tire on that car. I had, in fact, never changed a tire on any car in my life. So I thought to myself, "Well, here I am, going on an automobile trip with a Justice of the Supreme Court of the United States. Back in June I certainly would have felt complimented to take such a trip, but now I'm not so sure. I wonder what we'll talk about during our travels. At least, I'll let him do most of the talking."

The Justice soon proved to be an expert driver, despite his advanced years. On the way to Baltimore, we were weaving in and out of traffic at rates varying from fifty to sixty miles per hour. The auto was snorting and panting and chugging and jolting us, but nevertheless it was making good time. "I just had the garage at 2400 look the motor all over, so I guess it will be all right," volunteered the Justice.

"Gosh, I hope so!" I thought to myself.

Almost the next thing I heard, however, was, "My, my, we're almost out of gas. Mr. Knox, I shall expect you to keep your eyes on the gasoline gauge during this trip. We'll have to stop at the next gas station. Why didn't that fellow at 2400 fill up the tank before we left?" And so in a few minutes we halted before a small gasoline station on the other side of Baltimore. The Justice asked me to see that the attendant filled up the gas tank and checked the oil, and he excused himself to go to the washroom. While gasoline was being put into the car, I heard a voice asking, "Say, bud, where'd you get the low license number? How come?"

In obvious pride at riding in a car bearing a Supreme Court number, I could not resist saying, "Why, this is a car belonging to a Justice of the Supreme Court." And paraphrasing what the Justice had said at the beginning of the trip, I announced that numbers 50 to 75 were reserved for members of the Court.

"You don't say so?" said the attendant. "Now don't tell me you're a Justice of the Supreme Court!"

"No," I said in mock seriousness, "but the man with me is."

"Why, you don't say so," was the answer. And the next thing I heard was, "Hey, Ed, come over here a second."

A man of about fifty slowly ambled over and asked, "What's up? He's going to pay for the gas, ain't he?"

"Say, we got a real live Justice of the Supreme Court in the washroom. Look at this license number — 62. Watch the old guy when he comes out, and you'll see him."

This fascinating bit of information proved somewhat exciting to the newcomer. For the first time I felt that I had definitely spoken out of turn, and I vowed inwardly that never again during the trip would I mention low license numbers or Justices.

It was not long before I began to fear that McReynolds would be arrested for speeding. The car was being pushed to the limit, and the faster we went, the more difficult it became for me to study the map in my lap and to keep up with the road signs which kept flashing past. Being nearsighted, I kept adjusting my glasses to my nose and peering anxiously through them. Finally, in a moment of helplessness, I said, "I believe we took the wrong road about four miles back."

This information had a startling effect on the Justice, and the next thing I knew the car had ground to an abrupt halt — but on the shoulder of the road and not on the highway itself. "Let me see that map," he said impatiently. Without need of glasses of any kind, he finally said, "Yes, it's possible we are on the wrong road! I'll turn around and go back a ways. Mr. Knox, when I hire a law clerk, I expect to get one who can read road signs."

"Yes, sir," I said meekly.

Eventually we arrived at the Delaware Water Gap, and McReynolds decided to stay overnight there. We had separate rooms, and he paid for my accommodations. The next morning—which was a Saturday—we got an early start. This time I was not late in making my appearance, and before long we were on the outskirts of West Point. To this day I cannot recall one shred of conversation that took place after the Justice discovered we had gone some four miles out of our way due to my negligence in not noticing a certain road sign. At no time were we silent for very long, but I gather that the conversation from that time on centered mostly on the subject of not getting lost again. Certainly, there were no legal discussions about anything—least of all the petitions for certiorari. And even in the intimate surroundings of an automobile and a long trip together, the Justice never mentioned the Court, or any of the other Justices, or any of his experiences in the past. In fact, he never even mentioned Europe or that he had spent the summer there. I made a mental note that as regards conversational ability he certainly differed from Justice Van Devanter.

Once in the vicinity of West Point, McReynolds seemed immediately at home. We drove up to a large and fashionable restaurant, or inn, and there we ate a leisurely meal. A lady sitting at the next table a few feet away, evidently an army officer's wife, kept blowing cigarette smoke toward us while carrying on a lengthy conversation with a woman friend. The Justice became more and more annoyed, and finally, waving his right arm through the air and blowing some away smoke, he said in a voice which could be heard some distance away, "I certainly wish women these days would learn how to smoke without bothering other people!" I looked down toward the tablecloth in some embarrassment, and to this day I do not know whether the smoker did hear us and, if so, what her reaction was. At least, in a few minutes she got up and left.

In those days I always carried a camera with me and was in the habit of taking countless pictures. The sun was still high in the sky after we finished our meal, so the Justice walked out on a sort of veranda and sat down to enjoy the view. He picked out a bench which was empty, and after receiving his permission I took several pictures of him sitting there alone. The Justice looks like some forbidding senator of ancient Rome, resting after a brisk walk from the Coliseum.

At this moment a woman came walking by, carrying a small baby, and she sat down on the bench with McReynolds. I was at the time sitting on the bench, too, adjusting the roll of film in the camera. I glanced up, however, and then moved over to make room for her. After a few moments I noticed that McReynolds was eyeing the woman and child intently. Suddenly he became so gracious and gallant that I was almost transported back to the days of chivalry.

Nodding his head toward the woman he said, "Madam, you and your child would make a most charming picture. Would you mind if my secretary took a photograph of you holding the baby?"

To my genuine surprise, the woman consented to pose for such a photograph, even though she did not know who we were. For a fleeting moment I half expected her to bash us both over the head with her pocketbook and walk on. However, looking at the baby very proudly, she stood up and held the child toward the camera. After taking several pictures of the woman and baby, I closed my camera and asked to whom I should send the pictures—if they proved satisfactory. While she was writing down her name and address for the Justice, I thought to myself, "It's curtains for me if these pictures aren't a success!"

I passed her name and address on to the Justice, but even then he did not identify himself other than to state that we were from Washington, D.C.

In a short while we were again in the car, and the Justice announced his plans for the first time. While in the vicinity he expected to stay at the home of a friend. Arrangements had already been made for me to remain at Stone Ridge, New York, at the home of Mr. and Mrs. Service, who took in lodgers. [When we arrived at his friend's residence], McReynolds asked me to stay in the car while he went into the house. To this day I do not know whose home it was, nor did I ever see the hostess. In a short while the Justice returned with detailed directions as to where I was to spend Saturday night.

Monday morning came all too soon. Some minutes after I had eaten my last meal in the Service house, the Justice drove up at the exact moment which he had indicated would be the time of his arrival. He blew the car's horn twice, in an impatient sort of way, and he did not get out of the automobile. I had already reimbursed the Services for my board and lodging (this time I had insisted on paying), so I grabbed my satchel and hastened toward the Buick. "Good morning," I said, and then we started up with a jerk and were once again on our way. I expected that we would head straight for Washington, but soon the Justice said, "The weather's so nice that I've decided to drive over to Gettysburg and tour the battlefield. I haven't seen it for some time. Besides, there's no hurry in getting back to Washington."

By evening we had reached the vicinity of Hallam, Pennsylvania, and rather than drive farther on, the Justice decided to spend the night there. The next morning the weather was superb for a tour of the battlefield. We were soon standing at the spot where Lee hammered at the Union left wing the first day—July 1, 1863. On the third day of battle, the great Southern general smashed at Meade's center. Here was the very location, the ground on which they fought. The Justice walked slowly back and forth in silence, and I could almost see Pickett's fifteen thousand men staggering up a slope of land to reach the Union lines surmounting Cemetery Ridge. "Lee should never have done it," I said. "He exhausted his last and finest resources without any hope of reinforcements. Those men might have turned the tide of battle on the fourth day, but instead they were simply wasted. If Stonewall Jackson had not been killed at Chancellorsville, the outcome of Gettysburg would have been very different." This criticism brought no reply from the Justice, only a cool stare. He looked at me as if to say, "I suppose you could have managed things better?"

We arrived back in Washington at 6:30 that night. We had made the entire round trip without experiencing any motor trouble, and without even suffering the ill effects of a flat tire. How fortunate that was for him, the Justice never realized.

Later that day, I walked to the nearest drugstore and left some rolls of film to be developed. By chance, the pictures of the woman and her child turned out very satisfactorily—so much so, in fact, that the Justice had several enlargements made of one pose. He kept one enlargement for himself and sent the other copies to the woman. She must have been quite surprised to receive his letter written on Supreme Court stationery, but in a few days she replied and thanked him most sincerely for his generosity. At the time I thought that this incident revealed a deeply hidden facet of the Justice's character— namely, a liking for children and a regret that he did not have a family of his own. He never again referred to the incident after showing me the reply from the woman thanking us for the enlargements. He would have been the last to admit it, but the photographs did give him an immense amount of satisfaction.

Five days had been spent on the West Point trip. I had enjoyed it so much that it was difficult to get back into the routine of reading petitions again. Yet I threw myself into the task with a fervor which I marvel at even to this day. And with each passing hour I became more and more puzzled as to why the Justice never seemed to care whether I was going to finish reading all of the petitions or not. I failed to realize that all of my reading and typing was really quite unimportant after all. Even if I had not read and briefed a single petition, it would not have been too much of a loss for the Justice. I overlooked the fact that McReynolds and Van Devanter were the ranking senior Justices of the Court. McReynolds was next to the senior Justice in point of service, which meant that he had the privilege of voting next to the last at every conference of the Court—unless Hughes exercised his privilege of voting last by virtue of being Chief Justice. The youngest Justice in point of service had to vote first, [and so on up the seniority ladder]. So McReynolds and Van Devanter always had the benefit of the votes of at least six Justices, and perhaps seven, before they needed to cast their own ballots. Therefore, any recommendations which I might make in my digests of the petitions for certiorari were more or less superfluous. In a pinch, all McReynolds really needed to do was to listen to the Chief Justice's discussion of the facts of each petition and then wait for the Justices to vote. With his more than twenty years of experience on the bench, it was only natural that by 1936, petitions—even hundreds of them—would leave McReynolds quite unmoved. But they were a new experience for me, and like a salmon trying to swim upstream, I struggled on and on, briefing petitions even in my dreams.

On the way back from Gettysburg, however, despite the petitions that remained to be read, I decided that it was time to relax at least long enough to call on some people in Washington whom I had been wanting to see ever since my arrival in town. I also became intrigued with the idea of meeting some of the other Justices before the start of a busy term of Court. I made plans regarding which persons I would ask to meet first. The time was growing short, and because of the press of work I could only plan on going out two evenings a week at the most. I was beginning to feel a bit bored and in need of some friendly contacts. At Harvard I had lived a gregarious sort of life which was far different from what the days in Washington were proving to be.

2

THE NEXT MORNING McReynolds went out to play golf at Chevy Chase, and after he was gone Harry happened to stop by my office while I was typing. I looked up and said, "Harry, I hope nothing comes up to keep me working overtime on the seventeenth as I'm going to dinner that night at Mrs. Gann's."

Eyeing me somewhat suspiciously, Harry finally said, "I thought you didn't know many people in Washington. You mean 'Dolly' Gann?"

"Yes," I replied, "Mrs. Edward Everett Gann. Her brother, Charles Curtis, was Vice President under Hoover. She's an old friend of mine."

"Well, just don't let the Justice know you is looking up any old friends—especially lady friends," Harry cautioned. "And say, how come you know her at all if you never lived in Washington before?"

"That," I replied, "is a long story. Remind me to tell you sometime."

The summer of 1936 was now over. The Justices had already returned to Washington one by one. We were now on the eve of one of the most historic terms of Court ever to be held, but no one at the time seemed to suspect it. The Chief Justice and Mrs. Hughes had spent their summer driving leisurely through New England. Justice Van Devanter, as I already knew, had spent a goodly portion of his summer vacation at his farm near Ellicott City, Maryland. He owned 750 acres and had been busy raising a good crop of corn. That summer there was a shortage of corn, and he apparently sold his for a good price. His farm also produced wheat, oats, and hay. Van Devanter was also proud of a herd of thoroughbred Hampshire hogs which he had on the farm. Later on in the summer he and his sister, Mrs. Sanford L. Rariden, had gone North to the Seigniory Club near Montebello, Quebec. Mrs. Rariden was the Justice's younger sister and had been his companion since the death of his wife. McReynolds, of course, had been to Europe—but as yet he had made no mention of his trip aboard to me. I still didn't know what countries he had visited, whether or not he had enjoyed himself, or even why he had wanted to go—except perhaps to escape the summer heat in Washington. Justice Sutherland had also been abroad with his wife. He had been born in Buckinghamshire, England. I understood that he and his wife had walked in the hills around Buckinghamshire and had then gone on to France and Switzerland. Justice Brandeis had spent the summer as usual in his home at Chatham, Massachusetts, on Cape Cod. Justice Cardozo had vacationed at his home in Rye, New York. He, like Brandeis, had spent the summer reading and receiving friends. Cardozo had not only been reading petitions, however, but he had also covered a wide range of general literature. Justice Stone had apparently gone to the coast of Maine to spend the summer, but he had been stricken with an acute form of dysentery. His summer vacation had evidently been an unhappy one, and from time to time Harry had kept me informed of Stone's condition. Justice Roberts had spent the summer at his farm near Valley Forge. Here he had a prize herd of Guernseys and, like Van Devanter, had a great interest in being a gentleman farmer. Justice Butler had spent his summer vacation in southern Pennsylvania. He had played an occasional game of golf and had enjoyed happy family relationships with his grandchildren and other relatives.

[On Friday, September 18], the weather was oppressive. Scarcely a breath of air stirred in the apartment, and what breezes there were seemed always to be warded off by the mounds of petitions for certiorari which surrounded my desk. I typed on and on as if I were running back and forth on some kind of treadmill. And no matter how warm the weather became, I was never to remove my coat unless in the privacy of my own office and only then if the Justice were absent from the apartment. "If I am out, never answer the door with your coat off," Harry had cautioned, "and don't let the Justice ever catch you without your coat on, either!" Unfortunately I was not dressed for the occasion. I had brought with me from Chicago only my regular suits, and each day I kept thinking that the weather would turn cooler. At the same time, however, Harry and the Justice were wearing the lightest weight suits obtainable. They wore coats that, though black in color, were of a material which would have been very suitable for life in the tropics.

The loss of my eyeshade also bothered me considerably. "If only I could wear it like I used to do!" I sighed to myself. "But it's no use to hope for that as the Justice would never change his mind about eyeshades. If only I had never started to wear the darn thing while I was at Harvard!"

I kept watching McReynolds out of the corner of my eye that morning. First he took his usual "setting-up" exercises followed by a hearty breakfast. Then he made preparations to leave to play golf at Chevy Chase. Apparently he had decided to use to good advantage the last remaining days of vacation. Though in his mid-seventies, I understood from Harry that the Justice could still play a good game of golf. And the Chevy Chase Club, I also realized, was the symbol of the luxury and comfort and joy of life for many of those who held prominent governmental positions.

As more than three hundred petitions had by that time been carefully read and briefed, the "glamour" of reading learned pleadings filed in the Clerk's office of the most powerful Court in the world had become slightly dulled, to say the least. Besides I was anxious for the Justice to leave the apartment so that I could finish reading a magazine article which I had carefully hidden under a pile of documents. It was provocatively entitled "Is Roosevelt a Socialist?" and appeared in the October 1936 issue of *The American Mercury.* "I wonder if he is, but I'll never find out until McReynolds leaves for Chevy Chase," I pondered to myself. And with that conclusion reached, I typed out a few more lines of legal comment on the Justice's new and fine Remington Noiseless machine.

That same morning Harry Parker was in the kitchen of the Justice's apartment, but now and then his honest and heartwarming brown face would silently peer through the swinging door to see if McReynolds was advancing in his preparations to journey forth into the world of conflict and harshness and bitterness. Harry was anxious to inquire of me how the dinner at the Ganns' "went off" and just what had been served as the pièce de résistance. For had not Harry's late mother supervised state dinners during the McKinley and Taft administrations and then taught her son all the uncanny and devious ways of culinary skill? This son, let it be said, was never one to overlook the opportunity of discovering a new recipe. Such an inquiry, however, would have to wait until the Great Man had left the apartment. Soon, however, the moment of expectancy arrived. The Justice closed the door of his bedroom, walked rapidly down the long hall, carefully adjusted his tie as he glanced cautiously into a mirror, brushed a hair off his coat lapel, and then called out rather sharply, "Harry, where are you? My walking stick!"

"Oh, here it is, Mr. Justice. You didn't put it back in the right place when you came in last night."

To this statement McReynolds made no comment, but he gingerly took the stick. As he swept out of the front entrance of the apartment, while Harry was holding the door ajar, he announced, "Soft-shelled crabs for dinner to-night, Harry, and I'll be back at five."

Harry bowed in silence, and the door closed. And in the twinkling of an eye, I reached for the article on Roosevelt, and Harry took a few quick steps [down the hall to my office].

"Mr. Knox! Don't tell me you just sit there reading magazines!" exclaimed Harry. "Don't you know that the justice won't even let us read the newspapers while at work? Have you been reading a magazine all morning?"

"Of course not," I replied, "I just waited until you closed the door before reaching for this. In fact, here is an article that looks so interesting I think I'll give it to the Justice to read. Tell me, Harry, do you think Roosevelt's a Socialist?"

"Now how in the world should I know whether he's a Socialist? Why don't you ask him?"

"Say, I think you've got something there. I'll tell the Justice to call up the White House tomorrow and inquire if the President is a Socialist!"

"Oh, you will, will you?" exclaimed Harry in mock seriousness. "And now I'd like you to tell me something. Did you see your lady friend last night?"

"You mean Mrs. Gann?"

"Of course I mean Mrs. Gann. Wasn't you going to have dinner at her place?"

"Yes, I had dinner with Mrs. Gann and her husband. It was good to get out for a change, and I feel fine today. Maybe I'll step out again soon."

"Well, I'm warning you once more, Mr. Knox, the Justice don't believe in no secretaries having lady friends, and don't ever let him catch you going out there to dinner."

"Oh, I won't say anything about it, Harry," I replied, "Why, I suppose the Justice doesn't even know of Mr. and Mrs. Gann, or at least he's probably forgotten all about them. They're not written up in the papers any more. And, incidentally, we had meat and potatoes and corn on the cob—just an old-fashioned Mid-Western dinner."

"Corn on the cob!" said Harry with a disappointed smile. "Well, I guess that tasted better than all the chop suey you eat at that Chink restaurant over at Eighteenth and Columbia Road. But Mary and I figured out you would have something better than corn on the cob!"

"As for the Chink restaurant, they can fix up American food, too. I like their pork chops best," I replied.

Harry became quiet, looked at me intently for some moments, and then changed the subject of conversation. "Say, Mr. Knox, did you ever sort of notice anything different when you hear me talking to Mary?"

"Well," I replied, after a pause to collect my thoughts, "now that you mention it, I guess I did. Sometimes I hear you and Mary talking about funny things—like, for instance, pussy-willows and queens."

"That's just it," said Harry excitedly, "and Mary and me has now decided to initiate you into our secret!"

At this announcement I straightened up a bit in my chair and began to show more interest. "Secret?" I inquired, "You mean you want me to join a club or something?"

"Naw, it ain't nothing like that!" said Harry. "What I means is that once you is initiated, the three of us can talk about the Justice and all his friends without his knowing it or understanding us!"

"Indeed!" I declared with real interest. "I'm all ears. Just what do you have in mind?"

"Well, it's like this," said Harry triumphantly. "When Mary and me is getting dinner, the Justice often pokes his head in the kitchen door to give us some last-minute instructions. Or he sometimes hears Mary and me talking when we is cleaning up the dining room or fixing for me to go to market. Now all the time the Justice thinks we is just talking about some of our no-count colored friends, but we ain't at all. We is really talking about *him* and *his friends!*"

"Well, you don't say so," I countered. "But how do you talk about the Justice and his friends without his knowing it if he hears you?"

"That's easy," said Harry beaming, "and that's our secret. You see, we gives secret names to everybody. Take the Justice himself, for instance. We calls him 'Pussywillow.' Now his best lady friend is 'Madam Queen'—that's Mrs. [Camilla Hare] Lippincott."

"So that explains my hearing you two talk about pussywillows and queens!" I exclaimed. "Very clever, very clever indeed!"

"And now," Harry announced dramatically, "we have given you a name, too. You are going to be *Mr. Shoefenicks.* After this, when you hear that word you will know we are talking about you."

And so it came to pass that from that day forward I was always referred to in private by Harry and Mary as "Shoefenicks." Why they chose this name, or from whence it came, I was never to know. Nor did I ever question their selection of such a name. If the Justice, for instance, overheard Harry and Mary discussing Shoefenicks and whether he got sick after finding too many pussywillows yesterday, McReynolds must have wondered what sort of jungle dialect was being spoken in his presence.

Following this conversation, Harry began to refer at once to Justice McReynolds as "Pussywillow" in all subsequent conversation with me. Having been taken into the secret, I became a part of it at once. To this day McReynolds is, in reality, "Pussywillow" to me instead of "Mr. Justice." Several times, while serving as his secretary and law clerk, I narrowly avoided addressing him as "Pussywillow."

With the Justice, or rather "Pussywillow," gone to play golf, and it being a Friday, I continued my conversation with Harry in a leisurely manner. After a pause, during which I looked up toward Harry as I sat there at the typewriter, I said slowly, as if groping for words, "You know something, Harry. I think I'll call up Justice Brandeis and ask to meet him. He's not so busy now as he will be after the Court opens, and maybe he would have time to see me."

In one shattering moment, however, Harry's expression changed. His face took on a look almost of horror. "Justice Brandeis! Have you gone out of your mind?"

"Of course, Justice Brandeis. Why not? He's going to be eighty years old in November, and I'd like to meet him. Besides, his new secretary was at Harvard when I was there."[1]

Harry made a helpless, dazed sort of gesture with his right hand as he stood there in the doorway of my room, and he said, "Sometimes I think I never will be able to teach you nothing at all about Washington! Don't you know that we has absolutely no relations with Justice Brandeis?"

"What do you mean, we don't have any relations with him? Doesn't he come over here now and then to discuss cases that are up for decision?"

"Come over *here*?" exclaimed Harry in amazement. "Oh, you got so much to learn! Of course he never comes over here. Don't you realize that Justice Brandeis is Jewish?"

"Yes, but what about it?" I inquired innocently.

"Why," said Harry emphatically, "there's been only one Jewish fellow who ever got to come to this apartment, and he was Mr. Garfinckel who had the department store. You know, Garfinckel's downtown where they don't have no basement in the store."

---

1. [Editors' note: The secretary was Willard Hurst, later Vilas Professor of Law at the University of Wisconsin Law School. Like the author, Hurst was from Illinois (Rockford) and Harvard (LL.B., 1936).]

In a tone of quiet sarcasm I said, "And how did Mr. Garfinckel ever get in here? Did he sell some merchandise wholesale to the Justice?"

This question caused Harry to pause for some moments before replying. "Say, maybe that *was* why he came here. I always did think it kind of funny like. Pussywillow sure don't like to buy nothing if he can get out of it, and even some of the furniture here was given to him. Take that Japanese screen, for instance. One of his lady friends sent us that a couple of years ago."

"Now Harry," I ventured, "do you really mean to say that the Justice, I mean Pussywillow, is at outs with Brandeis because he's Jewish? And does that mean Cardozo doesn't come over here either?"

Without replying to the first question, Harry immediately commented, "Now Justice Cardozo, he's a sort of special case. He couldn't come over here even if he wasn't Jewish because the Justice is real mad at him."

"Mad at Cardozo? What did he ever do to upset Pussywillow?"

"Well," said Harry thoughtfully, "it was some time ago—soon after Justice Cardozo came to Washington. Pussywillow wrote an opinion and circulated it around to the other eight Justices, as he was supposed to do, of course, but Cardozo went and made a suggestion or two about improving the wording of a few sentences. That was when he was real new to the Court, too, and Pussywillow had been here for many years. Well, Pussywillow never had no more to do with Cardozo after that, and I guess they're not even on speaking terms to this day."

"Oh, Harry," I said, shaking my head slowly back and forth, "sometimes I wonder how these cases ever get decided at all. Is everybody mad at everybody else on the Supreme Court of the United States?"

"Course not! We is on real friendly terms with some of Justices. You'll see. They'll be coming here and calling on Pussywillow. Take Justice Butler, for instance. He'll come. And Justice Sutherland. Justice Van Devanter, too, and I like him to call because he's real nice."

Then after a moment's reflection Harry said, "Say, changing the subject, but what church do you belong to? You haven't said nothing at all about whether you go to church on Sundays since you got to Washington."

"Well, I'm an Episcopalian," I said.

"Is that so? And what church do you think I belong to?" inquired Harry in a triumphant tone of voice, as if I could never guess.

"Gosh, I don't know," I said, "but I suppose you're a Baptist."

"A Baptist, ha-ha! Now why would I be a Baptist?"

"To tell you the truth, Harry, I was just thinking that many colored people are Baptists, and I guessed that you might be one, too."

"Well, I ain't, because I'm a Roman Catholic!" said Harry with much pride. "Every Sunday morning I goes to mass before I come here to fix Pussywillow's breakfast. You never thought I was a Catholic, did you?"

"No, I didn't, Harry, but I'm sure we'll continue to get along fine even though I'm a Protestant and you're a Catholic and Garfinckel was Jewish. You can even keep on giving me all the advice you think I need."

"Well, then," said Harry seriously, "my advice would be that you should go to church every Sunday. You just don't want to sit around alone in this big building all the time. Don't go meeting any of Pussywillow's lady friends, but you should go and meet some nice church people. They may not be so high-toned, but they will be sincere."

"Aren't people in Washington sincere, Harry?" I inquired.

"Well, sometimes—sure—and sometimes—no," he replied.

Shortly after five o'clock on that Friday, the front door of McReynolds' thirteen-room apartment opened and the Justice himself entered. At the time Mary Diggs happened to be dusting some furniture in the hall. I was afraid that he might speak sharply to her, but this proved to be one of those times when McReynolds exhibited such unexpected friendliness that I was almost startled. Perhaps he had had a good golf game. In any event, he said, "Good afternoon, Mary," with real warmth in his voice. I could then hear the Justice stride down the long hall, and in a moment he had stopped at the door of my office.

"Can you step out here, Mr. Knox?" the Justice asked in a manner that betokened genuine friendliness. At this statement the thought flashed across my mind, "What's up now? He's certainly happy this afternoon! Maybe he won a golf trophy out at Chevy Chase!"

When I emerged McReynolds was seated on a rectangular bench which stood at the end of the hall near the door of my room. The Justice was leaning against the wall, and with his right hand he gave his thigh a few resounding whacks. I glanced rather intently at him to see if he might be suffering from the effects of sunstroke. I had never seen him exhibit such informality before.

Without further ado McReynolds said, "This afternoon I was wondering whether you would care to work here at the apartment or move down to the Court. Of course, I haven't used the office in the new building yet, but we *could* move down there if you wish. One or two of the other Justices are now using their offices, and we could use ours, too, instead of working here at home. What do you think of the idea?"

I little realized at the time that my answer to that simple question would have the most enormous significance for me during the coming year. With a naïveté bordering on what I later considered stupidity, I merely replied, "Well, sir, whatever you wish will be quite satisfactory with me. The Court is at least five miles away, and it might be disagreeable getting down there on a rainy fall morning or on a cold wintry day. You would either have to drive your own car or hunt for a taxi. Besides, Harry wouldn't be there to fix your lunch unless he made a special trip down. However, I have no fixed opinion one way or another in the matter. Either place will be quite satisfactory with me."

For some moments the Justice did not reply. Then he said, slowly and distinctly, "Perhaps you're right. It *would* be a ten mile round trip five or six times a week. Let's see, that's over two hundred miles of driving a month. I might catch cold, too, going out in all kinds of weather. Well, I guess we better continue to do our work here at 2400." And with that statement McReynolds suddenly stood up very erect—in the firm conviction that the matter was definitely settled in his mind. "One thing more," he said. "Come into my office as I want to show you how to write checks. Now that you will be keeping track of all household expenses, you must be very careful how you prepare checks for my signature."

As I was leaving the apartment that Friday evening—via the kitchen—I happened to mention in a casual way that the Justice had asked whether I wished to move down to the new Court building. "Well, what did you say to him, what did you say?" inquired Harry with great interest.

"Oh, really nothing," I replied, "except to point out that the Court is so far away that it might be wise to stay here and do our work at 2400."

"Mr. Knox," replied Harry with a note of anguish in his voice. "Do you know what you've gone and done? You've muffed your big chance! That's what you've done. Pussywillow sure must like you a lot to ask whether you want to move down to the Court, and then when you could do it, you didn't! Now why did you do a foolish thing like that?"

"Was it really as bad as all that?" I inquired in a surprised tone of voice.

"'Bad' ain't the word for it," Harry replied sadly. "It's worse than 'bad.' Don't you realize you're cooped up here in this apartment all day long with nobody else to see but me and Mary? But down at the Court you could meet other people, eat in the cafeteria, and get around more. You shouldn't just bury yourself here all year. And besides, if Pussywillow and you moved down to the Court, Mary and I wouldn't have it so hard here. We're cooped up here, too, you know?"

"Oh, gosh, Harry, I'm sorry," I replied. "I didn't realize it meant that much to you. I suppose I could tell the Justice tomorrow that I changed my mind about the matter."

"Naw, it's too late," said Harry. "He'll never change *his* mind now. We're stuck here, that's what we are! I shoulda warned you that if Pussywillow ever brought up that subject, you better try to get out of here and move down to the Court. Now every time you want to look at a book from the library, they've got to send it out here five miles in a truck."

Some weeks were to pass before I came to realize the true significance of what Harry had said, and the enormity of my error in not pressing the Justice in a vigorous manner to move down to the Court. Soon the constant need of referring to legal decisions while working five miles away from the Court's library presented problems that were serious enough in themselves, but coupled with the isolation of 2400 Sixteenth Street I gradually found myself becoming extremely lonely.

I have forgotten to mention that all during the summer of 1936, workmen had been busy renovating the entire building—which was then advertised as housing one of the most distinguished clienteles in Washington. Over two hundred rooms were redecorated. [Even with redecoration, as I complained to Harry,] "my apartment is ten feet, eight inches wide and thirteen feet, six inches long—not counting the bath and the hall entrance. It has one window which faces north and looks out on a court twenty-four feet wide."

"Well, don't look at me," Harry countered. "Remember, Pussywillow asked if you wanted to move down to the Court. We could be there right now, too, if you hadn't given him the wrong answer."

"I know, I know," I replied, looking very glum.

"And that isn't all," said Harry. "I been meaning to speak about something else for a long time. Your apartment may not be very big, but you should go and get yourself a typewriter. You can rent one if you ain't got one of your own."

"A typewriter?" I exclaimed. "What for?"

"Now don't be looking so innocent! Don't you suppose that ever since you came here I've seen you answering personal letters on Pussywillow's typewriter when he ain't around? Just don't let him catch you doing that, or you won't be writing any letters no more!"

"Oh *that*," I replied. "I guess I do write some personal letters on government time, but I'm too tired in the evening to try and answer every letter by hand."

"You sure must have a lot of girlfriends to write so many letters!" Harry ventured.

"I'm not writing all of those letters to girlfriends, Harry! If you don't believe it, here are some letters in the desk here that I am waiting to answer. And,
besides, I never type any personal letters on the Justice's machine unless I'm
pretty well caught up in my work here."

Harry's point about the typewriter, however, was well taken. In those days
I carried on a large personal correspondence with friends who lived as far east
as Finland and as far west as the Philippines. It was necessary to answer about
twenty letters a week in order to keep abreast of this correspondence. So a
short while later I did write to my parents and ask them to send on my typewriter from home. Upon its arrival I thereafter wrote most of my personal letters on my own typewriter in my own apartment.

I never mentioned to Justice McReynolds that I carried on a large personal
correspondence, and as the year progressed I had less and less time to devote
to letter writing. In college and law school it had been a delight to correspond
with people who were brilliant, witty, charming, and sophisticated. I had assumed, of course, that life in Washington would be just as interesting as that
which I had always known—or perhaps more so. But even as early as September of 1936 a chill was gradually descending upon my spirits. In the fabu-
lous city so long admired and spoken of, a door was slowly closing upon the
happy days of old. Yet I tried to keep that door open as long as possible.

3

IT WAS SATURDAY afternoon, the nineteenth of September, and Harry had just returned to the Justice's apartment. McReynolds was not at home, and I was typing a summary of the last petition for certiorari which I expected to read that day. As Harry walked down the hall from the kitchen, I called out and said, "Hello, Harry! Where have you been?"

"Why, I been to market. I sure needed somebody to help me tote back the groceries, too. They were heavy!"

"I'm leaving pretty soon," I said. "And I'm glad you came back before Pussywillow returned. I don't want to work next Wednesday afternoon. Do you think you can fix things so I can be gone for several hours that day? You know I've never asked for any time off until now."

"Getting married?" asked Harry with a grin as he walked into my little office.

"I thought you said the Justice didn't want me to get married while I worked for him."

"That's right, but just what are you aiming to do next Wednesday afternoon? Pussywillow's bound to be here, and he'll miss you for sure!"

"I want to see a parade."

"You want to see a parade!" asked Harry in genuine surprise. "And you expect the Justice to let you do that? What's the parade all about—is the circus coming to town?"

"It's the Grand Army of the Republic. Didn't you read about their convention in the papers?"

"I been too busy to read much this week. The Grand what?"

"Why, the Grand Army of the Republic! You know, the G.A.R. or Civil War veterans."

"Oh, those old men! Mr. Knox, you sure get interested in funny things! First you wanted to see Justice Brandeis, and now you are talking about some parade. We never had no secretary like you before."

"That's for sure," I said with a laugh. "But this is going to be a big event. Why, Harry," and I was bubbling over with enthusiasm, "tomorrow afternoon the seventieth annual reunion of the G.A.R. begins—with services at Mt. St. Albans at three o'clock in the afternoon. Then the convention will be held at the Mayflower Hotel on Monday, Tuesday, and Wednesday—with the big parade Wednesday afternoon. I've just got to see that parade!"

"Well, you won't be seeing it," countered Harry. "Why, if you asked Pussywillow to take Wednesday afternoon off to see a parade . . . !"

"You've just got to help me out," I replied earnestly. "It's the last time the G.A.R. will meet in Washington. The parade on Wednesday will be something unique, and I want to take pictures of it. I also know some of the men who will be coming to this convention, and I want to see them march. Why, they're all around ninety years old or more!"

"But what am I supposed to do about it?"

"I don't really know, Harry, but can't you figure out some way for me to be gone for a few hours next Wednesday?"

Then after a thoughtful pause Harry announced, "Perhaps I could! I been meaning to take you downtown so you can apply for a driver's license in the District of Columbia. Pussywillow may want you to drive his car, now that you and he are getting so friendly like, and you'll need a license. I could tell him I'm taking you downtown. We'd really have to go to the license bureau, but maybe you'd have time to see your parade, too."

"That's fine!" I said with enthusiasm. "I knew I could depend on you. Thanks so much."

And with a sigh Harry started to walk down the hall toward the kitchen door. "Don't mention it!" he called back as the door swung shut behind him.

The next morning was Sunday, but I did not go to church. It seemed to me the year was 1861, and that Abraham Lincoln was just over yonder in the White House. And weren't the very men who saw him, or who had at least served in his armies, relaxing just a short distance away—at the Mayflower Hotel?

And so I ate breakfast that morning with a feeling of quiet excitement while contemplating the spectacle which I would soon see. After breakfast I walked over to Connecticut Avenue and boarded a streetcar which would take me past the Mayflower Hotel. As I did so I felt that at last I was going back to the nineteenth century, which had always fascinated me so much. When the trolley was still a good city block away from the hotel, I could clearly hear the shrill notes of fife, drum, and bugle—playing Civil War marching songs. The Sons of Union Veterans were entertaining a knot of spectators gathered in front of the entrance to the great establishment.

I jumped off the streetcar when it stopped near the Mayflower, and I walked over toward the spectators. I never forgot the sight that met my eyes as I came in from the street. Nearly every chair in that lobby contained an old man who was neatly dressed in a faded blue uniform. Many other old men wearing the same uniform were standing about in groups, and there was a liberal sprinkling of wives, children, and grandchildren also in evidence. The air was filled with the busy hum of conversation, and the sight of this unique assemblage moved me very deeply.

I walked slowly and deliberately through the long lobby, gazing carefully to the right and to the left. Each face I momentarily scrutinized to see if I could recognize an old friend. Suddenly I spied an old man sitting alone in a corner. His name was Edward T. Abbott. He had a beautiful, sensitive face and seemed to be filled with the wisdom of age. Here was one of the last of the heroes of my youth, one of the most remarkable personalities I ever knew. As I approached he recognized me at once and exclaimed in a joyful voice, "My boy, how are you? It's good to see you again! You've come to our reunion, and all the way from Chicago, too!" And then he stood up and shook hands in a most friendly fashion.

Bent somewhat with age (he was then ninety-four), Mr. Abbott was about five feet, eight inches tall. He was wearing a blue tie with a white stripe, and in his coat lapel I noted the familiar bronze G.A.R. button. Pinned over his left breast was his Grand Army badge with ribbons, together with three other medals. Mr. Abbott had a neatly trimmed drooping white mustache and a white beard of medium length. His manners were gentle, and in all of his actions he exhibited a profound dignity of the spirit. There was an enchanting elegance about him, and to me he represented the rich magic of the long lost past. He had taken part in some of the bitterest battles of the Civil War and was a survivor of Sherman's March to the Sea. He was, in short, a knight of old who had somehow survived and become a living part of the present.

As I greeted him I explained, first of all, that I had not really come all the way from Chicago to attend the reunion. "I work in Washington now," I said.

Mr. Abbott and I sat in the lobby for a while, then walked around meeting other veterans whom he knew, and eventually the two of us strolled into the great dining room at the Mayflower. I never see that room now without thinking of Mr. Abbott and that Sunday afternoon in the long ago when time stood still and the past came alive once more. We had a leisurely meal and talked at considerable length. There was, however, very little mention of Justice McReynolds or of the Supreme Court. I wished to hear only about the War and of what had happened to Mr. Abbott nearly three-quarters of a century earlier. [He proceeded to tell me his memories of marching through Georgia with Sherman.]

As we finished our dinner I looked at Mr. Abbott more closely. I sought to fix in my memory each little detail about him. I also tried to remember his voice and mannerisms, so that later on I could bring back the words that he had spoken on that Sunday. "When you die," I thought to myself, "you shall live on, for you are a part of my memory now. And as long as I live and have my mind, I can recreate you at will."

The next day was Monday, September 21, 1936. I worked until 6:00 P.M., ate a hasty dinner in a nearby restaurant, and was back again in the lobby of the Mayflower at 7:30 P.M. There I spent the evening buttonholing any old soldier who would talk to me and hearing of battle experiences of every description from aged lips. The only veteran who did not seem inclined to discuss the War at all was a wizened up old man from Kansas. He regarded me with a rather suspicious eye, as if I were some newspaperman who expected to report on him adversely in the morning editions.

On Tuesday evening, I was again in the Mayflower lobby, though I made no mention of these evening visits to Harry. And then on Wednesday, thanks to Harry's diplomacy with the Justice, I was able to witness the entire parade of the Grand Army of the Republic—from 10:00 until 11:30 A.M. I snapped many pictures of that unique event, and even Harry seemed to enjoy the spectacle. "It is interesting after all," he commented. "I'm glad we came. But remember, we has just been to the license bureau and no place else if Pussywillow asks why we didn't get back sooner."

Everything, in short, had been a success, except that I had not yet taken Mr. Abbott through the Supreme Court building, [as I had promised to do on the first day of the reunion]. He expected to be one of the last veterans to leave Washington after the reunion, and he was not due to depart until Friday afternoon. So on the preceding Thursday afternoon, and with a feeling that I had nothing to lose and everything to gain, I walked into the Justice's office and said, directly and simply, "Would it be satisfactory with you if I didn't come to work tomorrow morning? I want to escort a Civil War veteran through the Supreme Court building, and then I would like to see him off at the Union Station as he will have no one to help him with his suitcase."

The Justice glanced up from some document he was reading and said, after first clearing his throat and peering across the room intently, "A Civil War soldier, you say? Why, I read about their reunion in the papers! Yes, it will be quite all right if you take him on a tour of the Court. And at his age he will probably need your help at the station, too."

"Thank you *very* much," I replied and walked out of the room.

The first time I saw Harry alone that day I said to him, "I think we've been trying to handle the Justice all wrong! Why, I just walked into his office and asked if I could take tomorrow morning off, and he said it was OK. Just like that! And think of all the trouble we went to on Wednesday to try and make him think we were at the license bureau all that time!"

"You don't say so!" replied Harry in surprise. "You sure musta hypnotized him! But now what are you going to do tomorrow morning that's so important?"

"I'm taking one of the Civil War soldiers through the Court and then on to the Union Station. He has to catch a 12:30 train."

Without registering any protest to this plan Harry replied, "Well, in that case I'll call up somebody at the Court so they can guide you around. I'm sure sorry I can't be down there myself to do it."

"And Harry," I said. "I bet Pussywillow isn't as easily fooled as we think. He probably suspects by now that we were gone too long yesterday to be just at the license bureau. The next time I want to do something, I'll just ask him if I can. There's no use beating around the bush!"

"Well, that's up to you, but Pussywillow is real unpredictable like. He just musta been in a good mood today."

On Friday I arose earlier than usual. After taking the Justice's mail up to him I caught a taxicab and met Mr. Abbott at the Mayflower Hotel. At exactly 10:30 A.M., our taxi drew up before the Supreme Court building. The old soldier and I slowly climbed the great marble stairs leading to the main entrance, and once inside the building, a Court attendant met us and took us on a leisurely tour of the huge edifice. Finally we reached the great room where the Justices sit to hear cases argued before them. This room is of marble, two stories high, eighty feet long, and nearly as wide. It also boasts thick marble columns, an ornate ceiling, and allegoric wall panels. In those days impressive crimson hangings were also in evidence, while in the rear of the room on a raised platform were the nine vacant chairs used by the "Nine Old Men." Each chair was different from the others and had been individually selected by the Justice who used it.

"Here, Mr. Abbott," I said as I slowly walked toward these chairs, "would you like to sit in the place reserved for the Chief Justice?"

"Yes," he replied, as I casually sat down for the first time in McReynolds' high-backed chair. It soon tilted to a dangerous angle, and I threw myself forward with a quick jerk, though apparently there would have been little danger of falling over backward. "How in the world can he sit in a chair like this one?" I thought to myself. "It must be just about as individualistic as he is!"

Mr. Abbott, however, was visibly impressed as he sat down very slowly in the Chief Justice's chair. "To think that I should ever live to sit here!" he said with awe. "Why, my boy, this is one of the happiest moments of my life! You've made the reunion a grand success for me!"

As we prepared to leave the building, I asked the attendant if he would mind, as a final favor, taking a Kodak picture of Mr. Abbott and me.

"Not at all! Not at all!" And as a sort of aside the attendant leaned over toward me and said in a low voice, "I hear you and Justice McReynolds drove all the way to West Point in his car."

"Yes, that's right."

"You sure are made! Why, I never heard of any other secretary going on an automobile trip with him. You sure are made!"

"Well, lots of things can happen between now and the end of the year," I replied. "Lots of things, you know."

"Perhaps. Say, did you hear what Justice Stone said when he heard McReynolds had a new secretary right out of Harvard?"

"No, I didn't," I replied with some surprise. "What *did* Justice Stone say?"

"Now let me see if I can recall his exact words. Oh, they went like this. He said, 'May Heaven have mercy upon him!' Hah, hah! Now isn't that something?"

"You mean, may Heaven have mercy upon *me*?' I replied, pointing to myself with my right forefinger.

"Yes, *you*!"

"Hmm," I answered. "I guess I'll ask to meet Justice Stone pretty soon."

Shortly after the photograph was taken, Mr. Abbott and I were boarding a train in the great Union Station in Washington.

In silence I leaned down and kissed his cheek. "Goodbye," I said. "I still wish I had lived in your time. I shall always wish that!" And with a smile I added, "Of course, if I had enlisted with the Confederates, you might have shot me dead!"

I then dashed down the aisle and jumped off the car as it was beginning to move. As I stood on the station platform I waved a final farewell to the old soldier.

And so, in silence and in thoughtfulness, I found a taxi and asked to be driven to 2400 Sixteenth Street. Upon my return Harry said, "Welcome home! Did you take your Civil War friend through the Court?"

"I certainly did," I replied, "and I shall always remember that tour! Those old men are among the greatest Americans who ever lived."

"Well, Pussywillow read his mail and then left."

And with a shrug of my shoulders I [returned to my work and tried to catch up for the time I had taken off].

People fascinated me, and every person I met was a challenge. So I had scarcely said goodbye to Mr. Abbott that Friday when I had the desire to meet some of the Justices of the Court. Within the next few days, therefore, I managed to see Van Devanter, Brandeis, and Cardozo, and for good measure I caught a brief glimpse of a former secretary to Justice McReynolds.

That Friday, after finishing dinner at a nearby restaurant I walked to a phone booth and rang up Justice Van Devanter's apartment. In a moment or two, I was talking with the Justice himself and asking if I could come over to see him some evening at his convenience.

"Glad to hear from you, Knox," Justice Van Devanter said. "I've just gotten up from the dinner table and expected to do a little reading, but why not come over this evening if you are free?"

This, of course, I agreed to do, and not many minutes later I was standing before the Justice in his study. "How nice of you to come," he said. "You know it isn't every day that I have a young caller who wants to see me and not just ask a favor about some case."

Hesitating a moment I ventured to say, "It's nice to see you again, too. It seems a long time since I was here last, and I thought perhaps you might have some further advice for me before the opening of Court."

Van Devanter was sitting at the same desk in his study where I had seen him at our very first interview. In his right hand he held a pipe, which he carefully placed in a tray on the desk while eyeing me somewhat intently at the same time. He paused for some moments before speaking, pushed back a law book which he had been reading, straightened up a bit in his chair, and then said almost abruptly, "Do you mind walking up and down the room a bit?"

Without replying, I rose from my chair with what must have been a puzzled look on my face, and I slowly walked to the door of the room and back again. I then remained standing rather awkwardly in front of the Justice's desk.

"Thank you. You can sit down now. I just wanted to be sure of something," were Van Devanter's next words, "but now I know that I did not make a mistake."

"A mistake?" I ventured.

"You will do," the Justice replied while nodding his head ever so slightly. "You know it would have been easy enough for me to make a mistake in choosing a secretary from Harvard for Justice McReynolds." Without waiting for me to reply, he hurriedly went on, "Oh, the Justice may seem a bit stern at times, but he means well. I think you will get along all right as his secretary. Some of his mannerisms may already have surprised you a little, but remember this is still vacation time. After the term begins we will all be so busy that we will forget everything but the work of the Court."

With these few words the Justice had touched upon the subject which I wanted most to discuss, even though I had not yet uttered one word about McReynolds. Though we talked on, there was never a mention of any particular incident which had ever taken place at 2400 Sixteenth Street.

"One of the reasons I asked you to walk up and down the room," Van Devanter next said, "was because I won't be seeing you any more—at least not for some time."

In genuine surprise at this statement I could only reply, "Have I offended you in some way, or made some mistake? You mean I can't see you any more this fall?"

"Yes, that's right, but not for the reason you might think. Of course, you haven't offended me, and as far as I know you haven't made any mistakes—at least not yet. I approve of my selection of you, and yet I shall not be seeing you again for some time to come. You see, John, if I may call you that, my duty was only to select a law clerk and private secretary for Justice McReynolds. Making this selection naturally occupied me for some time, but once the selection was decided upon my duties simply ended. I cannot continue on from there without offending Justice McReynolds. I feel that he would be very much put out if he ever discovered that I was giving advice from time to time to *his* secretary. You see, Justice McReynolds is the one and only one to give you advice from now on. His instructions and suggestions might not always be the same as mine, and you will have your hands full following the suggestions of just one Justice—let alone two."

There was a momentary pause. I glanced around the room and instinctively noted the picture of Chief Justice John Marshall, the many books, the pipe, even the telephone, and yet I did not speak. With the Justice still eyeing me intently, I finally bit my lip and said regretfully, "I suppose you are right.

In fact, you *are* right, but it's just that things are a bit new for me in Washington. I don't know many people here, and there is so much more I feel I should know in order to succeed in this work that I thought it would be nice to talk to you from time to time." And in a moment of youthful exuberance I ventured, "I do like you, you know—very much so."

Van Devanter sighed, and with a half smile on his face he stared absent-mindedly across the room. For some moments he made no reply, and then with a tinge of regret in his voice he slowly said, "Yes, I suppose you will need advice from time to time. Washington can be a strange and rather lonely city, but, well, I just *can't* see you again very soon without incurring the ill will of Justice McReynolds."

Feeling that there was little more to be said, I slowly stood up and prepared to leave the room. Van Devanter arose, too, and quietly took one or two steps toward the door, but he then paused. "One bit of advice, if it can be called that," he said. "You are now living in one of the great capitals of the world, and you may meet many people here. Some will be rich, others prominent, and some trying, shall we say, to get ahead. Toward them all I think you should be not only polite but sincere. Never be a 'four-flusher' in any way, and *never* be dazzled by either wealth or display. It all passes away soon enough, you know." Then, as if to clinch his argument, he gestured emphatically with his right hand and said, "There is that Senator—J. Ham Lewis—who has represented your State in the Senate for so long. Even if he were really sincere at all times, one could scarcely believe it because he is invariably putting on some kind of an act. Once in Court he kept the whole bench waiting, just prior to the argument of a case, while he calmly stood up and slowly removed finger by finger a pair of white gloves that he was wearing. He then ostentatiously tossed the gloves aside—almost, so I thought, as if he were tossing pearls before swine. Believe me, such a performance certainly made a bad impression on at least one member of the Court!" Then with a stern look and with eyes flashing, Van Devanter concluded, "I do not like such fakery! It is not worthy of an attorney and an officer of the Court. Never indulge in it. Always just be yourself—even with Justice McReynolds—and I am sure you will get along all right."

The next morning (Saturday, September 26, 1936), my first glimpse of Justice McReynolds was when he summoned me to his study and rather impatiently shoved a letter across the desk in my direction. "Take care of this. Somebody wants my autograph. I've signed my name on a piece of paper here, and you can send it to this child. It's nonsense, that's what it is, wanting strangers' autographs—and for what?"

This was my first introduction to a phenomenon that I was to see much of during the months to come—requests from strangers for the autograph of the Justice. It finally became rather burdensome to answer such requests by return mail and always accompany my answers with the autograph of the Justice. In the spring of 1937, these requests became very numerous following President Roosevelt's attack upon the Supreme Court. Yet never once did I venture to suggest to McReynolds that the matter would be simplified if he would only give me twenty-five or thirty autographs at one time, which I could keep in reserve for future requests. "If I asked him to sign his name on pieces of paper that many times and all at once, I suppose he would fire me for sure!" I rationalized to myself.

There was, however, something intriguing about this very first request for an autograph. In fact, the next time Harry stopped by the door of my office that day to ask if the Justice or I had any errands for him, I showed Harry the letter. "Nobody ever asks for my autograph," he said with a chuckle. "Say, why don't you send him my signature, too, along with your autograph and the Justice's?" And at the very thought of such a thing, Harry threw back his head, smiled from ear to ear, and gave a hearty laugh. McReynolds was at that time sitting in his study but not near enough to hear what we had been talking about. Yet almost immediately the buzzer on my desk began ringing with an insistent hissing sound. Grabbing my shorthand pad, I walked in at once to the Justice's study after throwing a knowing glance at Harry. He then turned and walked back toward the kitchen.

"I don't want to dictate any letter," McReynolds said rather impatiently, "but I do feel that this is the time to speak about one thing. I realize you are a Northerner who has never been educated or reared in the South, but I want you to know that you are becoming much too friendly with Harry. You seem to forget that he is a negro and you are a graduate of the Harvard Law School. And yet for days now, it has been obvious to me that you are, well, treating Harry and Mary like equals. Really, a law clerk to a Justice of the Supreme Court of the United States should have some feeling about his position and not wish to associate with colored servants the way you are doing." And with a genuine sigh McReynolds continued, "Of course, you are *not* a Southerner, so maybe it's expecting too much of someone from Chicago to act like a Southerner, but I do wish you would think of my wishes in this matter in your future relations with darkies." [1]

---

1. Later on during the year, the Justice received a letter of censure from an organization representing a group of negroes—because of his consistent use of the word "darkies." This letter he ignored, making no reply to it.

"Yes, sir," I said, in a low and almost inaudible voice. I then turned and left the room as the Justice indicated that he did not wish to discuss the matter further. Walking back to my office I sat down at the typewriter but began running my fingers absentmindedly through my hair and saying to myself, "What's the matter with me anyway? Am I a coward or something? Why don't I march right back in there and tell him that I *am* a Southerner! Of course, I wasn't born down South, I never lived down South, and I know very little firsthand about the South. But, at least many of my ancestors were born in North Carolina and Virginia during the 1700s, my great-great-grandfather was married in Warrenton, Virginia, after his return from the Revolutionary War, my grandfather was born in Richmond in 1833, and a small Confederate flag hangs on one of the walls in my home next to autographed pictures of Generals Lee and Beauregard. Why, I not only know many Confederate veterans personally, but I even know a member of General Robert E. Lee's staff. I'm not just a Northerner; I'm a Southerner, too!" But on second thought I decided not to go back into the Justice's study and revive the conversation, and in fact he was destined never to know anything about my ancestors, the Confederate flag, or my Confederate friendships. Nor did Harry or Mary ever learn of this conversation of mine with the Justice.

Later that same morning Harry again stopped at the door of my office and said in a rather excited tone of voice, "Say, I plumb forgot to tell you that this afternoon we're having a real nice caller. One of the Justice's former secretaries will be here, and I think you should meet him—especially as he was just about the most successful secretary that we ever had."

"Is that so?" I said with genuine enthusiasm. "I'll really be glad to meet him, and I have some questions I'd like to ask him, too!"

"He's a Southerner," said Harry, "from Georgia I reckon it was. Real polite like, though. Not like some secretaries we has had who never paid no attention to me at all."

"A Southerner and a former secretary, too," I thought to myself. "He is someone I really must meet!"

On the stroke of twelve, the Justice's lunch was announced, and I heard McReynolds walk briskly from his office into the dining room. As on all other days, he sat down alone at a small table and was served by Harry. In a few moments, however, the front door bell rang. I could hear Harry immediately excuse himself, answer the door, and then greet very cordially by name someone whom I suspected was the former secretary. I glanced out of my room and noticed a young man, presumably in his early thirties, black-haired, approximately five feet, ten inches tall, and neatly dressed in spite of the oppressive midday heat. He was directed by Harry to the doorway of the dining room, but on the threshold of this room the gentleman caller quietly stopped. Addressing the Justice by name, he carried on a conversation in rather inaudible tones which I could not have overheard even if I had tried. I presumed, of course, that the Justice would invite him to come into the dining room and perhaps even to sit down, but no such invitation was forthcoming. I had hardly expected him to be invited to sit at the same table with the Justice, but there were a number of chairs in the dining room—any one of which he could have been asked to sit in.

The conversation continued for some three or four minutes, during which time McReynolds' voice could clearly be heard. The Justice maintained a cool, detached formality toward his caller and scarcely gave any indication that he had even seen the young man before. "I thought this was supposed to be the Justice's favorite secretary," I said to myself. "Or maybe Harry said 'successful' instead of 'favorite.'"

Bowing slightly and politely, the young man then withdrew and would have left the apartment at once except that he was almost immediately snatched up by Harry and guided to the front door of my office. Introductions were made by Harry, enthusiastically and in plain hearing of the Justice. I realized in an instant that it would be virtually impossible to say anything. The caller seemed to sense my feelings, too, and after a few meaningless remarks he excused himself. My interview with him had occupied, perhaps, ninety seconds. The suddenness of his leaving left me disappointed, though there was nothing to prevent my subsequently learning his whereabouts from Harry. In fact, this was just what I did, though a long time elapsed before I had the opportunity to meet him again. Because of the press of work, it was not until eight months later that I saw him again—at lunch downtown in Washington. By then I had gone through so many experiences myself that there was no point in my asking him any questions about the life of a law clerk.

My first glimpse of him on that sultry day in September 1936, however, had left me in a very uneasy state of mind. I tried to conceal this feeling, of course, but for the remainder of that day I felt as if I were on the sinking *Titanic* immediately after that ship had struck the iceberg. There was really no hope that I could ever successfully penetrate the high wall of cold formality which the Justice had built around himself, and I felt that it was just a matter of time before my inevitable end as secretary to McReynolds. "If he is as formal and cold as that with a *Southerner* who was the most successful secretary he ever had, then there is absolutely no hope that I can ever be a success in this position," I said to myself. And yet, I also thought, "After all, the Justice is only human. He must have some feelings of good will buried somewhere within him! So I *will* get through or over that wall somehow!"

After lunch the Justice left the apartment, Harry went off to market, and Mary was busying herself in the kitchen—behind the swinging door and some distance from my office. With the apartment quiet and no one around, I decided I might as well telephone Justice Brandeis' household and ask to meet him. I ignored the fact that for anyone from McReynolds' household to ask to meet Brandeis was about as unheard of as it would be today if the Kremlin suddenly telephoned the White House and inquired whether the Soviet chief of state could have lunch with our President—say, perhaps, day after tomorrow.

Justice Brandeis lived at 2205 California Street, N.W. After I had looked up the telephone number, I wondered to myself what kind of building that address might be. "Probably some apartment as dull as 2400, or maybe it's a big private home like the ones out on Massachusetts Avenue. If Brandeis was so successful in the law before coming to the Court, I suppose he could afford to live in a mansion, too." I finally concluded that his address was probably a more impressive-looking establishment than where Justice McReynolds resided.

Everything was still quiet in the apartment, except that Mary had begun to wash some dishes. Now and then I could hear a saucer click as it was placed abruptly on the sink to await drying. "I'll telephone now!" I resolved to myself. "If Mary has started to wash the dishes, she won't be walking unexpectedly into the dining room, where she might overhear my conversation."

[I made the call, received an appointment with the Justice, and waited with anticipation for the day to arrive. When the day came, I] was able to leave McReynolds' apartment at 5:15 P.M. I hurried down one flight of stairs to my own apartment, glanced in the mirror to see whether I needed a second shave for the day, put on a clean shirt, and by 5:40 P.M. I was walking rapidly down the first floor corridor of 2400 Sixteenth Street. There being only twenty minutes left before the scheduled appointment, I jumped in one of the taxis which was standing near the entrance to the great apartment house.

A few minutes later the cab halted in a neighborhood that was strange to me. "This is your address," the driver said.

I paid my fare and looked around. "Why, it's just another apartment house," I said to myself, "and nothing like as grand as 2400! Oh, well, this must be the right address. Maybe he's only living here temporarily."

Rather hesitantly I knocked on the door of the Justice's apartment. To the best of my recollection, it was opened by a woman, and this rather surprised me, too. I thought the Justice's negro messenger would be at the door, or perhaps even his secretary.

And then in a moment I was facing Brandeis himself. He was sitting in a small room overlooking California Street—apparently a sort of sunroom. He greeted me cordially but a bit quizzically, and at first glance I thought he looked like one of the great Jewish prophets from out of the Old Testament. Without rising he said, "Do sit down."

"So you are Justice McReynolds' secretary?" he asked, while looking at me very intently. "And your name is John Knox? That is certainly a famous Scottish name you have."

"Yes, it is," I replied.

"And I understand you are from the Harvard Law School, too. Is that right? You graduated last June?"

Brandeis then straightened up a bit in his chair and proceeded directly to the point. "And how did you get here, Mr. Knox?"

"Oh, I came over in a taxi," I replied. "I just had twenty minutes to spare, too, and I was afraid I might be late."

"No," the Justice replied, "I am referring to the Court."

Even then for some strange reason I did not grasp what he meant, and after a momentary pause I said, "Well, you see I'm not at the Court. Justice McReynolds works at his apartment, and he has an office fixed up for me, too, next to his study."

With a somewhat benevolent smile Brandeis then shook his head slowly back and forth before speaking again. Finally he replied, "What I mean is— how did you get from Harvard to the Supreme Court?"

"Oh, I see what you mean now!" I replied in a tone of genuine embarrassment. "Well, one of the Justices appointed me to the Court."

And in a manner indicating the utmost curiosity Brandeis slowly said, "One of the Justices you say? Just which one?"

"It was Justice Van Devanter, and I was assigned to Justice McReynolds."

A momentary pause then ensued while Brandeis glanced across the room in a reflective manner. "I thought it was something like that," he finally volunteered. "I *thought* that was probably the explanation."

"Explanation?" I inquired.

"Why, yes. It seems that you came down here without being selected by Professor Frankfurter."

Immediately I answered, "Yes, I did. Was that something unusual?"

"It certainly was!" replied the Justice with emphasis. "There isn't one chance in a thousand for any graduate of the Harvard Law School to come to the Court these days without Professor Frankfurter's approval."

"But why should his approval be necessary?" I asked.

A trace of embarrassment crossed Brandeis' countenance, and rather hesitantly he replied, "Well, it is customary for law clerks who are graduates of the Harvard Law School to be chosen by Professor Frankfurter. This has been the practice in Cambridge for some years, you know."

"Oh, I see. Well, yes. I understand that Professor Frankfurter even chose the secretaries for Justice Holmes in years gone by." With a note of emphasis in my voice I continued, "I should think, however, that it would be satisfactory with Professor Frankfurter if one of the Justices personally selected someone from Harvard. After all, Professor Frankfurter is not officially connected with the Court."

Brandeis smiled and eyed me with a curious expression. Finally, with just a trace of humor in his voice he said, "Of course, a Justice *can* appoint a law clerk if he wishes. It is more convenient, however, for some of us to have a professor make the choice because he knows many of the students and associates with them for several years. Down here in Washington I don't get to see any students—from Harvard or from any other school."

"Well, Justice Van Devanter spent some months in considering a number of possibilities," I said, "and I wasn't informed of my appointment until the day I graduated."

Brandeis then gave me a piercing glance as if he could scarcely realize that all this had been going on in Cambridge, over a period of months, in secret, and under Professor Frankfurter's very nose. For the first time I realized with some surprise that the great Brandeis was evidently not on close confidential terms with any of the four "conservative" Justices—Sutherland, Van Devanter, McReynolds, and Butler.

"And how do you like your new duties now that you are here?" the Justice next inquired.

"I like them very much," I replied, "but reading and briefing all of the petitions for certiorari has been a pretty big job—at least for me. You see I didn't start work here until August, instead of in June, and I have been very pressed for time ever since. But I did want to meet you before the opening of Court."

"You digest all of the petitions in writing?"

"Yes, every one. I have now typed out about five hundred summaries of the petitions. I keep them all in a pile for Justice McReynolds to read."

Brandeis leaned forward, and I thought he was going to say, "Then Justice McReynolds doesn't bother to read the petitions himself?" But, instead, Brandeis paused and remained silent.

"Well," I said, "I keep the petitions near my typed summaries so the Justice can refer to them if he wishes."

"Oh, I see," replied Brandeis with a knowing glance in his eyes.

Feeling that the conversation was getting a bit too personal as regards Justice McReynolds, I then changed the subject. "At Harvard I was told that your scholastic standing while a student in the law school was so high that no one has ever been able to equal it since."

"Well, as far as I know that is true," said the Justice, "but of course that was many years ago, when law study was more simplified. It was easier for me to receive high grades in those days."

"What would you advise a young lawyer to do who is just starting out to practice at this time?"

Without a moment's hesitation Brandeis replied with emphasis, "Save your money! We have just been through a severe depression, and my advice to every young lawyer these days would be to save every cent possible."

I had already noticed the very modest furnishings in the apartment. I had also heard the rumor that another Justice, George Sutherland, supported a half-dozen relatives with his salary and, therefore, could not resign from the Court. Whether this rumor was correct or not I was never to know, but I suddenly thought to myself, "Brandeis must be hard-pressed for money, too! Maybe he has some relatives he is supporting. The poor man probably cannot afford to buy any new furniture, either. No wonder he is still hard at work even though nearly eighty years old!"

"When I was in law school, I wrote you a letter," I next said, "but you may not remember it. I asked you to autograph a copy of *Other People's Money*, which I sent along with my letter." This was a book of Brandeis' which had been published some years before in a cheap paper-bound edition.

The Justice did not remember the incident—he must have received a vast number of letters over the years—but he did show considerable interest when I said, "I'm almost sorry now that I ever asked you to autograph your book."

"You are sorry? Did I make some mistake in signing it?"

"Oh, no," I replied, "but now that I am with the Court I realize how many letters a Justice receives from strangers. I don't see how you ever had time to comply with my request."

"When I receive a request for Justice McReynolds' autograph," I went on,

"I try to give each correspondent the same consideration you gave me. It does, however, take time to write each person a short note and enclose an autograph of the Justice."

Brandeis nodded his head in approval while I glanced at my watch. "It was a real pleasure to call," I said, "especially as I had looked forward to meeting you for a long time. I knew that your advice would be helpful."

"Well," replied the Justice, "now that you are with the Court take very good care of your health, particularly of your eyes. A lawyer must use his eyes all his life. Also make sure you get plenty of sleep, and avoid late hours. And my congratulations on your appointment as a law clerk."

"Thank you," I said while making preparations to leave.

"Can you find your way out of here alone?" the Justice asked. After assuring him that I could, I bade Brandeis a cordial goodbye while he nodded his head again and looked at me rather quizzically. I reached the front door just as it was opened by Brandeis' new law clerk, Willard Hurst. In fact, the two of us almost collided. I drew back rather surprised and noticed that Hurst was carrying five or six heavy law books, and that he looked somewhat tired.

The two of us paused briefly and greeted each other politely. It was the first time I had seen Hurst since leaving Harvard, and though I scarcely knew him while in law school I was very glad to meet another Supreme Court law clerk. Hurst, however, gave me the impression that he was slightly ill at ease and that he desired to take the books in at once to Brandeis. I later wondered to myself whether he, too, felt a bit uncomfortable around his Justice.

As I strode down the hall toward the elevator, I thought to myself, "Tomorrow is Thursday. If I can get downtown before Brentano's closes, I'll buy that new biography of Brandeis. He's certainly different from McReynolds, and he's even different from Van Devanter, too. Brandeis seems to be very practical and a bit austere. Now Van Devanter would have talked about his early days in Wyoming and then become quite fatherly. Brandeis, on the other hand, never mentioned anything about himself or of his experiences in Boston, and in fact he talked very little. He let me do most of the talking. And I wonder when he lost his money—undoubtedly in the stock market crash seven years ago—but, at least, he and his relatives have his current salary to depend on."

The next day I did get to Brentano's before closing time, and the book, *Brandeis—The Personal History of an American Ideal,* by Alfred Lief, was in stock.[2] In thumbing through Mr. Lief's book, I noted with interest the de-

2. [Editors' note: New York: Stackpole, 1936.]

scription on page 423 of the room where Brandeis and his secretary worked:

> Only the twenty-seventh draft satisfied him. He tucked away the other drafts in a little storeroom which once was the kitchenette of a two-room apartment. This place was now his study, on the floor above his living quarters in Florence Court, an apartment house on California Street. Both rooms of the study were small, hemmed in by bookshelves reaching to the ceiling. In one the secretary-for-the-year worked; in the other, the justice. They were like two students in library alcoves. Light came in from a narrow courtyard. Up early, the justice sometimes entered with a magnifying glass in hand, looking for a particular volume of reports. When darkness came he switched on the green desk lamp; the top light was never used and it was in a state of disrepair. Here where the infinite pains of silent labor were applied some former tenant [had] slept. In the kitchenette reposed stacks of manuscript and corrected proofs. The *O'Fallon* opinion was not a unique product; Brandeis took as much care with less important cases. And he reminded the secretary to check up carefully every allegation of fact and every figure lest the respondents, when they petitioned for a rehearing, point to some "i" not dotted or "t" not crossed.

"I don't think I would care to work in that room," I thought to myself. "It sounds too much like two monks hidden away in some medieval monastery. McReynolds' apartment is much more to my liking than Brandeis' would be—even though I can't wear my eyeshade. I wonder if Hurst wears his shade. I suppose he had one at Harvard like the rest of us."

A little later I read the following words on pages 107 and 200 of Lief's book:

> A millionaire by 1907, he was earning more than fifty thousand dollars a year from his practice and he had his investments placed where anxiety did not need to follow them.... The Brandeises were living on no higher scale than when they married almost twenty years before. They still had their original furniture, mostly wedding presents. Indeed, their personal expenses were lower: formerly they had wine on the table, keeping up with the Jones and/or the Cabots, but as their circle of friends changed they found they could get on without elegance.

Other comments led me to believe that Brandeis had not lost his money in the stock market crash and subsequent depression. That news was the most surprising of all. He was, in fact, far wealthier than Justice McReynolds. "And yet he still lives in that old apartment house on California Street!" At that time I was too young to approve of Brandeis' living so simply under the circumstances. "Why hasn't he created some scholarships at Harvard for needy law school students? Why doesn't he get some good out of his money and move to a better location? He might as well not have any money at all if he just keeps it hidden away in a bank balance somewhere! What good has it ever really done him? Is he just saving it for the tax collector to take after he dies?" And this knowledge of Brandeis' wealth caused me to puzzle mightily for many a day thereafter.[3]

3. When Brandeis' will was admitted to probate, following his death on October 5, 1941, it was disclosed that his estate, before taxes, totaled $3,178,495.75. His charitable contributions, however, had been substantial. From 1890 until November 1, 1939, they had totaled $1,496,094.52. Of this amount contributions for educational purposes amounted to $109,900.02.

4

I HAD NOT as yet contacted Justices Butler and Sutherland—the two members of the conservative wing of the Court whom I had never met. After my latest interview with Justice Van Devanter, however, I decided not to get in touch with them—at least for the time being. I assumed that any attempt on my part to meet them would be known almost at once by McReynolds and probably misunderstood by him.

If I called on Justice Cardozo, however, there would be little likelihood that McReynolds or Harry would hear of it—especially if I saw Cardozo some evening when his messenger might not be present to report my call to Harry. There were only a few days left before the Court was scheduled to hold its first session of the new term. As matters now stood, Justice Van Devanter had requested that I not contact him again—at least for the present. I had so far met one of McReynolds' former secretaries, but the brief glimpse of him had been a disappointment. My first interview with Justice Brandeis had also proved to be a disappointment. I had failed to achieve any real warmth of understanding with him, and the reaction of Brandeis' secretary had intensified my feeling that I was an outsider to the Brandeis household. This feeling, of course, was not surprising in view of McReynolds' known hostility to Brandeis over a period of many years. At least I had tried, and later on that fall I would ask to call on him again. His eightieth birthday would be celebrated on November 13—an event which would undoubtedly hold little or no interest for Justice McReynolds.

What, then, of Justice Cardozo—a towering judicial figure who bore little resemblance to some of the other Justices. He was in many ways very different from them all but, like Brandeis, he was Jewish. The only thing he seemed to have in common with Justice McReynolds was that they both were bachelors.

And the only apparent similarity Cardozo had with Van Devanter was that he and Van Devanter were both friendly personalities who lived in the same apartment building.

In the 1960s, as I write these lines, it is hard for me to believe that a quarter of a century ago a great man was alive whose name was Benjamin Nathan Cardozo, and that I could call him up whenever I wished to do so. I had, in fact, even met him several years before going to Washington and at a time when I had no idea that I would ever be a Supreme Court law clerk. And since he was such an extraordinary personality, it is difficult at this late date to try and create by mere words any real understanding of him. I shall, therefore, write simply and at random as certain thoughts come to mind.

Cardozo, first of all, endeared himself to all who knew him. He had great warmth and charm and a brilliant mind. He was a man of genius who always kept in the background, and he was filled with tenderness, pity, and infinite compassion. The Justice, especially in his later years, was hampered by a weak physique and a failing heart. He was completely loyal in his friendships. He made no distinction between the unknown stranger and the high and mighty, and he was generous to each in his enthusiasms. His speaking voice was soft and beautiful, and the prose which flowed from his pen was often as sublime as poetry. His apartment was filled with books, and even the long hall entrance was flanked on both sides with bookcases which reached nearly to the ceiling. Here breathed the great and beautiful spirit, the lonely and shy scholar who found his refuge in the printed page and in his many friendships.

Few realize that Cardozo had a twin sister. When she passed away in 1922, she was the only one of six children who had ever married. The other five clung together in a close and beautiful relationship, perhaps due to a great shadow which had fallen upon the family. By the time Cardozo was three years old, the uncle for whom he had been named was murdered, and his own father had resigned from the Supreme Court of New York because of an alliance with the Tweed ring. This shadow never quite left the future Justice, and it contributed profoundly to the development of his personality. He became almost a recluse, and yet as he grew in stature his rare gift for friendship was demonstrated in many ways, especially among children. His amazing mentality was dedicated to his work, and he moved quietly through life like some lonely knight in shining armor. Eventually he became Chief Judge of the New York Court of Appeals, with offices in Albany. In 1932, when Oliver Wendell Holmes resigned from the Supreme Court of the United States due to old age, fate brought Cardozo face to face with the highest office attainable by a member of the bar.

While still a student in high school I was greatly impressed by Cardozo's reputation. Finally, when in college, I gathered enough courage to write the great jurist and ask to meet him. At that time he was living in Albany. He very graciously replied, acceding to my request, but the occasion did not present itself until after he had become a Justice of the Supreme Court of the United States. When the interview finally took place, long before I had the slightest expectation of becoming a law clerk, Cardozo blushed and said with a smile, "People seldom seem the same after close inspection. You probably will be disappointed in me." I was very young at that first meeting, and when I looked at him I thought, "You are my friend. I like you."

In a corner of one room there was a framed letter from Justice Holmes. When I expressed interest in this letter, Cardozo read it aloud, word for word, since Holmes' penmanship was often notoriously illegible. He talked of Holmes in awed tones and never once assumed to place himself in the same category as "the great judge."

After Holmes' death [in 1935], I saw Cardozo again. While seated in the library of his apartment, with only the desk lamp burning and the servants gone, Cardozo talked of Holmes' gradual physical decline, which had been coupled with slight mental deterioration. He fervently said, "I hope I shall never live to such an age. I would rather die in the full flush of powers!"

I never at any time felt the least bit ill at ease in Cardozo's presence, and we were friends from the first moment we met. Soon we began to correspond with each other. Busy as his life must have been, he wrote me ten to twelve letters a year. They were all penned in his beautiful handwriting—some on the stationery of the Supreme Court and others on his personal stationery with "BNC" in gray letters at the top of the first page. He would often write at length on the subject at hand, and he seldom confined himself to a single page. Each letter somehow managed to convey his tenderness and sweetness of character. To my everlasting regret, some of Cardozo's most treasured letters to me were lost just a few days before I left Harvard. I fastened the letters together with a rubber band and put them in my pocket, and later that day they were lost either in Harvard Square or in the subway on the way downtown.

[I corresponded twice with] Cardozo when I was busily studying shorthand in Chicago, but even then I had not yet informed him of my appointment as law clerk to McReynolds. I hesitated to say that I was going to Washington in case I failed to master shorthand sufficiently to be able to take dictation. And as things turned out, I did not contact the Cardozo household until Saturday, September 26, 1936. A second telephone call followed on October 8, and it was arranged that I call at the Justice's apartment at eight o'clock the next evening. I said nothing to anyone about this proposed visit. Everything went smoothly in the McReynolds household that day. I finished work at 5:45 P.M., ate a hasty dinner, put on the usual clean shirt for such an occasion, and promptly at eight o'clock I rang the bell of Cardozo's apartment at 2101 Connecticut Avenue, N.W.

In a moment or two the door was quietly opened by Cardozo himself. As the girl at the switchboard had told him I was on the way up, he had decided to meet me at the door, though a maid was in the apartment at the time. He was slender, dark-eyed, and his head was crowned with wavy white hair. He was about five feet eight or thereabouts in height. He had a fine aquiline nose and possessed a chin that seemed to indicate determination. His hair appeared to have been freshly washed, and it was unruly with little trace of a part in the hairline. He was wearing a black, lightweight summer coat, and the bow of his tie did not quite reach to the top of his collar or fill the collar opening. His hands were delicate and sensitive, and his whole appearance was almost fragile. Some have said that he looked like the poet Shelley. Perhaps he did.

As I was taller than the Justice, I glanced down at him as he stood in the open doorway. Then I smiled and said, "Hello! How are you?"

"I am fine. So good of you to call!" His glance was shy but direct. His eyes were full of candor, and they betokened friendship and even affection. For a brief moment we stood face to face, and then he said, "Do come in." After directing me where to put my hat, we both walked down the hall into the living room of his apartment. There he sat down on one end of a sofa and directed me to sit at the other end. We were thus facing each other. "It's very warm in here," he said. "Would you like a glass of water?"

The invitation of any other person would probably have been politely declined, but somehow I was led to accept Cardozo's offer. So off he went to fetch me a glass of cool liquid, which did prove very refreshing. As I sat drinking it and watching him intently I thought to myself, "Imagine McReynolds getting me a glass of water!"

"Well, I am so glad to hear you are in Washington. And with the Court, too! Tell me, how do you like your work so far?"

"Oh, I like it very much," I replied enthusiastically. And at that point in my experiences as a law clerk, I really did enjoy my work.

"And how do you like Washington?"

"Very much, too! I have been spending my spare time on Sundays seeing the sights." And at that time I also was fascinated by the city itself, despite the oppressive and continuing heat, though as the weeks slowly wore on I was to change my opinion of Washington.

And looking at me in a shy sort of way Cardozo replied, "I wish I liked it! I am lonely here. I do not care for Washington."

I glanced sharply at the Justice and thought he must be joking. Why, not to like Washington—how unheard of—especially when one was a Justice of the Supreme Court of the United States!

"I miss New York," the Justice went on. "Do you like the skyscrapers? There are no skyscrapers here in Washington," he said rather plaintively.

"I suppose you have not had time to do much reading outside of your Court work," Cardozo remarked.

"No, I haven't," I replied regretfully. "In fact, I have been trying to find time to read a novel which was published last May, but it is so long I don't dare begin it. It is called *Gone with the Wind*. Justice McReynolds' messenger asked me to stop in at some store and buy him a copy, and I got a copy for myself, too. I guess colored people aren't supposed to go shopping at some of the places here in town—especially at Woodward and Lothrop's."

Cardozo had begun to pale. But with sublime ignorance I went on.

"There are so many things to learn at Justice McReynolds' that I just can't do any outside reading—at least not now."

At the second mention of the name "McReynolds" Cardozo paled very perceptibly, and with delicacy he managed to change the subject under discussion.

"Well, just what else have you been doing with yourself here in Washington?"

With a smile I said, "I am afraid you may not approve of what I did a few days ago."

"Approve?" remarked Cardozo with interest.

"Yes. I went to the G.A.R. convention. I guess that sounds rather foolish for a law clerk to do."

"Why, I think that was a very nice thing to do. Are you interested in the Civil War? You must be if you are hoping to read this new novel about the South."

"I am enormously interested in the War," I went on enthusiastically. "Of course, perhaps not as technically interested as Dean Pound at Harvard. I guess he goes out and measures all the Civil War battlefields with a yardstick in order to find out where each person stood. That's the way it should be done, I suppose, but I only have time to read books about the War. Yet I have attended reunions of both Confederate and Union veterans."

"It must have been very interesting to see the old men who were meeting here."

"I saw their parade, too! And I took some Kodak pictures of it."

"Indeed?" said Cardozo, inclining his head forward ever so slightly.

[We reflected on the passage of time, how quickly historical moments are lost and how little the present respects what has come before. "It frightens me," I said, "that Time gradually destroys everything."]

Cardozo looked at me with a fascinated and rapt expression. "I have thought the same thing many times, but only in a different way! It is true that all things perish in time. Take Holmes, for instance. I believe even he is already forgotten, and yet he died only last year. The Court goes on without him, and seldom is his name mentioned any more. I sit in conferences with the other Justices and often think of Holmes and of how fleeting fame and everything else really is."

And so the conversation gradually turned to Justice Holmes. "I remember the framed letter from him, which you once read to me," I said.

"Yes," replied Cardozo with a nostalgic expression in his voice. "It *is* a wonderful letter."

Then the subject of conversation changed once more, and we began talking about how fast time flies and the age at which men die. "I think it is a great tragedy that man cannot live to be two hundred years old," I said. "As it is now he struggles and works and strives and then finds that life is all over before he really begins to live at all. He leaves some descendants who repeat the same process, and in a few years they are gone, too."

"How true!" said Cardozo. "When I was young, however, time did not seem to go so fast. I also remember when I was a little boy we had a relative who came to see us from time to time. 'How old he is!' I thought. 'How he totters into the room!' But do you know how old that relative really was—why, only seventy!" And with another shy smile Cardozo continued, "Do you think that I totter? At your age, you probably do! You see, I am already sixty-six."

"I shall not admit that you totter until you are at least ninety," I laughed. "But even at that age Holmes didn't exactly totter, either."

"I am afraid I shall never be ninety," Cardozo replied a bit sadly. "No, not ninety, not *that* old."

And to change the subject I said, "When I was in law school I read a book about you. It was a very interesting biography, too."

"Oh, so now you know all about me!" replied Cardozo.

"Do you mind," I said, "if I ask you about one statement in the book?"

"Why, not at all!"

"Well, in discussing the first case you argued before the New York Court of Appeals, this biography mentioned that you performed the task so well that the Chief Judge congratulated you afterward upon your fine presentation of the case. I have often wondered just what kind of a case that was. Do you happen to remember?"

"I must disillusion you," said the Justice. "Once I told you that you might be disappointed in me upon closer inspection, and now I must say that this story is a pure myth. I just don't know how it ever got started. It is like the report of my illness that appeared in the newspapers last July—saying I was in a hospital in Baltimore when I was not even in that city."

"You mean the Chief Judge never congratulated you at all?"

"Of course not. I guess one of the hazards of writing a biography is that all statements cannot be verified, even by a diligent author. This story is so well entrenched that Mr. Pollard must have considered it true and taken it on faith. But I must not take credit where credit is not due!"[1]

At that moment I happened to look at my watch. "Oh, I must be going! I did not intend to stay so long."

"But tomorrow is Saturday," replied the Justice as I slowly stood up and glanced around the room.

"I work on Saturdays, and sometimes it's hard for me to get up in the morning, too."

"Well, I hope you will stop by and see me again soon. And telephone whenever you can." Cardozo then rose and prepared to escort me to the door.

"You do not totter a bit," I ventured to say as we were walking down the hall together.

And with a laugh the Justice replied, "Thank you! It is always good to hear compliments like that."

After we had parted at the door of his apartment, I suddenly thought to myself, "How stupid of me! I forgot to ask him about his law clerks! And I never did get to meet them. Well, I guess they had gone home before I arrived."

Thus ended my first meeting in 1936 with the great man who became, for me, the symbol of the Ideal and Incomparable Judge. And in the months to come I knew that he was always just as close as the telephone. No matter how busy he might be, I could contact him merely by calling Decatur 1233. The visit with Justice Cardozo had, in fact, been much more satisfactory than the one with Justice Brandeis. I felt that I had a common ground of understanding to share with Cardozo.

1. [Editors' note: Joseph P. Pollard, *Mr. Justice Cardozo: A Liberal Mind in Action* (New York: Yorktown Press, 1935).]

5

ONE AFTERNOON toward the end of September 1936—a few days before the opening of Court—I ventured to inquire of Justice McReynolds what advice he would give to a young lawyer just starting out in the practice of his profession. The Justice had finished dictating some letters a few moments before, and he was now sitting silently like some member of the ancien régime awaiting the withdrawal of my presence from the room. He had also been unusually quiet that day, and his mind seemed absorbed by something far remote from the subject matter of the correspondence at hand. The morning newspaper still lay on top of his desk; perhaps an article about the current economic situation had caused him to be even more withdrawn than usual.

Upon hearing the unexpected question, McReynolds glanced sharply at the floor and remained silent for some moments. It may have been years since any of his law clerks had asked him such a question, or one similar to it, and I had the feeling that he was even pleased by such a request. In fact, it had been somewhat of an ordeal for me to ask the question in the first place, and the hush that now pervaded the room made me wonder if I had been a bit too forward in not leaving his study in silence after he had finished dictating the letters.

"Why, yes—umph—of course," said McReynolds at last, "I shall be glad to advise you about starting out in practice." And for just a fleeting moment the Justice seemed almost embarrassed. He began looking very intently at his left hand, and slowly and deliberately he closed and opened his fist and gazed at his fingernails as if he had never seen them before.(I had already come to recognize this habit of the Justice as indicating that he was indeed concentrating about some difficult problem at hand.) McReynolds suddenly cleared his throat, sat up even more erect in his swivel chair than he was accustomed to do, and then said in an impatient tone of voice, "There are many things I could tell you, but—umph—people seldom listen to advice any more these days."

I wanted to say, "I'll listen!" but the opportunity to offer such a remark was suddenly lost, for the Justice continued speaking. "Well, perhaps in a day or two I shall think of some things that a young lawyer should remember." And then as a sort of afterthought he concluded, "Yes, I'll do that!" With this final comment the conversation ended as abruptly as I had begun it. I said thank you and quietly left the room after closing my shorthand notebook.

There was something about this brief conversation that had succeeded in breaking through a barrier in McReynolds' personality—or at least I hoped so. Curious how difficult I had found it to be friendly with him. At first I had been attracted to the Justice and then somehow repelled. There was a certain brusqueness and arrogance about him that seemed to be infused into his temperament along with his good qualities. One instant he could be distinguished and a moment later unceremonious and almost crude. Nor had I as yet plumbed the secret of his rise to judicial eminence. Yet I had already concluded that he apparently cared for few people, that he had strong likes and dislikes, and that he was often taciturn and withdrawn. Of this I was sure. But of more I as yet knew nothing, though I was beginning to feel that his was truly a complex personality. Though I had already lived for several weeks in intimate and daily association with him, I still felt that I did not know him at all.

Three entire days passed, however, and the Justice never once referred to my request for advice. I finally concluded that he had either forgotten the incident entirely or had just decided to ignore it. For three days now he had sat in his study on those hot September days, and during this time I had read and summarized ever so many petitions for certiorari. He apparently was reading my typed summaries but was not commenting on same. "It seems rather odd," I thought to myself. "That question may have aggravated him a bit and maybe I should not have asked it after all."

On the fourth day, however, a strange thing happened. As soon as I began work that morning, I realized that McReynolds was much more animated than usual. [I also noticed that he] had on another of those gleaming white shirts with heavily starched cuffs. Then, after breakfast, and despite the heat, he put on a beautiful silk lounging robe and paced several times up and down the hall of his apartment. Never was I to see him walking around in his shirt sleeves, regardless of the weather, but the pacing up and down was unusual. He bore himself very straight and erect, and his arm and shoulder muscles seemed to quiver underneath the silk robe. Though nearly seventy-five years old, Mc-Reynolds was truly a magnificent specimen of a man—impeccably dressed at all times, remarkably well-preserved, and showing almost no signs of old age. There was indeed every indication that morning that he would outlive even the New Deal and would be calmly writing legal opinions at the age of ninety—as Justice Holmes had done.

Occasionally I would glance out of the door of my little office and then back to the typewriter. In fact it was becoming a bit difficult to concentrate, and yet it took me some time to realize that McReynolds was now ready at last to reply to my question. Then all of a sudden he marched quickly to the door of my office, entered, and sat down.

"You asked me—umph—about what advice I would give to someone just starting out to practice law."

"Oh, yes, I remember," I replied hastily.

I turned suddenly in my chair and looked intently at the Justice. I had, in fact, not even had time to rise upon his entrance into the room and then wait until he indicated that I should be seated again. There also flashed through my mind the realization that he could never be quite at ease in the presence of his law clerk—at least when he was talking to the clerk "man to man." And somehow at that moment I felt a genuine burst of admiration for him, for I suddenly realized the care he had apparently taken in mulling over my question.

"I'm glad to see you are so earnest about the law," McReynolds said in a brusque sort of way. "You must be or you wouldn't have asked the question in the first place." Then with an almost inaudible sigh the Justice continued, "I think, first of all, that honesty and integrity are the most important things for a young lawyer to keep in mind. A man must have sound principles and stand by them these days, and he should not endorse every wild scheme that comes along. I suppose you know that Washington is full of impractical lawyers, and I must say that many of them seem to have come from Harvard. You might as well realize right now that I think the Harvard Law School is highly overrated!"

McReynolds drew a long breath and then continued. "I also hope that you did not come under the influence of Frankfurter when you were in law school. There was some doubt in my mind about Justice Van Devanter's selection of any law clerk who graduated from a school where Frankfurter teaches. He is certainly one man not to be trusted! Even though he is dangerous to the welfare of this country, he evidently has a powerful influence at the White House."

"I only had Professor Frankfurter for one class at Harvard," I managed to reply. "There were about two hundred students in that class, and I am sure he did not even know that I existed." I was just about to add, however, that I did consider Frankfurter a very stimulating and interesting professor, but on second thought I decided to remain silent on this point.

"But with or without Frankfurter's help," the Justice continued, "the present administration has made many mistakes. Now just suppose we review a few of them. I was a Democrat when I was appointed to the Court, but I must recognize this administration for what it is. It began, for instance, by repudiating the campaign platform of 1932. That was the first betrayal. Then it recognized Soviet Russia. Imagine restoring diplomatic relations with that country! Justice Van Devanter was over there last year, and he saw even pregnant women working on the railroads in section gangs. And yet the Communists propose to infiltrate their ideas throughout the world. And Roosevelt recognizes them and installs the Soviets in the old embassy of the Czars right here on Sixteenth Street!"

I remained silent, fascinated by the flow of conversation that I had so unwittingly released. "Shortly after we recognized Soviet Russia," McReynolds continued, "we took another step down the road to Socialism and the destruction of states' rights!"

"What happened?" I ventured to ask.

"Why, a large bureaucracy began to mushroom here in Washington, and with this growth in the federal government there has been a greater and greater centralization of power in this city. And another thing! Before he was elected, the President pledged that he would cut government expenditures by, I believe, 25 percent. The national debt then stood at about twenty-one billion dollars. But the President did just the opposite of what he had pledged himself to do. In fact, he has squandered money so fast that Congress last year had to enact a law making forty-five billion dollars the national debt limit. Imagine: forty-five billion dollars! Why, this is a sum so vast that it cannot even be comprehended!"

I could not imagine the sum of forty-five billion dollars, either, except to assume that if this amount was all in dollar bills they would probably reach from Washington to the moon.

"I remember reading about your dissenting views in the gold clause cases last year," I said.

At this statement McReynolds' eyes began flashing, and memories crowded upon him with ever increasing rapidity. "We were assured that this country would not be taken off the gold standard![1] Not only Roosevelt promised that but also Garner and even Carter Glass. But these promises were repudiated! The dollar was depreciated to sixty cents. This meant that mortgages were depreciated, as were bank deposits and insurance funds. I want you to realize that this administration has deliberately sought to repudiate its national obligations and to confiscate private rights. As I said last year, when the gold cases were decided, this can only lead to the moral and financial breakdown of the country!"[2]

"What do you think the results of the *Schechter* decision have been?" I asked.[3]

"Well," McReynolds continued, "for one thing, businessmen throughout the country have become more and more confident because of the Court's decision in that case. The decision stimulated industry, which had been hampered by the N.R.A. laws." And then after a momentary pause McReynolds said, "But I guess I have strayed a little from the subject! I just want you to realize, however, that if it were not for the Court, this country would go too far down the road to socialism ever to return. We have been at the crossroads for several years, and it is our great misfortune to have a man as President who ignores the Constitution and dominates a weak and politically minded Congress. A man like Roosevelt can do great harm to this country, but I feel that the worst is now over. And so, getting back to what advice I would give you, let me see, well, I think a young lawyer should make all the contacts that he can—but in sincerity, of course. They will help him in building up a clientele later on. He should also be able to analyze the merits or defects of each individual judge before whom he may practice. This will be of great aid to him throughout his legal career."

1. [Editors' note: McReynolds ran unsuccessfully for Congress in 1896 as a "Gold Democrat," breaking with the Party's Presidential nominee, William Jennings Bryan, who campaigned for free silver and against the opposition's policy, which he derided as a "Cross of Gold."]

2. *Norman v. Baltimore & Ohio Railroad Co.,* 294 U.S. 240 (1935); *Nortz v. United States,* 294 U.S. 317 (1935); and *Perry v. United States,* 294 U.S. 330 (1935). Justice McReynolds' dissent begins at 294 U.S. 361 and ends at 381. In opposing the majority decision in the Gold Clause cases, the Justice is supposed to have declared from the bench that the Constitution "is gone." Five of the Justices were of the opinion that gold payments of private bonds could not be enforced. Four Justices dissented from this viewpoint: McReynolds, Butler, Sutherland, and Van Devanter. To my great regret, I failed to ask McReynolds whether he actually said that the Constitution "is gone." Some believe that he said, "The Constitution, as we have known it, is gone."

3. *A. L. A. Schechter Poultry Corp. et al. v. United States,* 295 U.S. 495 (1935). This famous decision, written by Chief Justice Hughes, declared invalid the National Industrial Recovery Act.

There was another momentary pause, and McReynolds now seemed to be groping for something to say next. Then he suddenly blurted out, "Also, don't be a bachelor! I think a lawyer can be more successful as a general rule if he has a wife and family to work for. They will keep him alert and on his toes, and there will be the companionship of his wife through the years. And another thing! Don't ever wear a red tie. It is much too effeminate for a lawyer to do. I don't like red ties!"

At this statement I could not refrain from glancing down at my own tie, even though I knew that it could not be red. While at Harvard I had heard that red ties were somehow taboo, and as a consequence I was careful never to purchase a tie with any red in it. The one I happened to be wearing on that particular September day was, I was glad to note, an innocuous blue in color.

The Justice then closed the conversation by saying that there were a lot of crackpot theorists in Washington who were bent on ruining the government if given half a chance. He enumerated several of them by name, and having done that he suddenly stood up and left the room. The conversation was over, but before he disappeared into his own study I did manage to thank him for answering my question in such detail. Then, as soon as he had gone, I began to sketch out on the typewriter a short memorandum of his conversation so that I would not forget what he had just said.

I had scarcely completed writing the summary of his conversation when McReynolds suddenly appeared once more at the door of my office. "I forgot to tell you," he announced, "that my brother is coming to Washington in a few days. He will be staying here at the apartment, and he may want to dictate some letters to you while he is in town."

"Yes, sir," I replied.

The Justice then walked to the kitchen door to break this news to Harry and Mary. It was received by Harry with somewhat less than enthusiasm, though of course he did not let McReynolds know his true feelings in the matter. "It means plenty more cooking, Mary," he commented later on, when the Justice was absent from the apartment. And then turning to me he said, "But maybe you are lucky. Pussywillow and his brother will probably be gone most of the time during the day, and this will give you a chance to finish reading all of those books on the floor of your office."

"What's the Justice's brother like?" I inquired of Harry. "And where does he live?"

"Oh, he's a doctor out in Los Angeles," Harry replied with a very glum expression. He was at that moment sitting in the kitchen, absentmindedly studying the wall.

"A doctor?" I said. "Do you mean an M.D.?"

"I suppose so," sighed Harry, "but if you ask me, I'd say he's a horse doctor."

At this statement I laughed. "Why do you say that?"

"Ah, I don't know," said Harry, "but he just don't act like a real sophisticated doctor. Why, one time he buttoned his vest and he had one button left over at the bottom. And he never even noticed it! He and Pussywillow went out walking that day, and it sure did look funny. Why, I woulda thought Pussywillow woulda told his brother about that vest!"

"Does the doctor have any children?" I next asked.

"Yes," said Harry. "He has two sons as far as I know. I understand Pussywillow is real friendly with one of his nephews but not so friendly no more with the other one. I don't rightly know what exactly caused the trouble, but I heard one of 'em turned on the radio late one night when he was visiting here. Or else he had a portable radio in his bedroom. Anyway, he got to playing all that jazz music they broadcast around midnight. Well, I guess Pussywillow was fit to be tied when that happened! The music musta wakened him up in the middle of his sleep, and he never had much use for this nephew after that. Too bad, as both those boys ought to keep in real friendly with their uncle. He's not going to live forever, and if he likes 'em well enough he might leave 'em a lot of money when he dies."

"Why, Harry Parker!" objected Mary, glancing back over her shoulder as she was bending over the stove. "Pussywillow ain't goin' to leave those boys nothing much, that's for sure. Just you mark my words! Some lady friends of his will get most all of his money—not no relatives like those two nephews way out in Los Angeles!"

"Maybe," said Harry in a casual manner, "maybe, but tell me, lady, how come you know so much about what he's going to do with all his money?"

"Why, I read his will!" exclaimed Mary. "You remember it was right on his desk one day. That was the time he got the will out to change it because one of his lady friends had died. She was goin' to get a heap of his money, too, but she up and died too soon. I think it was fifty thousand dollars. Imagine somebody making a will and leaving you fifty thousand dollars! And when he wrote a new will, I just bet Pussywillow never left his nephews no fifty thousand dollars!"

In any event, and despite any conversations that we may have had in the kitchen, McReynolds' brother did arrive from Los Angeles a few days later. He stayed with the Justice at 2400, dictated a few letters to me as had been predicted, spent several days in Washington, and then left. When the Christmas season came that year, Dr. McReynolds sent presents not only to the Justice but also to Harry, Mary, and to me. When this happened, I felt a little ashamed that there had ever been any discussion about how the Justice's relatives would fare when his will was finally read.

How calm and confident McReynolds appeared while in the presence of his brother! Less than two weeks remained before the opening of Court. Would it be another year in which the four conservative Justices would often succeed in thwarting the will of the man in the White House? What additional New Deal legislation would be nullified through the influence and persuasiveness of the Old Guard? Had not the National Industrial Recovery Act itself, and other acts and administrative policies, been found unconstitutional by a unanimous Court? Would not the man from Kansas be in the White House soon—the one whose name was Landon? Only a few months more, and things would be righted once again.

Occasionally, when I happened to be taking dictation in McReynolds' study, one of the other conservative Justices would telephone. How self-assured McReynolds sounded when he recognized the voice of the caller! "Oh, is that you, Butler? Splendid afternoon, yes, splendid afternoon. Have you seen Van Devanter or Sutherland lately? Yes, it looks like another busy year ahead, but the usual cases I suppose . . . the *usual* ones. Of course, I hope to see you soon. Why not come over here for a chat any time you are free? Perhaps, yes, we ought to dispose of at least three hundred petitions at the first conference. Most of them seem to be without merit as usual. No, I don't think I have received their calling cards yet. Of course, I shall acknowledge their cards. I do think his wife is very charming but perhaps on the talkative side. I shall look through all my cards tomorrow and see if theirs are here. No, no, it was no bother at all. I was just dictating a letter to my secretary when you called. Well, goodbye, then, but I shall hope to see you soon. Goodbye, goodbye! And now, Mr. Knox, where were we? Read back that last sentence I dictated just before the phone rang."

Despite the great differences in their early backgrounds, McReynolds and Butler found much in common while serving together as Justices of the Supreme Court of the United States. McReynolds had been born in the South in 1862 of Scotch-Irish Protestant parentage. Butler, on the other hand, had been born in the North in 1866 of Irish Catholic immigrant parents. His father and mother, residents of County Wicklow, Ireland, had migrated to Dakota County, Minnesota, where they lived the life of early pioneer farmers. He worked on his father's farm, which was fortunately only five miles from Carleton College at Northfield. The young Butler finally managed to attend this college, and he rode back and forth every day on one of his father's two farm horses. He studied law late at night, and then he would rise early in the morning when most of his classmates were still in bed and journey to a nearby dairy to wrestle milk cans before going to school. [Butler struggled but became a successful railroad lawyer and] was appointed a Justice of the Supreme Court of the United States by President Warren G. Harding. Though a Democrat, he was appointed to the Court by a Republican President. Butler took his seat on January 2, 1923. Along with McReynolds, Van Devanter, and Sutherland, Butler resisted any attempted infringement of the Bill of Rights and, in the absence of constitutional amendment, any centralization of government powers over the individual citizen.[4] Butler and McReynolds were especially close during the 1936 term of Court.

Thus did a dying age mirror itself in simple little incidents from day to day. Mary kept busy dusting the apartment and helping in the kitchen. Harry was off to market, back again, and then standing over a hot stove to help Mary prepare another meal for the Justice. "Good night," I would say to both of them when leaving at the end of the day. And with a nod of his head Harry would sometimes whisper, "Slip in the back door after you goes out! I've fixed something for you, and I don't think it'll spoil your dinner over at the Chinaman's. He probably never gives you enough to eat anyway!" In those twilight days before the opening of Court, I came to know Harry and Mary even more intimately than before, and a deep and yet unspoken camaraderie developed between the three of us.

Then one day when McReynolds was absent from the apartment, Harry came unexpectedly to the door of my office and said, "Mr. Knox, 'scuse my interrupting your typing, but how are you fixed for work today?"

"Busy as usual," I replied as I glanced up at Harry. "Why, what's on your mind?"

---

4. [Editors' note: Butler's record was in fact mixed. He was the sole dissenter (but without opinion) in Justice Holmes' notorious opinion upholding compulsory sterilization of the "feeble-minded," *Buck v. Bell*, 274 U.S. 200 (1927), and he wrote a sharp dissent in *Olmstead v. United States*, 277 U.S. 438 (1928), which found that illegal wiretapping did not violate the Fourth or Fifth Amendments. But he dissented in the first "Scottsboro Boys" case, *Powell v. Alabama*, 287 U.S. 45 (1932), which held that the right to counsel could not be satisfied by a sham appointment, and he wrote a vigorous dissent (for himself and the other three "horsemen") in *Near v. Minnesota*, 283 U.S. 697 (1931), which invalidated prior restraints on the press on First Amendment grounds.]

"Well," said Harry, "I think it's about time you met Mr. Bright."

"Mr. Bright? I never heard of him. Who's he?"

"Mr. Bright! You woulda heard of him if you worked at the Court building instead of being stuck way out here. Why, he's a real important fellow with the Court, and you just better see him before Pussywillow starts writing any opinions. Mr. Bright is the Supreme Court printer, and every time Pussywillow writes an opinion, you've got to take it to Mr. Bright to be set up in type. He runs the Pearson Printing Company down on Eleventh Street." [5]

"Oh, I see," I replied, "but why should I meet him now before Court opens? The Justice hasn't written any opinions yet."

"Because it's all done in secret, that's why!" insisted Harry. "You don't suppose those opinions are printed for just anybody to read! Mr. Bright don't run no regular printing plant. It's all done in secret, like I said, and he's got to tell you the rules. When he has an opinion all printed up and ready, you've got to go to his office and call for it. He'll give you a certain number of copies, and they must all be kept hid until Pussywillow reads the opinion in Court—except for the ones you circulate to the other Justices for their approval. Boy, will you catch it if one of them printed copies ever gets lost!"

And so it was decided that I would go downtown that very afternoon to meet Mr. Bright, since the Justice was not expected back at the apartment until dinnertime. In fact, I rather welcomed the chance to get out in the open air if only for a short time. So I caught a taxicab in front of 2400 and was soon driven to the office of the Pearson Printing Company [at] 519 Eleventh Street, N.W.

Upon alighting from the cab I noticed that the outside of the building had a somewhat drab and unimpressive appearance—so much so that no one would ever have glanced at it a second time. Here, indeed, was the perfect location where there could be printed in comparative secrecy the opinions of the world's most powerful judicial body. Even a lawyer would not have suspected for a moment that great and momentous occurrences in the printing world had been taking place for years behind a rather battered front door.

I walked to that door and, after a moment's hesitation, swung it open. After taking a step or two inside, I found myself in a small enclosure in which an elderly gentleman was standing. He was carrying on a most animated

5. [Editors' note: Clarence E. Bright, 1877–1949, began as an apprentice in 1891 and later became owner of the Pearson Printing Company, which printed Supreme Court opinions from the Civil War until Bright's retirement in 1946. "C. E. Bright, Supreme Printer, Dies," *Washington Post*, Feb. 22, 1949, at B2 (cited hereafter as Obit.).]

conversation with another elderly man, who was standing behind a sort of teller's window such as is found in any bank. But as soon as the door closed behind me, both men immediately stopped talking and looked at me very intently. I instinctively felt that I had somehow blundered in where I was not supposed to be. And then, in an instant, I realized that the man standing nearest me was the Chief Justice of the United States, Charles Evans Hughes. He looked at me quizzically and in silence, and for a few moments no one spoke.

I stood transfixed with interest as I gazed so unexpectedly upon the man who was acknowledged to be one of the greatest judicial minds of the age. The great Chief Justice's hair, which had once been a reddish brown, was now white. In that brief instant of silence, when time itself seemed to stand still, I noticed that he was approximately six feet tall, very well built, and with hair thinning on top but still thick on the sides of his head. There were very bushy eyebrows, in need of a trim, and a flowing white mustache. A goatee, which was neatly parted in the middle, adorned his chin. His eyes were open and candid, and yet they had an intense and almost restless expression. There was a small mole, or wart, to the right of his nose, and this proved to be the only disfigurement in an otherwise noble and arresting face. He did, indeed, look as if he could have been one of the twelve disciples, as I had often heard. And here was the lawyer of whom it had once been said that his equal had never before been seen at the American bar.

Looking squarely at the Chief Justice I managed to say, "I am Justice McReynolds' new law clerk, and I came here to meet Mr. Bright."

The Chief Justice's face broke into a broad smile, and in an instant his former attitude of silence and even suspicion changed to one of friendliness. "So you are Justice McReynolds' new law clerk!" he remarked, while eyeing me from head to foot.

"I am very glad to meet you," I replied with enthusiasm. "I recognized you at once from your pictures."

"Oh, you did, did you?" said the Chief Justice with a laugh and a glance toward Mr. Bright. That gentleman, however, did not laugh or even smile, and he continued to look at me with a serious and preoccupied expression.

Hughes certainly did look exactly like his photographs, and his sudden display of warmth toward a stranger puzzled me considerably. I had always believed that his was a very cold and aloof personality, but this unexpected meeting did not seem to bear out such a belief. He also possessed a beautiful and resonant voice, and the small room seemed to be filled with the magnetism of his personality.

Turning to Mr. Bright the Chief Justice then said, "Well, I think I'll leave now and let you and this young man get acquainted. I guess we understand each other pretty well as far as our printing problems are concerned. It looks like a busy term ahead."

At this statement Mr. Bright nodded his head in silent agreement.

Noticing that Mr. Bright was waiting for me to begin the conversation, I then said, "I didn't mean to interrupt your talk with the Chief Justice. I had no idea he would be here."

"Oh, that's all right. He was just getting ready to leave anyway. And now what exactly can I do for you?"

"Harry wants you to tell me how the opinions are printed up."

"That Harry's a corker! You'll be wise if you follow his advice, and he'll take a real interest in you, too. He's certainly a fixture at Justice McReynolds'," and peering at me intently Mr. Bright concluded, "but that's more than I can say about some of the secretaries who have been with the Justice."

To this comment I made no reply, so Mr. Bright came to the point at once. "Now when the Justice finishes writing an opinion you will, of course, type out a copy for me on legal-size paper. And if you can't type, I guess you better start learning right now. I used to have an awful time with Justice Holmes' opinions. He wrote them himself in his own handwriting, and sometimes I almost needed a magnifying glass to make out some of the words. He didn't believe in typewriters, and his handwriting was very small and cramped. But our Linotype men here need to have an opinion typed out—and double spaced, too. Do you understand so far?"

I nodded my head that I did.

"Try to use a typewriter that has big type, and don't put too many words on a page. Be sure to underline the names of any cases that are mentioned in the opinion, and also underline anything you want in italics. Say, do you know how to type at all?"

"Yes, I do. I can type pretty fast."

"That's good, but don't just type out part of an opinion and then bring me some volume of the *U.S. Reports* and expect us to copy a quotation directly out of the book. Every once in a while some law clerk does just that. If Justice McReynolds quotes a paragraph or two from some opinion that the Court has previously handed down, you must type out all the material that he wants quoted. And give us the quoted part, single spaced, of course."

Mr. Bright then paused for a moment before he said, "Now suppose you've got your opinion all typed up—quotations single spaced, and the opinion itself double spaced, and all the pages properly numbered and proof-read. You will then bring them down here and hand them to me—not to anybody else. I will count the sheets and take each page and give it to a *different* Linotype operator—so that no one man here can follow the sense of the opinion or be able to forecast the decision of the Court. That makes me the only person in this place who will know for sure what the entire opinion says. Then when each man has done his particular typesetting job, I will assemble all the pages that have been set in type and the opinion will be ready for you to pick up."

"Now, I want you to remember," Mr. Bright continued, "that there are about twenty-five people here in Washington who have knowledge in advance of all the Supreme Court opinions. It is, therefore, very important that there be no 'leak' before an opinion is read from the bench. I take pride in the fact that there has *never* been any such leak in all the years that this printing company has done work for the Court."

"Twenty-five people!" I said with some surprise. "I didn't realize there were that many."

"Well, let's see," replied Mr. Bright. "There's the nine Justices, of course. And this year there's sixteen secretaries and law clerks working for the Justices. That makes twenty-five right there, not counting me. Of course, some of the secretaries don't do any legal work and probably don't read the opinions in advance of their being handed down, but as I said, there are approximately twenty-five people in all."

"If there were ever a 'leak,' as you say, it would be pretty hard to find out which one of the twenty-five was the guilty party."

"That's right!" Mr. Bright replied with some emphasis as he nodded his head. "Some people could make money in the stock market if they only knew how certain cases were going to be decided before the opinions were handed down."[6]

"I guess I hadn't realized before how great a trust is placed in the hands of Supreme Court law clerks."

"And it is a trust which must never be violated!"

"Printing Supreme Court opinions must be quite interesting," I suggested.

"Yes, it is. Let's see now, I came here forty-five years ago when I was a

---

6. [Editors' note: See John B. Owens, "The Clerk, the Thief, His Life As a Baker: Ashton Embry and the Supreme Court Leak Scandal of 1919," 95 Nw. U. L. Rev. 271 (2000).]

young man, and I've been the owner of this business for thirty years. And during all those years I've seen them come and go, come and go. Some of the Justices have been really big men, but others were not—it just depends."

"Did you know Holmes pretty well?"

"Of course, and I didn't really mean to criticize the way he wrote his opinions. That was just his method—to write them all out in longhand—though it certainly was hard on us here at the time. Holmes was a very smart man even though he didn't believe in typewriters. You know, I even saw him after he was dead!"

"You did?"

"Yes. I wanted to call at his home over on Eye Street to pay my respects, but I didn't know whether they would let me in. But since we had printed his opinions for so long I decided to telephone his home, though as I said I hesitated to do it. But do you know, they said I could come after all!"

"Well, why shouldn't they have let you in?" I said with some surprise. "You are the official printer for the Supreme Court, and you had done his work for a very long time. Let's see now, Holmes came to the Court in 1903 and kept writing opinions until he retired in 1932. Of course you would want to pay your respects to him after he died."

Mr. Bright, however, could not understand my attitude that his desire to call at the Holmes' residence was something he should have been permitted to exercise as a matter of right. "I was mighty glad they let me in," he said once more. "They had to ask permission of Professor Felix Frankfurter, and he said I could come and see the Justice."

"Frankfurter!" I muttered. "What did he have to do with it?" And to myself I thought, "Don't tell me that you, of all people, had to ask a professor from Harvard whether you could pay your respects to the dead here in Washington!"

"Well," Mr. Bright continued, "Holmes' wife died in 1929, and he was left alone after that since they never had any children. And when he died I guess Frankfurter sort of ran the show—they had been pretty close friends through the years."

"Oh, I see!"

"After I saw the Justice I was mighty glad I had asked to come. He looked so peaceful, and he was very handsome even in his casket. I thanked them all for letting me see him."

By now Mr. Bright was in a reminiscent mood, and since no other callers had arrived at his office he continued, "They took Justice Holmes out to

Arlington and buried him all right. He was laid next to his wife, but it was raining on the day of the funeral. I understand they put his coffin in the wet ground protected by just a thin wooden box. Perhaps that was the way he would have wanted it, but water will eventually work its way through that box. I can't help thinking that some day the rain and the earth will fall in on the Justice as he lays there so peaceful and quiet. Yes, I've seen them come and go, and even the best of them finally die and are buried in the ground just like anybody else."

Just then an employee came from the rear of the plant to ask Mr. Bright a question about some typesetting problem. I thereupon thanked him for his advice and bade him a cordial goodbye. "I live out your way," he said as I was leaving. "On Sixteenth Street, too, but a long distance from Justice McReynolds and you. I'm at 7125 Sixteenth Street. Have a little place of my own where I manage to putter around in my spare time."

This was the first of numerous calls that I made at Mr. Bright's place of business during that term of Court. I also had occasion to call on him once at his home. Whenever I saw him, however, he was the serious and faithful government employee who prided himself on the fact that there had never been a leak in his printing plant during the many years that he had worked for the Court. But I never forgot the fact that he had had to ask Professor Frankfurter's permission before he could look for the last time upon the dead face of Oliver Wendell Holmes.

Mr. Bright served as the official Supreme Court printer for another ten years. When he retired in 1946, the opinions of the Court had been printed by the Pearson Printing Company for seventy-five years.[7] Mr. Bright had been associated with the firm for fifty-six of those years.

I had no sooner returned from my first visit to Mr. Bright than Justice McReynolds arrived back at the apartment! At once he summoned me to his study. "Mr. Knox," he said, "as you know, the Court will hold its first Saturday conference in a few days. At that time we shall probably dispose of at least three hundred petitions for certiorari, as I mentioned to Justice Butler on the phone the other day, and the remaining petitions will be voted on at the second Saturday conference. Now here is a list of all the pending petitions which I have just received. Tomorrow morning you can look over all your typed

7. [Editors' note: "Rather than trust any outsider with that job when he retired in 1946, the Supreme Court turned over direction of the highly specialized printing work to the Government Printing Office." Obit.]

summaries and put them in the same order as the titles on this list. Then give me the first 300, or 325, and I'll look through your notes hastily to see which pages I want to take to conference with me. There won't be many as most of those petitions seem to be unimportant."

"I'll do that," I replied. "In fact, some of the petitions are so lacking in merit that I wonder why all those clients ever paid their lawyers to appeal to the Supreme Court."

McReynolds glanced at me rather sharply. "Well, it's obvious the attorneys wanted to go on to the court of last resort so that their clients would feel entirely satisfied."

"Maybe," I replied, "but some of these petitions remind me of the story of the lawyer who kept a dead case alive so long that he used his fees from it to send his son through college."

The Justice made no comment to this remark but a rather pained expression crossed his countenance. He looked at me as if to say, "Mr. Knox! This is the Supreme Court of the United States! How could you say such a thing!"

"I must remember," I thought to myself, "that McReynolds doesn't have much of a sense of humor."

"And one thing more," McReynolds said as he frowned and looked in my direction. "I have a book here, and it's now time you knew something about it." Then reaching into a drawer of his desk he drew out a beautiful volume bound in red leather, the thick covers of which were fastened together by a swinging brass hinge. This hinge contained a tiny lock and key. "You will have charge of this book for the entire term of Court," McReynolds said. "As soon as a case is argued before us I want you to enter in black ink the title of the case, its number, etc. at the top of one of these ruled pages. Now at the bottom of each page you will notice that there is a blank space for me to record in pencil or ink the individual vote of each Justice. I often mark down the votes as soon as they are cast in our conferences. For a "Yes" vote I use a little check mark, and for a "No" vote, a simple "X." Now every time the Court is due to vote on any cases, I'll take this book with me. The reason I asked for samples of your handwriting when I hired you was that I am very particular about how you keep the record of the cases in this book. I want *every* page to be absolutely neat and clean—in your very best handwriting, and as I said in black ink. Each time that I return from a conference, I'll give the book back to you, and you can then put it away in your desk until I need it again."

"Yes, sir!" I replied.

"Now I hardly need warn you," McReynolds continued, "that confidential information of the most extreme importance will be written in this book. Sometimes I even use some blank pages to record the votes on important petitions for certiorari that are pending before the Court." And with a sigh the Justice said, "Voting is sometimes close in our Saturday conferences, but I am at least hoping that as regards questions which concern the future of this government there will be very little disagreement during the coming term."

I was now gazing at the book in real awe. McReynolds was still holding it in his hands, but suddenly he thrust it across the table in my direction. It was almost as if Moses had unexpectedly handed me the Ten Commandments. I remained silent as I slowly raised the brass hinge and opened the volume. I noticed that each page was printed on very heavy paper, and all the pages were gilded on top—which added to the general impressiveness of the book. "What a museum piece this would make in future years!" I thought to myself. "And during this term of Court it will contain information which may be dynamite! Gosh, where am I going to hide this thing? I should have a safe in my room! Imagine leaving it just in a drawer of my desk!"

McReynolds must have been reading my thoughts for he broke the silence by saying rather sharply, "That book will *not* be preserved after this term of Court! Next June I shall take it downstairs myself and stand before the big furnace in this building and watch it burn up. A book like that must be destroyed at the end of each term! I believe one or two of the books which [Howell] Edmunds [Jackson] used years ago are still around, but they certainly shouldn't be![8] That was a serious oversight by somebody—not to have those books destroyed!"

I finally managed to nod my head and say, "Yes, of course, the book should be destroyed." But as I glanced once more at the volume I thought to myself, "Maybe he will forget to burn just this one. Why shouldn't it be sealed in a box and given to the Library of Congress—to be opened up in fifty or a hundred years after his death!"

"You can take the book back to your office now," McReynolds said a bit impatiently. "I have no letters to dictate this afternoon." So I walked back to my office with this magnificent volume under my arm, and I slowly put the book away in the lower left-hand drawer of my desk. And at that moment I

---

8. [Editors' note: Howell Edmunds Jackson (1832–1895) was the first native Tennessean to serve on the Supreme Court (1893–1895). Jackson was a lawyer, judge, and Democratic Party politician. He served one term in the United States Senate, and during that period McReynolds briefly served as his private secretary after completing his law course at the University of Virginia. Jackson was named by President Cleveland to the Sixth Circuit Court of Appeals in 1887 and to the Supreme Court six years later by President Harrison.]

made a vow with myself never to write down in my diary the voting results of any case or petition for certiorari which McReynolds might thereafter note in this volume. And I faithfully held to this vow during the entire year. After President Roosevelt's Court-packing plan was made public in February 1937, I seldom even looked at the results of the voting in the Saturday conferences—when McReynolds would return to the apartment and give me the book once more for safekeeping. I was by then so afraid that I might inadvertently blurt out some Court secret, even in conversation with another law clerk, that I thought it best to avoid even looking at the voting results—except as regards the cases assigned to McReynolds in which he would have to write opinions. Today, however, it would be interesting—at least from an historical point of view—to be able to record in these pages just how each Justice voted in conference on certain important decisions handed down in 1936 and 1937. But I never made a notation of any such information and cannot, therefore, quote it here.

Once back in my own little office with the book safely tucked away in the desk drawer, I remembered for the first time that I had forgotten to tell the Justice of my interview with Mr. Bright. However, I did not return to his study to inform him of this meeting. In fact, I never did tell him. I was by now immersed in the problem of collecting together some 325 summaries of the petitions for certiorari. They represented a goodly part of my entire summer's work. "Life is going to be very nice around this place," I thought to myself, "when there aren't any more of these petitions to read and summarize! I wonder what it will be like when McReynolds starts writing opinions. I suppose the cases will be very important ones, and the entire country will probably be waiting to hear the Justice read his opinions in Court." And in my youthful enthusiasm it almost seemed as if the whole universe revolved around 2400 Sixteenth Street, or at least around the nine Justices of the Supreme Court of the United States.

It was not long before the first Saturday conference took place, and then the second Saturday conference. Like some giant Moloch, these two meetings devoured all of the petitions which were then pending before the Court. Weeks of toil in reading, briefing, and typing disappeared in the smoke of two afternoon conferences, and now all of the hundreds of pages that I had so laboriously typed were completely passé.[9] McReynolds merely threw them into

9. During the first four months of the term, the Justices granted 72 petitions for certiorari and thereby consented to hear these cases argued before the Court. In the same four-month period, 347 petitions for certiorari were denied.

the wastebasket. Like some budding author who dislikes to be permanently separated from his manuscript, I felt that perhaps these pages should have been preserved in some loose-leaf notebook to be referred to from time to time if need be. Only gradually did it dawn upon me that the Justice regarded all of my work on these petitions as little more than a mental exercise to keep me busy and out of mischief. It was undeniably true that a great many petitions were without merit, and even without any of my summaries before him in conference McReynolds could have held his own with the other Justices.

I was now very much aware of the fact that the day was drawing near when the first public session of the new term of Court would be held. But as the Great Event approached I grew more and more puzzled by McReynolds' behavior. He absented himself from the apartment for long periods of time—presumably relaxing at the Chevy Chase Club—and he seemed in no way disturbed by approaching events. I failed to realize that he had already seen more than twenty terms of Court come and go. I somehow felt that he should display more interest in this particular opening session. He also seemed surprisingly confident of the ability of the four conservative members to control the balance of power within the Court during the forthcoming months.

I had visions of Brandeis and Cardozo scarcely stirring from their apartments and pouring over the hundreds of petitions like students in some last-minute cram session. Whether they ever did or not, I was never to know. At that period of my life I just assumed that all the Justices should be bookworms, like some students I had known at the Harvard Law School. The fact that McReynolds was proving otherwise came as a bit of a shock, and I began to realize that I had really been looking at the Supreme Court through rose-colored glasses. At least one Justice, and perhaps more than one, was not proving to be the studious and scholarly type after all. In fact, he would sit in his study and carefully read what the *Literary Digest* had to say about the forthcoming Presidential election, and then seemingly assured that Landon was certain to win, he would casually take off again for the Chevy Chase Club. But then I tried to reassure myself that he had a perfect right to find what rest he could in those last hours before the Nine Old Men were due to meet together once more.

While I watched the Justice with a vague feeling of bewilderment, I was grateful that Harry wanted me to be present at that first session of Court—especially since he himself intended to be there. He had taken special pains to ask McReynolds some days before whether I could go. In a tone of some surprise at hearing this request from his messenger, the Justice finally replied, "Well, I suppose so. Yes, I guess it will be all right for Mr. Knox to be in Court that day. In fact, he can ride down with me."

In conveying this decision to me, which I had already overheard, Harry grinned and said in a low voice, "I was afraid Pussywillow would say no, but now you're finally going to see the Supreme Court in session!"

"That's good," I replied, "and many thanks for asking him. I was going to, but you saved me the trouble."

"Not much will happen the first day," Harry cautioned. "There won't be any opinions to be read, but a case or two may be argued. Also some new attorneys may get admitted to practice, and then they'll adjourn. I'll stay down there to fix Pussywillow's lunch for him, but you better hike on home." [10]

"How about my eating lunch in the cafeteria at the Court? I haven't been there yet."

"That will be all right," Harry replied after a moment's hesitation, "provided you're here when Pussywillow returns."

"I'll be here!" I said.

And so at last the great day finally dawned. It was Monday, October 5, 1936, and the Supreme Court of the United States was destined to hold its first meeting of the new term exactly on the stroke of twelve noon. I woke up earlier than usual and in more or less a flutter of anticipation. Now at last I would see all of the Justices in action. So I dressed hastily, shaved, and then opened the door of my small apartment and picked up the milk which was waiting for me there. A quart of milk constituted my sole breakfast each morning, and on this particular day I drank it slowly and then noted that I was still a good half-hour ahead of schedule. "Well, I guess I'll go upstairs anyway," I thought to myself. "The Justice is undoubtedly up, and perhaps he will have something for me to do before we go down to Court."

When my key turned in the front door, Harry poked his head out from the kitchen. "Why, man, you're early!" he said. "I haven't even fixed breakfast yet!" And pointing down the hall, Harry concluded, "He's just taking his bath."

"His bath?" I queried.

"Why, of course. He takes a bath every morning like most everyone else does. Only you never was here so early before. Say, you must be taking this opening session real serious!"

"I'll be in my room in case he needs me," I said, and then I walked down the hall to my office. Once there, however, I just sat, and I began to regret that I had arrived so early. There was no typing to be done, and it was evident that McReynolds had not eaten his breakfast. In fact, he had not even dressed. And

10. The Justices had their own private dining room at the Court.

now, for the first time, I realized that he was indeed taking a bath. It was impossible not to realize such a thing because of the noises which were issuing from behind the bathroom door—some twelve or fifteen feet from where I was sitting. I became a little embarrassed. For at least five minutes there was a sound of great splashing and gurgling—the likes of which I had never heard issuing out of any bathroom anywhere before. "This must be the way a Justice of the Supreme Court takes a bath!" I thought to myself. "But is it possible that he's splashing water carelessly all over the room without even using the shower curtain?" And so I quietly walked down the hall to the kitchen. Closing the swinging door behind me I glanced at Harry and Mary. "Say, Harry," I motioned, "did you say he's taking a bath or is he getting himself drowned on the opening day of Court?"

Without waiting for Harry to reply Mary spoke up. "Mr. Knox, you should get here early every morning! I guess you never noticed before how I have to clean up his bathroom everyday."

"No, I haven't," I replied, "because I don't use his bathroom."

"Well, the bath off the guest room which you use always looks pretty neat," Mary replied, "but then, of course, you don't take no baths here."

"You better get back to your office!" Harry now volunteered. "Pussywillow will be getting dressed soon, and then he'll be coming into the dining room to eat breakfast."

"OK," I replied as I left the kitchen.

Reaching my office once more, I now noticed that all was quiet in the bathroom. Shortly thereafter I heard the door open and then the Justice walked into his bedroom to dress. "One, two, three, one, two, three," I could hear him mutter under his breath. "It's his setting-up exercises," I thought. "Harry says that's what keeps him looking so young. If Roosevelt could only hear McReynolds counting off those numbers each morning!" "One, two, three, one, two, three," McReynolds kept repeating.

Ten minutes more passed, and now the Justice was finally ready to eat breakfast. I could hear him stroll from his bedroom, cross the hall, and then walk into the dining room. He had not as yet noticed that I had arrived earlier than usual.

"Good morning, Mr. Justice," Harry said in a very ingratiating tone of voice.

"Good morning, Harry," McReynolds replied pleasantly. "I'm certainly glad it isn't raining out. It looks like it's going to be a good day for the opening of Court." And then after sitting down at his small table in the dining room and adjusting his chair, McReynolds said, "Now what have you got for me this morning?"

"Sausage and two eggs," Harry replied, "and toast and grapefruit, too."

"The toast was too well-done yesterday," the Justice next volunteered. "Mary should know by now that I don't want toast to fall apart in my hands when I start eating it."

"Yes, sir, and say, Mr. Knox is here. He came in a little early since the Court is meeting today."

"That's good! Will you ask him to go downstairs to the garage and see if my car is in shape? I want it full of gas and then brought around to the front door. I shall leave here promptly at eleven. And he might also pick up the mail if he hasn't already done so."

A few moments later Harry formally conveyed this request to me, though I had already overheard the Justice's conversation. Then with a grimace and pointing silently toward the bathroom with his finger, Harry walked back into the dining room. I knew what he meant, so I tiptoed silently past the open door of McReynolds' bathroom before going downstairs to the garage. I could scarcely believe what I saw. Water seemed to be a quarter of an inch deep on the floor, and it was splashed all over the walls, too. Bath towels were tossed carelessly on the side of the tub instead of being hung up in their proper places. Everything, in fact, seemed to be a complete wreck, as if a tornado had just passed through that room. "Why, it will take Mary a half-hour to clean up this mess!" I thought to myself. "It's a good thing McReynolds is a bachelor. Imagine what any wife would do to him for leaving a bathroom in this shape!"

I then walked down the hall, but before I closed the front door behind me I heard McReynolds say, "Harry! I want to take my walking stick with me to Court. Look around and see if it's in the umbrella stand. It's either there or in my bedroom."

"Yes, sir!" Harry replied.

Once downstairs in the large garage at the rear of 2400, I volunteered the information that Justice McReynolds wished his car brought around in front so that he could use it at eleven o'clock. "So you're going out driving with the Justice again?" one of the men asked.

"Not very far this time—only down to the Court," I replied.

"Well, if he drives don't forget those long gloves he wears. There's nothing like getting all dressed up before starting out."

"Why don't you take along an umbrella, too?" some other mechanic volunteered. "Geeze—I'd think he'd get a new car and have you drive!"

After a few more minutes of conversation, during which I checked the amount of gasoline in the automobile, I returned upstairs to the apartment and let myself in as before. The Justice was still leisurely eating his breakfast. As I passed by the dining room door I stopped momentarily and said, "The garage will have the car around in front at eleven, and it is being filled up with gasoline now."

"Thank you," said McReynolds, who was just then in the midst of slicing a fat sausage in two.

I walked down the hall toward my office, but I had scarcely reached it when the telephone rang. It was the phone on my desk that was also connected with the one on the Justice's desk—the telephone with the unlisted number. Had it been the house phone at the end of the hall by the kitchen door, Harry would have answered it at that moment. Had it rung when McReynolds was in his study, he himself would have answered it. But now Fate decreed that I was to be the one to take this unexpected incoming call.

"Is the Justice in?" came a sweet-sounding feminine voice over the wire.

"Why, yes, he is," I replied, "but he is eating breakfast." I knew instantly that it was not an inquiry from some stranger or from any newspaper reporter, as such a call would have come through on the switchboard at 2400 and then on the house phone. And thinking that I recognized the voice of the caller being a certain lady in Washington who had already telephoned the Justice a number of times, I casually said, "Is this Mrs. ———?"

What happened next occurred so fast that I literally went limp. A voice in full feminine fury came back over the wire and snapped like a pistol shot. "Do you mean to say he's still going out with *that* woman? You get the Justice to the phone *this minute*! I want to speak to *him*!!"

"Oh, my Lord!" I thought to myself. "What have I gone and done now?"

I stalled for time but it was no use. I said once again that the Justice was eating his breakfast, that I regretted not having recognized her voice, etc. But all evasions were of no avail. I was directed in an imperious tone of voice to fetch the Justice to the phone *at once*.

Swallowing hard I walked down to the entrance of the dining room and announced in a weak tone of voice, "There is a lady on the phone who wishes to speak with you. She did not give me her name. It's the phone in your study."

McReynolds glanced down at his plate and frowned. Then, without making any comment, he slid back his chair rather noisily and walked down the hall. Instead of going to his own study, however, he stepped into my office and picked up the receiver which was laying on my desk.

At that instant I glanced helplessly at Harry, and I moved the forefinger of my right hand across my throat to signify my forthcoming fate as a Supreme Court law clerk. And to have it happen on the opening day of Court, too!

Harry glanced back with a rather quizzical expression on his face, not realizing just what I meant.

I stood deathly still and waited. The Justice was talking in a low tone of voice, and about all I could hear was, "Now, now . . . of course . . . but not at all . . . yes, yes . . . she only called to ask . . . just a few times . . . nothing, simply nothing at all . . ." And then the conversation was ended, and McReynolds slammed down the receiver.

For once in my life my nerve failed me. I could not look him in the eye as he emerged from my office. "Mr. Knox!!" he thundered in a tone of voice that I had never heard before. "I suppose you know what you have done! Don't ever, ever answer the telephone and try to guess who is calling! I did not hire you to conduct a guessing game!" And with that the Justice swept by me and went back into the dining room to finish his breakfast.

"I am sorry," was all I could say as I moved quietly away. "It won't happen again." I then walked back to my office.

"If it isn't one thing, it's another!" I could hear McReynolds say to Harry. "I don't know why I have a secretary who doesn't even know how to answer the phone. Oh, bring me another grapefruit!"

I sat in my office and looked down at the floor, and I wished that I could somehow recall the one fatal sentence which I had spoken over the telephone. But there was no turning back time itself. And now I remembered what Harry had once said: "If you ever get fired, it will come sudden like—just when you aren't expecting it. Like getting run over by an auto or something. Everything will be going along all right and then wham!"

"That time has now come," I concluded, "and on the very day the Court opens, too! I wonder what I can tell all the folks at home—when I get fired. It will mean I just failed, that's all, I just failed." And then my other nature began to assert itself. "Well, what of it anyway? It was just an innocent mistake, and I was only trying to be polite. She did sound exactly like Mrs. ———. If McReynolds wants to fire me for that, well, let him! I can find another job somewhere!"

For some strange reason, however, no further mention of the incident was ever made. Nor did I ever learn the identity of the woman I had talked to. But thereafter I was very careful not to guess the identity of anyone on the telephone again. Even when Justice Van Devanter himself happened to call when

I answered the phone, and regardless of the fact that I recognized his voice at once, I always made it a point to inquire politely, "Who is calling, please?" Thus I learned one of the basic lessons in how to be an efficient private secretary. And I was very thankful that I had somehow escaped from being peremptorily dismissed despite my First Great Blunder.

We finally did leave [for the Court] a few minutes past eleven o'clock that morning. With his walking stick grasped firmly in his right hand, the Justice strode majestically down the hall of the fifth floor while I trotted on ahead and rang for an elevator. I noticed that he had indeed neglected to take along his gauntlets, which he had used on the West Point trip, but I made no comment regarding them. The elevator door was just opening, and the colored girl on duty glanced at both of us as we prepared to enter her car. To her greeting McReynolds nodded his head ever so slightly in recognition—at the same time emitting a crisp but pleasant "Good morning."

I was glad there was no one else in the elevator. No society woman this morning holding a pampered dog in her arms. No retired general off for a brisk canter in Rock Creek Park. No, just the three of us, and we almost filled the car anyway. The Justice stood up very erect, eyes straight ahead, and he did look imposing indeed—just like some ancient Roman senator must have looked when on his way to the forum.

The Justice's red Buick coupe was carefully parked in front of the great apartment house—just as one of the garagemen had promised it would be. We climbed in and closed the doors. McReynolds was driving, as usual, and I noticed with interest that he did not start up with a jerk. Perhaps the absence of the gauntlets made some difference in his driving prowess. In any event, he negotiated with finesse the five-mile drive to the Court that morning. With nary an indication of speeding at any time, he moved along with the traffic at a dignified pace. And as we finally neared that great marble structure which was now the home of the nine Justices of the Supreme Court—after having ridden the five miles in almost complete silence—I wondered just where McReynolds would park his car. But in a nonchalant fashion he drove right past the front entrance of the great building without even so much as slackening speed.

"Here!" I wanted to cry out. "This is the Court building! Did you miss it? Or are we going to park over at the Union Station and walk all the way back?"

But by then the Justice had made a neat turn to the right, and then another turn to the right, and now we had suddenly darted into a driveway in the rear of the building itself. In another instant we were slowly and deliberately descending into the basement of the structure—by way of an entrance the existence of which I had not even suspected. Like an experienced engineer bringing the great *Twentieth Century Limited* to a gradual halt, the Justice carefully reduced speed as we reached an underground parking space.

"So this is the way the Justices get to Court without ever being seen by the public!" I said to myself in some surprise. "And they never need to worry about finding a parking space, either."

No person was to be seen that morning in this underground space, though a number of cars were already in evidence. Having chosen a likely spot wherein to park, McReynolds brought the car to final halt, pulled on the emergency brake, and then slowly and rather ponderously climbed out of the machine.

"Do you lock the doors?" I inquired—breaking our long silence.

"It won't be necessary," the Justice replied. "I don't think anybody would venture down here to steal a car!"

McReynolds then slowly turned to walk toward an elevator which would take us upstairs. In that brief instant of time there came to my mind the magnificent and stirring music which Bizet wrote to introduce the fourth act of *Carmen.* McReynolds seemed like some great matador who was entering Madrid's largest and most fashionable bullfighting arena. Inside the crowd was waiting, the music was playing, the people were shouting, and the fight was about to commence. The great moment had indeed arrived, and Destiny herself seemed to be waiting as I pressed the signal for the elevator operator to come down and fetch us up. And now the door of another car was opening. "Good morning," McReynolds replied to the colored man in a confident and pleasant tone of voice. And then turning to me the Justice said, "Mr. Knox, I am going up to the robing room. You can find yourself a seat in Court, and if Harry is already here he will find one for you."

"Thank you," I said, as we finally parted company.

I then walked alone through cavernous and austere corridors of white marble until I reached the vicinity of the Marshal's office. Harry was standing out in the corridor—apparently waiting for me to put in my appearance.

"Well, I finally got here!" I announced with a smile.

"Say, what happened this morning, anyway?" Harry inquired in a low voice. "Pussywillow was sure fit to be tied! Why, he even ate two grapefruit!"

At that moment I saw someone approaching so I merely replied, "Plenty happened, but I'll tell you about it later."

Without further comment on the subject, Harry then introduced me to several colored employees of the Court who happened to be standing nearby. One of them was, as I recall, the aged and infirm Arthur Thomas, who had for many years been the trusted messenger assigned to Justice Oliver Wendell Holmes. Thomas' duties consisted primarily of just sitting in a large chair at the entrance to the Courtroom and serving as official doorkeeper. He was by then too feeble for any more arduous work.

Harry next led me into a side entrance to the Courtroom itself, and here we came upon a row of pews reserved solely for relatives and friends of the nine Justices. "You can take a seat here," he said. "And every time you come to Court you can sit here."

I looked around as I sat down, but no other law clerks seemed to be present that morning. Or perhaps they were there and I did not recognize them. A number of well-dressed ladies, however, were sitting in the reserved section, and this section as well as the rest of the Courtroom was now gradually filling up with spectators. All of the visitors seemed impressed and even awed by their surroundings. Conversation was in low tones and reduced to a minimum. There was indeed a feeling of genuine majesty expressed by the architecture of the surroundings, and yet the great ionic columns, the huge red velvet draperies, and the extravagance of bronze and mahogany throughout the room appeared almost oppressive. I had also heard that this room was poorly lighted and suffered from bad acoustics. But I tried to remember, as I sat there that morning, that here was the meeting place of the most powerful judicial body in the entire world. I glanced at the nine empty chairs awaiting the arrival of the Justices, who were probably that very minute busily donning their black robes.

The great clock pointed to the hour of noon, and a warning gavel suddenly rapped for silence. Everyone present stood up. The huge curtains in the rear of the room parted, and Chief Justice Hughes and his eight associates slowly and deliberately entered—dressed in their traditional black gowns.

Mr. Frank Key Green, the Marshal of the Court, cried out in a loud and clear voice, "Oyez, Oyez, Oyez! All persons having business before the Honorable, the Supreme Court of the United States are admonished to draw near and give their attention, for the Court is now sitting. God save the United States and this Honorable Court."

The gavel then rapped again. Everyone sat down, and the Justices solemnly took their seats, too.

6

THE HISTORIC 1936 term of Court
had indeed begun, and a supreme moment in judicial history was rapidly approaching. I looked intently at the nine Justices who were assembled before
me, and on that day in 1936 I seemed to be gazing upon some great painting
unrolled for all to see. For several moments there was no sound, and even the
Chief Justice had not yet spoken. A sense of great drama filled the air. In this
stupendous shrine dedicated to the majesty of the law, however, no one that
day could have guessed how great a struggle would soon ensue over the question whether this Court, mighty as it seemed, could continue to function as
an independent agent of the government.

The Chief Justice of the United States was ready to speak. With a toss of
his handsome head and a quick glance around the vast room, Charles Evans
Hughes leaned forward in his chair and announced in a clear and loud voice
the first order of business: "Motions are now in order for nominations of attorneys to practice before the Supreme Court of the United States. The clerk
will read the names."

More than forty lawyers from all parts of the country then stepped forward one by one, while their sponsors made short stereotyped speeches introducing them to the Justices. While these placid proceedings were taking
place, I watched the nine men as they sat motionless and quiet in their high-backed, leather-cushioned chairs. Their average age was 70.8 years, and from
the audience they appeared seated in the following order [left to right]: Roberts (61), Butler (70), Brandeis (79), Van Devanter (77), Hughes (74), McReynolds (74), Sutherland (74), Stone (63), and Cardozo (63).

Six of these nine Justices had already served ten years, had reached the
age of seventy, and hence were eligible to retire on full pay at twenty thousand

dollars a year.[1] But there was, of course, no indication that any of the nine actually did intend to retire. During the months to come all of these men would, therefore, shape the policies of the country and influence the lives of millions of people as definitely as the Presidential election to be held on November 3, 1936. What course would their decisions take—these nine men who had already rendered adverse opinions in cases involving the National Industrial Recovery Act, the Agricultural Adjustment Act, "Hot Oil," the Guffey Coal Act, etc. and thus thrown the New Deal into startled confusion.

After studying the Chief Justice, I glanced at Justice McReynolds. His thoughts seemed to be far away as he gazed out over the crowded Courtroom. Proud and never-changing he sat, mysterious and strange: lonely, yet possessing the rewards of life withheld from so many of his fellow men. Like a gloomy Caesar he appeared—the Romanesque features of his granite-like expression conveying something forbidding and almost sinister. Here indeed was the man forever doomed to imperial isolation and yet somehow a vibrant and puzzling part of life. And on that day I was proud to be his law clerk, and my loyalty to him was undiminished.

I next looked at Justice Van Devanter. He seemed stern and forbidding— staring straight ahead with his thin lips tightly compressed. His bald head almost matched the color of the marble pillar near where he sat. And I could scarcely believe that one with his generous character and instinctive friendliness could seem so austere when sitting on the nation's highest tribunal and garbed in his robes of office. He appeared to be even more reserved than McReynolds.

At that moment Justice Brandeis began to fidget, and he slowly turned his swivel chair to the left until he was almost facing Van Devanter. Brandeis appeared more ascetic than any of the other Justices, with the exception of Cardozo, who sat quietly at one end of the bench, looking straight ahead, not moving a muscle and reminding me of Little Jack Horner. Or perhaps of teacher's pet at school. He had an almost imperceptible smile on his lips and was making no attempt to be a person of immense dignity. Unlike Cardozo, however, Brandeis appeared to be somewhat bored by the admission of so many attorneys. He continued for several minutes to look at Van Devanter with a rather cold and appraising eye. That Justice, however, gave no indication of awareness that he was being stared at.

1. [Editors' note: Unlike active judges, however, retired justices could have their pay reduced. See chapter 9, note 9.]

Owen J. Roberts, at the far end from Cardozo, was busily looking at a sheet of paper. Pierce Butler leaned over toward Roberts as if to see whether the junior Justice was merely doodling with his pencil. Butler exhibited a forbidding scowl while on the bench that day, and he seemed very displeased with the world. Whether he had the same lovable character of a Van Devanter remained to be seen. I then noticed that McReynolds had just slipped on a pair of horn-rimmed glasses, and that he and Butler were the only Justices wearing them. Even Cardozo, who had used his eyes so strenuously over the years, had no need of glasses while in the Courtroom that day.

My attention was then directed to Harlan F. Stone and George Sutherland. To my surprise both men appeared rather colorless. Justice Stone, stocky and perhaps even stodgy, sat in an informal and unconcerned fashion in his chair. He looked like a bored Wall Street executive patiently waiting for a business meeting to commence. Now and then he would shift his position as if he were not quite comfortable. No one studying him that day could have guessed the warmth of Stone's personality or the greatness of his heart. He appeared almost ill at ease.

Justice Sutherland looked exactly like the photographs I had seen of him, but despite his gray hair and rather striking beard, he did not exhibit any trace of the commanding presence that Hughes possessed. "But, of course, he might be impressive too if he were sitting in the middle chair and doing all the talking," I mused.

Little did I realize that Justice Stone would be stricken with a serious illness within a few days, and that he would be unable to attend to any court work until the following February.[2] Perhaps he was already ill. Nor did I suspect that Justice Brandeis would die exactly five years later—on October 5, 1941. But on that October day in 1936 they all sat before me—Nine Old Men—an incredible mirage of a million wonderful hopes.

I then glanced at one of the attorneys, who was busily engaged in sponsoring another candidate for admission. He appeared ill at ease, and his voice had begun to falter. I also noticed that he spoke with a marked Southern accent. A gentleman seated next to me leaned over and whispered, "A Georgia cracker! He's nervous and scared!" I nodded my head but said nothing. Harry had told me that even whispering was strictly forbidden while the Court was in session.

2. Justice Stone was absent from the bench, on account of illness, from October 14, 1936, until February 1, 1937.

Finally all the lawyers were admitted to practice, but no cases were to be argued before the Court that day. Presently Hughes adjourned the proceedings, and he and his eight associates left the room as ceremoniously and quietly as they had entered it.[3] After the Justices had disappeared from view, the spectators began to shuffle silently toward the doors. I slowly walked out into the spacious main hall, which was still crowded with latecomers who had not been fortunate enough to gain admission to the Courtroom itself. I failed, however, to catch any glimpse of Harry and concluded that he was busily preparing lunch for McReynolds. The public cafeteria also proved to be too crowded to enter, without a long wait in line, so I left the building by the main entrance. A surge of profound satisfaction engulfed me as I made my way to the nearest restaurant to eat some lunch. I was, in fact, very pleased with the world and with myself.

When I finally returned to McReynolds' apartment that afternoon only silence greeted me as I entered the front door, and I assumed that neither the Justice nor Harry had as yet come back from Court. The Justice's hat and walking stick were not in evidence and neither Harry nor Mary was to be found working in the kitchen. I then called Mary by name, and a pleasant voice cried out from the Justice's study, "In here, Mr. Knox!" Walking into McReynolds' room I found her busily dusting and polishing the chairs and bookcases. "Well, you finally got down to Court!" she exclaimed as she glanced at me without pausing in her work. "Was they all so high and mighty lookin' as you had expected?"

"I guess so," I replied a bit hesitantly. "At least they were very dignified. I certainly wish I could go down there every day."

"Humph!" said Mary as she stopped her work and let the dust cloth hang lazily from her right hand. "There won't be many more visits to the Court for *you!* We is just too far away for Pussywillow to let his secretary waste time trottin' down there. Why, I never even seen all the Justices myself while they was sittin'." And after a slight pause Mary exclaimed, "Say, Mr. Knox, how did Pussywillow look in that big black robe of his?"

"Solemn like all the others. I thought Hughes made the best impression."

"You don't say so? Then Pussywillow didn't stack up so good, eh?" And af-

3. The first case was set down for argument on Monday, October 12, 1936—just a week after the opening of Court. Arguments were to be made on October 12, 13, 14, 15, 16, 19, 20, 21, 22, and 23, after which the Court would adjourn until November 9 for the writing of opinions. Yet the Presidential election was to be held on November 3. It thus became apparent that the long-anticipated political contest would be decided before the Court handed down a single opinion during the 1936 term.

ter another pause, during which I made no comment, Mary suggested, "Why don't you just sit down and make yourself at home while I finish workin'? Pussywillow won't be comin' back for some time."

"Thanks, but where can I sit? Have you finished polishing my chair?"

"Why, sit in *his* chair, of course!"

So for the first but not for the last time I did sit down in McReynolds' big swivel chair that stood so forbiddingly in front of his desk. Then Mary turned, looked me over carefully, and laughed. "I just bet you feels like a real live Justice now, don't you—sittin' here in Pussywillow's chair."

"It takes more than a chair to make a Justice," I replied.

"Ain't that the truth now! For if it didn't, I sure would sit in that chair and be a Justice myself! And then Pussywillow could be the maid!" Mary exclaimed with a laugh. And after another pause she said, "Well, now that you is here, suppose you just pretend you is a Justice, too, and read that there letter layin' on top of his desk."

"You mean there's a letter here for me?"

"Naw, of course not! It's a letter from one of his lady friends in society. Go on and read it! We can always hear his key turnin' in the door if he should come home, but he ain't goin' to be gettin' here so soon."

"But I shouldn't read his letters, Mary, unless he wants me to. Is this one that I am supposed to answer?"

"What difference will it make? He'll never know, now will he? And besides he left it settin' right here on top of the desk where I'd be dustin' anyway. If he didn't want it read, why didn't he put it somewhere else, now I ask you?"

So I picked up the letter which was lying open in front of me. I glanced at Mary and then began to read the first page. She regarded me in silence and with a rapt expression.

Dear Mr. Justice:

How very nice it was to hear from you, especially since it is so lonely to be laid up in a hospital. But I am feeling quite fit again and hope to go home soon.

The head doctor on the floor must have sensed my loneliness as he has been in here a number of times to talk with me on one pretext or another. But he is a Jew! It's obvious. Imagine! I really did not know what to make of him at first, but I was, of course, *repelled*. He even touched me with his hands! What lengths these Jews will go to in order to make a conquest! And I certainly never expected one of them to turn up here in *this* hospital. . . .

I must have turned pale for Mary began laughing after I had completed reading the first page. "Mr. Knox, you sure do look surprised!" she exclaimed. "But you know he don't like no Jews and neither do his lady friends!"

In silence and with a strange feeling of guilt, I put the letter down on the desk again and replaced it exactly as I had found it. To this day I can recall from memory the complete wording of the first page of that missive, which came as such a jarring contrast to the impressive judicial proceedings which I had just witnessed. What the rest of the letter contained I never did know. McReynolds evidently answered it by hand for he never dictated to me any reply to this letter.

In a few moments we heard the sound of a door being slowly opened in the far end of the apartment. "Oh, oh!" Mary exclaimed under her breath, "That must be Pussywillow! How come he's home so soon?" She immediately stopped her work, and I arose from McReynolds' chair with the greatest of speed. I then strolled out into the hall as nonchalantly as possible and realized to my relief that it was Harry instead of the Justice who had just arrived. He had come in by way of the kitchen door. I called out to him, "Oh, it's *you*! I thought it was the Justice returning from Court. Mary and I were in his study when we heard the door open."

"He'll be home pretty soon," Harry replied pleasantly. "I think Justice Butler was going to take him for a short drive before bringing him back here. Anyway, I fixed Pussywillow's lunch at Court, and he didn't complain about nothing. And it was just like I told you—not much happened the first day but at least you were there. Next Monday they'll all start work in earnest when the lawyers begin arguing their cases."

I then explained the unfortunate mistake I had made in answering the phone that morning—when I had incorrectly identified one of the Justice's friends. Harry laughed heartily and said, "I thought it was *something* like that! But just don't go doing it again, and maybe he'll never even mention it. Some of his lady friends sure do get jealous of each other! Why, you shoulda been here at one of his Sunday morning breakfasts! When one of 'em arrived and found a certain other lady had also been invited, she stalked clear out into the corridor! She almost missed breakfast that morning before she decided whether to leave or come back in and stay. Pussywillow was sure embarrassed!"[4]

---

4. I never heard of Justice McReynolds going to church while I was his law clerk, although he may have attended services a few times. Instead it was his usual custom to have Harry prepare an elaborate Sunday morning breakfast for some of the Justice's friends. By 1936 these Sunday breakfasts

After greeting each other cordially, Harry and Mary then strolled out into the kitchen to prepare the evening meal. "Come along, lady," Harry said, "It's time for us to get to work."

Justice McReynolds did not return to the apartment that afternoon until a few minutes past four o'clock. While I was sitting in my office thumbing through a book from his library, I heard him enter, drop his walking stick noisily in the umbrella stand near the front door, and then proceed briskly down the hall and into his study. Presently, he rang for me. When I was anxiously seated before him with notebook and pencil in hand, he did not even mention the opening session of Court or my telephone mistake of that morning. Instead he merely proceeded to dictate three letters.

"Good. Now did any letter come in this afternoon's mail from Will McReynolds of Gracey, Kentucky?"

"No, not that I know of."

"That's strange. I expected to hear from him by now." And after a thoughtful pause McReynolds said, "Today at Court I was thinking about the repairs that need to be made to the family cemetery lot in Kentucky. My brother wrote to Will asking him to contact me, and I think we should hear from him shortly as to what I want done at the cemetery. The grave stones must be reset, for instance, and a new wall built around the lot. Remind me also to tell him that I want a low-growing ivy planted at frequent intervals—say, two feet between plants. Oh, well, if I don't hear from Will within a day or two, I shall write him.

"Yes, sir," I replied.

"In the meantime you better jot down some more points that I expect to take up with him. I want to tell him that there is a nursery about a mile out from Hopkinsville on the Cadiz Road. Also that bluegrass will not continue to live without much care. And in a short time the ivy should cover the ground and choke out the weeds. But, of course, it must also have some attention—especially during the first year. Mr. Knox, are you getting all this down in your notebook?"

"Yes, I am."

Then after a slight pause the Justice continued, "I want to put the family lot in shape before any more time goes by. When one is unmarried and getting along in years, he has no one to take care of matters like this except himself."

---

had become a real social event in Washington. To receive an invitation to one of these repasts was the fond hope of many a hostess allied with the "conservative set."

I remained silent, but I said to myself, "So *that* is what you were thinking about at Court today! Your parents' graves and your own inevitable death. I know now why you appeared so solemn and grim." I then looked across the desk at the Justice and felt a great surge of kindness toward him. But he was not gazing in my direction. Instead McReynolds was slowly opening and closing his left hand and examining his fingernails with care.

McReynolds then turned sharply in his chair and stared at me with a rather cold expression. "You know I don't approve of government employees collecting salary when they don't work!" he suddenly announced.

I was somewhat taken aback by this unexpected statement, and all I could mumble was "You don't?" It did not even occur to me that I was one of the employees he was referring to.

"Of course not!" the Justice exclaimed. "We have enough lazy people in Washington as it is—all living off the government! Well, what I mean is that you will need something to occupy your time for the next few weeks. You have now finished briefing all the petitions for certiorari, and the Chief Justice has not yet assigned me any opinions to write. While the Court is hearing oral arguments, I shall be gone much of the time from the apartment, and Harry will also be down at Court each day preparing my lunch. Now if you are going to be paid a salary for October you should have something to keep you occupied—at least part of the time. From now on, therefore, I want you to handle all the correspondence regarding invitations that are sent to me and calling cards that are left downstairs at the desk. So far I have been answering this correspondence myself."

I nodded my head and said, "I shall be glad to."

"Now it is extremely important," the Justice continued, "that an invitation to dinner be acknowledged promptly. The social rules in Washington must be strictly observed regardless of your other activities." And reaching into the top right-hand drawer of his desk, he slowly drew forth an envelope and then removed a letter from it. "Now here is an invitation, for instance, to a dinner later on this month. But I don't want to go! In fact, I shall probably decline nine out of every ten invitations that I receive during this term of Court. In your best handwriting, therefore, I want you to write an answer to this invitation—in black ink and on Court stationery. Say the following—well, let me see, now go on and copy this down in your notebook and use this form for all other similar invitations. You can write the following:

Mr. Justice McReynolds
thanks Mrs. ——

for her generous invitation
to the dinner to be given on
———— evening, October ————.
The Justice's engagements
do not permit him to accept.

2400 Sixteenth Street ———— October ————

After explaining in detail just how he wanted the reply spaced, line by line, McReynolds said, "Now before you leave today be sure and write an answer to this invitation and get it in the mail. I certainly don't want this woman to think I am coming! She is just trying to forward the career of her husband by inviting a Supreme Court Justice to dinner."

I was, however, thinking to myself, "This reply is too curt. It is not gracious enough. It should read, 'The Justice regrets' or 'The Justice sincerely regrets that his engagements do not permit him to accept.' Now if I were a hostess I would feel a bit hurt after I read the last sentence. It just doesn't sound right—at least to me." But I made no comment.[5] And after a brief pause, McReynolds continued, "Now I suppose it would be expecting too much to hope that you are familiar with the Washington practice of leaving calling cards."

"That is something I don't know anything about," I admitted.

"Well, I shall explain it *once,* and you can jot down some notes which can be used from time to time to refresh your memory. Harry will also be able to instruct you about the question of calling cards if some point should arise when I happen to be in Court. Now, first of all, when a new official comes to Washington, his wife must leave calling cards upon those high-ranking members of the government who are already here. In the fall of each year, cards are also left by many people who pay their respects to, let me see, well, first of all the President. Then comes the Vice President, the Chief Justice, the Speaker of the House, the Associate Justices of the Supreme Court, and finally the members of the Cabinet. And when a man and wife leave cards at the White House, for instance, they must leave, well, they must leave five!"

"Five?" I asked in surprise.

5. Throughout my term as secretary to McReynolds, I never knew just when to offer a suggestion and when to remain quiet. Sometimes I would speak up, but more often I merely kept silent. His moods were so changeable that a friendly attitude one moment might give way to hostility the next. This especially became apparent after the election of Roosevelt to a second term in the White House.

"Of course five! Now are you sure you are paying proper attention to all this? You can put 'five' down in your notebook, and then remember it."

"But why should a man and his wife want to leave five cards when they are calling at the White House? Why don't they leave just two cards?" I ventured to ask.

"They may leave two in Chicago, but they don't leave two here! The wife leaves two of her own cards, properly engraved, and one card is for Mrs. Roosevelt and the other is for the President's mother. The husband leaves three of his cards, and one is for the President, one is for Mrs. Roosevelt, and one is for the President's mother. That makes *five*."

"Oh, I see. I forgot about the President's mother and wife. But what happens when a new official and his wife call on *you*?"

"Well, don't interrupt me now. We were talking about the couple leaving five cards at the White House. There is another point to remember—if the cards are flat, then it means the chauffeur left them."

"Flat?" I queried. "Aren't all cards flat?"

By this time McReynolds was beginning to lose patience, and no wonder, but he continued, "Of course all calling cards are flat! What else would they be? But what I mean is that if the right-hand corner of a card is turned up—*turned up* mind you—then it indicates that the man and wife, or maybe just the wife, left the cards *in person*. In other words, they didn't send their chauffeur down to the White House but went themselves—or at least the wife went." By now the Justice was getting a bit confused himself regarding the calling card situation.

I then wanted to ask how "a wife" could gain admittance to the White House for the sole purpose of leaving five calling cards, but on second thought I concluded that perhaps silence on this point might be the best policy.

"I meant to say," the Justice continued a bit fretfully, "that the *upper* right-hand corner of the card must be folded up in order to indicate a call in person. If the lower right-hand corner is folded, that is the official way of expressing condolences in case of a death."

At this point I neglected to repeat my question about how many cards would be left by a man and wife calling on a bachelor Justice. I was thinking, "But suppose I wanted to leave cards on the President's *sons*, how would I do that? And what if the sons were married, too?" The possibilities involved in card-leaving seemed enormous and beyond my grasp that afternoon. Here was a world of mystery that had entirely eluded me heretofore.

And then, with a sigh, the Justice continued speaking, "Now then, Mr. Knox, if you have understood everything so far we can proceed."

"I have, sir!" I ventured to say—knowing full well that I hadn't.

"When all these people leave their calling cards for me here at 2400, it is then up to me to decide which cards I wish to acknowledge. Most of them will be ignored, as I haven't the time or the inclination to meet many people. The cards which have been acknowledged can be kept in a small pile, but the others should be thrown away. And my card will almost always be sent flat— meaning that it was delivered by Harry and not by me, or else sent through the mail. I very seldom make a special trip to leave my calling card in person with anyone."

I soon realized that McReynolds was indeed serious about the Washington practice of receiving and sending calling cards. This was no matter which could be treated lightly, at least with him. And as the social season progressed, I discovered that the proper and immediate dispatch of his calling card was second only in importance to the Justice's writing of Supreme Court opinions. If he wished to recognize a family socially, his card must be sent within twenty-four hours after such family had left cards with him. And once his card was received, the family he had acknowledged was then free to invite the Justice to teas, dinners, receptions, and the like. However, he often declined such invitations after the Court-packing controversy burst so unexpectedly upon the nation in February 1937.

My final questions to McReynolds that day concerned invitations from embassies. In 1936 there were fifty-four embassies and legations in Washington. The diplomatic representatives of the more prominent countries, he explained, usually sent him invitations to their receptions. The representatives from the smaller and less well known nations seldom included him in their guest lists.

"Will there really be any invitation from the Russian embassy?" I inquired with interest.

"Probably," McReynolds replied coldly, "but I shall accept no invitation to attend any affair held in *that* embassy! I wouldn't set foot inside their door! If any invitation arrives from the Russians, I want you to remember that it is to be promptly declined!"[6]

"How about the Spanish embassy?" I next inquired. Spain had suddenly been torn asunder by a violent civil war, which had begun in July 1936 and was then just three months old.

6. In those days invitations to the Russian embassy were much sought after by many members of official Washington society. Much as they might be embarrassed by this statement today, it nevertheless is true. Most people, including myself, were naturally curious to see what "those Russians" really looked like.

"Well, I don't think the Spanish ambassador will be sending out many invitations *this* year!" McReynolds replied with some emphasis. "In any event, I shall not accept any invitation from that embassy while their civil war is in progress."

Thus ended my first lesson regarding the subject of invitations and calling cards. But there was much yet to be learned.

I also discovered that many of the outsiders who were swarming into Washington during the heyday of the New Deal were simply ignored by a tightly knit inner circle of society called the Cave Dwellers. These were the old-fashioned families whose ancestors had lived in Washington for decades and who held themselves aloof from the hurly-burly cocktail parties and social goings-on of the New Deal parvenus—who would undoubtedly be leaving after Landon was elected President. Many of these families had voted the Republican ticket exclusively for years on end, and in October 1936 even the most pessimistic of them could not have dreamed that seventeen more years of unbroken Democratic rule were still to come.

While serving as secretary to Justice McReynolds, I tried earnestly to develop some small interest in the Washington social scene but this I was completely unable to do. On the evening of the judiciary reception at the White House in January 1937, for instance, I went instead to a movie. Even McReynolds was nonplussed at such utter disregard for an invitation from the White House. Though he detested the very name "Roosevelt," he nevertheless attended that reception, but I did not.

In the fall of 1936, however, I did venture to attend three Washington cocktail parties, but without the Justice's knowledge. These noisy affairs only served to make me even more allergic to the whole problem. Finally not even a White House invitation held any interest for me. All during that fall and winter there seemed to be something grotesque about Washington society during those early days of the New Deal. I constantly compared it with what I had seen in Boston only the year before. I longed many times for even one glimpse of the stately old homes on Beacon Hill, with their quiet and elegant drawing rooms where one met people who were not constantly "on the make," or at least who did not seem to be. The bread in Boston had long been baked, so to speak, while the dough was still rising chaotically and explosively in Washington.

Unfortunately for Justice McReynolds, he not only had a secretary who lacked the slightest interest in the mystery of Washington society but during that term of Court the Justice probably received more invitations than he was ever sent during any other social season before or after. As the glare of publicity focused more and more on the members of the Court, in their great struggle with the President, nearly every hostess in Washington appeared to be anxious to "snare" a Justice for one or more of her dinner parties or other social affairs. As a result a considerable amount of time, which I considered virtually wasted, had to be spent declining invitations in my best handwriting and on Supreme Court stationery, and occasionally in asking Harry to venture out "just once more" with the Justice's calling cards. Through it all, however, Harry remained ever faithful and always willing to tender whatever advice and assistance he could. Never once did he decline in any way to accede to my slightest request—a fact which seems amazing in view of my youthful inexperience. One afternoon I heard him laugh and say to Mary, "Shoefenicks is sure busy again answering some more of Pussywillow's invitations!" And I muttered under my breath, "Why in the name of heaven do all these people, many of them strangers, want to be bothered inviting McReynolds anyway!" What I failed to realize, of course, was that the invitations were being sent to a Supreme Court Justice and not just to a private individual. "Harry," I said one afternoon, "I suppose many women in Washington actually spend their entire time fooling around with this calling card business! What a useless life!"

Before I left the Justice's apartment on that long-to-be-remembered first day of Court, I typed the three letters he had dictated and then penned an answer to the dinner invitation. As soon as McReynolds approved my handwriting and the spacing of the words, I sealed up the reply and dropped it in the mail chute. "Well, the career of that lady's husband is not going to get advanced after all, at least by Justice McReynolds!" I thought as I saw the letter disappear down the chute.

When I finally returned to my little apartment that evening, I picked up and reread the letter which Justice Cardozo had written me five days before. Two sentences seemed to stand out above all others in that letter. They were "A hard year is ahead of us" and "Telephone me whenever you are free." "I'll call him this week for sure," I resolved. "Yes, I'll call him this week." And having made that decision, I decided to go to bed. It had indeed been a busy day.

The next morning, which was a Tuesday, brought with it an unexpected difficulty. It was not long before McReynolds' worst fears were confirmed— that I did not have enough work to keep me occupied all the time. There were simply no more letters that he could dictate, and I had no petitions for certiorari to read and brief. No cases had as yet been argued before the Court, and certainly there were no opinions to write. I could, however, have kept myself busy all that day just answering my own personal correspondence—which was always very extensive—but this was unthinkable under the circumstances. ["This is just the week I might start reading *Gone with the Wind*," I thought.] But I could not imagine myself sitting quietly in a chair perusing a novel on government time while McReynolds was pacing up and down the apartment, so in desperation I finally took down some volumes of the *U.S. Reports* and began to read them.

"Perhaps you might like to read this," McReynolds suddenly announced in the stillness of my small retreat. In some confusion I looked behind me and rose hastily to my feet. "Oh, I did not see you!" I exclaimed in surprise. "And what was that you said?"

"I said you could look into this book as long as you haven't got anything else to do," the Justice replied a bit impatiently as he held up for my inspection a slender volume enclosed in a red paper jacket. "In fact, you can keep it if you want to. Now let me see, yes, on page 22 there is some discussion of what the President did to the gold standard in this country." And handing me the book in an awkward and almost shy manner, the Justice left the room as abruptly as he had entered it and almost before I could thank him for his gift. "Well, I thought you might like to read it," he said just as he disappeared from view.

I found that I was holding in my hand a slender volume entitled *Hell Bent for Election*, written by James P. Warburg,[7] a former economic adviser to President Franklin D. Roosevelt. This book told of the President's many broken promises and why, in Warburg's opinion, Roosevelt had broken them. On the first page the Justice had written his name "McReynolds" in pencil to indicate his ownership of the book. Now he was giving it to me, but I did not realize at the time that this was a most extraordinary gesture on his part.[8] It was, in fact,

---

7. [Editors' note: Garden City, N.Y.: Doubleday, Doran, 1935.]

8. The Justice also gave me another book some time later. In January 1937, there was delivered to McReynolds' apartment a large volume entitled *Federal Justice*. The authors of this work were Homer Cummings, Attorney General of the United States, and Carl McFarland, Special Assistant to the Attorney General of the United States. The volume bore the date 1937 on the title page and had been published a few days previously by the Macmillan Company of New York. On the flyleaf there was written in ink, "To Mr. Justice McReynolds, with the best wishes of Homer Cummings, Jan 11/37." McReynolds, who had been dictating some letters to me when the book arrived by messenger, paused long enough to thumb through the volume, and he soon noticed his name in the index. Then turning back to page 531, he read: "Others have attacked the problem of age from another angle. 'Worn out judges ought to be respectably provided for, by allowing them to resign upon a competent pension,' recommended Attorney General Bates. After a retirement law had been passed, Attorney General McReynolds recommended in 1913 that when any federal judge, except justices of the Supreme Court, failed to avail himself of the privilege of retiring at the age provided by law, the President should appoint another judge to preside over the affairs of the

an indication that he had made some genuine, if slight, attempt to display an interest in his secretary which might lead to a closer relationship between the two men. For weeks I had been hoping that he would make some such gesture, and when he did so I wanted to respond at once with a warm feeling of friendship. There was so much to say, and I was already becoming lonely in Washington. But I still did not realize that McReynolds, unlike Van Devanter and Cardozo, for instance, resembled the character in a play who once said, "We're all of us sentenced to solitary confinement inside our own skins."

Mr. Warburg's book was only seventy-eight pages long, and I read it carefully since it was such a devastating indictment of President Roosevelt. The author would quote from Roosevelt's campaign promises of 1932 and show how they had been repudiated and ignored one after another.

The next time Justice McReynolds called me into his study for some dictation, I thanked him again for the Warburg book and mentioned my surprise at learning how many campaign promises the President had broken.[9] After some reflection the Justice slowly replied, "No trait in Roosevelt is more dangerous than the fact that he does one thing while planning just the opposite." And shaking his head back and forth he concluded, "I don't know where all this is going to end!"

Noticing a copy of the current issue of the *Literary Digest* on the Justice's desk, I chanced to remark, "It will probably end in Roosevelt's defeat. What does this week's *Digest* poll say about Landon's chances?"

---

court and have precedence over the older one. 'This,' said he, 'will insure at all times the presence of a judge sufficiently active to discharge promptly and adequately the duties of the court.'"

Upon reading this quotation harking back twenty-three years, McReynolds' eyes narrowed, and he spoke of the book in rather uncomplimentary terms. At the time, however, I did not know what statement he had taken exception to. "Here, you can have this book if you want it," he suddenly announced. "I wouldn't have it around the house! Take it away!" But little did either of us realize that in less than one month there would burst upon the country the Court-packing proposal of President Roosevelt—as approved by Attorney General Cummings.

I later spent some time reading this volume, as it showed a tremendous amount of research, and it did contain many facts of interest. However, the name of Cummings became unmentionable around McReynolds after the Court-packing idea was announced on February 5, 1937. At that time I even removed the book from the desk in my office, and I took it down to my bedroom on the fourth floor at 2400 in order to keep the volume out of sight.

9. The Justice was very interested in this book and considered it a most excellent one. Yet the author was Jewish. McReynolds' anti-Semitic feelings were rather puzzling at times. There was never any Jewish guest at his apartment while I was his law clerk, yet this interesting volume by a Jewish author was quite welcome. A book could enter Apartment 507 whereas a man could not, or so it seemed.

McReynolds then handed me the October 3 issue. On page 7 there was an article entitled, "Landon Holds Lead in 'Digest' Poll. Kansan Ahead in 21 States, Roosevelt in 10, Lemke in None."

"Landon seems to be gaining," the Justice ventured, "I think we may be due for a change. Let's hope so at least!" [10]

To this I replied, "I notice Roosevelt said last week that he expects to balance the budget in a year or two without imposing any additional new taxes."

"I suppose he said that in one of his campaign speeches," McReynolds remarked dryly. "Well, then, you can just be sure he is getting ready to spend some more money!"

I then left the Justice's study to peruse the copy of the *Digest* which he had given me. And at the moment it seemed that McReynolds might even be right in anticipating Landon's election. The *Digest* polls in the past had proved remarkably correct. In 1920, 1924, 1928, and 1932, not only had the *Digest* picked the correct Presidential winner, but it had forecast the actual popular vote within such a small percentage of error that the magazine's polls were considered extremely accurate by 1936. For instance, the percentage of error in the 1932 poll had been less than 1 percent.

Not only did the *Digest* predict that Landon was leading in twenty-one states, but these states carried an electoral vote of 290. On the other hand, the ten states in which Roosevelt was alleged to be leading contained only 111 electoral votes. Then, too, Al Smith had just made a stirring speech in Carnegie Hall telling a New York audience that "the remedy for all the ills that we are suffering from today is the election of Alfred M. Landon." The fact that the Democratic candidate of 1928 would endorse a Republican candidate in 1936 carried great weight with me. "Maybe he will influence several million votes throughout the country," I thought. "If Smith could swing New York State to Landon, Roosevelt might be seriously hampered."

In the evenings, however, I would tune in on some of Landon's campaign speeches [using the] small radio in my apartment. But when I listened to his voice and delivery, I began to have grave doubts again that he could win against Roosevelt. It was like trying to imagine a pygmy attempting to lasso an elephant. And all the while Jim Farley remained very calm and kept saying that whatever Al Smith or Alf Landon did was quite immaterial, and that Roosevelt's victory in 1936 would be an even greater one than his 1932 success. Yet

10. Neither Van Devanter nor McReynolds had ever asked me what my politics were. They just assumed that I was a staunch Republican, or at least anti-New Deal. McReynolds, however, did inquire as to what church I attended.

Justice McReynolds continued to place his faith in the *Literary Digest* polls. It was the only magazine that I ever saw on the desk in his study. He read each issue carefully and compared Landon's chances week by week with those of the occupant of the White House. The *Digest's* predictions were something to hold to, and to keep faith in. They were, in fact, like a guiding star, which seemed to forecast the early end of the four-year New Deal nightmare.

After leaving McReynolds' apartment at the close of the day on Thursday [October 8, 1936], I telephoned Justice Cardozo, and on Friday evening I called at his apartment. How delightful it was to see him again, but once in his presence I made no mention of the coming Presidential election or of the *Digest* polls. In fact, I did not even see a copy of the *Literary Digest* anywhere in Cardozo's apartment. It seemed strange that all the Justices were not busily perusing each weekly issue of that magazine.

Saturday, October 10, was my parents' wedding anniversary, and I did manage to type them a short note of congratulations even while the Justice was in the apartment. I had by now read nearly all of the important opinions of Justice Holmes from the books in McReynolds' library, and I had also thumbed through many other decisions written by late and sometimes lamented members of the Court.

Harry and Mary spent most of their time in the kitchen while the Justice was at home that week. It seemed almost as if they were deliberately avoiding having much contact with him. Occasionally, however, Harry would venture forth into the hall to answer the house telephone. After one such call, he walked quietly into my office and said in a low tone of voice, "Say, Mr. Knox, there's some reporter on the phone who wants to know if he can take a picture of the Justice next Monday morning when he is on his way to Court. What shall I tell him?"

I walked down the hall, picked up the receiver, and identified myself as the Justice's secretary. This time I was careful to learn to whom I was talking. The man had a pleasant voice and his request seemed reasonable enough, so I asked him to hold the line until I could pass on his request to the Justice.

When I entered McReynolds' study he was busily and carefully penning a letter by hand. I interrupted him just when he was in the middle of a sentence. "Pictures?" he gasped as he glanced up at me. "Absolutely not! No pictures, none at all! Hang up the phone. Don't talk to him."

That was my first but certainly not my last experience with photographers requesting permission to take the Justice's picture.

7

IT WAS MONDAY morning again—
October 12, 1936—and the first case was scheduled for argument before the
Court at twelve o'clock noon. It was like hearing the faint sound of a trumpet
at Gettysburg before the first shock of battle, and McReynolds was, so to
speak, wearing a uniform of gray. His cause had been primarily successful so
far, but how would he conduct himself when the defeat of his way of thinking,
and of everything in which he believed, began to manifest itself? It would indeed be a time to try a man's soul.

On that particular Monday morning I was careful not to arrive too early
at McReynolds' apartment, and by the time I entered he had, in fact, finished
his shower and was already eating breakfast. "Good morning," I said as I
walked down the hall. Harry was standing as usual at the entrance to the dining room—waiting for McReynolds to finish one course before serving him
another—and both he and the Justice answered my greeting in a very pleasant fashion. At times McReynolds was accustomed to respond in a most
friendly tone of voice, and since this was such an occasion I assumed that either the breakfast was agreeable or that the latest *Literary Digest* poll had
proved even more favorable to the Republican cause than the Justice had
anticipated.

McReynolds then cleared his throat, as he was sometimes accustomed to
do, and he continued speaking to Harry in a voice so friendly that it seemed
as if he were talking to his own brother. "I say, Harry," he continued, "I believe I'll change ties before going down to Court this morning. I guess I'll wear
a bow tie—what do you think? Do you think a bow tie would look all right?"

"Well, yes, I do," Harry replied a bit hesitantly. "Of course, though, you
can't wear a bow tie that don't match your suit."

"I know, I know!" McReynolds now answered a bit impatiently. "Naturally I wouldn't wear something that didn't match." And after a moment's pause the Justice continued, "Here, take this plate away, and bring me another cup of coffee. And when you've done that will you go into my bedroom and pick out a bow tie that I can wear with this suit I have on?"

Harry immediately complied with the first request, and I heard the swinging door between the dining room and kitchen creak on its hinges. And in a moment he was back. "Here's your coffee, and now I'll get the tie. Let's see, with your gray suit you should wear something sort of blue. Yes, I'll find your blue bow tie and put it out on the dresser for you."

"Thank you," McReynolds replied gallantly. "And tell Mary that the coffee is very good this morning. Sometimes she doesn't get quite the right flavor in it, but today it tastes just fine."

And at that moment all was indeed happiness and serenity in the McReynolds household. Then I heard the Justice say, "Oh, Harry, will you ask Mr. Knox what the temperature is going to be today? And is it going to rain?"

"Yes, sir!" replied Harry, and a few moments later he was standing at the door of my office inquiring very formally, "The Justice wants to know what the temperature is, and do you think it's going to rain?"

For a moment I was at a complete loss for an answer. I thought to myself, "Well, how would *I* know what the temperature is when I haven't been outside of 2400 this morning either? Doesn't he remember that I live on the fourth floor while he's on the fifth?" But finally, grasping at a straw and hoping for the best, I said, "The temperature will be in the 60s, and the sun will be out today. It won't rain."

After the weather inquiry I sat anxiously in my little office. And in due time the buzzer on my desk emitted a loud hissing sound so I immediately picked up my notebook and pencil and walked dutifully into McReynolds' study.

"I don't want to dictate any letters," he said—still in a very pleasant and friendly tone of voice. "I merely wish to review with you the cases that will be argued before the Court today. Let's see now, we will hear two and perhaps three." And then citing the names of the ones that would be heard, he continued, "Hereafter will you keep track of the ones that will be argued each day, and please order the briefs of these cases from the Clerk's office. I can glance at the pleadings before going on to Court, and the oral arguments of the attorneys will then make more sense. Some of these lawyers are certainly vague in their discussions these days!" And after a pause and a careful glance at the ceiling he then exclaimed, "But I suppose I should not criticize them. They are just trying to interpret these New Deal laws, and they are certainly vague, too." Looking me squarely in the eye he said, "Yes! Statutes carelessly drawn by young men just out of the Harvard Law School! Frankfurter's protégés, too, I suppose!"

I made no comment concerning this statement and must have looked quite foolish indeed. I could think of no brilliant example of repartee to offer at the moment, and so I just glanced down at a paper on the desk as if ashamed that I had ever heard of the Harvard Law School or even of Boston itself. One of my difficulties as secretary to McReynolds was that I often thought of what should have been said—but not until long after it was too late to say it.

It also must have been quite apparent to McReynolds that morning that the Chief Justice meant to start off the work of the term at top speed. From the number of cases scheduled for argument on the very first day, Hughes gave every indication that a busy year was indeed ahead. And as it turned out, on that particular Monday three cases were argued in their entirety and a fourth one was in the process of being argued when Court adjourned at 4:00 P.M. Another case involving a construction of the Bankruptcy Act was submitted the same day without argument. Not even President Roosevelt could have expected the Justices to work any faster than this. Therefore, on that twelfth day of October, 1936, even though there had been considerable loose talk in high places of a "horse and buggy" Court, I am sure that neither Hughes nor McReynolds suspected that anyone would ever seriously and repeatedly accuse the Court of handling its work in a slow and dilatory fashion—and then go so far as to hold them up to public ridicule before the entire nation. In fact, on that opening day McReynolds gave some indication that he resented the pressure that "the Chief" was apparently going to impose on his various Associates during the coming term.

As I sat before McReynolds following his breakfast that morning I wanted very much to ask if I could go down to Court with him. But somehow I found it impossible to broach the question even on a day when he was very friendly. Among the lawyers scheduled to appear was one of the Couderts of New York—Mr. Frederic R. Coudert, Jr. I was anxious to see a Coudert in action, but I made no request of the Justice to accompany him. And he did not suggest my going to Court with him, either.

"That will be all," McReynolds suddenly announced as I sat in his study.

Then the first sour note intruded itself into the morning scene. "Is my walking stick by the door, Harry?" the Justice inquired.

"I guess it is," was the answer.

"Well, I want you to know for sure! Go on out and look. When I get ready to start I don't want to be late for Court!" And the very thought of being late must have made McReynolds nervous for Hughes was accustomed to ascend the bench with his Associates on the split second of twelve o'clock noon—with no exceptions permitted.

"It's here, Mr. Justice," Harry called back from the hallway. "Yes, your walking stick is here all right."

Up until the very moment when he was ready to leave, McReynolds kept Harry almost constantly busy with one request after another.

Shortly before eleven o'clock McReynolds finally left the apartment alone. I stood quietly near the front door while Harry went through the ritual of handing the Justice his hat and walking stick, helping him on with his light-weight fall coat, and finally cautioning him about driving carefully.

"He certainly was in one good mood today," I said. "What do you suppose got into him? And on a Monday morning, too!"

"Well, maybe he's glad he's going to start workin' again," Harry suggested. "He's old, but it's still nice to have something to do—and his work is real important, too."

"You better fix him something good," I suggested. "Suppose he doesn't like what you have ready? In that case I would hate to be the lawyer who makes the first argument after lunch!"

"Lawyers aren't the only ones who argue cases before Pussywillow," Harry commented. "I been arguing lots of cases before him for years!"

"Changing the subject," I said, "but didn't he look a bit strange in that bow tie he was wearing? Do any of the other Justice ever wear bow ties to Court?"

"Naw," said Harry. "I never saw no bow tie on nobody but Pussywillow. I guess he thinks it makes him look younger."

"It does—a little," I replied, "but I still don't think a bow tie is dignified enough to wear on the bench. It looks, well, somehow it looks a little flippant."

"Suppose you just go and tell Pussywillow that!" Harry exclaimed as he walked into the kitchen to speak to Mary.

Some minutes passed, and I had just begun to read the only pending petition for certiorari when the telephone rang. It was the phone on my desk with the unlisted number. I thought, of course, that it was a belated call from one of the Justice's close friends—perhaps feminine—and so as I reached over for the receiver I was prepared to announce that he had just gone to Court. However, when I said in my best tone of voice, "Mr. Justice

McReynolds' chambers," I found to my great surprise that I was talking with McReynolds himself. "Oh, is that you, Mr. Knox?" he said in apparent surprise. And after a slight pause he continued, "Well, before I go on the bench I just wanted to call and ask Harry to make me a beef sandwich. Will you tell him to bring it along when he comes to Court?" This information I promised to relay at once to Harry, and the Justice then ended the conversation as abruptly as he had begun it.

When I walked down the hall I met Harry coming out of the kitchen. "I was just on my way to tell you that the Justice called," I said. "He wants you to bring him a beef sandwich when you go down to Court." And as an afterthought I commented, "Better slice the beef thick!"

"Oh, oh! It's begun," Harry replied with a grim smile. "It's begun all right!"

"What's begun, Harry?" I asked. "All he wanted was a beef sandwich."

"He don't want no beef sandwich—not really!" Harry replied with emphasis. "A beef sandwich—huh! All he wanted was to check up on *you*! He probably thought you had scooted out of here as soon as he took off to court. I was watching you, and I never heard you ask Pussywillow whether you could drive down to Court with him. You let the *whole morning* slip by without telling him that you wanted to go along. What did you do that for?"

"Of course I didn't ask to go," I replied, "because I thought he didn't *want* me to!" And then with a helpless gesture I said, "Is there no understanding this man? He was certainly friendly all morning, so why didn't he just come out and say, 'Mr. Knox, would you like to go to Court with me?' But no, he said nothing!"

"Well, you said nothing, too!" grinned Harry. "And so he thought you left as soon as he did."

"But what of it? Suppose I *had* decided to go to lunch just then?"

"Do you remember what I told you when you first came here last summer?" Harry replied. "If Pussywillow ever calls up and finds you gone, you will probably get fired! He just don't trust nobody! So always be sure to go to lunch five minutes after twelve, as the Justices go on the bench at twelve. And be back here not later than a quarter of two because the Court always adjourns at two sharp."

"You don't mean it!" I said.

"Of course I mean it! Why wouldn't I? If you always eat lunch like I say between twelve and two, you will never be gone when he calls up. Now remember what I tell you about this—that is if you want to stay on here."

"But Harry," I continued, "the very first time the Justice goes down to

Court alone and leaves us here, why does he have to rush to a telephone to call up and check on *me?* I don't see what difference it would make if I had gone to lunch just before he called—I still would expect to be back here promptly. Besides I haven't enough work to keep me busy all day anyway."

"He don't trust nobody—just like I said," Harry replied solemnly while shaking his head back and forth. "He don't even trust *me* to bring him his lunch on time, though I been doing it ever since he went on the Court over twenty years ago!"

I continued, "I just can't believe that a Justice of the Supreme Court of the United States would spend any time checking up on when his law clerk goes to lunch during the time Court is in session—unless, of course, he is expecting some important message or phone call. Maybe I should go to lunch now and get back here before two."

"That's right. I'll be gone when you return, but just be sure you are sitting by that telephone when Pussywillow leaves the bench."

"I'll be here!" I replied, "but now I suppose he won't even think of calling for another six weeks! Oh, well, it doesn't really make any difference, only I wish he would trust me just a little. Tomorrow I'll certainly ask to go to Court with him. I'd rather be down there hearing arguments than just sitting here doing nothing!"

Harry returned in the early afternoon, although the Court continued to sit until four o'clock, and McReynolds finally returned home about an hour later. Almost as soon as he opened the front door, Harry appeared from the kitchen. "I'm tired," McReynolds said with a sigh. "I think I'll rest for a while."

The Justice walked to the door of my little office and inquired, "Were there any calls for me this afternoon?"

"No," I replied, "no one called all day."

"Thank you," McReynolds said as he slowly turned to walk into his study. "I think I'll look at yesterday's *New York Times.* I haven't finished reading it yet." And after a momentary pause he continued, "If you wish, Mr. Knox, you can leave now. There really isn't anything to keep you here."

I thanked him sincerely for this unexpected expression of his generosity. "I briefed the latest petition and put the summary on your desk. It is not an important case, and I recommended that the petition be denied."

"I'll look at it a little later," McReynolds replied in a friendly tone of voice. "Good night." And as I prepared to leave the apartment that day I realized that the Justice had made no mention of what had transpired at Court, and I certainly hadn't either.

When an opportune moment arose [the next] morning, just as McReynolds began his elaborate preparations to leave once more for Court, I said, "Did Mr. Coudert finish his argument yesterday?"

"Mr. Coudert?' the Justice inquired in a seeming effort to place the name.

"Yes, Mr. Frederic Coudert," I replied with a show of enthusiasm. "I think he is arguing the three *Neidecker* cases—the ones involving an interpretation of our 1909 Treaty with France.[1]

"Oh, *that* case!" McReynolds replied. "It was being argued yesterday when we adjourned. I guess it will be the first case heard today."

"Well, I thought perhaps the Chief Justice might ask you to write the opinion in it," I ventured. "It is a very interesting case, and I am wondering whether the Court will decide to let the Americans be extradited to France to stand trial for crimes committed there."

McReynolds then replied a bit impatiently, "I won't know what opinions I shall write until a week from Saturday. The Chief Justice will assign the cases at that time—following our Saturday conference. I haven't the slightest idea who will get this treaty case." And then after a slight pause the Justice continued, "Why do you ask? Do you know Mr. Coudert?"

"No, in fact, I never even saw him, but I have often heard of his New York law firm." And feeling that the moment of decision was at hand I said, "I was wondering if it would be all right for me to go down to Court with you today. I'll leave after the first case or two is argued."

McReynolds became very thoughtful, and he even began to look at the fingernails of his left hand again. Then he said rather abruptly, "I think not! There might be some phone calls today, and I want you to be here to take them. I just don't trust Mary to get messages straight, and I don't want both you and Harry gone from the apartment at the same time."

I was tremendously disappointed by this statement, but I tried not to show it. "Of course," I replied. I knew from that moment on, however, that I need not expect to accompany the Justice to Court many times that term. But I tried to realize that it would indeed be best if his secretary were always at the apartment to answer any telephone calls that might come while McReynolds and Harry were downtown. I also felt that even if we had moved our offices to the Court building itself, the Justice would not have approved of my leaving my desk and walking only a few feet into the great room where hearings were

---

1. *Valentine, Police Commissioner of New York City, et al. v. United States ex rel. B. Coles Neidecker,* 299 U.S. 5 (Decided November 9, 1936).

held. After all, I wasn't being paid to listen to lawyers argue their cases, and a secretary's best place was near the telephone when his employer was absent.

Nothing of any further consequence happened until Harry returned to 2400 on Friday afternoon, October 16. "Say, Mr. Knox," he said, "did you know that Justice Stone took sick? Just like that, too! He hasn't been to Court since Tuesday, and I hear he may not come back for some time!"

"I wonder what his law clerk will do to keep busy if Stone is going to be sick very long," I commented thoughtfully.[2] "And suppose he gets so sick he has to resign! Do you know what that would mean, Harry? Roosevelt would appoint a new Justice, and the Nine Old Men would be broken up!"

"Oh, you're imagining things," Harry retorted. "Don't you know the Nine Old Men are going to keep going on and on—just on and on!" And with a solemn shake of his head Harry replied, "No, Stone won't resign! He's much younger than Pussywillow, so he'll get well soon."

But Stone was absent from Court the entire second week of arguments— October 19–23—and it became increasingly clear that he might not be able to work for some time to come. His illness, therefore, raised a serious and unexpected problem. With the loss of one Justice at the very beginning of the term, it was apparent that the remaining eight would have an even greater workload than originally anticipated. And during that second week of arguments, Mc-Reynolds seemed to sense this. Once he exclaimed rather unexpectedly, "It looks like more than twenty cases will have been argued by the time we adjourn this Friday. With Justice Stone sick, I may have to write at least two opinions this time—maybe even three."

All that week I deliberated whether to call Justice Stone's private secretary, Miss [Gertrude] Jenkins, and ask what the trouble was. Finally I decided against doing so—on the assumption that she might not want to give out such information on the telephone, especially when she would not be in a position to recognize my voice. It was not long, however, before Miss Jenkins

---

2. Stone's law clerk was a 1936 graduate of the Columbia Law School by the name of Harold Leventhal [later a judge of the United States Court of Appeals for the District of Columbia Circuit, 1965–1979]. Eventually I met Harold, and we soon became good friends. After Justice Stone returned to the bench in February 1937, I noted with interest that Harold's duties were very different from mine. He prepared, for instance, lengthy typewritten opinions regarding various points of law—something which Justice McReynolds never asked me to do. Harold also did not answer social invitations sent to his Justice or concern himself with the Washington world of society in the way I found it necessary to do. Justice Stone not only had the assistance of his wife in such matters, but both Justice and Mrs. Stone were fortunate in having a permanent and extremely competent social secretary to help them.

became one of my best friends in Washington, and at least once during the term she called on Harry and me at 2400—but at a time when McReynolds was absent from the apartment. Following Stone's return to the bench in February 1937, I called several times at his home. He always proved to be very friendly and informal, and I held him in the highest esteem. He was also the frankest member of the Court whom I was destined to meet. For instance, at our very first discussion in 1937 he commented in a quiet but firm tone of voice, "McReynolds has set the law of admiralty back a full century!"

But this was not all. It was common knowledge that Justice Van Devanter was seldom assigned many opinions to write because he had always found it extremely difficult to put his thoughts down on paper. Though he was considered a very able Justice in conferences, and one who contributed much to the regular Saturday discussions, Van Devanter had sometimes written only two, three, or four opinions during an entire term of Court. Of recent years he had somewhat increased his literary output, but this hardly altered the fact that the Supreme Court had suddenly been reduced to virtually seven Justices—and this unexpected state of affairs had arisen before a single opinion had been written that term.

I was careful, during the second week of arguments, not to mention anything about Justice Van Devanter's lack of literary prowess to Justice McReynolds. Already the latter was showing signs of temperament and increasing apprehension. He began calling to Harry in a rather sharp tone of voice, and he no longer made much effort to talk to me. He dictated very few letters, and each morning before going to Court he sat alone in his study and read over, or thumbed through, the hundreds of pages in the various briefs in the cases that were to be argued that day. And despite the fact that the Court was not at full strength, the Chief Justice was disposing of arguments at a pace which required McReynolds' utmost concentration—and at the very beginning of the term, too. It was all quite distressing.

During those disconcerting October days, however, it was comforting to know that one steadfast ray of hope remained—the *Literary Digest* poll was still predicting the election of Landon. So McReynolds took heart, and his spirits seemed to perk up whenever he read another issue of the *Digest*. No matter how burdened the Court might be during the 1936 term, things were going to work out all right in the end. The Justice was still reading the *Digest* from cover to cover, and each weekly issue was kept on top of his desk—sometimes open to the very page which contained the latest poll forecasts.

Then came Friday afternoon, October 23. The last case had been argued prior to the Court's first recess for the writing of opinions. Not until after the

Presidential election would the Justices assemble again. During the final stages of the battle between Landon and Roosevelt, the members of the Court would be sitting quietly in their homes or offices and busily studying hundreds of pages of legal briefs submitted to them by lawyers from all parts of the country. But on that particular Friday no Justice as yet knew just which cases he would be called upon to write opinions in. The allotment of all cases was in the sole discretion of the Chief Justice, and Hughes' decision would not be made known until shortly after the Saturday conference to be held on October 24.

It had been a tiring two weeks of arguments, and as soon as McReynolds arrived home on that Friday afternoon, he noisily dropped his cane in the umbrella stand by the front door and called out, "Harry! Are you here?" And as soon as Harry arrived from the kitchen, which was almost instantly, the Justice asked, "Will you help me off with my coat?" And before Harry could say more than "Yes, sir," McReynolds continued, "I hope you and Mary are going to have something good for me to eat tonight."

"Well," drawled Harry in a tantalizing fashion, "seeing that it is the last day of arguments, I fixed you some soft-shelled crabs. I thought you might like your favorite dish for tonight."

"That's good!" McReynolds replied with a sudden show of strength. "Why didn't you tell me that this morning? I would have felt better all day."

"Lots of arguments at Court?" Harry inquired diplomatically.

"Oh, yes, and very long and dull ones, too." And stifling a yawn McReynolds said, "I'm glad our recess is here." He then started walking briskly down the hall, but before he had taken many steps toward his study he noticed me standing by my office door.

"Good afternoon, sir," I said.

"Mr. Knox," McReynolds exclaimed while ignoring my greeting, "come into my study, and better bring your notebook, too. Tomorrow, as you know, the Court will hold a very important Saturday conference. Among other things we will be voting upon all the cases which have been argued during the past two weeks. But I want to be sure right now that you have listed all of these cases in that big red book I gave you some time ago."

"Yes, I have, every one," I replied eagerly.

"Well, bring the book in here and let me look at it," McReynolds said while peering at me intently through his glasses.

I disappeared at once into my office and was back in a few moments carrying the large and impressive-looking volume which was destined to contain so many secrets during the ensuing term of Court. All of the cases which had thus far been argued I had carefully listed by name and number at the top of each of the first twenty-three pages. A separate page was devoted to each case, and there was ample room at the bottom of each page for McReynolds to record the secret vote of the Court regarding the disposition of that particular case. The Justice inspected all of my entries very carefully and then commented, "Yes, this is satisfactory. Now as soon as a case is voted on in conference, I'll mark down the vote of each Justice here in this book. Later on we can always refer back to any particular case and know how each Justice voted in regard to it." And handing the heavy book back to me McReynolds continued, "Put this on my desk before I leave for Court tomorrow. You won't need to wrap it up—I'll just take the book with me in the car. I shall also need one of the two keys you have. In fact, you might as well give me one of those keys right now."

I fetched one of the two small keys that could be used to open the tiny lock in the swinging brass hinge which was so skillfully attached to the covers of the book. After I had handed the volume back again to McReynolds, he rather awkwardly inserted the key in the lock to see if it would work. Satisfied on this score he carefully put the key in one of his coat pockets. But in the next instant he exclaimed, "No, I better not do that. I don't think I'll wear this suit to the conference tomorrow. Here, I'll put the key in my desk, but don't let me forget it!"

"I won't," I replied.

For the second time the Justice handed me the book. "Always keep this locked up and out of sight somewhere in your office," he said. "Don't *ever* leave it on top of your desk! It's not a book for Harry and Mary to be seeing, and no telling who might be in the apartment some day and pick it up."

"Yes, sir."

"Now I shall also need something else before I go to the conference tomorrow. Let me see, we have some petitions for certiorari to vote on, and I have your summaries here. But before you leave today type me out a list of everything we shall consider at the conference. At the top of the first sheet write 'FOR CONFERENCE, SATURDAY, OCTOBER 24, 1936.' Put these words in capital letters, use legal-sized paper, and double space everything. You might also type the names of all cases in capital letters, too. List the petitions for certiorari first, and put the number of each petition to the left of the name of the case. Then leave enough space on the right-hand side of the sheet so I can write down the vote on each petition."

"Will you list the votes of each Justice after the name of every petition?" I inquired.

"No, the petitions aren't important enough for that," McReynolds replied. "I'll just write either 'Grant' or 'No.'" That will be sufficient as most of these petitions are without merit anyway." After a momentary pause the Justice continued, "After you have listed the petitions for certiorari, then list the petitions for rehearing together with any motions that may be pending before the Court. Also leave me enough room on the right-hand side of the paper so that I can mark down the votes on these petitions, too."

"I understand, and I'll type out the list at once."

"And one thing more," McReynolds replied. "Plan to stay here tomorrow evening until the Chief Justice sends over the numbers of the cases in which I shall be writing opinions. His darkey messenger will bring the list over here early in the evening. It will show the opinions assigned to each Justice."

For a moment I wondered whether McReynolds was actually going to invite me to dinner the next evening, but apparently the thought never even crossed his mind. As soon as he had approved the list which I had typed out I said, "Will that be all for today?"

"Yes, you can leave now, but I shall talk with you the first thing tomorrow. I may want to take several briefs with me to conference."

I then bade the Justice good night and left the apartment. Harry and Mary were busily at work in the kitchen, so I did not see them before I closed the front door behind me.

And at that moment I realized how abysmally ignorant I was regarding the problem of helping the Justice prepare for his important conference the next day. So far I had been of almost no help at all, but perhaps after a few Saturday conferences I would become accustomed to the work which had to be done in preparing the Justice for such an ordeal. We had already received from the Court all the briefs in the cases that had so far been argued. We had also been sent copies of all the accumulated petitions for certiorari, jurisdictional statements, motions, etc. that were pending. All of this printed material was arranged in a neat pile on the floor of my office, and I noticed that it was over two feet high. Yet how could McReynolds, or any other Justice for that matter, be held accountable for knowing the contents of every printed page in this vast array of legal material? It was all quite puzzling, and I began to appreciate how much work is involved in being a Justice of the Supreme Court of the United States.

Another thing of interest was that the Chief Justice had sent to McReynolds a list of those petitions for certiorari which Hughes considered to be without merit. This was the so-called black list, which would always be circulated among the Justices before each conference during the term. I was later to learn that about three petitions out of every five would usually be automatically denied and would not be discussed at all in conference unless one or more of the other Justices requested such a discussion. This, however, very rarely happened.

Several conferences had, of course, already been held to dispose of all the petitions for certiorari which had accumulated during the summer months, but the conference scheduled for October 24 was the first one at which the Court would vote on cases that had been argued during the term. I realized that Hughes would insist on keeping the Court abreast of its work, so the conference could be expected to continue in session until all matters that were pending had been disposed of at one sitting. The meeting, therefore, might not end until five o'clock or even later. Upon such adjournment, however, the Chief Justice's most delicate task would then begin. While the other members of the Court were on their way home, Hughes would be holding a quiet conference with his law clerk to decide just which cases to assign to each particular Justice. Once Hughes had decided which cases to give to McReynolds, the news of this decision would be conveyed to McReynolds' apartment by the Chief Justice's messenger.

"Now if I were a Justice," I thought to myself, "I would certainly try to keep the same law clerk year in and not go through all the agony of breaking in a new one each year. There is so much that I do not know, and McReynolds even had to tell me how to answer his calling cards! No wonder he acts a little cross now and then. I might, too, under the same circumstances."

Saturday dawned bright and clear. That morning I entered the apartment as McReynolds was again leisurely eating his breakfast. He had arisen earlier than usual, and he and Harry were busily talking when I passed by the dining room on the way to my office. We exchanged the usual greetings, and then I sat down at my desk to sort through the morning mail. "I shall want an extra suit," I heard McReynolds say, "but no second pair of shoes. They would make the suitcase too heavy."

"I won't put in the suit until the last minute," Harry replied. "Then it won't lose its press so much."

"That's odd," I said to myself. "What is McReynolds talking about a suitcase for when he's going to be right here working on opinions?" But I soon dismissed this thought from my mind as I began to read through the mail. Three bills to pay, two invitations to answer, several advertisements, including one about a winter cruise, and finally one personal letter.

"I mustn't forget to remind him to take the red book to Court, and he also left the key in his desk. And here are all the briefs in a pile in case he wants to read any of them this morning."

I then walked into the Justice's study, left the personal letter on his desk, and returned to my office to wait for McReynolds to finish his breakfast. He and Harry were still talking. "I say, Harry," the Justice exclaimed, "isn't this apartment near the edge of the taxi zone?"

"Yes, I think it is," replied Harry after a moment's reflection. "If you walk a block down Sixteenth Street, you are in another zone and can save yourself some money when going downtown."

"That's what I thought," McReynolds said in a serious but friendly tone of voice. "Of course with a suitcase along I won't do it, but next time when I have no luggage I'll walk down to the other zone. There is no use paying an additional fare when we are so close to the line."

"I 'spect not," said Harry. "If they set the edge of the zone so near 2400, there's no reason why a person can't walk to the cheaper zone before finding himself a cab."

"How odd!" I thought. "It would only save him ten or twenty cents, but maybe McReynolds wants the extra walk anyway before the weather turns cold. And what is all this talk about a suitcase? He certainly won't be going anywhere now."

"I'll be leaving for market soon," Harry next said. "I expected to get some lamb today. Will that be all right?"

"Yes, lamb is good," the Justice replied. "Only I would like green mint jelly with it. Don't forget to buy some of that. Better plan on dinner being a little late. I should be here not later than 6:00, but I'm not sure. At least by 6:30 I hope I'll be ready to eat."

"Dinner at 6:30 then," Harry concluded. "And I'll have lamb and mint jelly."

"And potatoes and gravy, of course," McReynolds suggested. "Also two vegetables, but no more cauliflower. Try something else for a change." And with that statement, and Harry's assent, the Justice arose from the table and walked leisurely across the hall and into his study. Some minutes passed, however, before he rang for me—and during this interval I could hear Harry rattling the dishes and cleaning off the small table in one corner of the dining room where McReynolds always sat when dining alone.

As soon as I had entered the Justice's study, in response to his summons, he exclaimed in a friendly tone of voice, "I'll need a good pencil to take to Court with me. I want one with a soft lead, too."

"I have several no. 2 pencils in my desk," I replied. "I'll get one of those for you."

As soon as such a pencil had been brought to the Justice, he examined it carefully and then exclaimed, "Thank you! I don't like pencils that make a weak-looking mark. They are just like some people who are never quite able to accomplish what they set out to do." And then after a pause McReynolds continued, "Now let's see what more I need before going to the conference. Better bring me the red book now, so I won't forget it. And I've already put the key in my pocket. Your typed summaries are here, and I've marked a few I shall take with me. And, oh, yes, bring in the briefs in the *Wood* case. I think I'll glance through them once more."[3]

As soon as I had handed him the red book and the briefs McReynolds said, "That will be all. I guess I won't dictate any letters this morning. And I'm not just sure when I shall be returning from this conference, but plan to stay here until I know just which opinions I have been assigned to write."

"There is one thing more," I ventured. "Two invitations arrived this morning, and here they are."

I handed the invitations across the desk to the Justice. After reading them carefully he exclaimed, "Decline both of them." And referring to one in par-ticular he said, "This hostess gives nice dinners, but I won't have time to go anywhere for the next few weeks. So send the usual regrets. She should understand."

Before I left his study McReynolds concluded by saying, "Will you send Harry in? I forgot to ask him something."

Eventually all preparations were made for McReynolds to leave for his first Saturday conference which would be devoted primarily to voting upon the cases already argued before the Court. Since he expected to drive down to Court alone, Harry showed genuine concern in getting him off to a good start. It was almost as if a fond mother were preparing her firstborn for his opening day of school. And at the last minute McReynolds was forced to leave his walk-ing stick behind as he wished to carry the red book under his arm, [even re-fusing to] allow Harry to trudge on ahead and take the book out to the car, even though the volume was quite heavy.

3. *United States v. Wood*, 299 U.S. 123 (1936). This case concerned the constitutionality of an Act of Congress prescribing qualifications for service as jurors in the District of Columbia, as applied to criminal prosecutions. The opinion was ultimately written by Chief Justice Hughes. This was a 5-3 decision with Stone taking no part in the consideration or decision of the case. McReynolds, Sutherland, and Butler dissented, and strangely enough Van Devanter cast his vote with Hughes, Roberts, Brandeis, and Cardozo to constitute the majority of five.

"I worry about you driving alone," Harry said.

"Well, don't," McReynolds replied. "Even though it's Saturday, I can certainly drive down to Court unless some young fool gets in front of me."

"I asked the garage to check the tires and to fill the tank with gas," Harry said as a sort of afterthought.

"I'm ready then!" McReynolds exclaimed. And armed with the red book, a few of my typewritten notes, a key, a pencil, and a new supply of ink in his fountain pen, James Clark McReynolds, at the age of seventy-four, set out alone for the Supreme Court of the United States to cast his vote in more than twenty cases which had recently been argued and were now awaiting decision. It was an historic moment, at least for me.

"I wonder how he's going to vote in all those cases," I said after Harry had closed the door behind him.

"Well, I sure don't know, but just you wait until Pussywillow starts writing some opinions!" Harry retorted. "Then things will get plenty serious around here!"

"Oh, you're just trying to scare me," I replied. But on second thought I wasn't so sure.

I ate a hasty lunch that Saturday, but the Justice did not call from Court either during my absence from the apartment or after I had returned. Undoubtedly he had more important matters to attend to that day. The time passed very slowly.

About five-thirty that afternoon McReynolds finally returned to the apartment. Harry had long been back, and he immediately appeared from the kitchen to help the Justice off with his coat. McReynolds then walked straight into my office and handed me the red book. "Put this out of sight somewhere," he said in a relieved tone of voice. "We've finished voting on all the cases. And don't leave tonight until I hear from the Chief Justice." He then strolled into his study without making any further comment.

Before slipping the volume into a drawer of my desk, I carefully opened its pages and idly studied how the various Justices had voted. "Very little dissenting today," I noticed with some surprise. "Either these first cases of the term are not too important, or else Hughes has succeeded in establishing harmony among the brethren. Or maybe everybody just felt in a good mood today."

It was not long before Harry strolled down the hall from the kitchen and announced at the door of the Justice's study, "Dinner is ready. I served it a little sooner because you got here before six."

"I'll be there in a moment," McReynolds called out as he noisily crinkled together the pages of the evening paper which I had placed in his study earlier that afternoon.

I then heard the Justice stroll once more across the hall and sit down at his small table in the dining room. And for some forty minutes he ate at a leisurely pace while I remained in my office studying the floor. I just did not feel in the mood to thumb through any more volumes of the *U.S. Reports.*

"This lamb is very good," I could hear McReynolds comment to Harry. "And so is the mint jelly. I'm glad you got enough of it this time."

"Now, if he were Van Devanter," I thought, "I just bet he would at least toss me a potato to eat while we are waiting to hear from Hughes." And the smell of the dinner floated tantalizingly across the hall and into my room. "And if he were Cardozo—well, I know he would even invite me to eat with him." This conclusion I reached while feeling quite sorry for myself. Perhaps I was far too sensitive, but the fact that McReynolds let me sit idly by without even suggesting that I might be hungry, too, was something which was hard to accept. "Maybe he doesn't want to sit at the same table with his secretary," I mused. "Yet, I ate with him on the West Point trip. But that, of course, was always in a restaurant. Since he asked me to stay late tonight, he could at least send Harry in here with a piece of meat." But no lamb was forthcoming, or anything else for that matter.

After finishing his repast, the Justice walked back into his study without further ado. Some fifteen minutes later, however, the doorbell suddenly rang. I at once stood up and looked down the hall. In a moment Harry had emerged from the kitchen, and upon opening the door I heard him say almost in a whisper, "Hello there!" I then noticed that he was conversing in low and earnest tones with a colored man whom I assumed to be the Chief Justice's messenger.[4] They talked together for perhaps forty-five seconds, at the end of which time Harry was handed an envelope. He did not, however, invite the caller into the apartment at any time, and once the envelope was delivered the door was quietly closed and the messenger left.

Harry walked down the hall and made no comment as he stopped for a brief moment near where I was standing. He merely held up the envelope as if to say, "This is it!" And all I noticed was that the envelope was brown in color, that McReynolds' name and address were printed on the face of it, that it bore no postage stamp, and that the Chief Justice had written "Hughes" in ink near the top left-hand corner and underneath a few lines which had been

---

4. This was George Robinson, 1025 Park Road, N.W., Washington, D.C., messenger for the Chief Justice. He lived next door to Justice Stone's messenger, E. Joice, 1027 Park Road, N.W.

printed in very small type. After a momentary pause, Harry then walked in where McReynolds was, and I quietly turned around and sat down once again.

Some three or four minutes later the buzzer on my desk emitted its familiar low hissing sound. I promptly picked up my notebook and pencil and walked at once into McReynolds' study. "Oh, Mr. Knox," he exclaimed, after first pausing to clear his throat, "the Chief Justice has just sent me this." And reaching across the desk he then handed me a paper which I glanced at with the greatest of interest. It was four and one-half inches wide and eight inches long. At the top was printed "October Term, A.D. 1936." Below that the names of all members of the Court had been printed on the left side of the paper— with the names of the Junior Justices appearing first. Following the name of each Justice certain numbers had been typed. The whole effect, therefore, was as follows:

October Term, A.D. 1936

October 24, 1936.

Justice Cardozo,	. . . . 11, 23, 29
Justice Roberts,	. . . . 18, 21, 51
Justice Stone,	. . . .
Justice Butler,	. . . . 19, 27
Justice Sutherland,	. . . . 2, 3
Justice Brandeis,	. . . . 17, 22
Justice McReynolds,	. . . . 9, 31
Justice Van Devanter,	 10
Chief Justice,	. . . . 4 and 5, 6, 34, 48, 271
Per Cur.	. . . . 12, 13, 30 46, 54

I noticed at a glance that no opinions had been assigned to Justice Stone on account of his illness.

"What cases are numbers 9 and 31?" McReynolds asked.

"I don't remember," I replied. "I'll have to look through the briefs in my room."

"Well, do that at once," the Justice said.

I went back to my room, stooped down to the pile of documents on the floor of my office, and scattered them about hurriedly in order to find cases numbered 9 and 31. Soon they were located and I took them back into McReynolds' study.

"This is case number 9," I said as I handed him several briefs.

"Hmm," McReynolds replied slowly as he glanced at the documents.

"This is the *Carlin Construction Company* case regarding an explosion on a ferry boat.[5] Yes, I recall that case. Now where's the other one?"

"Here it is," I replied as I gave him the briefs in case number 31.

"Oh, this was the insurance case about a fire in Puerto Rico," McReynolds exclaimed.[6] "It looks like I've been assigned one maritime case and one insurance case in which to write opinions."

And at the moment I was thinking, "I wonder who was given the *Neidecker* cases that Mr. Coudert argued. They were number 6." And glancing hurriedly at the list I noticed that the Chief Justice had taken that number for himself. This was somewhat of a disappointment to me, but I made no comment about it to McReynolds. Then for the first time I noticed that Hughes had assumed the burden of writing five opinions instead of just two or maybe three. "Evidently he is going to do Stone's work as well as his own," I thought. "Five cases will be quite an assignment in addition to his administrative duties."

"I think I'll take case number 9 first," McReynolds then announced following a few moments of reflection. "That is the Carlin Construction Company matter."

"Yes, sir," I replied in a mechanical sort of way for by then I was studying the five cases listed under the heading "Per Cur." for per curiam. I remembered that [the Chief Justice nearly always wrote the opinions in] such cases . If this were so, then Hughes had decided to write not just five opinions but ten! And even though some of them would be relatively short, this was still more than three times the number of cases that Hughes had assigned to any other member of the Court. For the first time I began to appreciate the stature and ability of Charles Evans Hughes.

"Mr. Knox," McReynolds said once more—as if to awaken me from my reverie. "I think I'll take number 9 first!"

"Yes, sir!" I replied upon glancing up from the list which I held in my hand. "And do you wish to start working on that case this evening?"

At this question McReynolds quietly leaned back in his chair, and while eyeing me with a cat-and-mouse expression he casually announced, "No, not this evening. I am leaving for New York tomorrow morning, and I shall be away until Tuesday afternoon. While I'm gone, however, I wish you would

5. *P. J. Carlin Construction Co. et al. v. Heaney et al.,* 299 U.S. 41 (1936). This case had been argued on October 13, 1936.

6. *Jose Rivera Soler & Co. v. United Firemen's Insurance Company of Philadelphia,* 299 U.S. 45 (1936). This case had been argued on October 20, 1936.

write the opinion in case number 9 and have it ready for me when I return to town. I have an appointment in New York on Monday, but I expect to be back here not later than five o'clock on Tuesday."

For some unaccountable reason I rose admirably to the occasion. I was not in the least daunted by the magnitude of the Justice's remarks, and so I casually replied, "I'll have the opinion ready when you get back." In fact, the assignment was one which greatly appealed to me, and I regarded it as a rare opportunity which should be accepted with the greatest of pleasure. I had always been very much interested in creative writing anyway, and the prospect of composing an opinion—all by myself—for the Supreme Court of the United States seemed like a heaven-sent opportunity. And I thought to myself, "What a whale of an assignment when I am only four months out of law school! Gosh, I hope he lets me write all of his opinions during this term of court. But what a surprise! Harry never told me anything like this would happen!"

McReynolds then glanced at me very intently as if annoyed that I had not yet exhibited any signs of a fainting spell. "Well, of course," he hedged, "I want you at least to write the facts of the case even if you do not have time to write the law part."

"Oh, I'll have it all ready when you return," I calmly announced, "but just how did the Court vote in this case?"

"Well, go get the red book and see!" McReynolds replied with a trace of annoyance in his voice. "That's what the book is for."

I at once walked into my office for the book, and upon returning to his study I handed the volume to the Justice. It was open to the page which listed the votes in case number 9.

"We voted to affirm," McReynolds announced after a momentary examination of [his notes]. "The judgment of the Court of Appeals of New York will be affirmed, and the award of workmen's compensation will be sustained."

For a few moments there was an unexpected silence in the room. McReynolds appeared more and more surprised that I had received his request so casually and almost as a matter of course.

Then looking up at the Justice once again I said, "I hope you have a nice trip to New York." But my voice was so enthusiastic that this statement almost sounded like, "I'm glad you're going to New York, and I hope you stay away a long time."

"Thank you," McReynolds replied while shifting himself in his chair. There was a puzzled expression on his face, and now he began to tap the fingers of his right hand on the desk. [After a moment of distraction, he recollected his thoughts and] said, "I appreciate your staying late this evening, but you might as well leave now. And I'll be here on Tuesday not later than five o'clock. I've already told Harry about my plans. And if you finish the opinion before I get back, just leave it here on top of the desk so that I can read it."

"I'll do that," I replied. I then bade him a cordial good evening as I left his study with the briefs of the *Carlin* case safely tucked under my arm. And despite the fact that I had not yet eaten any dinner, I was like a fire horse waiting to start running to the nearest conflagration. I was immensely pleased about being asked to write an opinion for the highest court in the land, and I had already decided to do my very best at such a task. "I'll take one of these briefs with me to dinner," I thought to myself. "In fact, I might as well start writing the opinion tonight!" So I canceled plans to go to the neighborhood movie at Eighteenth and Columbia Road that evening, and I also decided to spend all the next day—a Sunday—working on the opinion instead of seeing some more of the interesting sights of Washington.

And that is exactly what I did. I worked ten hours that Sunday—October 25, 1936—and by the end of the day I had composed on the typewriter in my own room at 2400 three complete drafts of the entire opinion in the *Carlin* case. And I was quite pleased with the way the third attempt read. It was brief, to the point, and the sentences all flowed evenly. And holding the finished product out before me I thought, "This may not sound like Justice Holmes in the Rosika Schwimmer case, but I'll sleep on it tonight and work it over again tomorrow."[7]

I laid down the third draft and walked over to the nearest drugstore and asked for a malted milk and a sandwich. My literary endeavors had somehow spoiled my appetite, so I did not go to the Chinese restaurant to eat my customary dinner. I sat in that drugstore, looked at the clerks and the other customers, and realized that they were all strangers to me. And yet, oddly enough, I did not experience my usual feeling of loneliness that evening. "It is because McReynolds has given me some real responsibility at last," I said to myself. "As long as he treated me as an inferior I could not help but withdraw and feel at a loss for words. But now that he has raised me to his own level and even asked me to write an opinion, the situation is different. I guess he is going to be all right after all—despite what some people say. In fact, he may end up as nice as Cardozo."

---

7. [Editors' note: The reference is to Holmes' dissent in *United States v. Schwimmer*, 279 U.S. 644, 653 (1929).]

The next morning, a Monday, it seemed a bit odd to enter the Justice's apartment and know for the first time that he would not be there. But I made it a point to arrive on time—for fear he might have changed his mind and not gone to New York after all. In fact, I was secretly hoping that he was still in Washington so that I could walk into his study and proudly hand him the finished opinion as soon as I had reported for work.

But when I closed the door behind me I noticed with some disappointment that the Justice's hat and walking stick were not in their usual places in the hall. "I guess he went to New York after all," I thought. I then poked my head into the kitchen door and said good morning to both Harry and Mary. In fact, I wondered why they didn't take the entire day off and go downtown or get out in the open air. On second thought, however, I concluded that McReynolds might even telephone from New York to check on whether the three of us were on duty that day.

No invitations had arrived in the morning mail, but even if there had been any, I would have held them until I could ask McReynolds whether they should be declined as usual. So I enthusiastically sat down at the typewriter, took off my coat now that the Justice was not in the apartment, and began typing out the fourth draft of my opinion. Soon I was busily at work, referring back from time to time to certain statements in the briefs and concentrating so intensely that I ignored the customary sound of Harry's and Mary's footsteps as they walked from one room to another. It was with some surprise, therefore, that I suddenly became aware that Harry was standing quietly behind me. "Oh, I didn't hear you come in," I said. "I thought you were working in the dining room." And noticing that Harry was gazing at me very intently I exclaimed, "What can I do for you this fine morning? I hope you are not here to ask me about the weather!"

"Who said anything about the weather?" Harry declared. "I can look out the window and see it's not going to rain. Even Pussywillow could do that if he wanted to." Then after a momentary pause Harry continued, "I bet I know what *you* are doing!"

Looking up and noticing that he had a broad grin on his face I replied, "Well, I just bet you don't! But if you are so smart today, tell me what I am doing."

"Ha, ha!" Harry laughed. "Why, you're writing one of Pussywillow's opinions for him!"

"Harry Parker!" I said in genuine surprise. "But how did you know? What did you do—sneak in here and look over my shoulder while I was typing?"

"I didn't need to look over your shoulder. I could tell by the way you was acting—so serious like, and sittin' in here alone even when Pussywillow is in New York."

"You win," I conceded, "I might have suspected it. You certainly know just about everything that goes on around here!"

"Well, talking about knowing something," Harry drawled, "I suppose *you* know that Pussywillow just gave you something to write so as to keep you busy while he is out of town. He wanted to make up for all the time you didn't have much to do when he was in Court recently."

Looking intently at Harry I asked in surprise, "Just what are you saying?"

Without answering my question Harry continued, "He's done the same with other secretaries, too, but no matter how hard you work he'll just throw your opinion away. It won't do you no good at all to write it."

"But I spent all day yesterday working on it!" I protested. "I stayed in my room on a Sunday when I could have been out seeing the sights. Do you mean to say he won't use it *at all,* and that it was just some sort of trick to keep me busy over the weekend? Not that!"

"That's all it was," Harry replied solemnly while looking at me with a sympathetic expression. "Just how much of the opinion have you got finished?"

"Why, all of it! In fact I'm now on my fourth revision!"

"Fourth revision!" Harry exclaimed in surprise. "You sure rose to the bait! Just like a fish in the sea you rose to the bait! Or like one of those ducks that flies right in front of Pussywillow's gun when we go out hunting!" Then after a brief pause Harry said, "You might as well take it easy today and just show him what you have already written when he comes back tomorrow."

"But maybe you're wrong," I exclaimed stubbornly. "Perhaps I should re-write it once more because I did want it to be the very best opinion that I could get together. Now that I have gone this far, I suppose I might as well revise it again."

"Well, do as you like," Harry replied, "but don't say I didn't warn you the first thing on Monday morning. It just don't mean a thing—all this work. Pussywillow did it to make you stay in on Sunday while he was having a nice train ride to New York."

But I doggedly insisted on refusing to face the inevitable. All that day, therefore, I continued to labor on the fourth draft of my opinion—even though my enthusiasm had by now been considerably dampened by Harry's unexpected remarks. And by the close of work on Monday, I had managed to complete what I regarded as a very tolerably written opinion in the *Carlin* case. After reading it over once more to myself, I thought, "This sounds good!

And he probably will use part of it anyway for his own opinion. I've checked all the facts and the legal sources, and the case is summarized as well as I could do it. So what I have written should have some real value after all, and it will prove that I can write a Supreme Court opinion even though I am just out of law school!"

The three of us remained in the apartment all that day, but the Justice did not telephone from New York to check on our activities. Harry and Mary ate their lunch in the kitchen, but I went out as usual for mine. By five o'clock, however, I had finished all the writing and typing that I intended to do. The complete opinion was now ready for McReynolds' inspection, and I had also made a carbon copy of it for myself. Both copies I then slipped into the drawer of my desk—intending to read them over the first thing Tuesday morning for any possible changes.

When I bade Harry and Mary goodbye that evening, Harry replied by saying, "You sure typed plenty today. You was like a wound up top that had to run down."

"Who's run down?" Mary inquired as she shut off the kitchen faucet while washing the dishes. "Is Mr. Knox run down?"

"Not that kind of 'run down,'" Harry explained. "Mr. Knox has been taking Pussywillow's place today in writing opinions. His enthusiasm is just run down, that's all, and by tomorrow it sure will be dead."

"Oh, maybe not!" I said to Harry and then left.

The next morning—a Tuesday—I casually entered the apartment and unthinkingly slammed the front door behind me. Then to my enormous surprise I noticed the Justice's hat and walking stick reposing in their usual place. I almost froze to the spot where I was standing. Not a sound was to be heard anywhere in the apartment, and a hasty glance down the hall disclosed nothing. I looked hurriedly at my watch. "Twelve minutes late! Yet he *can't* be here! He evidently isn't eating breakfast, but maybe he ate on the train before coming from the station."

I then walked silently and slowly toward my room. No one was in the dining room, and if Harry and Mary were working in the kitchen they were certainly making no sound. Once in my office, however, I could stand the suspense no longer so I walked quietly to the door of the Justice's study and looked in. There he was—sitting at his desk as big as life and perusing a copy of the *New York Times*. The mere sight of him made me almost speechless for some unaccountable reason.

"Good morning, Mr. Knox," McReynolds said casually as he glanced up from the paper. "I came in on the night train. A little sooner than I expected, but there was no sense in wasting most of today just looking out of a train window."

"Oh, good morning," I replied after regaining my composure. "I saw your hat and walking stick in the hall and thought maybe you were here. Is there anything that I can do for you?"

"You might bring in the briefs in that case I was supposed to write an opinion in. What was the name of it again?"

"The Carlin Construction Company matter," I replied. "The one about the explosion on the ferry boat."

"Yes, I remember now," McReynolds replied. "That was the case I was going to work on first."

"I wrote the opinion," I ventured a bit timidly.

"Oh, you did?" the Justice answered in an inquiring tone of voice. "All of it, too?"

"Yes, all of it."

"You can bring it in along with the briefs."

This I proceeded to do at once, and I then walked back to my own office. For the next hour all was silence from McReynolds' study, and then suddenly the buzzer on my desk rang. I picked up my notebook, pencil, and the carbon copy of my opinion and walked hurriedly in where the Justice was sitting. I noticed at a glance that the original copy of the opinion was resting on top of his desk—to the right of the briefs. Whether or not he had read it I could not determine, but I presumed that he had. I also noticed that McReynolds had evidently been studying a number of the briefs for they had paper markers inserted in their pages.

"Sit down and open up your notebook," the Justice directed. Then reaching for the Transcript of Record he exclaimed, "We will now start writing the opinion as it should be written!" And that was the closest reference he ever made to the fourth draft of my own masterpiece, except that in a few minutes he quietly reached across the desk and silently, almost gently let my opinion glide downward into his wastebasket. When this happened I hurriedly glanced back at my notebook and clutched my pencil a little more tightly. "All of Sunday wasted!" I thought. "I might just as well have spent it standing on my head in the Capitol Plaza! I guess Harry was right after all. In fact, he's *always* right." And then I experienced a terrible sinking feeling in the pit of my stomach— as if something had just died that I had once very much believed in.

8

MCREYNOLDS BEGAN dictating very slowly as he continued to examine the Transcript of Record in the *Carlin Construction Company* case.[1]

"Now be sure to get every word, Mr. Knox, every word!" he exclaimed.

"Yes, sir!" I replied.

"All right then. Here we start. The respondent Heaney instituted a proceeding before the New York State Industrial Board against his employer P. J. Carlin Construction Company and its insurance carrier, The Travelers Insurance Company, wherein he sought an award . . ." At this point McReynolds stopped and hesitated as to what to say next. "Oh, yes, now let's continue. Wherein he sought an award for injuries received in the course of his employment. That's the end of the sentence—after the word 'employment.' And stay in the same paragraph and continue. The Board granted an award, and this was approved by the Appellate Division and by the Court of Appeals. The matter is here on writ of certiorari. Make that the end of the paragraph—the first paragraph."

"Now we are starting a new paragraph. In September 1932, the Construction Company, whose principal place of business is in New York—make that New York City—was engaged in constructing buildings on Rikers Island, which lies in [the] East River about a mile or two from the Manhattan Shore."

There was another pause at this point. McReynolds began drumming the fingers of his hand on the corner of the desk, then suddenly commenced

---

1. This description is based upon extensive stenographic notes which I made at the time and which are still preserved.

dictating again. "Respondent Heaney and other workers engaged about this construction were transported daily from New York City on the S.S. *Observation*, owned by Captain Forsythe." After another pause the Justice said, "Better change that to: ' . . . were transported to New York City and back on the steamer *Observation*, owned by Captain Forsythe.' "

At this point I asked the Justice how to spell "Forsythe," as I thought he said "Forsyte." He told me and then said, "You can always check on the spelling of any names later on from the Transcript itself—after I finish dictating." After pausing for a few seconds, McReynolds continued. "For the round trip each of them paid a fee of 10 cents. The steamer was operated under an agreement with the Construction Company, which among other things provided. . . ." After another pause, McReynolds said, "Put a colon after the word 'provided.' In fact, you better read me that sentence again."

"The steamer was operated under an agreement with the Construction Company, which among . . ."

"Stop there," McReynolds exclaimed, "I want to insert something. Make it read: ' . . . under an agreement with the Construction Company, embodied in a letter from the Company, which among other things provided. . . .' Yes, that's the way I want it to sound, and be sure to put a colon after the word 'provided.' And now at this point copy the words on pages 46 and 47 of the Transcript of Record beginning with the sentence, 'You are hereby licensed. . . .' This is the part providing that the owner was to operate the steamship for five days in each week upon a schedule to be furnished by the Construction Company and that there was—and now put in another quote—'You are to be compensated therefore by collecting fares from the men at the rate of 10 cents a round trip' end of quote. Also that the owner was licensed—colon—put in a quote again and the figure (1)—reading '(1) to operate a ferry service for the transportation of the men engaged upon the construction of the Rikers Island Penitentiary Buildings'—end of quote.

"I am still on pages 46 and 47. And the third point should read: quote '(3) and the understanding that your boat is warranted to be in first-class condition'—end of quote—etc., etc."

"Now, Mr. Knox, did you get all that? Remember this first draft must be typed correctly!"

"Yes, I have it all here in my notes."

"All right. So far so good. We are now starting a new paragraph. Are you ready?"

"Yes."

"September 9, 1932, respondent boarded the steamer with Heaney on board the steamer. No, change that to 'and with Heaney on board, the steamer started for Rikers Island.'"

There was then a short pause, after which McReynolds said, "Better read the beginning of the second paragraph back to me."

"Yes, sir," I replied, [and did so].

"Now we better begin another paragraph. Are you ready?"

"Yes."

"All right then. Here petitioners rely for reversal of the action of the court below upon the theory that the rights and obligations of the parties arose out of the maritime law, and that the State Compensation Act does not apply under the—no—change the end of that sentence to 'has no application.' They rely upon *Knickerbockers etc.*, 253 U.S. 149; *Spencer, etc.* 285 U.S. 502; and generally upon that line of cases here which have laid down the general doctrine that the admiralty rules control in respect to torts upon navigable waters."

"Now begin another paragraph. The Court of Appeals pointed out that— no—begin typing the quote reading, 'No recovery is sought . . .' on page 56 of the Record. 'No recovery is sought against the employer in this case . . .' down to the words ' . . . gives a right to recovery.' Also copy 'An award under the Workmen's Compensation Law' and continue copying the rest of the paragraph on page 56. After you have finished typing out those quotations then say: See, also, *Industrial Commission v. Nordenholt Corporation*, 259 U.S. 263 at 271. After you write this sentence, then type in the state cases at this point."

McReynolds sighed, straightened up in his chair, thumbed through the briefs some more, and then said, "Now begin another paragraph. This Court has often pointed out that rights and liabilities arising out of the maritime law cannot be so modified—no—change that to 'changed' by a state statute as to bring about interference with—no—change that to 'as materially to interfere with'—the settled maritime law as would be destructive of the uniformity and consistency with the essential uniform operation of that law.[2] Then copy the *Nordenholt* case citation—259 U.S. 263. But we think that doctrine has no application here where the only attempt is to enforce liability against the employer and the insurance carrier. The effort was to enforce a contract entered into by an employer and an employee non-maritime in character where all the parties and the scene of the accident were within the limits of the State of New

2. This statement, of course, does not make sense, but it was altered by McReynolds when he saw my first typed draft of the opinion.

York. End of sentence. Then begin a new sentence in the same paragraph. The contract had no direct relation to navigation, and to enforce it against the parties now before us would not materially interfere with the uniform operation of the maritime rule."

At this point McReynolds paused for several more minutes. During this pause I hurriedly corrected a number of shorthand symbols—such as "doctrine", "has", "application", etc. "Now, Mr. Knox, read that back where I start talking about the effort to enforce the contract."

So I began, "The effort was to enforce a contract entered into by an employer . . ."

"That's the place I want to change," McReynolds suddenly exclaimed. "I want it to read 'The effort was to enforce a contract between an employer and employee non-maritime in character' . . . etc. The rest of the sentence can remain the same."

"Now where did I end at the last sentence?"

"You said, 'The contract had no direct relation to navigation, and to enforce it against the parties now before us would not materially interfere with the uniform operation of the maritime rule.'"

"All right," the Justice replied. "Your next sentence then is, 'No claim has been made against the ship or her owner.' Now that's the end of the paragraph."

After another pause McReynolds continued. "We are now starting a new paragraph. The principle approved in *Spencer v. Hicks*, 285 U.S. 502, is not acceptable. There the owner of a vessel was rendered liable for injuries received from a tort on navigable waters—strike out 'from a tort' and just say 'on navigable waters because of improper navigation.' Here the effort is to enforce a non-maritime contract of employment which has no immediate relation to navigation."

"Now I'm ready for the last paragraph!" the Justice next said. "It should read, 'We think the court below reached the correct conclusion, and its judgment is affirmed.'"

McReynolds now leaned back in his chair. Approximately twenty-five minutes had elapsed. "Well, Mr. Knox," he said, "that's the end of the opinion. You can type it out now, and once the first draft is ready I'll start revising it. And be sure and get the correct heading on the case. Also remember that I shall read this opinion in Court on November 9—so put that date just before my name. After my name begin typing the opinion itself."

"I'll type it right away," I said. I walked back to my office and began to type the opinion just as it had been dictated by the Justice. Double spaced on legal-sized paper, [the opinion] reached five pages in length. I made no carbon copy as I assumed that such copies were strictly forbidden in view of the confidential nature of Supreme Court opinions. I had no difficulty deciphering my shorthand notes as McReynolds had talked very slowly at all times. However, I very carefully proofread the opinion for possible errors, and nearly an hour elapsed before I was ready to submit the first typed draft to the Justice.

As soon as I took the initial draft into McReynolds' office, he began at once to make his penciled corrections. As soon as he had finished correcting the entire opinion, which took him about a half-hour, he rang for me to retype the whole opinion once more.

I spent about forty-five minutes typing the second draft of the opinion. When I had submitted this draft to the Justice, he labeled it "2" and began to correct it at once also. The second typewritten draft proved satisfactory to McReynolds, and as far as he was concerned the writing of the opinion had now been completed. He asked me to take it down at once to Mr. Bright's printing shop and have the opinion set up in type. At this point the Justice had spent a total of about two and one-half hours working on the opinion—not counting the hour he had spent studying the briefs of the case before he had begun his dictation.

When I reached Mr. Bright's office, he inspected my typing very carefully and approved it. "Nice work for your first case," he said. "I'll get right to work having it set up in type."

Mr. Bright telephoned as soon as his own draft was ready, and I went downtown once more to the Pearson Printing Company. To the best of my recollection, Mr. Bright only gave me two or three copies of the first printed draft as I expected further changes would be made in it by the Justice.

[That same afternoon I took the printed draft, marked with a number of very minor corrections,] back to Mr. Bright's office. I told him there would be no more changes, so he printed up about a dozen copies of a final draft for me—after having made the corrections indicated. Justice McReynolds approved the wording of this final draft, so I circulated copies of it among the other seven Justices—Justice Stone being ill and taking no part in the case. These circulating copies were not sent through the mail but were picked up at 2400 by the various messengers of the other Justices. Each copy was folded, and on the back I had, for instance, written: "For Roberts, J., From McReynolds, J."

Eventually all circulating copies were returned to me by the other seven members of the Court. No Justice objected to the wording of McReynolds' first opinion of the 1936 term of Court so work on it was completed as far as he was concerned. He had spent far less time in writing this opinion than I had in completing my four drafts. At that time he had been on the bench for over twenty years, and he had much experience in dictating opinions. On the other hand, I had never attempted to write a Supreme Court opinion before. Our basic approach was also different. McReynolds, for instance, had made use of quotations from the various briefs in the case. This was something I had not done. I also did not approve of some of the grammatical structure of his opinion. In short, I felt that my opinion read more smoothly than his. On the other hand, his summation of the case was at least as good or better than mine.

McReynolds' final effort did not measure up to my expectation of what a Supreme Court Justice should be able to write. I had not expected him to be another Justice Holmes but, on the other hand, I had looked forward to a more scholarly approach on his part. I also felt that scores of members of the 1936 class at the Harvard Law School could have produced a better opinion than the one McReynolds wrote. When the opinion was ultimately published in the bound volumes of the Supreme Court reports, it appeared in volume 299 at pages 41–45.

[When McReynolds] went to work on the second case he had been assigned, [he followed] exactly the same procedure. I shall not impose upon the reader's time or patience with a detailed analysis of the composition of this second opinion. Suffice to say that the title of it is *Jose Rivera Soler & Co. v. United Firemen's Insurance Company of Philadelphia*.[3] It took McReynolds about two hours longer to produce this opinion than it did to compose the first one.

During the time that McReynolds was busily working on his two opinions, Justice Sutherland was also writing two. Yet the Chief Justice, who was the same age as the other two men, had assigned himself five cases plus five more "per curiams"—or a total of ten opinions to write. McReynolds never mentioned the fact that Hughes had assigned himself so much more work. Apparently if the Chief Justice wanted to take on those added duties, it was up to him. But at the time I marveled at the country's good fortune in having a Chief Justice like Hughes.

There was also something else that I could not fail to take note of. While McReynolds and I worked in our ivory tower on his two opinions, the Presidential campaign was drawing to a whirlwind close. Alf Landon spoke at

3. 299 U.S. 45 (1936).

Madison Square Garden on Thursday evening, October 29. The Republican candidate then returned to Topeka, Kansas—making speeches all along the way. The biggest meeting was held in St. Louis. President Roosevelt, on the other hand, was in eastern Pennsylvania at the time. A great crowd heard him in Philadelphia, and his last major address was in New York at Madison Square Garden on the evening of Saturday, October 31. On Monday evening, November 2, both candidates made brief and last-minute appeals for their respective parties. And on that day I noticed for the very last time a copy of the *Literary Digest* on McReynolds' desk. That magazine was still predicting Landon's election.

Of course, permanent residents of the District of Columbia could not vote. This excluded Harry, Mary, and even the Justice from casting their ballots. Had they been able to go to the polls, however, I naturally assumed that Harry and Mary would have preferred the Democratic ticket and that McReynolds would have cast his lot with the Republicans—even though he was a lifelong Democrat himself. I had already voted a split ticket by absentee ballot. I felt that Roosevelt would win but that the contest would be a close one. And just before the election I wrote to my parents, "I think Roosevelt is going to win by a small but decided margin. . . . He is cheered tremendously when he is thrown on the screen here in Washington because so many people are here who have federal jobs. Landon is booed something awful. I feel that there is just no chance of Landon's winning." In any event, Landon finished the campaign still sounding as if he were reading some of his speeches for the very first time. As for Roosevelt—no one who heard his masterly delivery in that campaign could ever forget the sound of his magnificent voice. It was sheer magic over the airwaves.

The historic Presidential election of 1936 took place on Tuesday, November 3. There was an almost ominous silence in McReynolds' apartment on that long-to-be-remembered day. I was hurrying to get proofs of the second opinion circulated to the other Justices and approved by them prior to the end of the week. Harry and Mary moved quietly from one room to another in their appointed tasks. The Justice remained in his study, and he did not inquire whether I had voted or not. On that afternoon, when I returned to 2400 from an errand, he reminded me of Jefferson Davis—sitting in the Confederate White House at Richmond and anxiously but quietly waiting for news of the battle of Shiloh.

In those days, of course, there was no television to watch. And rather than stay alone in my little apartment, to listen to the returns on the radio, I decided to take another streetcar ride downtown. [As] I arrived near the White

House, I stopped in at a nearby drugstore and heard some election returns being broadcast over a portable radio. All the early returns indicated a sweeping victory for Roosevelt.

The next morning I went downstairs to pick up the Justice's mail as usual. Not until then did I grasp the enormity of the Republican defeat. In cold and glaring type the morning paper announced the startling news that Landon had carried only two states—Maine and Vermont—and that a mere eight electoral votes were all that the Republicans could muster from the entire country. Roosevelt's popular majority was also well over ten million. I could scarcely believe that the President had achieved such a stunning victory. Under the circumstances, how could I face the Justice when I went upstairs? What would he say? Would this terrible defeat of Landon's make McReynolds more difficult to work with?

I stood near the newsstand at 2400 and read the paper more carefully. I knew all too well that there was far more involved than just Landon's ignominious defeat. The election results meant that Franklin D. Roosevelt would be in office until January 1941, and I was certain that all nine members of the Supreme Court could not continue in their positions until then. For the very first time, therefore, Roosevelt would be in a position to appoint a new Justice to the Court. Of the "liberal" Justices, Brandeis was already eighty years old, Cardozo was in ill health, and Stone was on the sick list and would be absent from the Court indefinitely. Of the four "conservatives," Van Devanter was seventy-seven years old, McReynolds and Sutherland, seventy-four, and Butler, seventy. All four were in fine health, but could they remain active on the Court until 1941? "This election is curtains for the Nine Old Men!" was all I could think of as I tossed the morning paper into a nearby wastebasket. I did not want to take it upstairs with me.

When I opened the front door of McReynolds' apartment I saw no one— not even the Justice stretched out unconscious on the floor as a result of the election. I walked quietly to the end of the hall, went into my little office, and listened intently. There was no one in the dining room, but I could hear sounds coming from the kitchen. I gathered, therefore, that the Justice had already eaten breakfast and was sitting in his study. A few letters had come in the morning mail. Two letters appeared to be personal. I did not open them, but I stood up, adjusted my tie unconsciously with my left hand, grasped the two letters in my right hand along with some other correspondence, and walked into McReynolds' study.

"Good morning, Mr. Knox," the Justice exclaimed in a friendly fashion as

I entered the room. He was sitting at his desk and making a few notes on a sheet of paper.

"Here are some letters that came in the morning mail," I announced.

"Thank you," McReynolds said with scarcely a glance at me or at them. "Just leave them here."

He made no mention of the election or gave the slightest hint that he was even upset by it. And thereafter he maintained an air of nonchalance, which I could not help but admire. In the days to come there was never any mention of the election results, but I did notice that copies of the *Literary Digest* were conspicuously absent from the top of his desk from that time on.

I had by now reached the very nadir of my loneliness in Washington, and I could only assume that the future would become progressively worse. If I had ever felt like resigning, the time to have reached the decision would have been on Sunday, November 8, 1936. That was the loneliest day I was ever to spend in Washington. In the afternoon I took another streetcar ride downtown and just looked at the people and wondered why they ever lived in such a dull and tiresome city. I missed Boston and Harvard acutely and all of my pleasant associations of the year before. It was now November, and I had not yet been able to achieve any real rapport with Justice McReynolds. The extent of Landon's defeat had been a jolting surprise, too, and in the future the Justice would undoubtedly be more difficult to work with than ever before.

[On Monday, November 9, the Court met to hand down the first opinions of the 1936 term. Strangely enough, the Justice had given me permission to accompany him, and we drove to Court together in his car. After parking, the Justice] walked to the robing room as usual. I looked for Harry near the Marshal's office. On this particular morning there was a great crowd seeking to enter the Courtroom itself. Harry had been on the lookout for me, however, and he whisked me into a space in the very first row of the reserved section. He had found a place for me next to three middle-aged women whom I had never seen before. Just before I sat down Harry turned to me and said, "Oh, Mr. Knox, I would like you to meet Mrs. Savage. She lives at 2400, too, and she is a friend of the Justice's." I glanced to one side and looked more closely at the three well-dressed and distinguished-looking women, one of whom identified herself as Mrs. Savage. [I had at once] recognized her name as she had called a number of times on the Justice's private phone—regarding golfing appointments with McReynolds. She appeared quite friendly and regarded me with more than passing interest. For years she had resided at 2400, and now here was another secretary of McReynolds who had come to work for him. Mrs. Savage turned and introduced me to her two friends.

After lunch I showed the three women the suite of offices assigned to Justice McReynolds. They were completely furnished though unoccupied and included what would have been my own private office had the Justice and I ever moved down to the Court. The elaborate surroundings impressed the women. Apparently Mrs. Savage had never seen McReynolds' chambers before.

Court began again promptly at 2:30 P.M., and a case had been set down for argument at that time. But my new friends and I did not finish our tour of the building until nearly 3:00 P.M., so we made no attempt to return to the Courtroom. Instead we left and were met by a chauffeured limousine.

As I walked into the lobby I thought to myself, "Yesterday I was very downcast, but today things are finally looking up at last. I never expected one of McReynolds' 'lady friends' to be as friendly as Mrs. Savage is. I wonder what the Justice would think if he knew she drove me home!" And I congratulated myself at having had the good fortune to sit next to her at Court. "But I suppose she never really will get in touch with me," I concluded. "After all, why should she?"

Mrs. Savage did contact me again, however, and from that day forward my life in Washington underwent a magical change. On Wednesday, only two days after I had first met her, she telephoned while McReynolds was at Court. I was invited to have dinner with her in the dining room at 2400 on Friday, November 13, after which we would attend a lecture by Lowell Thomas, which was sponsored by the National Geographic Society. And on Saturday, November 14, I was asked to be one of her guests at a more elaborate dinner in her apartment—for a number of her friends, including an Admiral from the Navy Department.

All had been changed in the twinkling of an eye because of one woman's desire to be of help to a stranger in distress. Without asking, she seemed to sense that life with Justice McReynolds had been very difficult and lonely up to that time. Now she would open up a new world for me, and the Justice need never know. I would work for him in the daytime but meet a number of her friends in the evening. They would be among the most interesting and intelligent people in Washington, but I would not be invited on any evening when McReynolds was scheduled to be her guest, too. He would, in short, never realize that I had even met his "lady friend" from the apartment one floor above his own. The Justice had a thirteen-room apartment on the fifth floor, and she maintained a similar establishment on the sixth floor. He was a bachelor and she was a widow, and they both had a right to invite to dinner whomever they pleased. Mrs. Savage would, therefore, include me in her guest list, and I gladly accepted despite Harry's early warning that I was never to "mix socially" with any of "Pussywillow's lady friends." "The Justice will never know," I thought to myself. "After all, why not? So far he has never raised a finger to lessen my loneliness in any way. Maybe he doesn't even know I am lonely down here in Washington, but even if he did he wouldn't be interested." Thus did I rationalize the question of accepting invitations from Mrs. Savage. Meeting her, in fact, now seemed to have been almost providential. I, therefore, decided to accept the offer of hospitality, which she had so unexpectedly extended.

When I first beheld Mrs. Savage's apartment later that week I was genuinely surprised. It was exactly the same type of apartment that the Justice had, but what a contrast it presented! She had installed exquisite stained glass windows in the dining room, and they gave this room a cathedral-like aspect. Oil paintings centuries old hung in the hallway and living room. Superb Louis XV furniture contrasted with beautiful carpeting. And there was a small library in [which] I noticed a number of old books of considerable rarity. I had never even realized that such a place existed only one floor above where Harry, Mary, and I worked each day.

At dinner on Saturday, November 14, I sat near the Admiral from the Navy Department. I noticed Mrs. Savage's maid eyeing me rather sharply. She was busily serving someone on the opposite side of the table, and she had just heard me tell the Admiral that I was Justice McReynolds' secretary. In no time at all this same maid informed Harry of what she had learned. A few days later he took me aside in the kitchen of McReynolds' apartment and in a very serious tone of voice asked me if I had ever heard of a Mrs. Francis M. Savage.

"Why, Harry," I exclaimed in surprise. "Don't you remember? You introduced me to her when I went to Court the other day."

"That I did," Harry replied glumly, "and I'm real sorry to hear you have become a gigolo so soon."

"A gigolo?" I inquired in surprise. "Just what do you mean?"

"You know what I mean!" replied Harry. "Mrs. Savage is a widow twice your age. She is also a friend of Pussywillow's. You were seen eating with her in the dining room downstairs—right out in public where everybody could see you! And then you even went to dinner in her apartment! I know because her maid told me."

It took some time and considerable discussion before Harry was prepared to concede that perhaps I wasn't exactly a gigolo after all, but he was certain that the whole affair had an element of great disaster in it. "No good will come of this!" he said, shaking his head from side to side. "Mark my word, when

Pussywillow hears about you and Mrs. Savage, you will really be in trouble—and just when everything is going nice and calm like now that the Court is hearing arguments again. In fact, you won't last until Christmas. You'll be looking for a nice new job by the time snow comes!"

"The Justice won't need to hear of it," I said, "that is unless somebody tells him."

"Well, nobody's going to snitch on you," replied Harry, "but some day soon Pussywillow will come walking down the lobby swinging his cane and see his secretary as big as life eating right there in the dining room with his lady friend from upstairs. And when that happens it sure will be curtains for you!"

"I'm prepared to take the risk," I finally replied. "After all, he only plays golf with Mrs. Savage. He isn't married to her, and he can't tell her who to invite to dinner."

"OK," Harry concluded with a sigh, "but don't say I didn't warn you! Pussywillow is real jealous of all of his lady friends—even the ones he only sees on a golf course." And with that statement the subject of Mrs. Savage was closed for the time being. In fact, a few minutes later McReynolds arrived home from Court, and soon he was immersed in dictating a letter to me.

"Mr. Knox," I heard the Justice exclaim, "are you getting all this down in your notebook? This letter must go out in the mail today you know."

"Yes, it's all here," I replied, and thoughts of Mrs. Savage were forgotten for the time being.

There was in Washington at this time a virtually unknown member of the State Department by the name of Alger Hiss, and I called at his home during the same week that I first met Mrs. Savage. I was late in arriving at the Hiss household. On the way there I had stopped at a florist's shop and placed an order for two dozen long-stemmed roses to be sent to Justice Brandeis on his eightieth birthday the next day.

Of course, I had no idea that I was calling on anyone whose name would later be of great national significance. Yet in the years to come a book would be written by one Whittaker Chambers alleging that at this very time his friend, Alger Hiss, was an active participant in a Communist spy apparatus in Washington. I was, in fact, so naïve in 1936 that it did not even occur to me that there was any really significant Communist spy apparatus in Washington or anywhere else for that matter. In those days the U.S.S.R. seemed to be a weak, famine-stricken regime far, far away which had been recognized by the United States only three years before. About the only real thought I had given to the Russians was to wonder how they could afford such elaborate parties in their Washington embassy when their country as a whole presented such a dreary picture to the world.

There was no special reason why Alger Hiss and his wife should have cared to set aside an evening to chat with me. I was the one who had asked to call on them in the first place, and I had resolved to stay for only a short while. Yet once I was in their home something made me linger, and I remained there until 11:30 P.M. Since both Hiss and I had to go to work the next day, it seems unbelievable to me now that I should have imposed on their hospitality for three entire hours. Perhaps they sensed that I was very lonely, for at no time did either of them give any indication that they would be happy if I left so they could retire for the night. As I sat down and looked at Alger Hiss and his wife I thought of the time when I had first met him, in September 1930 at the Beverly Farms, Massachusetts, summer home of the venerable Justice Oliver Wendell Holmes. My memories of Hiss were, therefore, inextricably bound up with my recollections of Holmes.

At that time Holmes was a veritable legend. He had graduated from Harvard College in 1861 as Class Poet (his father had been Class Poet in 1829), [was wounded three times in the Civil War], graduated from the Harvard Law School in 1866, [and published] his monumental work *The Common Law* in 1881. [A year later he was appointed] to the Supreme Judicial Court of Massachusetts, and in 1902 his appointment to the Supreme Court of the United States followed almost as a matter of course. So legendary had Holmes become by 1929 that one of my English instructors at college said in class one day that as far as she knew, the son of the "autocrat of the breakfast-table" had passed away some years before. In my next letter to the Justice, I mentioned that he had been pronounced dead by no less an authority than a member of the faculty of the University of Chicago. By return mail he wrote:

> You may tell your teacher with my compliments that the son of Dr. Holmes referred to, a Justice of the Supreme Court of the United States, is still alive and working. I know because I am he. If she still doubts, the Clerk of the Court I am quite sure will inform her that I am not mistaken. . . .
>
> I shall be at the above place (which, as it is not clearly written, I write again, Beverly Farms, about half or three quarters of an hour by train from Boston) through September. If you come this way I should be glad to see you. . . .

The Justice's letters were written on stationery that was unique for one in his exalted position. Members of the Supreme Court have their choice of several varieties of official writing paper, but in his later years Holmes made use of pads that could be purchased at any ten-cent store. His envelopes were the ordinary post office variety. His handwriting was also unusual. Words were written very closely together and were at times almost illegible. His judicial opinions were all penned by hand, as the Justice abhorred a typewriter, and the Supreme Court printer often had to use a magnifying glass in order to decipher the wording of some decision. I once commented on his handwriting, and with his characteristic tang he replied, "Young man, when the Justices of the Supreme Court tell me they can't read my handwriting, I advise them to go to business school and study penmanship."

In response to my inquiry as to which law school to attend, Holmes wrote: "I shouldn't worry too much about which Law School to go to. The result depends on the fire in your own belly, though no doubt one school may do more than another in kindling it."

In the summer of 1930 the Justice wrote again regarding my plans to visit Beverly Farms while on a trip to Boston:

> You probably have received a letter from my secretary [Alger Hiss], but I am so touched by what you write that I add a word. He has told you of the time that would be most convenient, I believe, or that the last week in September would probably be crowded for me and inconvenient. I doubt if it occurred to him to suggest that my telephone number is Beverly Farms (not Beverly) No. 14, and that if you get near here you had better telephone. I do not venture to express an opinion as to whether it will be worth your while to come. The only recommendation that I offer for myself is that I am a survivor from great events.

At the age of eighty-nine, when Alger Hiss was serving as his secretary, Justice Holmes walked very slowly and with a slight stoop. He almost shuffled along under the burden of his years. Yet when seated in a chair and smoking a cigar he appeared ten or fifteen years younger. He had lost none of his hair, which was then snow white, and an impressive white mustache set off his finely chiseled features to great advantage. Beneath his forehead glistened a pair of the most remarkable eyes I have ever seen. They could be so piercing as almost to drill through steel, and yet when his wit brought laughter into the conversation his eyes twinkled with all the benignancy of nine decades of gracious living. He was also extremely alert mentally. At Beverly Farms he complained that in almost every mail the postman brought a fresh bundle of petitions for certiorari to be read, and yet the Justice found time to delve into the great literature of the past. I remember him saying, in reference to Alger Hiss, "Do you know what I was doing before your train came in? My secretary was reading Goethe to me. I find Goethe very stimulating in my old age."

As a college student in 1930 I had been considerably impressed when I had first met [Alger Hiss] at Beverly Farms. My eyes had followed with interest this well-dressed young man with dark hair, a pleasant expression, and exquisite manners. [As I sat and conversed with Alger and Priscilla Hiss for three hours on that November night in 1936,] we talked of Holmes in considerable detail. I then told the Hisses some but certainly not all of my experiences with Justice McReynolds. At no time did they ask any prying questions, for which I was thankful. I also mentioned Harry Parker and the great help he had been to me. When I left that evening, I expressed the hope of seeing them again and my regret at having stayed so long. Hiss kindly offered to introduce me to some of his attorney friends, and this gesture I much appreciated.

The day after my call at the home of Alger Hiss, the Washington papers mentioned the eightieth birthday of Justice Brandeis. I wondered if he had received my flowers. It was not long, however, before I received [a] short [thank you] message [from Justice Brandeis, and] I thought to myself, "I'm glad now that I did send those long-stemmed roses, though it seemed a little foolish to do at the time."

It was some time later before I learned that Brandeis managed to keep abreast of a large correspondence by writing very brief notes—always right to the point—but never dictating any replies to his law clerk or to a secretary. In fact, he had no private secretary. I still have more than a dozen letters written to me by Brandeis—precise one-page missives of only a few lines each. The message was always so condensed that it resembled a "night letter" sent over the telegraph wires.

Another Saturday conference was held on November 14, 1936. Justice McReynolds surprised me by asking that I drive him to the Court. We made the usual formal preparations for his leaving, and after all the necessary papers and documents were gathered together for his use at the conference, McReynolds and I started out in his car. This was the first time I had driven it in his presence, and it was not without some anxiety that I took the wheel. However, I negotiated the five miles to the Court without any untoward incident, and McReynolds finally alighted from the machine when I had reached the underground parking space at the Court. After the conference he expected to be driven home by Justice Butler, so I was instructed to return the car to the garage at 2400. This I did, but not before I went on a short detour of several miles. It was a beautiful day so I drove over to the Lincoln Memorial and was soon standing before the towering and brooding statue of Abraham Lincoln.

On December 7, 1936, the Court met to hand down opinions for the second time. McReynolds again permitted me to drive to Court with him, but this time Mrs. Savage and her friends did not attend. The Courtroom was crowded as usual, and Chief Justice Hughes delivered two opinions under his own name and also handed down two per curiams. To one of these opinions there was a short dissent by Justices McReynolds, Sutherland, and Butler, but neither of these three conservative jurists had stirred himself sufficiently to write a detailed dissent.[4]

On the same day, Van Devanter handed down one opinion, McReynolds three, Brandeis one, Sutherland two, Butler three, Roberts one, and Cardozo two. With Stone ill and still absent from the bench, even McReynolds was being given more assignments than usual. His three opinions were not lengthy, but they were an indication that he was working at top speed.[5] Though Brandeis delivered only one opinion that day, it was an absolute model of clarity.[6] I also noticed with interest that Butler's opinions showed the same awkward grammatical construction that was so evident in McReynolds' opinions.

By this time it was painfully evident that Edward VIII had finally decided to abandon the throne of England. In fact, as soon as the Justices had handed down their opinions on December 7, I thought of little else but the forthcoming abdication on Thursday, December 10. The proposed action of the uncrowned monarch was something I considered very unwise, but at the same time I concluded that Mrs. Simpson must be the most interesting woman who had ever lived since the death of Cleopatra. While walking through the lobby

---

4. This was the case of *United States v. Wood,* 299 U.S. 123. Hughes' opinion was so lengthy that it fills twenty-one pages in the official reports (130–151). The dissent, however, merely reads: "Mr. Justice McReynolds, Mr. Justice Sutherland, and Mr. Justice Butler are of opinion that the case is controlled by our decision in *Crawford v. United States,* 212 U.S. 183, and that the rule there laid down should not now be departed from. They think the opinion of the court below is sound, and that its judgment should be affirmed."

5. *Helvering, Commissioner of Internal Revenue v. Fried,* 299 U.S. 175; *Algernon S. Schafer v. Helvering, Commissioner of Internal Revenue,* 299 U.S. 171; and *Mountain States Power Co. v. Public Service Commission of Montana et al.,* 299 U.S. 167. In the two Internal Revenue cases, the name of Charles A. Horsky appeared on the Government's brief. [Editors' note: Knox had recently been introduced to Horsky through Alger Hiss.]

6. *John Hancock Mutual Life Insurance Co. v. Yates,* 299 U.S. 178.

of 2400 that week I heard two fashionably dressed women discussing the forthcoming abdication. I can still remember their exact words. "Imagine," said one, "what Mrs. Simpson is in for—keeping a King of England satisfied for the rest of his life!" "You're quite right!" replied the other woman. "I certainly wouldn't want that job!"

There was a large console radio in the living room of McReynolds' apartment, and Harry, Mary, and I looked forward with panting anticipation to listening to a rebroadcast of the abdication speech. On the day of the broadcast, Harry hurried to market so as to be back in time to hear the speech. Mary arranged her work so that she, too, could stop long enough to listen to the talk, and I was certain that I was going to hear it regardless of how much work I might have on hand. Our interest, in short, was at fever pitch. But as the hour drew near, Justice McReynolds unexpectedly returned to the apartment. I was, of course, somewhat disturbed by this unforeseen development, but Harry was not. Talking to me in a low tone of voice he said, "Now don't worry! I'll ask Pussywillow if it's OK for us to listen to the King step off the throne. I'm sure he won't say no."

"That's fine," I replied. "Of course, he will want to listen, too."

Just before the broadcast, Harry walked quietly into McReynolds' study to ask permission to turn on the radio in the living room. In a few moments, however, he returned looking very downcast. McReynolds had casually announced that we could not hear the King's farewell speech, nor did he want to listen to it, either.

At this news I walked into my office and sat down, and Harry and Mary strolled quietly back to the kitchen, closing the swinging door behind them. The time for the broadcast came and went, but the Justice's radio remained silent and no one in the apartment listened to the famous words which began, "At long last. . . . " In fact, I despaired of ever hearing them at all, but in a few weeks some recordings of the speech were on sale in Washington and I purchased one of them. At least I then had the King's words available on a record. But my feelings for McReynolds, which were already in a confused state, were never quite the same again. He went down still another degree in my estimation. The Justice had, I felt, prevented our listening to the broadcast out of sheer unadulterated cussedness—and at a time when there were no opinions for him to write and when he was completely abreast of all of his work at the Court. And during the time of the actual broadcast, McReynolds just sat alone in his study and did not even ask to dictate a letter to me. From then on, however, Harry, Mary, and I had no doubt as to who was "boss" in that apartment.

"Perhaps he was upset by the letter from that fellow in Michigan," I thought to myself. I then turned to a typewritten letter on my desk which had just arrived and had not yet been answered. It was a request for an autograph. To this day I can still see McReynolds studying that letter until its contents seemed almost to hypnotize him. This particular request proved to be the last straw. Following its receipt it was almost impossible to discuss the subject of autographs at all with the Justice. The letter [was addressed to the] "Honorable Jason C. McReynolds." Shortly before the King's abdication speech was scheduled to be broadcast, McReynolds had regarded this literary effort with care. "Why, he doesn't even know my name!" the Justice exclaimed. "I suppose he'll come here on the train if we don't send him an autograph!"

During the broadcast, I busied myself in typing a reply and enclosing an autograph of the Justice written on a small sheet of paper. I also thought to myself, "I wonder what the Justice would say if he knew I am seeing so much of Mrs. Savage lately!" And suddenly I remembered Harry's dire warning of what McReynolds' feelings would be in such a situation. "I'll have to be more careful in the future when I eat dinner with her in the dining room downstairs," I concluded.

John Knox, age seven, child of promise.

(LEFT) Knox as a guide at the World's Fair of 1933–34
in Chicago, a few weeks prior to his departure
for Harvard.

(RIGHT) Knox's graduation photograph,
Northwestern School of Law, 1934.

(LEFT) Knox and Justice Oliver Wendell Holmes, Jr.,
age eighty-nine, at Beverly Farms, Massachusetts, 1930
(photograph by Alger Hiss).

(RIGHT) Justice Holmes and his law clerk, Alger Hiss,
at Beverly Farms (photograph by John Knox).

Knox with Civil War veteran Edward T. Abbott,
age ninety-four, at the seventieth reunion of the Grand
Army of the Republic, Washington, D.C., 1936.

MR. JOHN KNOX

Secretary to
Mr. Justice McReynolds

MR. JOHN KNOX

2400 Sixteenth Street N. W.

Professional and personal calling cards of John Knox.

Meridian Mansions, 2400 Sixteenth Street, N.W., Washington, D.C.
Opened in 1918, the beaux-arts apartment building housed diplomats,
cabinet officials, and members of Congress until World War II. Amenities
included a dining room, a ballroom, rooftop pavilions, tennis courts,
and a garage. Renovated in 1983, the 302-unit complex is now called the
Envoy (Theodor Hordyczak Collection, Library of Congress).

Typical foyer of an apartment at "2400" during the period McReynolds
lived there (Theodor Hordyczak Collection, Library of Congress).

Harry N. Parker, messenger to Justice McReynolds
from 1919 to 1941 and to Justice Robert H. Jackson from
1941 to 1953, photographed in one of the internal
courtyards of the Supreme Court Building, spring 1952
(photograph by Sam Daniels, Collection of the
Supreme Court).

Parker, flanked by law clerks to Justice Robert H.
Jackson (spring 1952): C. George Niebank, Jr. *(left)*, and
William H. Rehnquist (photograph by Sam Daniels,
Collection of the Supreme Court).

Justice James Clark McReynolds in the sitting room of his apartment in Meridian Mansions, posed to highlight his prized bird prints (Collection of the Supreme Court).

Justice Benjamin N. Cardozo, for whom Knox had
great affection, on his way to work, April 10, 1937
(International News, Collection of
the Supreme Court).

Justice Willis Van Devanter, Knox's longtime pen pal
and his conduit to a clerkship (Harris & Ewing,
Collection of the Supreme Court).

The Supreme Court of the United States, October term 1936.
Front row (from left): Louis D. Brandeis, Willis Van Devanter, Chief Justice
Charles Evans Hughes, James C. McReynolds, George Sutherland.
Back row: Owen J. Roberts, Pierce Butler, Harlan F. Stone, Benjamin N.
Cardozo (Harris & Ewing, Collection of the Supreme Court).

McReynolds relaxing during his motor trip to West
Point with Knox, 1936 (photograph by John Knox).

"Inauguration, President F. D. Roosevelt, January 20, 1937.
Taken during a torrential cloudburst. J. K."
(inscription on the back of the photograph taken by Knox).

Knox in his office about the time he began to
write his memoir.

9

AT THE TIME of the 1936 election, President Roosevelt was at his home in Hyde Park, and it was there that he heard the news of his great victory. He returned to Washington almost immediately, and his arrival was marked by a triumphant ride in an open car past cheering crowds of federal employees who lined the sidewalks to catch a glimpse of the victor. Neither McReynolds nor I heard those cheers or saw the smiles of the President, but the newspapers printed some unforgettable pictures of the occasion. Yet the Justice, as I have already mentioned, gave no indication that he was disturbed in the slightest degree by the astonishing results of the election. A few days later, in fact, he even bestirred himself to accept an invitation to dine at the French embassy. I was genuinely surprised by this decision to show himself so soon after Landon's catastrophic defeat. Despite the turn of events, life at 2400 remained in the same placid groove immediately after the election as just prior to it—even though the resident of the White House was now enjoying the first fruits of his great victory. Within a matter of days Roosevelt had turned over to [Attorney General] Cummings the delicate task of finding a satisfactory answer to the troublesome judicial problem—after which the President left Washington on November 18 for a goodwill trip to the Argentine. He was not due to return to the White House until the middle of December.

The Court had met on November 9 to hand down opinions for the first time in the 1936 term. On that occasion no decision was announced that was of outstanding national importance or that ran counter to any basic New Deal theories. The cases decided were more or less routine and a bit disappointing in content. Justice Stone was still ill, and the other eight members of the Court were working at top speed hearing arguments and preparing to write more opinions. Since the election, however, I had been anxiously waiting for the growing struggle between the President and the Supreme Court to become more acute. Yet nothing of any consequence happened until a case entitled *United States v. Curtiss-Wright Export Corp. et al.* was set down for argument on Thursday, November 19, 1936. Now at last, I thought, the battle would begin.

The *Curtiss-Wright* case concerned a direct test of the President's powers in conducting foreign relations. Arguments in this case were not completed on November 19, and they were continued until Friday, November 20. The case concerned a Joint Resolution of Congress, which had been approved on May 28, 1934, together with the provisions of a proclamation issued on that same day by President Roosevelt. The South American countries of Bolivia and Paraguay were then engaged in an armed conflict in the Chaco region. The Joint Resolution provided that if Roosevelt considered that the prohibition of the sale of arms and munitions of war in the United States to the countries engaged in fighting in the Chaco would contribute to the reestablishment of peace between those countries, he could then issue a proclamation to that effect after consulting with the governments of other American republics and cooperating with them. The President did issue such a proclamation—on the date of the Resolution—and the defendants were later indicted for selling fifteen machine guns to Bolivia in violation of the Joint Resolution of Congress and of the President's proclamation. There were various other questions involved, but in any event the lower court held for the defendants and the government appealed.

One of the questions before the Supreme Court was whether the Joint Resolution was an unconstitutional delegation of legislative power to the Chief Executive. I had expected the Court to split about four to four when deciding this question—since Stone was ill and not voting. When McReynolds returned from the Saturday conference during which a vote on the case had been taken, I looked at the results which he had marked in pencil in the red book. I was surprised to find that the vote had been 7 to 1 in favor of Roosevelt. Only McReynolds, in fact, had voted in opposition to the President.[1]

Chief Justice Hughes assigned the writing of the opinion in the *Curtiss-Wright* case to Sutherland, and that Justice soon began work on a voluminous decision sustaining the viewpoint of the seven Justices who had voted to

1. Since I never made any written notations of the secret votes in the Saturday conferences, I do not now recall whether 7 to 1 was the first vote taken or whether it was the final result achieved after several prior votes.

reverse the decision of the lower Court.[2] While Sutherland's opinion was being written, however, McReynolds decided to file a written dissent of his own. Here, then, was the first real opportunity during the 1936 term for him to write a brilliant summary of his own personal views concerning the extent of the President's powers in such a situation. He had no backlog of his own as he had completed all of the opinions assigned to him, and hence there was plenty of time to devote to the dissent. In fact, there had been so much spare time that he had gone on a duck hunt. But instead of composing a stinging dissent—as I had half expected him to do—McReynolds merely dictated the following words: "Mr. Justice McReynolds does not agree. He is of the opinion that the court below reached the right conclusion and its judgment ought to be affirmed."[3] It was an easy way out.

It was now December of 1936. We were abreast of our work, and I was having a difficult time appearing busy. One day during the first week of this month the Justice was sitting in his study and had not rung for me for some time. Harry had gone to market and Mary was busily working in the kitchen. Along about four o'clock in the afternoon, however, I suddenly smelled smoke. At first I did not pay much attention to the matter as I assumed some food was probably burning in the kitchen. But then I recalled that the swinging door between the kitchen and the dining room was almost always shut, and since Mary was in the kitchen she would have smelled anything burning long before the odor could reach my office. By then the odor was very strong, and I was becoming somewhat alarmed. I knew the Justice was sitting in his study—but certainly he could not be smoking a cigarette or a cigar. "Perhaps he fell asleep and set something on fire!" I suddenly thought. So I stood up

2. A few days before the vote on this case was taken, Harry celebrated his twenty-second anniversary as a messenger for McReynolds. Harry had begun work for the Justice on November 22, 1914. [Editors' note: But see chapter 14, note 6.] By 1936 he was a bit wistful as he recalled the early days in Washington when McReynolds rode around in a horse and buggy. "Pussywillow even complained then!" Harry remarked. "He didn't like the upholstery in the buggy. He thought it was not comfortable to sit on. It's been a long time since then, and now we have autos, but he's still complaining about something."

I might also mention that on November 23, 1936—a Monday—the Justice announced that he was going on a duck hunting expedition, that he would leave on Thursday, November 26, and that he would expect Harry to accompany him. I did not inquire where the "hunt" would take place, but winter was approaching, and I was afraid that Harry would catch cold if he had to wade into any icy waters to fetch some dead ducks the Justice might shoot. Later that week the duck hunt did take place on schedule, and I was relieved that Harry brought no ducks home as a result of this particular trip. Perhaps the Justice failed to hit any, but I did not ask him as this might have been construed as a reflection on his prowess as a hunter.

3. [Editors' note: See *United States v. Curtiss-Wright Export Corp.*, 299 U.S. 304, 333 (1936).]

and walked hurriedly to his office. On the threshold of his study, however, I brought myself to a sudden halt. "Good afternoon," McReynolds said while looking up at me in a rather cold fashion. In his right hand he was holding a metal tray on which he had been burning personal letters one at a time.

"Oh! I thought something was on fire in here!" I said.

"Well, something is on fire," McReynolds replied, a bit nettled, "but I'm not on fire, the furniture isn't on fire, and the only thing on fire is what I am now disposing of. So you can go back to your office."

"Thank you," I replied as I backed away, feeling a little sheepish.

This incident was my first experience regarding the Justice's burning of personal letters. Later on, however, I became quite accustomed to smelling smoke from McReynolds' study soon after the morning mail was received and read. This smoke increased in intensity after President Roosevelt's attack on the Supreme Court in February 1937. By then some of the mail which McReynolds was receiving was highly uncomplimentary.

[On each of the first three Mondays in December, the Court announced decisions, including, on December 21, Justice Sutherland's opinion for the Court in] the *Curtiss-Wright* case—which he had completed a few days before.

It was now almost Christmas, and I was anxious to return to Chicago and spend the holidays with my parents and relatives. For days all eight Justices—Justice Stone still being ill—had been busily at work on some sixteen opinions which they expected to read on Monday, January 4, 1937, the fifth opinion day of the term. Of these sixteen cases, McReynolds had been assigned two, and as soon as his opinions in these two cases were completed and approved by the other Justices I walked into his study and asked if I could go home for Christmas. To my surprise he replied very pleasantly, "Of course you may!" He then mentioned that he would probably go out of town himself over the holidays—now that the two opinions had been written, set up in type, circulated to the other Justices, and approved by them. I thanked him sincerely and wished him a happy holiday season, too. In fact, I was delighted to be able to get away from Washington, and I soon telephoned my parents that they could expect me home.

I left Washington by train on the afternoon of December 21, 1936, and the next morning arrived at the Union Station in Chicago. I was met at the train by my father and younger brother—neither of whom I had seen since the previous August. My father beamed with pride as he saw me, and he mentioned that he was sure that I had been very successful with the Justice during the past months. "In fact," he exclaimed, "McReynolds appears from his pictures to be the ablest-looking member of the Court!" I made no comment.

It was a happy Christmas homecoming for me, but I still made no adverse comments to any relatives about Justice McReynolds. I could not bear to spoil the wonderful illusions which my parents in particular held about him and, in fact, about the Court in general. [Over the holidays I had luncheons with several friends who were now working in Chicago, including Otto Kerner.[4]] Kerner and I talked for an hour. "John," he exclaimed with enthusiasm, "with your Supreme Court experience I bet you could come back to Chicago and even command a starting salary of fifty dollars a week in some law firm!"

"Fifty dollars!" I said. "Who'd pay me that much just for having associated with McReynolds!" In those days Harvard graduates were starting work in Chicago law firms at salaries as low as fifteen dollars a week, but Kerner still insisted that I would be in a unique bargaining position once I returned home. After I left Kerner's office, I saw two other young lawyers—Lee Freeman and Abbott Phillips. They, too, regarded me as a rather unique commodity because of the Supreme Court clerkship I held. I had seldom felt happier on any Christmas Eve before. It was good to be home again with relatives and friends.

My train ride back to Washington was uneventful, and I arrived on Sunday, December 27. The next day McReynolds was at his desk as usual. There had apparently been a trip to Tennessee over the holidays, but I did not question him about it. Nor did he make any inquiries regarding my experiences in Chicago other than to express the hope that I had had a pleasant trip.

There was little for the Justice to do that week except to dictate a few routine letters. He remained friendly and even gave me permission to accompany him to Court on the following Monday. And on New Year's Eve I wrote a letter to Justice Van Devanter and then went alone to a movie to "celebrate" the end of 1936.

The following weekend Justice McReynolds caught a rather severe cold. Though he was feeling unwell, he nevertheless drove me to Court on Monday, January 4, 1937, for the fifth opinion day of the term. There was a great crowd as usual. The session was lengthy, and decisions in sixteen cases were announced. McReynolds read the two opinions which he had completed some days before Christmas.[5] None of the sixteen cases is of sufficient importance

---

4. [Editors' note: Otto Kerner (1908–1976), later governor of Illinois, 1961–1968, and judge of the United States Court of Appeals for the Seventh Circuit, best known for chairing the National Advisory Commission on Civil Disorders, which produced the "Kerner Report" in 1968. Kerner was later convicted of multiple crimes in conjunction with racetrack stock deals and imprisoned. Kerner's father also served on the Seventh Circuit, and Knox declined a clerkship with him following his work with McReynolds.]

5. *Liggett & Myers Tobacco Co. v. United States*, 299 U.S. 383; and *Hauge v. Chicago*, 299 U.S. 387.

to be considered here. All were average, run-of-the-mill Supreme Court opinions that did not run counter to the New Deal. McReynolds, for instance, handed down one tax opinion and one opinion dealing with an ordinance of the City of Chicago.

On Wednesday, January 6, 1937, President Roosevelt delivered his annual message to Congress on the state of the Union. This message contained veiled references to the nine Justices of the Supreme Court, and apparently they were considered obstacles in the path of social progress. McReynolds, however, made no reference to the President's address, and I did not mention it either. For perhaps a week longer life at 2400 continued at its slow accustomed pace.

[About that time,] the Justice dictated another letter—to a negro living near Hopkinsville, Kentucky. He wished this negro to secure some rock from a quarry near Elkton, and the Justice explained how he wanted the rock used. But he was in somewhat of a quandary as to how to address the letter and how to end it—since it was, after all, a letter from a Justice of the Supreme Court of the United States to a "darkey." So he directed me to begin the letter as follows:

> Mr. Gano ———, colored,
> near Hopkinsville, Kentucky.
> My dear Gano:

I am omitting the last name of the recipient of this letter, but the point is that I was asked to type the word "colored" after the man's name. This word was also to be put on the envelope—to facilitate delivery of the letter, so the Justice said. In ending the letter McReynolds decided it would be best for him not to sign it, so I was asked to type the following:

> I feel that it would be distinctly to your advantage to give this your immediate attention.
> I am dictating this letter and asking that it be sent at once without my signature.

To the best of my recollection, I then indicated at the bottom of the letter that it had been typed and sent by the Justice's secretary while he was at Court.

The Justices met for a Saturday conference on the afternoon of January 9—after a week of hearing arguments. On that same afternoon I had my tuxedo pressed and got everything in readiness to slip into formal clothes for the reception [honoring the judiciary] at the White House on the following

Tuesday. But on that day McReynolds made no comment about the White House reception when he arrived home from Court. Instead he casually suggested that he begin dictating an opinion which had just been assigned to him by the Chief Justice. We had never before begun work on an opinion so late in the day, and since the case was not of any outstanding importance I was somewhat surprised by the unexpected display of scholarship on his part.[6]

The Justice dictated on and on with no apparent regard for the passage of time. At intervals I typed out his dictation and brought it back to him for correction. Five o'clock came and then 5:30 and finally 6:00. By 6:30 Harry announced that dinner was ready, but the Justice said that the meal would have to be delayed for a while. At 7:00 McReynolds was still at work on the opinion, and by then I had been at his apartment for ten hours. Not until 7:30 P.M. on that Tuesday did the Justice finally indicate that we could stop work for the day. He then merely announced that I could leave, and this I did. When I bade him good evening, I still had made no comment about the reception. Nor had he.

By the time I reached my room, it was already 7:45. The reception was scheduled to begin in an hour and a quarter. I had as yet eaten no dinner, and by the time I could walk to a restaurant and return it would be nearly nine o'clock. And then I would have to change into formal clothes and find a taxi to take me to the White House. Under the circumstances I did not spend more than a minute deciding what to do. I gave up any idea of going to the reception, and soon I was leisurely walking over to the Chinese restaurant at Eighteenth and Columbia Road. On the way there I purchased the evening paper and after looking at the current offering of movies I decided to go to a nearby theater after finishing dinner. This I did but not before I had cherished some very negative thoughts about the Justice. "That bastard," I said to myself, "he deliberately kept on dictating to see if I would squirm and finally mention the reception. But I never gave him that satisfaction, even though he managed to make me miss it entirely. He probably thought that I was so eager to go to the White House that I would rush there without eating any dinner—even though Harry had fixed him a nice meal. I can't figure McReynolds out! Ever since he came back from Court today he acted like a cat toying with a mouse."

The next morning I had not been in the Justice's apartment for long before he rang for me. When I walked into his study McReynolds said, "Good morning," in an unusually pleasant tone of voice. He then casually inquired,

---

6. This was the case of *Elmhurst Cemetery Company of Joliet v. Commissioner of Internal Revenue,* 300 U.S. 37.

"Well, how did you enjoy the reception at the White House last night?" This reference, incidentally, was the first time he had mentioned the reception to me.

I replied in a nonchalant manner while casually looking him in the eye, "The reception? Oh, I didn't go."

McReynolds stopped rocking back and forth in his swivel chair and said in unfeigned astonishment, "You mean you did not go to the reception at all?"

"Why, no, I didn't," I replied. "It was a little late when I left here, so I just ate some dinner and then went to a movie."

The Justice could still not disguise his astonishment, and presently he replied, "You will regret not going for the rest of your life. You should have gone!"[7]

"Well, perhaps," I admitted, and then the conversation turned to another subject. But I felt like replying, "How do you think I could have gone? You know damn well that you kept on dictating until it was too late for me to eat dinner, walk back here, change clothes, and get to the White House by the time the reception began." But perhaps the Justice had not even given any consideration to the matter. In many respects his secretary was in the same category as a piece of furniture, and it is possible that the Justice had never cherished a thought as to how I might organize myself so as to arrive at the White House under my own power and on time. But even after taking the most generous approach possible to the subject, I did feel that Justice Cardozo, for example, would have handled the matter far differently with his own secretary. And if I assumed that the worst was true, then McReynolds had deliberately made me miss the reception by dictating so long that it would be almost impossible for me to attend it. At least I ultimately noticed that it was not until much later in the year—during the Court-packing episode—that he ever again worked on an opinion until 7:30 in the evening.

I had by now resolved to move from 2400. Ever since Christmas I had been looking around the northwest section of Washington for a room in a private home. This, at least, would give me some modicum of companionship with congenial people. Three days before the White House reception, therefore, I had informed McReynolds that I intended to move. He made no objection to the suggestion at the time, and he gave no indication that he cared whether I remained at 2400 or not. Harry had already seen and approved of

---

7. McReynolds was correct. The White House reception was held on the very eve of President Roosevelt's attack upon the Supreme Court. I regret now that I cannot describe how the President appeared that evening and what was said by some of the guests.

my proposed new living quarters. I told the Justice where they were located [2700 Conn. Ave., N.W.], but he appeared to be only mildly interested.

Not long after the White House reception, I noticed a subtle change beginning to take place in the Justice's conduct of his affairs, and as the month progressed he began to exhibit marked signs of irritability and uneasiness. I finally wrote in my diary as follows:

"The Justice has been tipped off to something, but I don't know yet what it is. He is either fearing inflation or being forced to resign. He has had me go through his records back to 1903, he has been calling up his stock brokers, etc. A millionaire from Wall Street came down to advise him to ship part of his money to Canada and England. Beyond that I don't know what happened but will find out in due time, I suppose. . . . Something is wrong somewhere. . . . There may be a blow-up somewhere along the line."[8]

Since McReynolds was in contact with a number of prominent people in Washington, I finally assumed that someone from Capitol Hill was upsetting him considerably by forecasting what the President's plans for the country might be. The Justice, for instance, was a friend of Representative Hatton W. Sumners of Texas, the able Chairman of the House Judiciary Committee. Was Sumners the one who was causing the Justice such uneasiness? I assumed that he was, and for years I felt that Sumners was the one who had warned the Justice, [but Congressman Sumners denied "ever discussing the matters" when I corresponded with him in 1961]. In any event, shortly after President Roosevelt's message to Congress on January 6, 1937, Sumners revived a bill which he had previously introduced in the House of Representatives. He may have read between the lines of the President's message and anticipated Roosevelt's impending assault upon the Supreme Court. In his revived bill Representative Sumners looked toward the day when some of the Justices might resign but still need a guaranteed income each year. This bill, therefore, sought to establish a retiring Justice in a new position in which he would exercise certain minor judicial functions. In return, the Justice would be guaranteed a certain salary which would not be subject to reduction.[9]

---

8. [Editors' note: Knox wrote a letter to his parents that contained the same paragraph during the first week of February 1937. Knox to Folks, n.d., D'Angelo Law Library, University of Chicago Law School.]

9. A law already in effect provided that any retiring Justice should receive his full salary until death. However, after Justice Holmes resigned in 1932, his retirement salary had been reduced by the economy bill of 1933. He also became subject to the income tax. Sumners' bill would have made it impossible to reduce the stipend of a retiree. The income tax would also not have applied to such a retiree.

Now it so happened that while serving as Attorney General in 1913 Justice McReynolds had recommended the passage of a bill providing that when any federal judge, except justices of the Supreme Court, failed to avail himself of the privilege of retiring at the age provided by law, the President should appoint another judge to preside over the affairs of the Court and have precedence over the older one. "This," said McReynolds, "will insure at all times the presence of a judge sufficiently active to discharge promptly and adequately all the duties of the court." McReynolds had made this recommendation to President Wilson in 1913, but no action had ever been taken on it. Now in 1936 McReynolds, as the arch conservative member of the Supreme Court, was on the verge of finding these words turned against him by the occupant of the White House. Whether he knew this or surmised it during the month of January 1937, I have no way of knowing for sure. But for many years I have assumed that he did know, for he became more and more uneasy as he occupied himself with day-by-day routine Court work. He was busily preparing three decisions which he expected to read at the next opinion day—February 1— but writing these decisions was certainly not the cause of his growing uneasiness. I finally began to wonder just what was really going to happen after the inauguration scheduled for Wednesday, January 20.

I had been sent two reserved-seat tickets for the inaugural ceremonies, and my guest was to be a cousin of mine from New York City. The two seats that had been allotted us were directly in front of but a long distance away from the location where the President would be taking the oath of office in the presence of the Justices of the Supreme Court and various other dignitaries. I did not know just how I was going to transport my cousin to the inaugural ceremonies, or whether it would be best to meet him there despite the vast crowd that was expected, but in any event my plans did not include Justice McReynolds. After the fiasco of the judiciary reception I naturally assumed that the Justice would scarcely be interested in how I would arrive at the Capitol— providing I ever got started at all. Two days before the scheduled event, however, McReynolds surprised me considerably by announcing that his friend, Mrs. Jacob L. Loose of Kansas City, was putting her car and chauffeur at his disposal on January 20, so that he could be driven to the inauguration in comfort. I was welcome to accompany him if I wished. I replied rather hesitantly that a relative would be with me, but in a gallant tone of voice McReynolds said that he, too, would be most welcome to ride in Mrs. Loose's limousine. In fact, Harry would also be along and would be ready to attend to whatever needs we might have for the occasion. I thanked McReynolds for his unexpected offer, and I genuinely appreciated it. "Apparently," I thought to myself, "he is going to make sure this time that I attend the ceremonies instead of taking in another movie!"

So much has been written about the second inaugural of Franklin D. Roosevelt that it would be superfluous to recount it in detail here. Suffice to say, however, that by the time I arrived at McReynolds' apartment on the morning of January 20, it was evident that the entire ceremonies would undoubtedly have to take place amid torrents of rain. This meant that the President would be forced to ride down Pennsylvania Avenue in an open car at the mercy of a violent cloudburst, deliver his address in the rain, sit on a wet reviewing stand, and watch a drenched inaugural parade. Despite the very threatening weather, however, McReynolds calmly continued his preparations for departure and gave no evidence of canceling his plans to attend the ceremony. As for me, I was ready to call off the whole project but naturally said nothing about doing so.

My cousin reached 2400 by taxi—having come directly from Union Station—and Mrs. Loose's limousine was driven to the front entrance of the large apartment house when the hour of departure finally arrived. I introduced my relative to McReynolds, and the Justice, my cousin, Harry, and I walked solemnly to the car while the chauffeur stood waiting in attendance. Despite the rain McReynolds was his most charming self—polite, attentive, and interested in carrying along the conversation. Harry sat in the front seat of the limousine next to the chauffeur and said nothing. McReynolds, my cousin, and I sat in the back seat. [We] were wearing raincoats, hats, rubbers, etc., but we carried no umbrella. I felt that an umbrella would be unwelcome in the crowded reserved-seat section where we expected to be.

Upon our arrival at the Capitol, the Justice and Harry disappeared in the direction of the balcony where the ceremonies would take place while my cousin and I found our way to a soggy row of wooden benches. It was by then raining so hard that it almost meant sitting in a puddle of water just to take advantage of our reserved seat space. We did sit down, however, amid a gathering crowd of people who were very unhappy looking and who were all strangers to me.

The inaugural balcony was so far away from where I sat that I could not even see a trace of any members of the Supreme Court—let alone McReynolds. And I could not imagine how Justices Van Devanter and Cardozo, for instance, could dare expose themselves in such a rain—especially since Van Devanter had told me once that he had been afraid even to take his hat off at Justice Holmes' funeral for fear of catching cold. And Cardozo was too frail a man to risk sitting out long in such weather.

Shortly before President Roosevelt was ready to take the oath of office, I saw Harry making his way laboriously through the downpour to where my cousin and I were sitting. He was carrying a large blanket, and when he reached us he exclaimed triumphantly, "Here, Mr. Knox, I brought you this to keep off the rain. Wrap it around both of you!"

"Where did you get it?" I asked in surprise.

"Never mind where," replied Harry rolling his eyes, "I just knew you would need it on a day like this!" And with that statement he walked away.

My cousin turned to me in surprise and remarked, "He certainly must like you a lot!"

I cast an affectionate glance after Harry as he was departing slowly through the crowded reserved seat section. He was probably wet to the skin but as faithful as ever. I never did inquire where he had obtained the blanket, but it was probably from McReynolds' own linen closet. In that event Harry had put it in the limousine before we began our trip to the Capitol. At least I ultimately returned the blanket to him with thanks.

Shortly after the ceremonies began the assemblage of distinguished persons on the inaugural balcony and also those in the reserved seat section rose to its feet and solemnly stood as the Chief Justice of the United States administered the oath of office to the incoming President—who repeated the words of the oath in a load, clear, and ringing voice. After the oath was administered everyone sat down. The President made a slow turn on his paralyzed legs, faced the audience, and began reading his second inaugural address as he gripped the sides of the speaker's stand with his strong arms. His words flowed from the microphones over the heads of the drenched audience while the patter of the rain kept up.

As soon as the ceremonies ended—which was shortly after the reading of the inaugural address—the crowd hastily began to disperse. It was still raining, and my cousin and I decided to walk over to the Supreme Court building. Once there we went to McReynolds' unoccupied suite of offices and tried to dry out. I was, however, thoroughly chilled, and by the time we returned to 2400, we both thought it wise to bathe our feet in hot water. I began to wonder if the Justices who had sat out in the rain would soon be ill with pneumonia.

The next day I was very puzzled to note that both McReynolds and Van Devanter appeared to be in excellent health. In fact, I was the only one ailing, and two days later I was even forced to go to bed—the first time I had been ill since coming to Washington. On Sunday, January 24, I was too sick to leave 2400 and go out to eat. I had some food sent up, and during the afternoon

Mary walked from the Justice's apartment down one flight of stairs to where I stayed. To this day I can still see her standing in the hall as I opened the door. "I'se brought you a nice cherry pie," she exclaimed proudly. "Now I sneaked it out so don't ever mention to Pussywillow that I give it to you. I left him a couple of big pieces, and he won't ever miss the rest!" I thanked her profusely as she hurried back upstairs.

On Monday, January 25, I was back at work and during that week my cold gradually got better. I did not give it to the Justice, and strange to say he gave no indication that he was afraid I might. He inquired as to my condition, but at no time did I indicate that the cold amounted to much. I hated to admit that the weather had laid me so low when it had not affected McReynolds or Van Devanter at all. In fact, Cardozo had not even been sick as far as I could ascertain. And thereafter McReynolds never mentioned the inauguration again, though Harry told me that Vice President Garner had fortified himself with a shot of whiskey shortly before he took the oath as Vice President.

Thus did the second inauguration of Franklin D. Roosevelt pass into history. I had occupied a rain-drenched seat, seen him at a distance, heard his address, missed the real significance of it, and had been thoroughly miserable during the entire proceedings. I also did not see any of the inaugural parade.

On Thursday, January 28, a distinguished Chicago lawyer was in Washington on a business trip, and I talked with him privately for more than a half hour at the offices of the United States Chamber of Commerce. He was Silas Strawn, the senior partner of a prominent Chicago law firm. Among other things, we discussed the political situation and the second inauguration of Franklin D. Roosevelt. Mr. Strawn was convinced that one or more of the nine Justices of the Supreme Court would be forced to retire due to age during the President's second term in office. This would then give Roosevelt his first opportunity to appoint a new member of the Court. "Some of the Justices are too far along in years to be able to hold out until 1941!" Strawn commented with a pessimistic shake of his head.[10] And then looking at me ever intently he inquired in an anxious tone of voice, "Do you think Roosevelt will ever appoint Professor Frankfurter of Harvard to a vacancy on the Court? I am afraid that he might!"

To this question I replied without a moment's hesitation, "I am sure that he will not! Even though Congress has been called a 'rubber-stamp' one at

10. [Editors' note: A few days later, when the president's plan was announced, Strawn—a former president of the American Bar Association—denounced the bill as a "short cut to a dictatorship," "Strawn Scores Proposal," *New York Times,* Feb. 6, 1937, p. 10.]

times, the Senate would surely reject Frankfurter if such a nomination were ever made. I feel that he is much too radical for even the Democratic Senators to stomach."

"Well, I'm certainly glad to hear your opinion," Mr. Strawn replied in a more relaxed tone of voice. "If there is anything that I would consider a real disaster for this country, it would be that man's elevation to the Supreme Court of the United States!" Yet as matters turned out, I was wrong in my opinion, and Strawn did live to see the day when Frankfurter was sworn in as a Justice of the Supreme Court [January 30, 1939].

On Monday, February 1, 1937, McReynolds drove me to Court to attend the seventh opinion day of the term. Once again there was a great crowd in the building—many of whom were evidently expecting the Justices to hand down some important decisions concerning the New Deal. Every available seat was occupied in the Courtroom itself, and the session was lengthy. I noticed with great interest that when the members of the Court filed in to take their seats, there were now nine Justices instead of eight. Harlan F. Stone had finally returned to the bench. The Supreme Court was once again functioning at full strength. The significance of this very important fact I did not, of course, fully comprehend at the time—but we were now on the eve of the President's famous attack upon the Court.

Decisions in twenty-four cases were announced [that day].[11] On both February 1 and February 15, [however,] many of those who attended the Court session must have been acutely disappointed and perplexed because not a single important New Deal decision was announced.[12] This meant that the earliest date such an announcement could be made would be the session of March 1, and it was far from certain that such an opinion would be handed down even then.

Events in general, however, were now moving rapidly. Two things of especial significance took place on Wednesday, February 3. Not only was the

11. McReynolds read three opinions: *Elmhurst Cemetery Company of Joliet v. Commissioner of Internal Revenue*, 300 U.S. 37; *United States v. Giles*, 300 U.S. 41; and *Kelly, Trustee in Bankruptcy v. United States et al.*, 300 U.S. 50.

12. [The Court handed down just one opinion, written by Justice Brandeis, on February 15.] The case was *Helvering, Commissioner of Internal Revenue v. Midland Mutual Life Insurance Co.*, 300 U.S. 216. In this tax case the Court split seven to one—McReynolds being the lone dissenter and Stone being ill and not taking part in the decision. McReynolds' dissent concluded, "Divorced from reality taxation becomes sheer oppression." This statement sounded like an excerpt from some distinguished opinion of Justice Oliver Wendell Holmes, and for once I concluded that McReynolds' literary style was definitely improving.

annual dinner for the judiciary held at the White House on that date, but February 3 also marked Justice McReynolds' seventy-fifth birthday. McReynolds, however, took no particular note of the day and went to Court as usual to hear arguments. After he left he received a few personal messages of congratulations on his private telephone. His personal mail also contained what appeared to be some birthday cards. And in the afternoon, while the Justice was still at Court, a newspaperman called on the house phone. Harry answered this call and then referred it to me. The voice at the other end of the wire asked if Justice McReynolds had any particular comment to make to the newspapers on the occasion of his reaching seventy-five. I answered, as politely as possible, that the Justice was enjoying a very quiet birthday and that he would have no comment to make to the press.

As soon as the Justice arrived home from Court that day, he began immediate preparations to attend the dinner for the judiciary. Harry flitted about and answered various questions as to whether McReynolds' formal clothes had "really" been cleaned, pressed, etc., and by the time I left the apartment at 5:30 P.M., Harry had already announced to the Justice that everything was in readiness whenever he wished to begin dressing. It was apparent that McReynolds considered this dinner to be an occasion of considerable importance. The members of the Court had somehow managed to survive the dampness of the inaugural ceremonies, and now they were ready to assemble at the White House to meet the President again. And since it was the Justice's birthday, his presence at the dinner would indicate that he was certainly hale and hearty at seventy-five.

I had not, of course, been invited to the White House to attend this dinner. Nor did I realize that it was destined to be one of the most unusual repasts of the kind ever held, and that at the time when the Justices would be dining in the presence of Franklin D. Roosevelt there remained only some thirty-six hours before the plan to attack the judiciary was to be made public. And in view of the President's ultimate display of supreme confidence in the outcome of the struggle, at the time when he announced his plan two days later, I do not consider it unfair to say that he really must have had an almost contemptuous disregard for the Justices as his unsuspecting guests and future adversaries sat down with him for their last meal together before the opening of hostilities. At least they were supposed to be unsuspecting, though for some weeks McReynolds had been displaying an acute awareness that something was amiss. But even he could not have foreseen the exact type of attack the President contemplated making upon the Supreme Court.

The day after the White House dinner McReynolds barely commented on what had happened, but the newspapers of February 4 contained write-ups of the affair. It was noted, for instance, that Justices Brandeis and Stone had been absent. Brandeis made it a practice not to attend evening social functions, and Stone was just recovering from his lengthy illness. The dinner list had comprised almost eighty guests. Some of those present included Attorney General Cummings, Solicitor General Reed, Senator Henry F. Ashurst, Representative Hatton W. Sumners, Donald Richberg, Judge Samuel I. Rosenman, Mrs. Warren Delano Robbins (a cousin of the President), Judge Irving Lehman, Gene Tunney, George Harrison (President of the New York Reserve Bank), and representatives of the Army and Navy. After the dinner there had been music and a reception. All the ladies present were elegantly gowned in the height of fashion, and there were newspaper comments on some of the dresses that had been worn. In fact, the whole affair had been a great social success, though I seemed to read between the lines that it had also been a trifle dull.

Unknown to McReynolds or to me, of course, President Roosevelt, on the afternoon of February 4, contacted Senate Majority Leader Joseph T. Robinson of Arkansas and Speaker of the House William B. Bankhead of Alabama and told them that there would be an important cabinet meeting the next morning. They were asked to bring along with them to this meeting the following three Congressmen: Representative Sumners of Texas (chairman of the House Judiciary Committee), Representative Samuel Rayburn of Texas, and Senator Ashurst of Arizona (Chairman of the Senate Judiciary Committee). The secretarial staff of the White House also received instructions to report for work at 6:30 A.M. on Friday, February 5. The staff did assemble at that early hour and found (a) Roosevelt's message on the judiciary; (b) Attorney General Cummings' accompanying letter, and (c) the proposed court bill—all waiting to be mimeographed. Hundreds of copies were needed before noon on that day so that they could be distributed to Congressmen, members of the Cabinet, Justices of the Supreme Court, etc.

I arrived for work as usual on Friday, February 5, and McReynolds did his setting-up exercises as usual, ate his breakfast at the usual time, and then left for court [alone by] car. Another routine day had begun—or so we thought. But on that morning President Roosevelt held his 342nd press conference, which followed close on the heels of a brief Cabinet meeting. The President disclosed his proposed bill—first to the Cabinet and to a few congressional leaders and then a few minutes later to members of the press. For weeks he had been completely aloof in working out the details of his plan along with a few picked subordinates—perhaps because he considered that it would be adopted in any event without much opposition. Mr. Roosevelt now represented his proposed bill as a reform to correct certain injustices and to relieve the courts of congestion—especially the Supreme Court of the United States. He had inferred that elderly Justices were only able to keep abreast of their work by rejecting many petitions for review which should have been allowed. The President, in fact, was now calling for an infusion of entirely new blood into the judiciary. The crux of the whole matter, however, was that the bill contained a provision giving the President authority to name an additional federal judge for every incumbent who had been on the bench for at least ten years and who had not resigned within six months after reaching seventy years of age. Six members of the Supreme Court of the United States had been Justices for at least ten years and were already beyond the age of seventy, so the bill would have allowed the President to appoint six new Justices at once. If the six who were over seventy had then insisted upon remaining on the Court, the membership would have been increased from nine to fifteen Justices.

In his proposed bill, therefore, the President placed his emphasis on judicial delay and inefficiency and on the incapacity of elderly judges to keep abreast of their case load. There was no direct reference to his primary purpose to solve the problem created by the Supreme Court of the United States in its relations to the New Deal. The President, in other words, was attempting to pack the Court and yet was pretending not to. He also had consulted no one in the Senate or House on his plan prior to its being made public.

Copies of the plan were distributed to the members of the Supreme Court while they were on the bench hearing arguments that day. Yet when Justice McReynolds arrived back at 2400 late in the afternoon, he made no comment to me on what had happened. I left his apartment at 5:30 P.M., and it was not until I saw the evening newspapers that I learned of the President's message.

On Monday, February 8, 1937, McReynolds had still not mentioned the President's plan when he consented to drive me to Court. I commented on it briefly, however, once we were in the car. Yet the Justice indicated that he did not want to discuss the matter—at least just then—so I changed the subject. The Justice drove on slowly and in silence, his eyes on the traffic ahead and his thoughts far away. He was, in fact, on his way to work as usual, but now the President of the United States was proving most disconcerting by attempting to oust him from his lifetime job. And this so soon after the White House dinner for the judiciary!

Now and then I would pretend to look at something passing by in traffic and then surreptitiously glance at the Justice from out of the corner of my eye. His facial expression was grim, and he reminded me of a general in the midst of a decisive battle who is sorely puzzled as to just what move to make next. Thinking to change the subject again and at least say something, I asked if he would mind if I enrolled in a review course for a couple of nights a week—to prepare for the District of Columbia bar examination to be held in June. Few questions, however, could have been more ill-advised at such a time. The Justice finally grunted his approval of the idea, but at the moment I did not realize what a near-fatal mistake it was even to suggest attending such a course. The Court was now beginning a momentous battle, and the last thing McReynolds was interested in was for his secretary to study for a bar examination at such a time. And it was unwise on my part to think of doing so as I would not have sufficient opportunity to study—especially as I was still accepting all the invitations which Mrs. Savage and others were now extending to me. But in the exuberance of youth I assumed I could handle my work as a secretary, study for the bar examination, go out socially in the evening as much as possible, and at the same time watch from a reserved seat the battle which was rapidly shaping up between the President and the Supreme Court. I was, in fact, planning to burn the candle at both ends, though I did not quite realize this at the time.

When McReynolds reached the Court building he left his car in the lower-level parking space as usual and walked silently to the robing room while I met Harry and found a reserved seat in the Courtroom. I remained there from noon until 2:00 P.M. to be present during part of the arguments in the much-publicized *Angelo Herndon* case.[13] That day all nine Justices seemed to be unusually solemn and quiet as they sat hearing arguments in this case. Perhaps all of them were mulling over in their own minds the President's plan as they went through the motions of listening [to counsel]. The public was already responding to the publicity being given the President's plan by thronging to the building in large numbers and hoping for a firsthand look at the nine Justices as they sat upon the bench. Yet only a portion of the great crowd could be accommodated.

Just a week later—on Monday, February 15—I attended my first bar review class. And on the evenings when I would not be studying for or attending [the] sessions, I expected to be spending my time circulating around

---

13. *Herndon v. Lowry*, 301 U.S. 242. The decision in this famous 5-4 case was handed down on April 26, 1937. [Editors' note: See chapter 12.]

Washington with some newfound friends. Washington was finally becoming endurable after so many months of loneliness. For this I was especially indebted to Mrs. Savage.

And then—all of a sudden and without warning—the gates began to close, and Justice McReynolds decided to withdraw completely from contacts with everyone but his most intimate friends. And though he did not specifically request it, he gave indications that he expected me to do the same. Letters and postcards of an astonishing nature had already begun to arrive in the mail each morning. Many of the postcards were from anonymous senders, some were threatening, and all were hostile. I finally decided not to give any more of these cards to the Justice, but the sealed envelopes from many different states I did have to place unopened on his desk each morning. Soon after he had completed reading the daily mail, I would smell smoke coming from his study. He was burning his correspondence again—and doing so each morning. This unsolicited correspondence was causing both of us embarrassment, and the Justice soon became quite difficult to work with.

Among the postcards which I still have, and which he never saw, are the following:

- An anonymous card mailed from Denver, Colorado, and addressed to "Just-Ice J. C. McReynolds, Washington, D.C." A newspaper photograph of a head and shoulders picture of the Justice is pasted on the reverse of this postcard. A bandit's mask is drawn to cover the Justice's eyes. On his forehead is printed the word "R E S I G N." And on the edge of the card is written "Enemy 'No One.'"

- An anonymous card mailed from Chicago, Illinois, and addressed to "Judge McReynolds, U.S. Supreme Court, Washington, D.C." On this card is written "Some people never learn anything—*human* or *real*—. You old Crab are one of them. If you'd had some heart, some sense, some regard for the rights of the poor the Lord would not now have left you like Cardinal Wolsey—to a well deserved fall. May you *land hard*. People's Lawyer."

- A signed card mailed from Mt. Pleasant, Texas, and addressed to "Justice J.C. McReynolds, Washington, D.C." On this card there is written in ink "Mt. Pleasant, Texas, Justice J. C. McReynolds, Washington, D.C. Dear Sir:—I am writing you as an American citizen. I do not wish to be in 'contempt' of court, but I sincerely believe that the most patriotic thing you can do is to resign *at once*. Respectfully, J. R. Reynolds (Ph.D.)"

But not even a Doctor of Philosophy from the South was going to be able to influence Justice McReynolds to resign from the Supreme Court of the United States on which he had been serving since the year 1914. He was determined to stand his ground, but he had by now resolved to withdraw into an ivory tower and wait out the hurricane.

Some days, after burning his morning mail, McReynolds would become unusually restless and then decide to go out for a walk. At such times he always carried his walking stick with him, which was made of strong wood and was rather heavy. Soon after the anonymous letters and postcards began arriving, however, Harry announced that the Justice should not go out alone for fear of his being assaulted in broad daylight. "Better let me go with you!" he would say. "Somebody might hit you over the head if you go walking alone!"

"I'll go alone—like I always have!" McReynolds would reply heatedly. "If anybody dares hit me, why, why, I'll strike him with this walking stick! I can put up a good fight yet!" With that statement he would open the front door of the apartment with a vigorous tug on the knob and look back for just a moment toward Harry and me. And once he said, "To think that the President would bring us to this!" Then he recovered his composure and started out. Harry, faithful servant that he was, showed growing anxiety and genuine concern over the Justice's welfare as the weeks went by. I could not help but admire McReynolds for his grit and nerve, though I felt a strange compassion for him, too. Then I would go into my little office and sit down and remember that while the Justice was slowly walking up Sixteenth Street alone and bitterly lonely, striking automobile workers in Detroit had seized physical possession of certain plants and were chanting derisively day after day, "Nine Old Men! Nine Old Men!" It was all very strange indeed—this business of being a Supreme Court law clerk.

10

~~~~~~~~~~~~~~~~

ONE DAY DURING the middle of
February, Harry and Mary invited me to eat a pork chop lunch with them in
the kitchen of the Justice's apartment. McReynolds had gone out and was not
due back for some time, and Mary had unexpectedly announced that she
would "put an extra chop on the fire" and also fix me some potatoes and gravy.
This was the first invitation to eat with them that they had ever extended, and
I accepted with pleasure. It meant that I would not have to walk clear over to
Eighteenth and Columbia Road on a wintry day to eat lunch as usual.[1]

"Everything's ready!" Mary finally called out to me while I was typing in
my little office. I thereupon stopped work, walked down the hall, went into the
dining room, and swung open the door leading from there into the kitchen,
but on the threshold of the kitchen I suddenly stopped. Mary had set two
tables—one with two chairs in front of it and a second table with one chair
beside it. "This is your place," she said as she motioned me to sit at the table
with the single chair. I noticed that my lunch was already served and on this
table. "I'll pour you a glass of milk, too," Mary said smiling. "Milk is always
good for young men your age." However, I remained standing where I was, so
she motioned again and said, "Here, sit down! Don't let your lunch get cold!"

"But where are you and Harry going to eat?" I said in surprise.

Harry motioned toward the table with the two chairs in front of it and
said, "Why, over here at this table. Mary and I eat here and you eat there." He
then pointed to the table with the single chair.

"But why two tables?" I inquired.

1. I had previously eaten in the kitchen but always alone.

At this question Mary became somewhat embarrassed and made no reply. I realized in a flash that she had set two different tables as she and Harry were negroes and I was white. She had assumed that I would not care to eat at the same table with two colored persons, regardless of how well I might know them.

I decided to ignore the negro question which had so unexpectedly arisen, so I merely said, "Mary, I don't want to eat alone. I'm not the Justice, you know, and he always looks so lonely sitting there in the dining room all by himself. So let me sit with you and Harry. There's enough room at your table for the three of us." And with that statement I began to move some of the dishes from the place that had been set up for me to the table before which Harry and Mary were standing.

Mary thereupon broke into a broad smile and exclaimed in genuine surprise, "Why, you mean you're going to eat with us—with Harry and me—and at the same table?"

"Why not?" I replied. "It would look pretty silly for us to sit at two separate tables in this small kitchen—now wouldn't it?"

"Well, I guess it would," Mary replied after some hesitation. And turning to Harry she said with a dignity that I had not heretofore noticed in her voice, "Now let's all of us start eating before these chops get good and cold!"

And so the three of us did sit down at the same table, and at first we began to eat in a rather embarrassed silence. I wondered for a fleeting moment if some of my friends would not derisively call me a "nigger lover" if they could only see me sitting at that table with two negro servants. I really wasn't sure what their attitude might be in such a case. In a few moments, however, I lifted the glass of milk to my lips, and as I began drinking Harry said, "I suppose you know that Mary asked Pussywillow for a raise."

"Why, no, I don't," I replied with interest. "And what did he say?"

I am now recalling Harry's reply from memory—as his exact words are not quoted in my diary—but to the best of my recollection he said, "Mary wanted a raise of five dollars a month, and he finally decided to give her two dollars more."

I put the milk down and looked intently at Mary. "You mean Pussywillow gave you a raise of twenty-four dollars a year—just like that?"

"Yes," Mary replied a bit sheepishly, "but I guess that's better than nothing."

"But I thought you needed to save two hundred dollars for your funeral!" I exclaimed. "Let's see—at twenty-four dollars a year your funeral will simply have to be delayed for a long time!"

"It's not as funny as it sounds," Harry replied glumly. "Pussywillow could sure have afforded to give Mary five dollars more a month instead of just two dollars! Don't you think so?"

"That's for sure," I said, whistling softly under my breath. And as I said these words, I had visions of the tens of thousands of dollars which the Justice had "stashed away" at that very moment in various bank accounts, etc., which he would probably never spend, and, in fact, which he never did spend.[2] He could, of course, have easily afforded to give Mary an increase of a hundred dollars a month if he had wanted to. But to Justice McReynolds, an increase of two dollars a month for his hard-working maid was, in fact, all that he evidently felt she deserved.

I never forgot this incident, even though McReynolds had a perfect right to pay his maid whatever he thought was a fair amount — providing she would accept it. And it is true that salaries were low in the 1930s, along with living costs. But nevertheless the incident became fixed in my mind — especially when I compared the way the Justice treated his friends whom he considered his equals when they called at his apartment.

An uncle and aunt of mine came to town [shortly thereafter] and introduced me to a Mr. and Mrs. Robert M. Macy, who lived in Washington; [Mr. Macy was my uncle's stepson]. On Sunday evening, February 21, my newly found "cousin," Robert Macy, suggested taking me to a club meeting. I did not wish to go and at first declined since it was late in the day and I was tired. Macy's wife, however, insisted that I "get out and meet some of these interesting young men in Washington," so I finally consented to accompany her husband to the home of a Mr. Quigg Newton.[3] He was playing host that evening to perhaps twenty or twenty-five enthusiastic young "New Dealers" who met once or twice a month at the home of one of the members of the group to discuss various national problems.

Macy drove me to the home where Quigg Newton lived — a large residence which apparently had been rented by a group of men who shared similar interests. We entered the living room, and I was introduced to Newton, who was at that time serving as legal secretary to one of the members of the Securities and Exchange Commission [William O. Douglas]. I noticed various groups of men standing around and chatting amiably in both the living room

2. In his will the Justice made *cash* bequests totaling [over $190,000].

3. [Editors' note: Quigg Newton (1911–), later mayor of Denver, 1947–1955, president of the University of Colorado, 1957–1963, and president of the Commonwealth Fund, 1963–1975. See Ann Carnahan, "Ex-Mayor Remains Modest at 90," *Rocky Mountain News,* Aug. 4, 2001, p. B1.]

and a large adjoining room. I soon concluded that here before me was a glittering group of personalities the likes of which I had never before seen in Washington assembled under one roof. Each appeared to be an outstanding attorney or economist who had come to Washington in the heyday of the New Deal to take part in the reshaping of America. Almost at once, however, I felt ill at ease in the midst of such a group—being a law clerk to the arch conservative Justice who was so intensely hostile to everything the New Deal stood for. I therefore remained noncommittal and as unobtrusive as possible when I was introduced to the various guests. Each one instantly showed considerable interest upon learning of my connection with the Court. This embarrassed me all the more until I finally felt like a Confederate officer who had accidentally blundered into one of General U. S. Grant's staff meetings during the siege of Vicksburg.

As I rather aimlessly drifted from one group to another I was eventually introduced to a G. Mennen Williams and to a Charles Fahy.[4] Williams, a resident of Michigan, was in Washington serving as an attorney for the Social Security Board. Fahy, the oldest of those present, was General Counsel of the National Labor Relations Board. No one in the room, however, was more impressive looking than Williams.[5] He was tall and handsome with a vibrant personality and a zest for bubbling conversation. I was soon informed that he was a wealthy young lawyer who had forsaken a Republican background in order to embrace the theories of the New Deal. And during the course of the evening I could not help but turn and gaze at him from time to time as he walked from group to group with a smile on his face and a hearty handshake. I soon concluded that Williams was a very unusual personality, and I thought to myself, "How generously the gods have endowed you with everything— brains, looks, talent, personality, money—all the things, in fact, to make you a success."

By then Robert Macy had drifted off into one of the various discussion groups, and I found myself on my own. I was at that moment standing in a corner of the living room. I still felt ill at ease and did not know exactly what to do with myself, so I glanced around and carefully appraised each man who

4. [Editors' note: Charles Fahy (1892–1979), general counsel of the NLRB, 1935–1940, solicitor general of the United States, 1941–1945, and judge of the United States Court of Appeals for the District of Columbia Circuit, 1949–1979.]

5. [Editors' note: G. Mennen Williams (1911–1988), later governor of Michigan, 1949–1960, assistant secretary of state for African Affairs, 1961–1966, and justice on the Michigan Supreme Court, 1970–1986.]

was in the room at the time. All were in animated and noisy discussion except one. In the opposite corner of the room one of the guests was sprawled lazily in a large upholstered chair, with one leg draped over an arm of the chair, talking to no one and showing no interest whatever in the proceedings. I had no idea who he was, but I gradually made my way over to where he was sitting, and I introduced myself. Without moving or stirring from the chair he looked up at me and smiled, shook hands, and replied in a very friendly Southern accent, "I am Travis Brown from Charlotte, North Carolina, and I am an attorney with the Federal Trade Commission." I sat down near him, and soon we were lost in such an animated discussion that we were oblivious to our surroundings. He resembled Williams—brilliant, charming, and handsome—but he also seemed to have a wonderful sense of humor. I forgot about my embarrassment at being present at such a gathering, and Brown soon released a flood of conversation that had long been bottled up within me. I learned, for instance, that his grandfather had served as a Confederate officer from the State of Mississippi, and this information led to a brief discussion of the War between the States. In a short while we exchanged names, addresses, and telephone numbers and agreed to meet again within a few days. In fact, when the speaker of the evening finally began talking in the next room, we paid no attention to him and remained where we were.

The following week I attended two sessions of the bar review course and also went out to dinner to a home on F Street. I noted in my diary that February 28 was the first Sunday in nine weeks it had not rained in Washington. I spent the afternoon of that day at the Supreme Court building reviewing my bar examination notes. There I met and chatted with [the] law clerks to Justice Sutherland and to Chief Justice Hughes. They were busily working even though the day was a Sunday.

The next day—Monday, March 1, 1937—was the ninth opinion day of the term. Fortunately Justice McReynolds consented to drive me to Court again. He still had not referred to the Court-packing struggle, and even on the drive downtown he did not mention it in any way. Nor did I. After parting company with him I met by appointment Mrs. Robert Macy, her mother-in-law (my aunt), and my new friend, Travis Brown. All three had been waiting for me—in the midst of an enormous crowd which was seeking to gain admittance into the Courtroom itself. There was an air of great expectancy among the visitors to the building that morning, and it was evident they felt that some very important decisions affecting the New Deal might be announced when the Justices assembled at noontime. Through Harry's intercession I was fortunate in securing front row seats in the reserved section for my three guests.

Decisions in thirteen cases were read to a tense audience on that day. [All thirteen were] run-of-the-mill cases, [with the exception of an opinion] delivered by Justice Cardozo in the case of *Holyoke Water Power Co. v. American Writing Paper Co.*[6] Here the Court split 5 to 4, and Justices Van Devanter, McReynolds, Sutherland, and Butler dissented without writing an opinion. This case involved an interpretation of the Joint Resolution of June 5, 1933, which declared in part that "every obligation payable in money of the United States, whether theretofore or thereafter incurred, should be discharged upon payment, dollar for dollar, in any coin or currency which at the time of payment was legal tender for public or private debts, irrespective of any provision contained therein whereby the obligee was given a right to require payment in gold or in a particular kind of coin or currency, or in any amount in money of the United States measured thereby."

The Court had for consideration certain leases of water-power rights to be enjoyed in perpetuity provided that the grantee should pay as rent "a quantity of gold which shall be equal in amount to" a stated number of "dollars of the gold coin of the United States of the standard of weight and fineness of the year 1894, or the equivalent of this commodity in United States currency." The five majority Justices held that the lessee's obligation under the contract was for the payment of money, and not for the delivery of gold as if gold had been sold as a commodity. Cardozo made reference to the famous 1935 "gold decision"—*Norman v. Baltimore & Ohio R. Co.,* 294 U.S. 240.

When all the decisions had been announced, some of the spectators [seemed to be quite disappointed]. Someone near me, for instance, asked a friend when he thought the Justices were going to tackle "some real live issues." Apparently the public was becoming impatient for the Supreme Court to show some reaction to the President's great frontal attack upon it. Laymen were evidently ignoring the fact that cases could only come before the Court for decision after they had first slowly worked their way up through the lower courts.

As soon as the session was over, Mrs. Macy and her mother-in-law left the Supreme Court building. Travis Brown, however, remained with me, and we had lunch together in the cafeteria of the Court. McReynolds returned to the bench for the afternoon session. I took Travis to the Justice's apartment and showed him the little office where I worked. Mary then invited us into the kitchen, and Travis and I ate ice cream and cookies which she set before us. He

6. 300 U.S. 324.

laughed and joked and brought happiness into that chill apartment, and I was glad that I had met him at Quigg Newton's home.

I was now undergoing a gradual deterioration in my position as a law clerk, but at first I did not realize this. The opinions being written by McReynolds were not proving of much interest to me and were probably of little interest to him, too. I also noticed that the Chief Justice was assigning him cases of less and less importance, and I assumed that Hughes considered McReynolds a weak reed indeed on which to lean in the midst of the national storm that was now howling around the corners of the Supreme Court building. The Court-packing fight was indeed at its height, but despite the fact that it was the main topic of conversation in many Washington circles the subject was never once mentioned to me by McReynolds. I sensed that he was undoubtedly deeply worried about the trend of national events, but I no longer made any effort to penetrate the wall of austerity and silence behind which he had now retreated. His failure to mention the Court struggle to the only office associate he was in daily contact with caused me to think even less of him than before, and perhaps he had come to think less of me, too. We were now formally compatible but that was about all. Yet despite the glare of publicity we were living in, he never inquired how I was spending my time after office hours. Nor did he attempt to restrict my outside activities in any way. He had also proved unusually cooperative of late in driving me to Court whenever I asked to accompany him.

Each day was now filled with events of such interest that I scarcely had time to note them in my diary. On Thursday, March 4, for instance, I had lunch with Harold Leventhal—law clerk to Justice Stone. I had contacted Stone's household some weeks before, [just after the Justice had returned to the bench]. I found his law clerk very congenial, and I hoped to call soon on the Justice himself. Leventhal was a 1936 graduate of the Columbia Law School and had evidently been an outstanding scholar in his class.[7] Since he was Jewish, however, I did not invite him to visit 2400 or to see where I worked as I had invited Travis Brown to do. Even with McReynolds absent from the apartment that day, I did not wish to risk his arriving home unexpectedly and finding Stone's law clerk on the premises. Hence I met Harold at a location convenient to both of [us; it] was the first of a number of meetings that we were to have.

After parting with Leventhal, I took time to call at a nearby law firm where I met one of Justice Cardozo's former law clerks—Percy Russell. He was the

---

7. [Editors' note: See chapter 7, note 2.]

first Cardozo law clerk I had seen, and we had an interesting chat. In fact, it was after 4:00 P.M. when I arrived back at 2400, shortly before McReynolds himself returned. He never knew, of course, that I had been absent from the apartment so long, nor had he telephoned during the afternoon to check up on me. On this particular day the Justice was evidently thinking of more important problems, and he walked silently down the hall to his office after giving his hat and coat to Harry.

That evening a great Democratic Victory dinner was to be held in the grand ballroom of the Mayflower Hotel, and the President himself was to address this dinner. What would he say on such an occasion? Would he mention the Supreme Court? Perhaps he might even mention Justice McReynolds, who remained closeted in his office for the rest of the day and did not ring for me even once. However, I did walk to the threshold of his office to say goodbye when I left the apartment that day. He nodded and replied, "Goodbye, Mr. Knox."

At the Mayflower Hotel that evening, thirteen hundred Democrats paid one hundred dollars apiece to be present at the Victory dinner. Eleven hundred similar dinners were held simultaneously in different parts of the country, and the President's speech was a direct appeal for national support in his efforts to subjugate the Supreme Court. He accused the Justices of vetoing the New Deal program—an accusation which was essentially correct up to that date.

[Five days later, on] Tuesday, March 9, President Roosevelt delivered a very important fireside chat—discussing with the nation his plans for reorganization of the judiciary. He spoke in part as follows:

> Like all lawyers, like all Americans, I regret the necessity of this controversy. But the welfare of the United States, and indeed of the Constitution itself, is what we all must think about first. Our difficulty with the Court today rises not from the Court as an institution but from human beings within it. But we cannot yield our constitutional destiny to the personal judgment of a few men who, being fearful of the future, would deny us the necessary means of dealing with the present.
>
> This plan of mine is no attack on the Court; it seeks to restore the Court to its rightful and historic place in our system of Constitutional Government and to have it resume its high task of building anew on the Constitution "a system of living law." The Court itself can best undo what the Court has done. . . .

During the past half century the balance of power between the three great branches of the Federal Government has been tipped out of balance by the Courts in direct contradiction of the high purposes of the framers of the Constitution. It is my purpose to restore that balance. You who know me will accept my solemn assurance that in a world in which democracy is under attack, I seek to make American democracy succeed. You and I will do our part.

I listened on my own radio at 2700 Connecticut Avenue, N.W. After the President had finished, I felt that he was now definitely on the defensive.

Each week I was still trying to attend two evening sessions of the bar review course, but on other evenings I was not spending enough time in concentrated study. It was not possible to do any studying in McReynolds' apartment during the day, and by the time I attended the evening session held on Thursday, March 11, I noticed that I was no longer keeping abreast of the classroom work. This, however, was a warning signal which I failed to heed.

Another opinion day was scheduled for Monday, March 15, but I did not ask McReynolds if I could accompany him to Court, as I knew that only one decision would be handed down. When Harry returned that day, after serving the Justice his lunch, he mentioned the great crowd that had been in the building. The disappointment of many of those who gained entrance to the Courtroom itself must have been very keen. The single opinion delivered on that day was merely a decision involving taxation of the salary of an engineer.[8] It was now the middle of March, and from all outward appearances the Supreme Court was continuing on its way as serene and detached as ever despite the vast pressures being built up by the President's attempt to reform the judiciary. The heaviest artillery the White House could muster was being fired point blank at the nine Justices, and yet all they produced on that March 15 was a single tax opinion.

The next move in the great battle came, surprisingly enough, from Justice McReynolds himself. His college fraternity was Phi Delta Theta, and each year the Washington members of this fraternity renewed old acquaintances at a banquet. Of course, they invited the Justice to attend their annual dinner, which was scheduled for Tuesday, March 16, at the Carlton Hotel. McReynolds actually accepted this invitation, and it was one of the very few invitations he

8. *Brush v. Commissioner of Internal Revenue*, 300 U.S. 352.

did accept during the strenuous weeks of the Court-packing struggle. I do not know whether he had been accustomed to attending other annual fraternity dinners, but he resolved to be present at the 1937 banquet. Naturally it was evident that he would cut quite a figure at this dinner and perhaps be the most distinguished guest present. And he probably expected that he might be called upon to say a few words, but even so he did not dictate any prepared speech to me.

In any event, the Court was in session on Tuesday, March 16. When McReynolds arrived home I did not hear him make any comment to Harry about the impending fraternity dinner. I did some studying that evening for the bar examination and never once thought about the dinner. Just how impressive a figure McReynolds did cut at the banquet, however, was apparent when the newspapers appeared the next day. They carried the startling news that the first [public] statement [by a Supreme Court justice] since Reconstruction Days had unexpectedly been made the evening before by none other than Justice McReynolds while attending a fraternity banquet.

I was considerably surprised when I read the newspaper accounts. The Justice had indeed been called upon to speak, and perhaps he had prefaced his remarks with some general comments about the fraternity. However, he had then changed the subject to a reference to the Supreme Court's struggle with the President. Perhaps a newspaperman was present, or a guest may have taken down the gist of the Justice's comments and reported them to the press. In any event, McReynolds told his fraternity brothers that the life of a judge was not a pleasant one. He said that some attorneys lose cases and then complain about the unfairness of the courts. He believed, however, that when a man had presented a fair case to a fair tribunal he must be a good sport and accept the outcome. Such acceptance was evidence of good sportsmanship. This was, of course, a direct reference to President Roosevelt's refusal to accept the decisions of the Supreme Court in various cases concerning the New Deal. McReynolds' comments were printed in newspapers all over the country,[9] and in two or three days he began to receive letters and postcards—both signed and unsigned—about the subject of sportsmanship.

[By this time] the Senate Judiciary Committee was holding hearings on the proposed court bill. The Committee was composed of some eighteen members—with Senator Henry F. Ashurst of Arizona acting as Chairman.

9. [Editors' note: See the foreword, note 37.]

These hearings had begun on March 10, the day after the President's fireside chat, and Attorney General Cummings was the first witness who testified in favor of the President's proposal. He was followed by Assistant Attorney General Robert H. Jackson. For a week and a half other witnesses favoring the bill also appeared and were closely questioned by the Committee members. On Monday, March 22, however, the first witness in opposition to the plan was scheduled to testify. This was one of the most prominent members of the Senate—Burton K. Wheeler of Montana.

Wheeler and several other opposition senators had already contacted Chief Justice Hughes and inquired if he would consider testifying before the Committee. Hughes, however, declined to appear in person, but he did consent to draft a letter. When the Senator appeared before the Committee the next day he read this letter from the Chief Justice, and its production was a masterly stroke of timing. Hughes very adroitly struck down a number of arguments which had been made by both the President and Cummings. The Chief Justice also pointed out that the Supreme Court was actually abreast of its work, and furthermore that the efficiency of the Court would be lowered if it were enlarged. This letter was so skillfully written that it soon had a marked effect in strengthening growing opposition to the proposed bill—much more so than Justice McReynolds' speech before the fraternity could ever have done. In fact, the letter dealt a devastating blow to the President's proposal. Hughes had, in fact, begun his ultimate triumph over Roosevelt.

I remember vividly those six days which elapsed between McReynolds' comments at the fraternity banquet and Senator Wheeler's statements before the Judiciary Committee. During this period the Justice and I were busily working on a long dissenting opinion which will be mentioned shortly. I was also still trying to attend sessions of the bar review course. I was likewise attempting to accept all of the invitations extended by either Mrs. Savage or her sister.

My frequent meetings with Mrs. Savage, however, had now reached a point where Harry could not remain silent any longer. Once more he solemnly warned me to stay away from her for fear the Justice would learn that I was acquainted with one of his lady friends. However, I refused and told Harry there was no reason why I should decline her invitations. But because of Mrs. Savage's wealth, and the fact that she was a middle-aged widow living alone in a large and elegantly furnished apartment, Harry now became more insistent than ever that I really must be a gigolo after all. He felt that I was either accepting money from her or had even gone further than that. After all, people in Washington were not all lily-white and chaste, even though some of them might pretend to be. And because of my youth I was probably being swayed in the wrong direction.

"Why, Harry Parker!" I replied in real surprise. "How many times do I have to tell you that I am no gigolo! She may be a widow and a wealthy one, but I have never accepted one cent from her. I like her for herself and just as a friend and not for what money I might get out of her. And as for your other suggestion, that is impossible. Mrs. Savage is just trying to make this city a more enjoyable place for me to live in. In fact, someone should put up a monument to her for trying to help secretaries to Justice McReynolds!"

Harry looked very glum but made no reply, and there was never any further mention by him of my friendship with Mrs. Savage. Even though [that friendship] was as unsullied as the driven snow, I was never to know for sure whether Harry really believed this. For weeks it had seemed to him that she must have some ulterior motive back of all the invitations she showered on me. And since I never discussed any Supreme Court problems with her, of course, it was a genuine puzzle to Harry just what this unusual friendship was all about.

More than six weeks had now passed since the President had announced his proposal. To the general public it appeared that the Justices were mighty slow in responding to the fierce attacks upon them. But to the twenty-five people who had advance knowledge of future Supreme Court opinions, it was apparent by Sunday, March 21, that the long-awaited moment of decision was now at hand. Opinions of the greatest importance were either being written or had just been completed, and a number of these decisions would be announced on the next opinion day—Monday, March 29. And once these decisions were made public, they would paralyze the attempts of the White House to secure passage of the proposed Court bill.

First of all, the Supreme Court had actually [voted to] reverse itself on the issue of minimum wages for women. The *Adkins* case—dating from 1923— [was to be] overruled. That case had been a 5-3 decision holding that the Minimum Wage Act of September 19, 1918, was invalid as an unconstitutional interference with the liberty of contract. This Act, which was passed during World War I, fixed minimum wages for adult women engaged in any occupation in the District of Columbia.[10] Now, however, the Court had reversed itself in a 5-4 decision holding that a statute of the State of Washington, which

---

10. *Adkins et al., Constituting the Minimum Wage Board of the District of Columbia v. Children's Hospital of the District of Columbia*, 261 U.S. 525 (1923). Majority opinion by Justice Sutherland. Dissenting opinion by Chief Justice Taft in which Justice Sanford concurred. A second dissent by Justice Holmes. (Justice Brandeis took no part in the consideration or decision of this case.)

set minimum wages for women, was valid. This new case was *West Coast Hotel Co. v. Parrish et al.*[11] The *Adkins* case was finally [to be] overruled and another case distinguished.[12] Chief Justice Hughes [was writing] the majority opinion in the *West Coast Hotel Co.* case, and Justice Sutherland had [responsibility for] the dissent—in which Justices Van Devanter, McReynolds, and Butler concurred.

Two other very important cases were also scheduled to be announced on March 29.[13] One decision would uphold the Railway Labor Act, and the other would approve the revised Frazier-Lemke Farm Mortgage Moratorium Bill. And, surprisingly enough, both of these decisions would be unanimous—with not even McReynolds registering a dissent. The President was indeed due for a real surprise. The Court was at last favoring the New Deal—or so it would appear.

Overshadowing the above cases, however, were the five immensely important Labor Board cases that had been argued before the Justices on February 9, 10, and 11.[14] One of these cases involved the Jones & Laughlin Steel Corporation in its dealings with the National Labor Relations Board, which had been created by the National Labor Relations Act of 1935. The Board had decided that the corporation violated the Act by engaging in unfair labor practices affecting commerce. The company was found to have discriminated against members of a labor union with regard to hire and tenure of employment; also that the company had coerced and intimidated its employees in order to interfere with their self-organization. The Board ordered the corporation to cease this discrimination and coercion, to reinstate ten employees, to make good their losses in pay, and to post for thirty days notices that the company would not discharge or discriminate against any employees who were members of, or who desired to become members of, the labor union in question. The Jones & Laughlin Steel Corporation, however, ignored the orders of

11. 300 U.S. 379 (1937).

12. *Morehead v. New York ex rel. Tipaldo*, 298 U.S. 587 (1936).

13. *Virginian Railway Co. v. System Federation No. 40, Railway Employees Department of the American Federation of Labor et al.*, 300 U.S. 515 (1937); *Wright v. Vinton Branch of the Mountain Trust Bank of Roanoke et al.*, 300 U.S. 440 (1937).

14. *National Labor Relations Board v. Jones & Laughlin Steel Corp.*, 301 U.S. 1 (1937); *National Labor Relations Board v. Fruehauf Trailer Co.*, 301 U.S. 49 (1937); *National Labor Relations Board v. Friedman-Harry Marks Clothing Co.*, 301 U.S. 58 (1937); *Associated Press v. National Labor Relations Board*, 301 U.S. 103 (1937); *Washington, Virginia & Maryland Coach Co. v. National Labor Relations Board*, 301 U.S. 142 (1937).

the newly created National Labor Relations Board. The Board then petitioned the Circuit Court of Appeals to enforce the order of compliance. The Circuit Court denied the petition and held that the Board's order lay beyond the range of federal power. The Supreme Court of the United States granted certiorari and heard arguments in the case. Previous opinions of the Supreme Court indicated that production was a purely local matter—whether in mining, manufacturing, or agriculture. The government, however, contended that the Steel Corporation's production was national in scope, subject to federal regulation, and that the Court should discard its earlier doctrines.

The four other Labor Board cases concerned the Fruehauf Trailer Company, the Friedman-Harry Marks Clothing Company, the Associated Press, and the Washington, Virginia & Maryland Coach Company. All five cases related to the question whether the National Labor Relations Act of 1935 (also known as the Wagner Act) was or was not constitutional. The Court's decision would be of great importance to the entire nation.

When McReynolds arrived home from conference on the Saturday that the vote was taken, he made no mention of the National Labor Relations Act when he handed me the big red book. After he walked to his office I opened the book and noticed that all nine Justices had been present at the conference and that the decision had been 5 to 4 to sustain the Act. As I locked the covers of the book together before putting it away in my desk, I could not help but agree with the decision of the five majority Justices. I had read the briefs carefully and felt that the power of the federal government extended, for instance, to the Steel Corporation. The four conservative Justices had voted otherwise, but they failed to win over Justice Roberts to their side. This meant a severe defeat for the conservatives, but McReynolds made no mention of it. He remained quietly in his office and did not ring for me. I left the apartment shortly after Harry called him to dinner, and I said goodbye to the Justice as he sat alone in the dining room. He responded but did not look up from the table.

The Chief Justice decided to write the majority opinion in the *Jones & Laughlin* case, in the *Fruehauf* case, and in the *Friedman-Harry Marks* case. Justice Roberts, who had deserted the four conservatives, was designated by the Chief Justice to write the majority opinion in the *Associated Press* case and in the *Washington, Virginia & Maryland* case.[15] Soon both Hughes and Roberts were busily at work. The Chief Justice began composing a majestic draft

---

15. At this time the Constitution was just about what Justice Roberts said it was. He held the balance of power between the two rival Court factions—each composed of four Justices.

of his three opinions—the proofs of which he circulated to the other eight Justices. Roberts also sent proofs of his two opinions to the other members of the Court. Hughes reviewed the facts, examined the constitutional arguments, launched into a discussion of the interstate commerce clause and its applicability to the Jones & Laughlin Steel Corporation, and finally declared in favor of labor regulation by the federal government [through] a new interpretation of the commerce clause. He discarded the earlier doctrines of the Court and decided in favor of the New Deal.

The senior dissenting Justice was Van Devanter, and it was his obligation to determine which one of the conservatives would be assigned to write the dissent or dissents in four of the five cases. (The *Washington, Virginia & Maryland* case was a unanimous opinion so no dissent was required.) I gave no particular thought to the matter one way or the other and assumed that Sutherland would be assigned to write whatever dissenting opinions might be necessary. He was a good reliable wheel horse who could always be depended upon in an emergency. It never occurred to me that Van Devanter might select McReynolds as well as Sutherland, but this is exactly what he did. McReynolds, in fact, was chosen to write a dissent which would apply to three of the cases: *Jones & Laughlin, Fruehauf,* and *Friedman-Harry Marks.* Sutherland, on the other hand, was to write the dissent in the *Associated Press* case.

When McReynolds was informed of Van Devanter's decision I was astounded, and it was evident that the Justice himself was considerably disgruntled. The news that he had been selected as the white hope of the conservatives was just about the last thing he wanted to hear. It would have to be a very lengthy opinion. The writing of it would be very arduous and time consuming as the dissent would be an immensely important one. It would be, in effect, the swan song of the four conservative members of the Court. Composing it would mean hours and hours of work which McReynolds had not been planning on doing. But Van Devanter soon made it clear that he would assist McReynolds and, in fact, the four conservatives eventually decided to hold conferences in McReynolds' apartment.

And so work on the great dissent began, but McReynolds moved like a dinosaur while Hughes and Roberts were busily at work on their majority opinions. Hughes finished his three, Roberts completed his two, all five opinions were circulated, and the Labor cases were ready to be announced as far as the five majority Justices were concerned. Sutherland then concluded his dissent, and the cases could have been read from the bench at the March 29 opinion day had Justice McReynolds completed his assignment. But unfortunately his dissent was far from ready. Finally one of the Chief Justice's law clerks telephoned me at a time when McReynolds happened to be out of the apartment. "Say, when are you going to finish that dissent?" I was abruptly asked. "The Chief completed his opinions days ago, and you have the final drafts. What is holding up your Justice? Can't you get those four fellows together long enough to decide what to say?"

"Just give us time," I replied. "Just give us time. After all, Rome was not built in a day." Or perhaps I should have said "unbuilt."

The whole nation was now anxiously awaiting the decision in the Labor Board cases, and the fact that McReynolds had not completed his assignment was delaying the entire proceedings. He had burned the preliminary drafts of Hughes', Roberts', and Sutherland's opinions, but he did not destroy their final drafts, which had been printed by Mr. Bright. Yet McReynolds did not want to keep these drafts in his desk for fear Harry or Mary might find them. He just did not trust them and felt there would be a fearful scandal if any leak in information developed. Nor did he wish me to keep the drafts in my desk. Finally McReynolds handed the drafts to me and said, "Here, see that they are hidden away where no one can ever find them!"

I wrapped the opinions in a piece of brown paper and carried them to my room at 2700 Connecticut Avenue, N.W. I hid them in the closet among my belongings. Not even the maid who cleaned my room ever disturbed anything in that closet. And there the opinions rested—for days and days—while the whole country waited for the Court's decision in the Labor Board cases, and while McReynolds fumed and the four conservatives continued to hold conferences about what should be said in the dissent.

All day Tuesday, March 23, McReynolds and I worked on the dissent. On Wednesday, Justice Van Devanter arrived at McReynolds' apartment to discuss the dissent in more detail. And at 8:30 that evening I called at Justice Cardozo's for another visit with him. No other person was in the apartment at the time, as far as I knew, and Cardozo answered the doorbell himself. We talked for an hour, but there was no mention of McReynolds or of the Supreme Court or even of the labor cases. We merely chatted about the latest books, literature in general and of his early experiences.

Events [then] began to happen so fast that it would lengthen this book unduly to review them in detail. [The] three other conservative Justices came to McReynolds' apartment and held another conference. Each one arrived separately and was solemnly ushered into the living room by Harry, who then disappeared into the kitchen. Once all four Justices were assembled together, Van Devanter, Sutherland, and Butler each contributed something to the conversation in an effort to help McReynolds with his dissenting opinion. No one, however, led the discussion. There was no argument, and all statements were made in solemn tones. Without doubt the four Justices were in agreement on what to say, but the problem was just how to say it. The dissent would have to come right to the point and show how obviously wrong the other five Justices were in their views. And from the discussion I gathered that McReynolds and I would have to spend considerably more time working on the dissent. The *Adkins* case would be overruled on March 29. McReynolds' dissent would have to be completed shortly thereafter as the Court would be busy hearing arguments in other cases. Besides, the Chief Justice was waiting.

When the conservatives held their conferences in McReynolds' living room, it was natural that I felt a bit privileged to be the only other person present—even though I was not in the same room with them and was certainly not invited to take any part in the discussions. I was, however, witnessing the end of an era in the law and the death of an entire way of thinking. Never again would the views of Van Devanter, McReynolds, Sutherland, and Butler prevail in the Supreme Court of the United States. America was indeed at a turn in the road.

The conservatives felt that the various orders of the National Labor Relations Board in these cases clearly lay beyond the range of federal power. They were sure that the power of Congress under the commerce clause did not extend to relations between employers and employees who were engaged in mere manufacturing. Therefore, Hughes' opinions were contrary to established legal precedents and would have the gravest effects upon multitudes of employers who were engaged in a variety of private enterprises. Congress had no power to authorize by statute what the Labor Board was commanding these companies to do. A three-man Board had been illegally given vast powers over purely local industries. The Tenth Amendment to the Constitution recognized the existence of states with indestructible powers, and the Board's orders went far beyond permissible constitutional limitations. In fact, the Board was attempting to manage the internal affairs of manufacturing plants—which was something distinct from commerce and not subject to state authority. This could not be done because of some vague possibility of distant interference with commerce. In other words, the right to contract was fundamental and included "the privilege of selecting those with whom one is willing to assume contractual relations." [16] Private manufacturing plants such as these could not be deprived of the right to manage their own properties by

16. [Editors' note: See 301 U.S. at 103.]

freely selecting employees agreeable to them. The National Labor Relations Act violated this right, and Congress had exceeded the powers granted it in the Constitution. The Act should, therefore, be declared unconstitutional. It was, in fact, unthinkable to believe otherwise.

I heard no mention of the name of Roberts or any comment about that Justice aligning himself with the so-called liberal wing of the Court. And when the conference ended I noticed that Van Devanter, Sutherland, and Butler left together. McReynolds ushered them down the long hall to the door of his apartment and then returned to his study. He immediately began work again on the dissent and soon rang for me. Following this latest conference with the three other conservatives, the "paste and shears" method of writing was to be resorted to. In other words, McReynolds now announced that we were to quote verbatim the three opinions of the lower courts instead of summarizing them in his own language.[17] I was, in fact, to cut these opinions out of the briefs and paste them on our latest proof so as to avoid any error in typing. (No such error had occurred as far as I knew.)

The cutting and pasting was done. The Justice then dictated changes in other paragraphs, and gradually a new draft of the opinion was developed. By now the dissent was in nine separate sections, and each section was numbered. McReynolds, of course, dictated whatever went into his dissent. I merely typed his dictation and contributed nothing to the substance of the opinion. Nor did I attempt to. In the first place, I would not have had the opportunity to do so, and in the second place I agreed with the five majority Justices that the National Labor Relations Act should be declared constitutional. Of course, McReynolds did not know of my views in this matter.

As the days went by, McReynolds continued to labor on the dissent—dictating, revising my typing, dictating again, and revising again. And I was, as far as I knew, still operating as an efficient secretary and law clerk—despite the late hours that I had been keeping. The duties of the job had now become so routine that I almost never made an error either in taking dictation or in transcribing my shorthand notes. And on straight copy work of material that had already been typed and then revised by the Justice in ink, I could retype it at one hundred words a minute if need be. I was also never late to work in the morning, and I never left early at the end of the day. I had not been ill since

17. (1) The opinion handed down on June 15, 1936, by the Circuit Court of Appeals (Fifth Circuit). See 83 F. 2d 998; (2) The opinion handed down on June 30, 1936, by the Circuit Court of Appeals (Sixth Circuit). See 85 F. 2d 391; (3) The opinion handed down on July 13, 1936, by the Circuit Court of Appeals (Second Circuit). See 85 F. 2d 1.

catching cold at the January inaugural ceremonies and had not missed any time from work since then. And during the day I did not leave the apartment without permission unless McReynolds happened to be away, too, and I always tried to be back before his expected return. I also kept my conversation at a minimum and seldom spoke unless spoken to. In short, I had now become little more than a machine and an efficient one at that.

Occasionally, however, I actually did have some "brain" work to do. Petitions for certiorari, of course, were being received all during the term of court. I enjoyed reading them, reviewing the briefs, and then summarizing the arguments in one page of typing—concluding with my recommendation either to deny or allow. If several petitions arrived in the morning delivery from Court, for instance, my typed summaries would generally be on the Justice's desk shortly after lunch on the same day—except during the weeks we were working on the dissent in the Labor cases.

Despite all this effort, however, the gradual deterioration in my position as a law clerk continued. It was as if the very floor were slowly slipping out from under me—try as I might to prevent it. I kept reminding myself that, after all, I really did like the work itself. I was also in an extremely favorable position to watch at close range the continued progress of the battle between the President and the Court. But the difficulty was that I had by now simply lost all interest in the Justice as a man. I had finally come to realize that we were light years apart in our ways of thinking and in reacting to people—even though we worked together each day in close surroundings and in ostensible harmony. And being human I now began to feel sorry for myself. I kept thinking about Harold Leventhal and envying him his work with a Justice like Harlan Fiske Stone. "Now why can't my Justice be a little more like Stone?" I kept asking myself. But all this was merely wishful thinking for there was never the slightest "improvement" in McReynolds.

On the evening of Thursday, March 25, I managed to attend another session of the bar review course. However, by now I was no longer making any real effort to do the assigned reading, and I realized that I had long since fallen behind in my attempts to keep abreast with the class. Nevertheless I still felt that I could pass the June District of Columbia bar examination without much difficulty.

The next day was Good Friday, and that evening I [went to a] a movie and [then enjoyed] a midnight supper. And just as I had expected, the Justice decided not to work [that] Saturday, but to spend part of Easter Sunday laboring on the dissent. As a result, after being at his apartment for the usual time on Saturday, I also reported for work at 9:30 A.M. on Sunday. McReynolds dictated and then revised my typing until 2:30 P.M. At that time, however, he adjourned for lunch and said I could leave and need not return. I walked over to Eighteenth and Columbia Road, ate lunch myself, and caught a streetcar downtown. It was a lonely Easter. "Either Pussywillow just cannot work any faster or else he is deliberately stalling to delay the announcement of the majority opinions," I thought. But then I decided that even he would not dare to institute a slow-down in view of the Chief Justice's anxiety to announce the majority opinions to an expectant public. However, as of today I am not so sure.

Then came Monday, March 29, the eleventh opinion day of the term. I asked McReynolds if I could drive to Court with him, and without any protest at all he said I could. [At Court were] hundreds of people milling about in the main hall of the building—all seeking to enter the Courtroom itself. I later learned that a total of eleven thousand persons [had] jammed into the building on that day. I could, in fact, scarcely make my way through the crowd. Eventually, however, I located Harry, and as usual he had saved a choice seat for me.

Promptly on the stroke of twelve there was the usual rustle of robes, and the nine Justices appeared once more from behind the great curtains at the rear of the room. A warning gavel was suddenly rapped for silence, and everyone present stood up. Mr. Frank Key Green, the Marshal of the Court, cried out in his loud and clear voice, "Oyez, Oyez, Oyez! All persons having business before the Honorable, the Supreme Court of the United States are admonished to draw near and give their attention, for the Court is now sitting. God save the United States and this Honorable Court."

The sound of the gavel was then heard again. Everyone quietly sat down, and the Justices—dressed in their traditional black gowns—solemnly took their seats, too. As I watched the proceedings, the Chief Justice straightened up slowly in his chair, leaned forward, looked very intently at the people seated directly in front of him. A moment before he began to speak I thought to myself, "Well, today is the day for the *Adkins* case to be overruled, and what a surprise that will be for some people! But it is only the beginning—only the beginning!"

11

⁓⁓⁓⁓

THE CHIEF JUSTICE appeared as a towering figure that day, and it was also soon evident that he was a man with a purpose. He resembled the captain of a great ocean liner trying to save his ship in a sudden storm by turning it around as rapidly as possible and following another course. Had he not be able to do so at the eleventh hour, [thanks to Justice Roberts' alignment with the four liberal Justices in a number of important cases,] the Court as it was then constituted might well have foundered in the hurricane caused by the President's proposal.

A great moment in American judicial history was at hand. Seventeen opinions were waiting to be read. After Hughes had made the usual preliminary announcements, Justice Cardozo—the junior Justice in point of service—began reading first. In ill health and destined to serve on the Court for only a few months more, the great Jewish jurist read his four opinions in a shy and almost diffident manner but in a voice that could be clearly heard throughout the Courtroom. *Highland Farms Dairy, Inc. et al. v. Agnew et al.,* [Cardozo's fourth case, was a 5-4 decision in which] the Justices had considered the question of whether the Virginia Milk and Cream Act was constitutional.[1] This Act created a commission with power to establish market areas within the state and to determine, after hearing, the need for regulation of milk and cream prices within each area. If satisfied of the need, the Commission could also fix prices accordingly. Cardozo held that there was no basis under the federal Constitution or under the Constitution of Virginia for objecting that this Act was an unconstitutional delegation of legislative power. He

---

1. 300 U.S. 608.

felt that the State of Virginia could fix a minimum price for milk and cream in order to save producers, and with them the consuming public, from a practice of price cutting which was so destructive as to endanger the supply. The price-fixing and licensing provisions of the Act would not apply, however, to transactions in interstate commerce. Sales would not be affected by any restriction as to price unless made within the boundaries of a designated market area in the State of Virginia.

This case was, in short, the first indication that day that the Supreme Court was now changing course. At the end of the opinion, however, there followed a terse paragraph stating that Justices Van Devanter, McReynolds, Sutherland, and Butler did not assent to that portion of the opinion which attributed to the State of Virginia the power to fix minimum and maximum prices to be charged for the sale of milk and cream. These four dissenting Justices based their views on what had already been said in their behalf by Justice McReynolds [dissenting] in the 1934 case of *Nebbia v. People of the State of New York*.[2]

It was then Justice Roberts' turn. He had only one opinion but it concerned an important question of federal criminal law which had never before been settled by the Supreme Court. Did retraction neutralize false testimony previously given and thus exculpate the witness of perjury? In an interesting decision concerning a Resolution of the United States Senate, Justice Roberts held that a witness who commits willful perjury in violation of the federal Criminal Code cannot purge himself of the offense by appearing at a later stage of the inquiry and recanting his false testimony.[3]

[Following Justice Roberts, Justice Stone read three opinions, the last of which] was of national importance. It concerned not only the constitutionality of certain provisions of the Railway Labor Act of May 20, 1926, as amended by the Act of June 21, 1934, but also relating to the nature and extent of the relief which the courts were authorized by the Act to give.[4] The railroad in this case was a common carrier, a public utility, and Stone held in a lengthy opinion that the Railway Labor Act may, among other things, be applied constitutionally to cover persons employed in the "back shops" of a carrier even though such persons are not themselves engaged in interstate commerce. "Back shop" employees were engaged in heavy repairs on both locomotives

2. 291 U.S. 502 at 539–559 (1934).

3. *United States v. Norris*, 300 U.S. 564.

4. *Virginian Railway Co. v. System Federation No. 40, Railway Employees Department of the American Federation of Labor, et al.*, 300 U.S. 515.

and cars withdrawn from service for long periods of time. Their duties bore such a relation to the interstate activities of the railroad as to be regarded as part of them—all subject to the power of Congress over interstate commerce. The Act, therefore, required the railroad to "treat with" the authorized representative of such employees, to meet and confer with him, to listen to the employees' complaints, and to make a reasonable effort to compose differences. This duty to treat with such a representative was enforceable by injunction.

One could have heard a pin drop in the Courtroom that day when Justice Stone arrived at the climax of this opinion and announced that the Act was indeed constitutional. The Chief Justice had by then quietly leaned back in his chair, and as I studied him closely I noticed a barely perceptible smile on his face. It was one of those never-to-be-forgotten moments in time. And strangely enough, this was a unanimous decision. Not even McReynolds had ventured to file a dissent.

Pierce Butler was the next Justice to speak, with one opinion to read.[5] He looked just as sour and forbidding as ever. The government, he announced with a grim expression, was seeking to tax certain alleged income of an oil company. In a lengthy decision which would later fill seventeen pages in the official volume of Supreme Court reports, the Justice held that no tax was due. It was evident that Butler had worked a long time in writing this opinion. This tax case, in fact, may very well have been the reason why Justice Van Devanter had not assigned Butler to write any part of the dissent in the Labor cases. A battery of prominent attorneys had appeared in the case, and Butler undoubtedly had enough to keep himself busy in writing this one opinion. The oil company's position, for instance, had been argued before the Court by Mr. John W. Davis of New York—the 1924 Democratic candidate for the Presidency. Davis was the senior partner of a prominent New York law firm. He was also a friend of Justice McReynolds. He had, in fact, called at 2400 on one of his trips to Washington, and much to my surprise McReynolds had introduced me to him. Davis was the only guest McReynolds ever introduced me to during the entire time I was in Washington.

[After Justice Sutherland finished reading his two opinions, both of minor importance,][6] Justice Brandeis slowly straightened up in his chair. Eighty years of age but still at the height of his mental powers, the Justice had only

---

5. *Helvering, Commissioner of Internal Revenue v. Tex-Penn Oil Co.,* 300 U.S. 481.

6. *Atchison, Topeka & Santa Fe Railway Co. v. Scarlett,* 300 U.S. 471; *American Propeller & Manufacturing Co. v. United States,* 300 U.S. 475.

one opinion to read. It was an important one, however, and like Butler's single opinion it, too, would fill seventeen pages when printed in the official volume of Supreme Court reports.[7] In this case Brandeis upheld the constitutionality of the revised Frazier-Lemke Mortgage Moratorium Act, and the decision was unanimous. The exact question for consideration was whether Section 75, subsection (s), of the Bankruptcy Act, as amended by the new Frazier-Lemke Act of August 28, 1935, was constitutional. The Justice stated that the language of the Act was not free from doubt and that he had sought further enlightenment from reading reports of congressional committees and explanations given on the floor of the Senate and House by those in charge of the measure. When the legislative history of the bill was thus surveyed, Brandeis concluded that the revised Act was constitutional. It was obvious that the Justice and his law clerk had done considerable research before writing this learned opinion. And while Brandeis was reading it in a clear voice that carried to all parts of the Courtroom, the Chief Justice occupied himself by looking very intently at the people assembled in front of him—glancing carefully from one side of the room to the other.

After Brandeis finished reading, [McReynolds gave] three opinions, but they were short and of minor importance. In fact, I was almost ashamed for "my Justice" to read such insignificant opinions in the midst of the great Court-packing controversy. When printed in the official volume of Supreme Court reports, all three cases would occupy less than twelve pages.[8] There were no dissents to the three opinions.

The next Justice to read was Van Devanter. It was well known that he had great difficulty in expressing himself in writing, and he had only one opinion to read. It would, in fact, have been almost unthinkable for him to deliver two opinions on the same day. [His opinion disposed of] an involved and dull case which appeared to be of little interest to the persons present.[9] There was also a one-sentence dissent, which had been filed by the Chief Justice and by Justice Cardozo, and it was noted that Justice Stone had not participated in the consideration or decision of the case.

7. *Wright v. Vinton Branch of the Mountain Trust Bank of Roanoke et al.*, 300 U.S. 440.

8. *Matos v. Alonso Hermanos et al.*, 300 U.S. 429; *General Banking Co. v. Harr, Secretary of Banking of Pennsylvania et al.*, 300 U.S. 433; *Stroehmann et al. v. Mutual Life Insurance Company of New York*, 300 U.S. 435.

9. *Dugas v. American Surety Co.*, 300 U.S. 414.

Only the Chief Justice remained to be heard from. Hughes leaned forward and picked up his single opinion. "This case," he said, "presents the question of the constitutional validity of the minimum wage law of the State of Washington." [10] With this single statement Hughes immediately recaptured the attention of the audience, which Van Devanter had almost completely lost. Hughes then raised his head and looked at the audience for a moment or two before glancing back at the sheets he held in his hand. As he continued to read I carefully watched the reaction of the attorneys who were seated in the front of the room. They did not move a muscle, and their attention was riveted on the Chief Justice.

The first minimum wage law which the Court had declared unconstitutional was that of the District of Columbia in 1923 in the *Adkins* case. [11] The Court invalidated a similar Arizona law in 1925, an Arkansas law in 1927, and a New York law in 1936. [12] In the New York case the decision had been 5 to 4 with Justice Roberts siding with the conservatives. The latest controversy to reach the Court was now the *Parrish* case, and it too was a 5-4 decision. However, Justice Roberts had now transferred his allegiance to the four liberal Justices. Because of this change in Roberts' vote, Hughes was ready to announce that the Supreme Court had finally reversed itself upon the very important subject of minimum wages for women.

A chambermaid by the name of Mrs. Elsie Parrish, a grandmother at thirty-seven, had sued the Cascadian Hotel of Wenatchee, Washington, for $216.19 in wages due her under the minimum wage law of that State. This sum represented the difference between the wages paid her and the minimum wage fixed pursuant to the State law. Her own minimum wage was $14.50 for a work week of forty-eight hours.

At one time or another some fifteen states had passed minimum wage laws for women or children or both. Laundry workers, for instance, were among the most earnest advocates of minimum wage legislation. Many women known as "feeders" were employed to feed wet clothes through ironing machines. If these women worked for a union shop they received at least

---

10. *West Coast Hotel Co. v. Parrish et al.,* 300 U.S. 379.

11. *Adkins et al., Constituting the Minimum Wage Board of the District of Columbia v. Children's Hospital of the District of Columbia,* 261 U.S. 525 (1923).

12. *Murphy v. Sardell,* 269 U.S. 530 (1925); *Donhan v. West-Nelson Co.,* 273 U.S. 657 (1927); and *Morehead v. New York ex rel. Tipaldo,* 298 U.S. 587 (1936).

$14.00 a week. Non-union feeders, however, earned as low as $6.00 a week. The messiest job in laundrying was starching. This was generally done by women of middle age or older. While the New York minimum wage law was in effect, all starchers received at least $12.40 a week. When, however, the law was invalidated in June 1936, in the *Morehead* case, the wages of these women dropped to as low as $6.00 a week. A question of vast social implications was, therefore, involved in the *Parrish* case. Only the change in Justice Roberts' vote had saved the Washington statute from also being declared unconstitutional.

Chief Justice Hughes continued reading:

[W]hat can be closer to the public interest than the health of women and their protection from unscrupulous and overreaching employers? And if the protection of women is a legitimate end of the exercise of state power, how can it be said that the requirement of the payment of a minimum wage fairly fixed in order to meet the very necessities of existence is not an admissible means to that end? The legislature of the State was clearly entitled to consider the situation of women in employment. . . . The legislature had the right to consider that its minimum wage requirements would be an important aid in carrying out its policy of protection. The adoption of similar requirements by many States evidences a deep-seated conviction both as to the presence of the evil and as to the means adapted to check it. Legislative response to that conviction cannot be regarded as arbitrary or capricious, and that is all we have to decide. Even if the wisdom of the policy be regarded as debatable and its effects uncertain, still the legislature is entitled to its judgment.

There is an additional and compelling consideration which recent economic experience has brought into a strong light. The exploitation of a class of workers who are in an unequal position with respect to bargaining power and are thus relatively defenseless against the denial of a living wage is not only detrimental to their health and well being but casts a direct burden for their support upon the community. What these workers lose in wages the taxpayers are called upon to pay. The bare cost of living must be met. We may take judicial notice of the unparalleled demands for relief which arose during the period of depression and still continue to an alarming extent despite the degree of economic recovery which has been achieved. It is unnecessary to cite official statistics to establish what is common knowledge through the length and breadth of the land. While in the instant case no factual brief has been presented, there is no reason to doubt that the State of Washington has encountered the same social problem that is present elsewhere.[13]

By now the Chief Justice's eyes were flashing and his voice was booming. He read a few more sentences and concluded that *"Adkins v. Children's Hospital, supra,* should be, and it is, overruled."

It was done, and the Court had reversed itself at last on the question of minimum wages for women. Charles Evans Hughes leaned back in his chair and carefully appraised the audience for a moment or two before glancing to his left where Justice Sutherland was sitting. That Justice was now prepared to read his dissent. He first looked at the people directly in front of him in a calm and almost detached manner and then casually picked up his opinion and began reading. When Sutherland was on the bench, he always appeared to be the very model of a comfortable and secure English gentleman. In fact, he had been born in England in the same year as Hughes and McReynolds. How long ago it now was—1862—and his quiet voice, which also could be easily heard throughout the Courtroom—was now the voice of the "old" Supreme Court—the "conservative wing" which had lost its power forever: "Mr. Justice Van Devanter, Mr. Justice McReynolds, Mr. Justice Butler, and I think the judgment of the court below should be reversed." With this statement Sutherland began reading the dissent, which when published in the official Supreme Court reports would fill more than thirteen pages:

> The principles and authorities relied upon to sustain the judgment were considered in *Adkins v. Children's Hospital,* 261 U.S. 525, and *Morehead v. New York ex rel. Tipaldo,* 298 U.S. 587, and their lack of application to cases like the one in hand was pointed out. A sufficient answer to all that is now said will be found in the opinions of the court in those cases. Nevertheless, in the circumstances, it seems well to restate our reasons and conclusions.
>
> Under our form of government, where the written Constitution, by its own terms is the supreme law, some agency, of necessity, must have the power to say the final word as to the validity of a statute assailed as unconstitutional. The Constitution makes it clear that the power has been intrusted to this court when the question arises in a controversy within its jurisdiction; and so long as the power remains there, its exercise cannot be avoided without betrayal of the trust.[14]

13. 300 U.S. 398–400.

14. [Editors' note: 300 U.S. at 401.]

[He turned to the statute in question, found it wanting, and concluded:] "A more complete discussion may be found in the *Adkins* and *Tipaldo* cases cited *supra.*"

With this statement Justice Sutherland slowly placed the dissenting opinion on the dais in front of him, and with a grim expression he leaned back in his chair.[15] The conservative wing of the Supreme Court of the United States had spoken for the last time concerning minimum wage laws for women. Hughes adjourned the session for lunch, and the audience filed out of the Courtroom into a very crowded lobby. [During lunch] I weighed in my mind the President's attempt to pack the Court as against the merits of the four conservative Justices. "Of course, I cannot agree with Roosevelt, but how immovable these four men must be in conferences!" I thought to myself. "They are all former corporation lawyers who met with success in the old laissez-faire days, and their philosophy dates back to the Civil War." Yet I could not forget that the Chief Justice was also the same age as McReynolds and Sutherland, and Brandeis—another "liberal"—was older than any member of the Court.

Each of the conservatives was at the time receiving an annual salary of $20,000.00, while some of the women who were working in laundries—without the benefit of a minimum wage law—had been laboring for as little as $6.00 a week. This amounted to a grand total of $312.00 a year if one were paid for all fifty-two weeks.[16] A tide of sit-down strikes was also beginning to flood the country, and employers themselves had been staging another sit-down against the National Labor Relations Act. Yet for all practical purposes the four conservatives still remained immovable and aloof to changing

15. During the reading of his dissent, Justice Sutherland is supposed to have "pounded on the dais" at least once. However, I do not recall his doing so, nor did I make any mention of it in my diary. On the other hand, my gaze may have been elsewhere in the Courtroom at the time. [Editors' note: According to Franklyn Waltman's by-lined story in the *Washington Post,* Sutherland "rapp[ed] his knuckles on the desk before him to emphasize his words." (Supreme Court Upholds Minimum Wage, 5-4, in Dramatic Overruling of Former Decisions, March 30, 1937, p.1.) Waltman also reported that Sutherland's "remarks quickly captured the attention of spectators who had become restless on completion of the majority opinion. They seemed to annoy Justice Roberts, who several times glanced in the direction of Justice Sutherland and then held a handkerchief to his lips." Id. at 8. Either due to discretion or distraction, Knox failed to report what the *Chicago Tribune* highlighted in the sixth paragraph of its lead story on the decisions: "Mr. Justice McReynolds . . . refused to stay on the bench and hear the majority opinion read today. He left just before the chief justice began reading." Chesly Manly, "Uphold Three New Deal Acts," March 30, 1937, p. 1.]

16. Even with the protection of the minimum wage law, Mrs. Parrish, for example, expected to receive only $14.50 a week, or a total of $753.00 for fifty-two weeks.

conditions—even to Roosevelt's landslide victory at the polls in the fall of 1936. I could now understand why McReynolds had given his maid only a two-dollar monthly increase in salary. If he had felt this way toward someone with whom he was in intimate and daily contact, why should the plight of laundry workers whom he had never even seen be of any interest to him?

Of course, the newspapers gave much publicity to the overruling of the *Adkins* case, and on the surface it did appear that the Court had actually reversed itself because of the pressure of outside influences. Even the President himself concluded that this might have been the case.[17]

Was the President correct in his conclusions? Did the Court, for instance, overrule the *Adkins* case because of the pressure of outside influences? The answer is no.

It is true that the *opinion* in *West Coast Hotel Co. v. Parrish et al.* was handed down at the height of the Court-packing controversy. However, *arguments* in this case were heard on December 16 and 17, 1936, at a time when Justice Stone was ill. Eight Justices were at the Saturday conference when the *vote* was taken, and it was 4 to 4. The date of this tie vote was apparently Saturday, December 19—long before the President's proposal of February 5. Hughes then temporarily shelved the case to await Stone's return to work. The situation [was later] described in a well-known biography of the Chief Justice.[18]

It is evident, therefore, that the *West Coast Hotel Co.* case was neither the result of the November election returns nor of the February 5th proposal of the President. It is true, however, that the four other important opinions which were also announced on March 29 were cases that had been argued and voted upon *after* February 5.[19] Yet all nine Justices were men of such pronounced individuality and honesty that it can certainly be assumed their decisions were in no way influenced by the election returns or by the President's proposal.

When Court adjourned on March 29, Justice McReynolds arrived home soon after I reached his apartment. The dissent in the Labor cases demanded his immediate attention despite the fact that he had spent a strenuous day

17. *The Public Papers and Addresses of Franklin D. Roosevelt, 1937: The Constitution Prevails* (New York: Macmillan, 1941), 66–68.

18. Merlo J. Pusey, *Charles Evans Hughes*, vol. 2 (New York: Macmillan, 1951), 757–758.

19. The *Virginian Railway Co.* case (Stone) was argued on February 8 and 9, and the *Wright* case (Brandeis) on March 3 and 4. The *Highland Farms Dairy* case (Cardozo) was argued on March 8 and 9, and [*Sonzinsky v. United States*, 300 U.S. 506] (Stone) on March 12. [*Sonzinsky* unanimously upheld an annual license tax imposed upon firearms dealers by Congress in the National Firearms Act of June 26, 1934.]

at Court. He therefore assembled the latest galley sheets sent him from the printer, and ate a hurried dinner. At 6:00 Justice Van Devanter arrived once again to discuss the wording of the opinion. This was my cue to bow out of the picture, and by 7:00 I was at Mrs. Savage's apartment on the floor above to attend a dinner for a half-dozen guests. The evening proved very enjoyable, and I remained until 11:00 P.M.

The next opinion day was scheduled for Monday, April 5, but it was apparent that McReynolds' dissent would not be ready by then. The Chief Justice had already been informed of the continued delay, and Monday, April 12, had therefore been set as the date when the decisions in the Labor cases would positively be announced. This date now began to appear on the latest proofs received from the Supreme Court printer, and it meant that the final deadline for last-minute changes would be Saturday, April 10. In fact, the delay gave Hughes an opportunity to make a [minor] change in one of his opinions.

Despite the pressure now being built up to finish the dissent, the four conservative Justices still could not agree on the exact wording of the opinion. When it had first been assigned to McReynolds, he had dawdled along as if in a fit of resentment. Now, however, time was closing in on him, and he found himself in a very unenviable position.[20] He would, in fact, have to curtail all social activities even though they had been very limited of late. I decided to do the same—without McReynolds requesting it—and I remained at his apartment on Wednesday and Thursday evenings (March 31 and April 1) to type and take more dictation. All day Saturday was also devoted to more typing and revisions. Mrs. Savage had again invited me to dinner that evening, but I canceled plans to attend without giving her a specific reason why.

On Sunday, April 4, I was at McReynolds' apartment from 10:00 A.M. until 4:00 P.M. I then took a cab to the Pearson Printing Company, where Mr. Bright was patiently waiting for me. I handed him the latest revisions and remained at his office until 5:00 P.M. By now McReynolds' tardiness in completing his opinion was not only causing the Chief Justice acute inconvenience, but it was also forcing the Supreme Court printer to open up his office

---

20. He was also still receiving [severely critical] letters and postcards [though I continued to keep the postcards from him]. [Editors' note: Perhaps as a response to his critics, McReynolds wrote a friend in Santa Barbara and allowed part of the somewhat cryptic contents to be made public: "Against my inclinations to seek freedom from the incessant demands on my time and strength, it is not my purpose at present to retire from the bench in the immediate future. But the situation is a very grave one and, unless the public demands another course, there is not much to hope for—according to our standards." "McReynolds Tells Friend He Intends to Stay on Bench," *Washington Post*, April 3, 1937, p. 1.

to work on a Sunday. But Mr. Bright, as usual, made no complaint. He was not only a dedicated employee of the Court but had undoubtedly labored on many a Sunday in the past to meet important deadlines. "We're on the home stretch now," I told him, "and the dissent should be finished in plenty of time for April 12."

"That's good," Mr. Bright replied. "You will receive copies the first thing Monday morning to circulate to Van Devanter, Sutherland, and Butler."

At this stage of the proceedings the dissent was still being printed on galley sheets, which measured seven inches in width and twenty-three inches in length. At the top of the first sheet was listed the day on which it was printed in order to avoid confusion with other proofs. Most of these sheets were destroyed by Justice McReynolds as soon as new proofs arrived from Mr. Bright's office. However, I did manage to salvage a number of sheets—there being so many—and these I still have.[21] They apparently are the only remaining clues as to just how the dissent was written as I presume the other three conservative Justices also destroyed their copies.

On Monday, April 5, McReynolds consented to drive me to Court again, and I very much appreciated his doing so. There was, of course, a great crowd in the building, and those who gained access to the Courtroom that day must have been considerably disappointed as only one opinion was handed down. This was a case of Justice Stone's in which McReynolds had written a short dissent.[22] Another opinion day, therefore, had come and gone and still there was no decision in the Labor cases.

That evening Bob Macy had invited me to attend another discussion meeting at Quigg Newton's home. However, I declined to go. I decided not to call at Newton's again until the opinions in the Labor cases were announced as I would obviously be the only one present who had advance knowledge of them. During my last visit I had been considerably embarrassed because of this fact. Early in the evening I strolled over to a group of five or six men who happened to be engaged in a lively discussion of the National Labor Relations

---

21. [Editors' note: Numerous draft proofs, including Justice Sutherland's editorial suggestions for the "Labor Board" dissent, survive in Box 20, John Knox Papers, Georgetown University.]

22. *District of Columbia v. Clawans*, 300 U.S. 617. A 7-2 decision with McReynolds and Butler dissenting. A dealer in secondhand personal property had engaged in business in the District of Columbia without first obtaining a license to do so. Stone considered that this was a petty offense which, consistent with the Constitution, could be tried without a jury. McReynolds, however, dissented on the ground that the defendant should have had a right to trial by jury. His dissent concluded with these words: "This cause shows the grave danger to liberty when the accused must submit to the uncertain judgment of a single magistrate."

Act. Upon my approach they looked intently at me, hesitated what to say next, and then I noticed that one of the group was Charles Fahy, the able General Counsel of the National Labor Relations Board. Fahy and I smiled at each other, and I then withdrew to another part of the room. "This is the last time I shall come here," I said to myself, "until the opinions in these cases are announced! Just what would McReynolds say if he knew I was here tonight with all these New Dealers! And if a leak developed from whatever source, he would be justified in firing me. Caught red-handed in the enemy's camp—that's what it would look like!"

On Tuesday, April 6, I took the time to note in my diary that it was the twentieth anniversary of America's entry into "the World War"—or what later became known as World War I. Mrs. Savage had arranged for me to occupy a box seat that evening at Constitution Hall to attend a concert of the Philadelphia Symphony Orchestra. However, I declined to go, and by now she obviously suspected that something really important was brewing. Of course, I made no comments, and she was thoughtful enough not to inquire whether she should attend Court the following Monday as a spectator in the reserved section.

The next day was also a busy one. I canceled plans to attend a formal dinner. [Even at that late date,] proofs were still being returned to us in long galley sheets. [Justice Sutherland wrote to McReynolds:] "I think this is a strong opinion and I fully agree." [He and Van Devanter suggested minor stylistic changes, some of which conflicted which each other.] By April 9 the galley sheets had finally been reduced in size to separate page proofs, [but they were not yet final]. [Four changes from Justice Sutherland] arrived less than twenty-four hours before the final deadline. One paragraph—poorly worded—he wished to omit entirely:

> The right to contract is fundamental. This we think is unduly abridged by the Act now upheld. A private owner is deprived of [the] right to manage his own property and the other under review forces him to accept an undesired employee who may cause loss of property and life by careless or unskillful action, whose presence indeed may cause serious trouble and eventually disrupt the business. Other employees may refuse to work with him.

Under this paragraph Sutherland wrote in pencil: "I think this had better be left out."[23]

---

23. [Editors' note: The document survives in the location identified in note 21, *supra.*]

Van Devanter, on the other hand, wanted to change the paragraph to read as follows:

> The right to contract is fundamental and includes the right to select those with whom one is willing to enter into or renew contractual relations. This we think is unduly abridged by the Act now upheld. A private owner is deprived of [the] right to manage his own property and to select those to whom his business and manufacturing operations shall be committed. This we think cannot be done in instances of the type shown in these cases.

Van Devanter also wrote in pencil in the margin: "I should either leave this paragraph out or change it substantially as here suggested. The majority opinion concedes that employees may be discharged for incompetency or other causes than that of being a union man. Besides, we have assented to a like act as applied to strictly interstate commerce. See opinion in *Virginian Ry.* case." [24]

The conflicting last-minute suggestions of Van Devanter and Sutherland caused McReynolds considerable inconvenience and confusion. Telephone calls had to be made, and by Saturday the paragraph had been changed to read as follows:

> The right to contract is fundamental and includes the privilege of selecting those with whom one is willing to assume contractual relations. This right is unduly abridged by the Act now upheld. A private owner is deprived of power to manage his own property by freely selecting those to whom his manufacturing operations are to be entrusted. We think this cannot lawfully be done in circumstances like those here disclosed.

This was the wording of the paragraph as I made preparations to take the latest corrections at 1:00 P.M. on Saturday, April 10. I expected to go downtown in a cab, but when I reached the lobby of 2400, I noticed that Mrs. Savage and her sister, Mrs. Driggs, were just leaving the building for an afternoon of shopping. They offered to drive me to Mr. Bright's office, and I was glad to ride with them. I was carrying the typewritten manuscript in my hand so as not to let it out of my sight. Therefore, it must have been obvious to both women that McReynolds was writing an important opinion of some kind—especially since the day was a Saturday. No comment was made, however, as to the

24. [Editors' note: Ibid.]

purpose of my errand. Under normal conditions it would have been unthinkable for the Justice to work on a Saturday.

When the Driggs' limousine pulled up at the office of the Pearson Printing Company, I said goodbye to Mrs. Savage and her sister and then hurried inside. As soon as I opened the door, however, I received an unexpected surprise. Chief Justice Hughes was in conference with Mr. Bright, and the two were alone in the outer office. They were apparently discussing the Labor cases, but both ceased talking and looked up as I entered. "Here's the last of it!" I said after nodding to both men. "There may be one or two more changes later today, but if so I shall return with them. Everything will be ready for a final printing not later than this evening."

This news, of course, was of the greatest importance to the Chief Justice. It was now certain that the decisions could be announced on the following Monday. When Hughes realized that the deadline had actually been met, he smiled but made no comment. Mr. Bright, however, replied that he would be expecting a telephone call from me, and that if there were any more changes in wording he would wait for my return regardless of the hour. I promised to telephone him not later than 5:00 P.M.

I remained at McReynolds' apartment until nine o'clock that evening after alerting Mr. Bright that further changes would, in fact, be made. Not until then was the dissent finally completed to the Justice's satisfaction, and he felt that the wording would also meet with the approval of the other three dissenting Justices. It was nearly ten o'clock when I once more arrived at Mr. Bright's office. He was now alone and waiting for me. I do not know how late he worked that night on the Linotype machine, but he expected to deliver the final proofs to McReynolds the next day—Sunday—and apparently to the Chief Justice, too. In any event, my work on the dissenting opinion was finally completed as I had not been asked to report to McReynolds' apartment on Sunday. So on that day I had waffles for breakfast and then saw the cherry blossoms in bloom, walked around the Tidal Basin and later visited the Corcoran Art Gallery. It was an enormous satisfaction to be able to look at something besides the latest proof of the dissent. That dissent would never disturb me again, for at noon on Monday the entire country would finally learn that the National Labor Relations Act was constitutional. Even though the Court's decision was 5 to 4, the majority opinion would naturally be of great benefit to the New Deal. It remained to be seen, however, what immediate effect this would have upon the President's proposed bill. I suspected that the decision would be a near-fatal blow. Why should the Court be "packed" when it was now deciding in favor of the New Deal on such vital issues?

On Monday, McReynolds was just finishing breakfast when I arrived for work. There was such an air of indifference about him that morning that one would never have guessed he was preparing to drive five miles to read the carefully prepared swan song of the conservative wing of the Supreme Court of the United States. Shortly before eleven o'clock, however, the Justice and I finished assembling the final draft of the dissent along with various other papers he would need to refer to that day. There was little conversation that morning as we drove to the session which I later described in my diary as "the most famous Court day since the N.R.A. decision of May 27, 1935."

When we reached the Court, I parted company with [the Justice] and then made my way to the Marshal's office where both Travis Brown and Harry were waiting for me. There was, of course, an enormous crowd in the building that morning. Harry had managed to save two choice seats for us in the reserved section, but he was anxious that we occupy them at once. As I sat down I noticed Mrs. Charles Evans Hughes in the same pew and just a few feet from us. Her husband had evidently suggested that she watch the proceedings, too. I also glanced at her once again as the Justices filed into the Courtroom on the stroke of twelve. She was looking intently at Hughes with an expression of endearment.[25]

After the nine men sat down I noticed that the room was filled not only with the usual number of sightseers who had managed to gain admittance but also with attorneys, officials, reporters, legislators, and relatives and friends of the Justices. As nearly as I could ascertain, the steel company attorneys were on one side of the Courtroom and the government lawyers on the other side. Among those present were Solicitor General Reed; William D. Mitchell, former Attorney General; Robert H. Jackson, Assistant Attorney General; Charles E. Wyzanski, Jr., Special Assistant Attorney General; and Charles Fahy, General Counsel of the National Labor Relations Board. I also noticed Mrs. J. Borden Harriman, who was soon to become Minister to Norway; Mrs. Gifford Pinchot; and Mrs. Mabel Walker Willebrandt, former Assistant Attorney General.

As soon as some unimportant preliminary matters were disposed of, Justice Roberts began delivering the first opinion of the day. This was a 5-4 decision—the case of *Associated Press v. National Labor Relations Board*.[26] Roberts

---

25. Mrs. Hughes had also been in Court on March 29, the day the *Adkins* case was overruled. Her appearance again on April 12 was a signal to those in the know that the long-delayed Wagner Act cases would probably be handed down on that day.

26. 301 U.S. 103.

spoke for the majority in a clear vigorous voice, did not look at the paper before him, moved his head up and down, and now and then shifted his position in his swivel chair. The Associated Press, said the Justice, was a non-profit-making corporation whose members were owners of newspapers published for profit throughout the country. It was also the agency of these papers in exchanging news between them, in using the telegraph and telephone and other means of communication, and in supplying them in like manner with domestic and foreign news collected by itself. One of the employees in the New York office of the Associated Press had been discharged. The American Newspaper Guild, a labor organization, then filed a charge with the National Labor Relations Board alleging that this employee's discharge was in violation of the National Labor Relations Act. Justice Roberts held that the Associated Press was engaged in interstate commerce within the meaning of the Act and of the Constitution. The discharged employee's duties were editorial, having to do with the preparation of news for transmission in interstate commerce, but nevertheless the Board had power to require that he be restored to employment and his loss of pay made good. The Act, as applied in such a case, did not unconstitutionally abridge the freedom of the press as safeguarded by the First Amendment.

Justice Sutherland then followed with a vigorous dissent delivered in an unusually distinct voice and with considerable earnestness. He kept closely to his written opinion and from time to time would shake his head as he stressed a particular point. He concluded with these words:

> Do the people of this land—in the providence of God, favored, as they sometimes boast, above all others in the plenitude of their liberties—desire to preserve those so carefully protected by the First Amendment: liberty of religious worship, freedom of speech and of the press, and the right as freemen peaceably to assemble and petition their government for a redress of grievances? If so, let them withstand all *beginnings* of encroachment. For the saddest epitaph which can be carved in memory of a vanished liberty is that it was lost because its possessors failed to stretch forth a saving hand while yet there was time.[27]

Roberts then referred to his second opinion—the case of *Washington, Virginia & Maryland Coach Co. v. National Labor Relations Board*.[28] This was

27. [Editors' note: 301 U.S. at 141.]

28. 301 U.S. 142.

a short opinion, and there was no dissent. [The company was clearly in inter-state commerce and therefore within the Board's jurisdiction.]

As Roberts finished speaking, the Chief Justice then straightened up in his seat with an Olympian dignity and began to read the first of his three opinions in the Labor cases, the *Jones & Laughlin Steel Corporation* decision.[29] The audience showed intense interest as soon as Hughes identified the case by name. Those present seemed to understand at once that long-awaited decisions of the greatest importance were now to be announced.

The *Jones & Laughlin* case involved the question of the extension of federal powers to a corporation which was claiming that the National Labor Relations Board had no right to interfere with its activities. The Company had sued to keep the Board out of its plants on the theory that production—whether in mining, manufacturing, or agriculture—is a purely local matter. Previous holdings of the Supreme Court sustained this position. As Hughes read on and on, however, in a loud and clear voice and with a superb delivery, it gradually became evident to those present that the Court had actually decided the Company's activities were national in scope and in their effect upon the nation's economic structure. The Chief Justice was overruling prior decisions as well as announcing that the National Labor Relations Act of 1935 was constitutional.

A number of employees had been dismissed for union activity, and the National Labor Relations Board had ordered them reinstated. However, the Company had ignored the Board's order and had claimed that such an order was beyond the range of federal power. Hughes, however, noted that the Corporation operated a vast industrial empire. It had, for instance, iron and steel plants in Pennsylvania; mines in Michigan, Minnesota, West Virginia, and Pennsylvania; limestone properties in West Virginia and Pennsylvania; steamships on the Great Lakes; railroads which it owned—the Monongahela, the Aliquippa, and Southern Railroad, etc.; and it also had nineteen subsidiaries. Tens of thousands of people, in fact, were therefore beyond the reach of state powers, and Congress clearly had a right to protect interstate commerce from labor disturbances under such circumstances.

Hughes went on to say that it was not necessary to relate the Company's business to the "stream of commerce" cases:

> [G]iving full weight to respondent's contention with respect to a break in the complete continuity of the "stream of commerce" by reason of respondent's

---

29. *National Labor Relations Board v. Jones & Laughlin Steel Corporation*, 301 U.S. 1.

manufacturing operations, the fact remains that the stoppage of those operations by industrial strife would have a most serious effect upon interstate
commerce. In view of respondent's far-flung activities, it is idle to say that
the effect would be indirect or remote. It is obvious that it would be immediate and might be catastrophic. We are asked to shut our eyes to the plainest
facts of our national life and to deal with the question of direct and indirect
effects in an intellectual vacuum. Because there may be but indirect and remote effects upon interstate commerce in connection with a host of local
enterprises throughout the country, it does not follow that other industrial
activities do not have such a close and intimate relation to interstate commerce as to make the presence of industrial strife a matter of the most urgent national concern. When industries organize themselves on a national
scale, making their relation to interstate commerce the dominant factor in
their activities, how can it be maintained that their industrial labor relations
constitute a forbidden field into which Congress may not enter when it is
necessary to protect interstate commerce from the paralyzing consequences
of industrial war?[30]

. . . It is not necessary again to detail the facts as to respondent's enterprise. Instead of being beyond the pale, we think that it presents in a most
striking way the close and intimate relation which a manufacturing industry may have to interstate commerce and we have no doubt that Congress
had constitutional authority to safeguard the right of respondent's employees to self-organization and freedom in the choice of representatives for col-
lective bargaining.[31]

When Hughes finished reading the majority opinion in the *Jones & Laughlin* case, it was evident that the Court had now discarded various earlier doctrines, had opened up a broad area of labor regulation by the federal government, and had also set up a new interpretation of the commerce clause.
The Corporation's attorneys must have been almost choking with incredulity,
though of course they did not show it. In their briefs these lawyers had quoted
an impressive list of precedents which had now been overturned.

I then glanced from the attorneys to Justice McReynolds. His face was
set in granite, and he was staring straight ahead—seeing nothing. Already the
news that the Court had upheld the National Labor Relations Act had been

30. [Editors' note: 301 U.S. at 41].

31. [Editors' note: 301 U.S. at 43].

sent through the tubes by the reporters present and was being carried to Capitol Hill and to every other part of the country. And the telephone must even now be ringing in the White House to let Mr. Roosevelt know that a majority of the Justices had reversed themselves in the midst of the Court-packing controversy.

It was obvious that the liberals had won a resounding victory. Hughes then began reading his second decision, which held that the National Labor Relations Act was applicable to a trailer company.[32] This case was followed by the reading of a third decision holding that the Act was also applicable to a men's clothing manufacturer.[33] Since the basic principle of protecting interstate commerce from labor disturbances had been established in the *Jones & Laughlin* case, the Court was now applying that principle wherever interstate commerce was substantially affected by labor strife.

When Hughes finally finished reading his three opinions, he glanced at McReynolds. That Justice then cleared his throat and began speaking in a voice louder than usual. I assumed that he would pick up his dissent and begin quoting from it. In fact, I knew his opinion so well that I could have recited certain paragraphs of it almost from memory. I also assumed that the reading of this lengthy dissent could only be an anticlimax to what had just gone before. The tension of the audience had long since subsided—as soon as it became evident that the National Labor Relations Act was constitutional—and I expected that McReynolds' recitation would be little more than extending the courtesy of the floor to the representative of the defeated opposition.

But McReynolds took advantage of the situation in a way that I did not anticipate. He began speaking extemporaneously, and what happened then was described as follows in the next day's issue of the *New York Times*.[34]

"The field opened here is wider than most of the citizens of the country can dream. The cause is so momentous, the possibilities for harm so great that we felt it our duty to expose the situation as we view it." . . . . His voice was drawling but in vigorous accents, he scoffed at the idea that the Friedman-Harry Marks Clothing Company had really been in the "stream-m-m-m-m" of interstate commerce, talked about the "pants" made in the factory and asserted that if, under the decision, Congress could control the relations

32. *National Labor Relations Board v. Fruehauf Trailer Co.,* 301 U.S. 49.

33. *National Labor Relations Board v. Friedman-Harry Marks Clothing Co.,* 301 U.S. 58.

34. "Supreme Court Upholds Wagner Act," *New York Times,* April 13, 1937, p. 20.

between employers and employees, it could exercise supervision over marriage and birth. Sardonic smiles played about his lips as he sketched what he and his three associates thought of the Wagner Act. At times he rested his head against the back of his leather chair and leveled his forefinger at his listeners to make a point. Again he would lean forward, rest his black-gowned arms on the bench, gaze intently at the spectators and continue his argument in calm but bitter and incisive tones.

Ordinarily the celebrated dissenter speaks in a low voice, often difficult to hear, but today almost every word came clearly and with feeling.... "This court has decided again and again within the last fifty years, and particularly in the last two years, that manufacturing is only incidentally related to interstate commerce and that Congress has no authority to interfere with manufacturing, operating as such. ... It is now said that Congress has the right to remove any obstruction to the free flow of commerce. In the proper sense it has, but the interference must be direct and substantial. It has been gone over again and again and again. It is perfectly true that in the Standard Oil and tobacco cases Congress removed threatened interference with interstate commerce." In his written opinion, Justice McReynolds had said that, under the conclusion of the majority, "almost anything—marriage, birth, death—may in some fashion" be held to affect commerce. In speaking, he said that "marriage and babies" could be regulated, and that the marriage of "Mary Jones and John Smith" might be considered in the stream of commerce. The other justices sat listening to Justice McReynolds, but their expressions were mask-like.

The hour of 2:00 P.M., customary time for the justices' luncheon, passed before Mr. McReynolds completed his remarks. He finished just after 2:10 P.M., after speaking about half an hour.

For weeks the four conservative Justices had labored on a dissenting opinion which had been very carefully worded. But when McReynolds arrived in the tense and crowded Courtroom to deliver the dissent, he ignored the printed word and spoke extemporaneously.

His voice and general attitude had clearly shown implacable hostility to the majority opinion in the *Jones & Laughlin* case. He seemed as convinced as Hughes that his side of the argument was the only correct one, and seldom had the cleavage in the Court been more evident than in the delivery of the majority and minority opinions in this case.

As soon as Court was adjourned, Travis and I ate lunch in the cafeteria of the building, after which I returned alone to 2400. At that moment none of the nine Justices could have been happier than I was that we were rid of the Labor cases. No longer would it be necessary for me to hide Hughes' and Roberts' opinions in the closet of my room or decline to attend meetings at Quigg Newton's home. In fact, I was completely relaxed, and I looked forward to a resumption of the usual routine. The term of Court would be over in two months, and no opinion comparable to the troublesome dissent in the Labor cases could possibly plague McReynolds from now on. The Court was abreast of its work, the city looked beautiful in the springtime, and I felt that henceforth my life in Washington would be very interesting. The only real problem on the horizon appeared to be the June bar examination, but I would come to grips with that in due time.

The Justice arrived home from Court at 5:30 P.M., and I left shortly thereafter. Somewhat to my surprise he made no comment on the events of [the day], and I did not refer to them either. I also noticed that he did not even seem to be tired. He simply appeared indifferent, and he probably spent that evening alone in his apartment. However, I had already returned to active social life for at 8:00 P.M. I was at the Earle Theater with Mrs. Savage and her sister, Mrs. Driggs. Afterward the three of us stopped in at the Occidental Restaurant to eat oysters and drink beer in a leisurely fashion until nearly midnight.

The Court had been in adjournment since April 12, and McReynolds was spending the time in his apartment working on some routine matters and dictating a few letters. Even though it had not been necessary for him to drive to Court each day to hear lengthy arguments, he announced on Friday, April 16, that he was not feeling well. And by the next morning, he said he just was not able to attend the usual Saturday conference at Court. This news surprised me—especially as it meant that he would not be on hand to congratulate Justice Van Devanter on the occasion of his seventy-eighth birthday. After leaving work that afternoon I ordered a basket of flowers sent to Van Devanter's apartment.

Court was still in adjournment for another week, but by the time McReynolds recovered from his temporary illness I noticed that he was no longer acting merely indifferent. Instead, he was now showing deep irritation at nearly everything in general, and I finally concluded that the reason for this change was the way the Justices had been voting of late in the weekly Saturday conferences. In a number of very important cases, for instance, the four conservative Justices had naturally voted together as a unit. The four liberal Justices had also stood together. But the ninth Justice—Owen J. Roberts—had become the key man or the "swing man" on the Court. In every recent 5-4 case he had cast his vote with Hughes, Brandeis, Stone, and Cardozo. However, if he had continued to vote with Van Devanter, McReynolds, Sutherland, and Butler—as he had done in a number of important cases in the past—then ultra-conservative theories would have dominated the decisions of the Court at the very time it was being so vigorously attacked by the President. The loss of Roberts by the conservatives was, therefore, destined to have an incalculable effect upon the future of the Court, upon the laws of the land, and upon the President's proposal of February 5. As more and more important cases became 5-4 decisions—with Roberts always casting the deciding vote—McReynolds' irritability smoldered and grew even though he never once mentioned Roberts by name when referring to one of these cases.

The next opinion day, for instance, was scheduled for Monday, April 26, and a very important 5-4 decision would be handed down at that time. Roberts had voted with the liberals in a matter involving the distribution of Communist literature to negroes in the State of Georgia. This was the *Herndon* case, which was destined to become one of the best-known decisions of the term.[35] Van Devanter, surprisingly enough, had actually managed to write a lengthy dissenting opinion in which he was joined by McReynolds, Sutherland, and Butler.

The latest disaster for the conservatives involved an extremely important case which had been argued on April 8 and 9.[36] This particular case—which would have the most far-reaching effects upon Americans for generations to come—involved a tax imposed by the Social Security Act of 1935 upon employers of eight or more persons. Once more Roberts cast the deciding vote—in favor of declaring the tax constitutional. Cardozo was destined to write the majority opinion in this case, and there would also be three separate dissenting opinions.

As the power struggle between the conservatives and the liberals continued, I watched it with an almost hypnotic fascination. When McReynolds returned home after each Saturday conference, he would hand me the book in which he had kept an account of the afternoon's voting. Before putting it away, I would glance at the record. There always seemed to be some new defeat for the conservatives. It was soon necessary, therefore, for McReynolds to announce that there would be more dissents to write. Work must start at once, for instance, on a dissenting opinion in the Social Security case. This time,

---

35. *Herndon v. Lowry, Sheriff,* 301 U.S. 242 (April 26, 1937).

36. *Steward Machine Co. v. Davis, Collector of Internal Revenue,* 301 U.S. 548 (May 24, 1937).

however, the dissenting Justices would not write one general opinion—the wording of which all four would have to agree to. Such an opinion had become much too involved and had taken too long to write in the Labor cases. A separate opinion, therefore, would be written by each Justice. McReynolds would compose his own dissent, and so would Justices Van Devanter, Sutherland, and Butler.[37]

It was now crystal clear that the position for the four conservative Justices had been permanently shattered—and by none other than Owen J. Roberts. The conservative way of thinking had been superseded by the power of one vote, and a new kind of Supreme Court was in the process of being born—for better or for worse.

On Monday evening, April 19, Bob Macy and I went once more to Quigg Newton's home. One of the guests present happened to be [Mennen] "Soapy" Williams, and after the meeting was over Soapy drove me to my room at 2700 Connecticut Avenue, N.W., where we talked until nearly midnight. What did the future hold? How would the struggle between the President and the Court ultimately resolve itself? Who would win the Spanish Civil War? Would Germany ever be a menace to the peace of Europe? And what would the outlook be for us in the years to come? Although all of our lives lay before us we could not forecast for a certainty one single day ahead.

37. As matters turned out, however, Van Devanter did not write a separate dissent but joined in the opinion written by Sutherland.

12

AN INCIDENT NOW occurred that proved so embarrassing I did not even mention it in my diary, and as a result I cannot recall the exact day when it happened. However, on Saturday, April 24, the sole entry in my notes reads as follows: "Situation with McR. reaches crisis." All too well I remember a crisis that did happen at about this time, so I presume the entry refers to the week when the Great Misunderstanding occurred.

In those days a newsreel entitled *The March of Time* was shown monthly in motion picture houses throughout the country. Each new installment of this film covered the latest and most important current events. Therefore, it was not long after the Court-packing controversy began that the creators of *The March of Time* conceived the idea of photographing the Justices individually for a newsreel that would be released during the very height of the crisis caused by the President's proposal. As I recall, someone from the Chief Justice's office telephoned to inquire whether McReynolds would consent to appear in such a film if the other Justices agreed to do so. At the first opportunity, therefore, I casually mentioned the request to him, and after a brief discussion he agreed to pose *providing all the other eight members of the Court were photographed first.* I thanked him and then informed the person who had called that McReynolds would agree to be photographed under these conditions.

For some days—or perhaps several weeks—I heard nothing more about the matter. I did not know whether the other Justices were or were not being photographed, and eventually McReynolds and I became so involved in miscellaneous work that I gave no further thought to the request. I assumed that if the other eight Justices were photographed, then it would naturally follow that McReynolds would be.

McReynolds is supposed to have said that he would "consider" posing "after the other Justices had been photographed." The word "consider," of course, implies that he did not actually promise to pose. As I recall my conversation with him, however, he definitely said he would pose if movies were first taken of the other eight members of the Court. Thus the groundwork was laid for a very serious misunderstanding, but if McReynolds had been halfway cooperative in the first place, he would not have hedged about being photographed. He was well aware that the Chief Justice approved of the whole project, and yet the request from the representatives of *The March of Time* apparently came at just the wrong moment as far as McReynolds was concerned.[1]

When the cameramen finally arrived, McReynolds did not happen to be home. There were, as I recall, three or four men. I distinctly recall talking with the men once they had entered, and it was not long before one of them suggested setting up the camera. It would be placed only in the hall and not, of course, in McReynolds' study. Then everything would be ready by the time he arrived, and the movies could be taken at once and the equipment removed with a minimum of inconvenience to him. This suggestion sounded sensible—at least when it was made.

The easiest course for me to follow would have been to insist that the men wait until the Justice returned and not set up any equipment without his specific permission. Then he could have handled the situation in any way he saw fit, and I would have assumed no responsibility for any misunderstanding that might occur. But after some further discussion I gave permission for the equipment to be installed. Once everything was in place, however, the appearance of the hall began to cause me considerable uneasiness. There were so many more lights, reflectors, etc., than I had imagined would be necessary—to say nothing of the bulky camera itself. Cords were also spread haphazardly across the floor and plugged into wall sockets. By now, however, it was much too late to ask that everything be dismantled only to be set up a second time. Hence there was nothing to do but wait until McReynolds returned.

The Justice returned all right, and he surveyed the scene in genuine dismay and demanded to know just what was going on. McReynolds had evidently forgotten about the appointment with the cameramen. He looked

1. [Editors' note: The incident is recounted in Drew Pearson and Robert S. Allen, *Nine Old Men at the Crossroads* (Garden City, N.Y.: Doubleday, Doran, 1937), at 25–29. According to Knox's diary, the Pearson-Allen account "over-emphasized" the dialect of Harry Parker and Mary Diggs, "especially as to Harry's conversation." The implication is that Pearson and Allen turned Parker and Diggs—who were concerned that cigarette-smoking by the photographers and other journalists would irritate McReynolds—into shuffling caricatures. Knox Diary, n.d., D'Angelo Law Library, University of Chicago Law School.]

first at the cluttered up appearance of the hall, then at me, then at the men, and naturally he resented this unexpected invasion of the privacy of his home.

I now realized the serious error I had made, but I reminded McReynolds as nonchalantly as possible that men from *The March of Time* had merely arrived to take some movies of him since all the other Justices had now been photographed. There was also some conversation between McReynolds and at least one of the cameramen, but this ended with the Justice demanding that everything be gotten out of the hall at once. Such instructions, of course, left the men and me in an extremely embarrassing position. They began quietly dismantling the equipment—with a raised eyebrow here and there—but before they left I told them the Justice could be photographed some morning while walking from the front entrance of 2400 to his car. All that would be necessary would be to place the camera in a strategic location across the street in what was known as Meridian [Hill] Park. Whether they also discussed this idea with the Justice I do not know. Eventually some belated movies were actually taken of McReynolds, but [not that day].

When the newsreel was finally released, of course I made a point of seeing it at least twice. I was also grateful that McReynolds did not discharge me as a result of the incident. Even though he may have had sufficient justification for doing so at the time, I suspect that it would have been rather inconvenient for him to find another law clerk so late in the term. Neither of us ever spoke of the incident again, but it embarrassed me so much I did not even mention it in my diary. However, I immediately resolved to spend the rest of the term being nothing less than a perfect secretary, and so I merely noted in my diary that the situation with McReynolds had reached a crisis. That, however, was the understatement of the month.

Then came Sunday, April 25. On this day Travis Brown and I were invited to have dinner at [the home of Leila McKnight, an "ardent New Dealer," recent Vassar graduate, and daughter of a family friend.] Mrs. Savage, however, was giving a tea that afternoon, and she suggested that we first stop at her apartment before going to Leila's home.

When Travis and I arrived at Mrs. Savage's, we were warmly greeted by the hostess and were soon chatting with a number of interesting people who were in the living room at the far end of the apartment. From time to time the bell in the hall rang announcing the arrival of other guests. After one particular summons, however, the maid found that none other than Justice McReynolds himself was at the door. He was, of course, uninvited and apparently did not know that Mrs. Savage had guests at the time. It was Sunday afternoon, and since he lived in the same building and only one floor below Mrs. Savage's apartment, he had probably decided to call on her for lack of something else to do. The maid, however, had presence of mind enough to ask him to wait, and she then quietly informed her employer of the Justice's arrival. Upon hearing this unexpected news Mrs. Savage took me hurriedly to one side and advised that I retreat at once into a nearby bedroom while she would delay McReynolds' entrance into the living room. Every second would count!

Travis accompanied me on my precipitate exit even though he was a stranger to the Justice. Before we could get to the nearest bedroom, however, we had to walk across one end of the long hall—at the other end of which the Justice was standing. I saw him but as far as I could determine he did not see us. Perhaps he was looking in another direction—I do not now recall—or Mrs. Savage may have distracted his attention elsewhere. In any event, once Travis and I were in the bedroom we remained there until our hostess could pilot the Justice into the living room via the dining room. Then we looked out, saw the coast was clear, and left the apartment as unobtrusively as possible.

I was never to know for certain whether McReynolds did or did not see us at Mrs. Savage's tea that afternoon. At least he never made any mention of the incident to me, but during the next few days I spent many an anxious hour wondering if he really had noticed me. I kept remembering Harry's long-standing warning that I would be dismissed at once if McReynolds ever learned that I was accepting invitations from any of his lady friends. When several anxious days passed, however, and nothing happened, I finally concluded that the instantaneous reactions of the maid and of Mrs. Savage had saved me from disaster—but only by a hair's breadth. I also assumed that never before in the history of the Court had a law clerk hidden himself in a hostess's bedroom to avoid being seen by his Justice—especially when everything was very proper indeed and had always been so.

The next day—Monday, April 26—was the fourteenth opinion day of the term. Despite recent events, which had been rather embarrassing to say the least, I ventured to ask the Justice if I could drive to Court with him again. To my surprise McReynolds was as cooperative as ever in agreeing to take me along. He acted as if nothing out of the ordinary had ever happened. When we left 2400 and got into his car as usual, I was very thankful that I was still his secretary and law clerk. I had somehow managed to survive two catastrophes in a row, so under the circumstances I considered that silence was the better part of valor and hence did very little talking on that particular drive to Court. When we arrived I noticed another great crowd in the building, but as soon as

I found Harry he announced with a grin that he was holding the usual "fine place" for me in one of the reserved pews. So I entered the Courtroom at once and sat down to survey an interesting and rather tense audience.

Fifteen decisions were to be announced that Monday. I knew, however, that only one of these cases would be of national importance. [That] one decision involved the Communist party and a negro who had been arrested in the State of Georgia and sentenced to a prison term of eighteen to twenty years. This would become widely know as the *Herndon* case.[2] It was a 5-4 decision which had undoubtedly merited careful consideration in the conference room before the vote was taken. And yet the four liberal Justices had once more voted together as a unit, [as had the conservatives. Justice Roberts] again sided with the liberals and hence had cast the deciding ballot in the case. Roberts had also written the majority opinion, and Van Devanter had composed the dissent. I looked forward with great interest to hearing both.

On the stroke of twelve the Justices entered and sat down. I noticed that one chair was vacant—Sutherland was absent. When the reading of opinions began, Cardozo as usual read first. After his two cases were announced, he was followed by Roberts, who then delivered the important opinion of the day.

Angelo Herndon was a young negro Communist who had been charged with violating a Georgia law dating back to 1866 during Reconstruction Days. This law barred "any attempt to persuade or otherwise induce others to join in any combined resistance to the lawful authority of the State." During the depth of the depression in 1932, Herndon had led a successful demonstration of about a thousand negroes and whites in demanding food from the City of Atlanta. The next day the city voted six thousand dollars for relief, but about two weeks later Herndon was arrested while leaving the Atlanta post office. He had in his possession certain Communist literature which had been especially prepared for negroes. Action was taken against him on the theory that membership in the Communist party meant revolutionary opposition to the State, and that organizing the work of the party constituted forceful revolution within the terms of the above mentioned law.

Herndon was subsequently convicted under the Georgia law, but he appealed on the ground that such a conviction unduly restricted his freedom of speech and of assembly as guaranteed by the Constitution. The Georgia Supreme Court, however, affirmed the conviction. The case was then brought to the Supreme Court of the United States, but that Court at first refused to assume jurisdiction because the defense attorneys had failed to raise certain

2. *Herndon v. Lowry, Sheriff*, 301 U.S. 242 (1937).

matters involving Herndon's rights. The defendant then swore out a writ of habeas corpus and won in the Superior Court of Fulton County, in which Atlanta is situated. He was again defeated by the Georgia Supreme Court, and the case came once more before the nine Justices in Washington.

Herndon's bail had been set at seven thousand dollars, but this amount was raised in his behalf by the [American] Civil Liberties Union and by the International Labor Defense. Since December 1935, therefore, he had been free on bail and was living in New York City and engaged in active work as a member of the Communist party. In February 1937, he journeyed to Washington to be present while his case was argued before the Supreme Court. The case had by now aroused nationwide interest.

In his opinion Justice Roberts admitted that Communist literature had been found in Herndon's possession but held that there was no evidence to show that Herndon had actually distributed any of this literature. Roberts was also of the opinion that the power of a State to abridge freedom of speech and of assembly is the exception and not the rule, and he added that the Georgia law was vague and uncertain. He also stressed the fact that under such a law any person's fate would be subject to the particular jury before which he happened to appear. The old Georgia law had, therefore, been wrongfully applied to the defendant, and the evidence did not warrant his conviction. The decision of the Georgia Supreme Court was reversed, and this meant that Herndon would be freed.

The four conservative Justices, however, vigorously dissented in an opinion written and delivered by Van Devanter. That Justice insisted that Herndon had been rightly convicted and that he was, in fact, guilty of agitating against the lawful authority of the State of Georgia. Van Devanter announced that constitutional guarantees do not shield or afford protection for acts of international incitement to forcible resistance.

On Monday afternoon, as soon as the decision became known in New York City, Herndon was interviewed in the office of the Young Communist League at 35 East Twelfth Street. He said, "The decision today is a decisive victory for all the progressive forces in the country. . . . It strikes another heavy blow at the Jim Crow oppression of the Negro people." And the fact that he was freed by the narrow margin of "one lone Justice, who switched to the side of the four liberals," was indicative, as far as he was concerned, of the "political set-up of the Court."[3]

3. *New York Times,* April 27, 1937, p. 10.

During the week I had much free time on my hands as Court was in session. I did not realize, however, that the Justice was making careful note of this fact and that he would refer to it later on. Each morning he left the apartment not later than eleven o'clock, and he was so preoccupied in keeping abreast of new cases that there was no time in which to write opinions or dissents in other cases that had already been argued and voted upon. This meant a gradual accumulation of work which would have to be disposed of during the month of May. I knew that my spare time would be very limited once he began writing opinions again so I tried to make the best possible use of each day. In fact, I was now studying for the bar examination during office hours—but not, of course, while he was in the apartment. I did not mention the examination to him, and he had evidently forgotten [about it].

On Wednesday, April 28, Col. John Henry Wigmore of Chicago—the internationally known authority on the law of evidence—was in Washington, and he invited me to lunch at the Cosmos Club. As we strolled near the White House, Col. Wigmore continued his discussion of the possible outcome of the Court-packing struggle. He was strenuously opposed to the President's bill and was hopeful that it would be defeated. He also expressed disappointment that the Dean of the Northwestern University School of Law in Chicago [Leon Green] had come out publicly in favor of the bill.

After leaving Col. Wigmore, I hurried back to 2400 and was there only a short time before McReynolds arrived home from Court. He soon summoned me to his study but did not ask me to be seated since he did not expect to dictate any letters. As I remained standing in his presence he leaned back in his swivel chair and announced in a courteous tone of voice that my term as his secretary and law clerk would end on either June 1 or July 1. When I heard this news my first thought was that he had seen me at Mrs. Savage's tea after all, but apparently this was not the case. McReynolds made no mention of her and did not appear upset in any way. He merely commented that I should make my plans accordingly and that he would know later on just when the expiration date would be.

I assumed that my successor would be a June graduate of some distinguished law school—possibly Harvard—but I was puzzled that he might arrive on June 1. How could he graduate that early in the month? And who might he be? The very thought of his identity intrigued me, but there had been no reference as to who he was, and I had not ventured to inquire. Nor had I been asked to spend a few days breaking him in, but then I remembered that my own predecessor had never met me either. It was now April 28.

How amazed I would have been on that day had I known the real identity of my successor! For he was to be none other than J. T. McHale, the long-time law clerk and secretary to Justice Van Devanter. But why was McHale being transferred to McReynolds when he was a valued employee of another Justice? Simply because Willis Van Devanter had finally decided to retire from the Court. He was seventy-eight years old and had served as a Justice since 1911. Van Devanter, being a thoughtful person, had sought to keep McHale in Court employment by having him transferred to McReynolds. The Nine Old Men, however, would pass into history upon the resignation of one of the arch conservative Justices, and this resignation would also take place at the very time when the Court-packing issue was being most vigorously debated. The four conservative Justices would no longer vote together as a unit, and liberalism had finally triumphed in the Supreme Court of the United States. But for some days yet I was not to know of this very important fact, and at no time did McReynolds ever indicate to me that there was soon to be an important change in the personnel of the Court.

After leaving work that day—April 28—I had dinner with Travis Brown and his roommates at their home. A date with Leila McKnight followed on Thursday, April 29, beginning with dinner at 2400. The bar review course was attended on Tuesday and Friday of that week, and Sunday, May 2, was spent at the Court studying for the forthcoming examination in June. The building was closed to the public, but Justice Stone's law clerk, Harold Leventhal, was also working there that Sunday. We had lunch together at a nearby restaurant.

The fifteenth opinion day of the term took place on Monday, May 3. This Monday, however, was not scheduled as a regular opinion day and I knew only two cases were to be announced. I therefore decided not to ask McReynolds if I could drive to Court with him. Both opinions were written by Justice Sutherland. One was a lengthy tax case, and the other involved the ownership of a sum of money which had been deposited by a Russian corporation in a New York bank prior to the Russian Revolution of 1917.[4] After McReynolds left for Court and Harry had gone to market, I began studying once again for the bar examination. That evening Bob Macy took me to another club meeting at Quigg Newton's home.

One more day of leisure followed. On Tuesday, May 4, Justice Stone's social secretary, Gertrude Jenkins, arrived at 2400 shortly after McReynolds left for Court. After chatting briefly with Harry and Mary, she drove me to Mary-

---

4. *Cincinnati Soap Co. v. United States*, 301 U.S. 308; *United States v. Belmont et al., Executors*, 301 U.S. 325. Apparently these cases had not been completed in time to be read on April 26. In fact, Sutherland may have been ill as he was absent from the Court on April 26 and 27.

land for lunch. In fact, we did not return until 3:00 P.M., but fortunately the Justice had not telephoned while I was absent. Of late I had been taking more and more chances in this regard.

On Wednesday, May 5, McReynolds was again in Court, but at the close of arguments that day the Chief Justice announced an adjournment until Monday the seventeenth. Since the seventeenth would also be the next opinion day, I assumed we would be very busy until then. As soon as I learned of the adjournment, I canceled a dinner engagement for the fifth. This proved wise, for just as I had expected, McReynolds decided to tackle some accumulated work as soon as he arrived home from Court that Wednesday. He was tired, but there were a number of invitations which would have to be answered without further delay. Among them was an elaborately engraved piece of cardboard which had arrived from the British embassy. After carefully examining this invitation, the Justice took a pencil and wrote in the upper left-hand corner "Please Decline." He then handed it to me, and it proved to be the most coveted invitation of the spring social season in Washington: [A garden party May 12 at British embassy celebrating the coronation of George VI.]

On Thursday morning, May 6, the Justice began work in earnest. Shortly after he rang for me to come to his office, he gathered together all of the accumulated briefs, etc. and placed them in a pile on his desk. Some had been in my office and some in his. He then asked me to be seated while he leaned back once again in his swivel chair. A few moments of silence followed. He looked first at the documents in front of him and then at his hands while he seemed to be lost in contemplation. I had my shorthand notebook in front of me and was holding a freshly sharpened pencil in my right hand. The Justice was now seventy-five years old, and he had been producing opinions every year since 1914. But perhaps he was thinking that they just did not seem to matter any more — especially since Justice Roberts, after some wavering, had finally abandoned the four conservatives to their fate.

McReynolds slowly emerged from his reverie and leaning forward in his chair announced in a tired voice, "Mr. Knox, as you know I dissented in the *Anniston* case. I have now decided to file merely a notice of dissent instead of writing an opinion. So ask Mr. Bright to have the words 'Mr. Justice McReynolds dissents' follow the Chief Justice's opinion."

"Yes, sir," I replied as I made a note of his instructions. I knew that McReynolds was referring to *Anniston Manufacturing Co. v. Davis, Collector of Internal Revenue.*[5] This was a very important case involving a suit to collect taxes

5. 301 U.S. 337 (May 17, 1937).

paid under the Agricultural Adjustment Act of 1933. Eight Justices had decided that the right to sue the Collector of Internal Revenue for the recovery of taxes exacted under an unconstitutional statute may be abolished—consistently with the Fifth Amendment—if a fair and adequate remedy directly against the government is substituted. It was held that the taxpayer had an adequate remedy by suing the United States in the District Courts or in the Court of Claims for a refund of the "floor stock taxes" collected under the A.A.A.

McReynolds, in fact, did not have time to write a satisfactory dissent in this case. His lone opinion would also have followed a learned dissertation by the Chief Justice, and Hughes expected to read his decision on May 17—the next opinion day. Therefore, the easiest and wisest solution to the problem was for McReynolds to record his dissent without an opinion. In so doing he also disposed of a very troublesome case in the matter of a few minutes.[6]

The Justice then began to dictate an opinion in a suit involving the Revenue Act of 1928 and the computation of the net income of a trust.[7] Several days were spent in getting this opinion in shape and then attention was given to two other cases. One was a unique 5-4 decision in which McReynolds had been assigned to write the majority opinion while Roberts was composing the dissent.[8] Roberts had as usual voted with the liberals, but in this particular instance Chief Justice Hughes sided with the four conservatives—thus giving them the victory in at least one more case. In fact, it was the last "victory" the four conservative Justices were ever to have. The majority opinion held that a Georgia statute of 1935 was unconstitutional because it discriminated between two different types of insurance companies—mutual and stock. Such discrimination violated the equal protection clause of the

---

6. McReynolds' dissent is of considerable interest because it shows his implacable hostility to the New Deal. Had the other Justices agreed with him a very serious burden would have been placed upon the United States Treasury. Processors of farm products were seeking a refund of $963,000,000.00 of processing taxes which had been unconstitutionally collected under the original farm program. Some two hundred similar suits were pending in other courts throughout the country.

In the opinion written by the Chief Justice the Court declined to rule on whether the Anniston Manufacturing Company, processors of cotton textiles in Alabama, was entitled to recover $270,000.00 of invalidated A.A.A. taxes. It was held in substance that the Company must first demonstrate the validity of its claim and prove that it had not shifted the burden of the tax to purchasers of its products or to those from whom it bought the raw cotton.

7. *Old Colony Trust Co. v. Commissioner of Internal Revenue*, 301 U.S. 379 (May 17, 1937).

8. *Hartford Steam Boiler Inspection & Insurance Co. et al. v. Harrison, Insurance Commissioner*, 301 U.S. 459 (May 24, 1937).

Fourteenth Amendment. Before finishing work on this case, however, Mc-Reynolds began dictating a dissenting opinion in a controversy of immense importance involving the constitutionality of the Social Security Act of 1935. This Act imposed a tax upon employers of eight or more persons.

This suit was the *Steward Machine Company* case.[9] The District Court dismissed the complaint, and the Circuit Court of Appeals affirmed. The case then came to the Supreme Court of the United States where it was argued on April 8 and 9, 1937. The subsequent vote in the conference room was four to four, with Roberts again casting the decisive ninth ballot and siding with the liberals. Justice Cardozo was assigned to speak for the majority (of one), and in weaving a mantle of constitutionality around the Act he produced an opinion which subsequently filled twenty-six pages in the Supreme Court reports. However, when McReynolds was dictating his dissent he decided to refer to Cardozo's reasoning as a "cloud of words" and an "ostentatious parade of irrelevant statistics."[10] In composing this dissent McReynolds was not as pressed for time as he had been in writing the dissent in the Labor Board cases. There was also no need to secure the consent of the other three conservative Justices to every word that he was writing. In the Labor Board cases all four had joined in writing one common dissenting opinion, but in the Social Security case McReynolds was writing only his own dissent. Sutherland was composing another dissent, and Butler was busy with a third. As for Van Devanter, he was already hard at work composing a lengthy opinion regarding the Chippewa Indians of Minnesota.[11] Any dissent in the Social Security case would apparently have been beyond his capabilities at the time, and he ultimately decided to join in Sutherland's opinion.

Unfortunately the more McReynolds became involved in writing his dissent in the Social Security case, the more difficult he was to work with. This case seemed to crown an entire year of judicial frustrations for him. It was also obvious that he was keenly aware of the fact that the majority decision was the result of Justice Roberts' vote. Nevertheless he did not once mention Roberts by name. However, McReynolds fretted day after day during this particular

9. *Steward Machine Co. v. Davis, Collector of Internal Revenue*, 301 U.S. 548 (May 24, 1937). [See also chapter 11, note 36.]

10. [Editors' note: 301 U.S. at 599.]

11. *Chippewa Indians of Minnesota v. United States et al.*, 301 U.S. 358 (May 17, 1937). This opinion fills nearly twenty pages in the Supreme Court reports. The Chippewa Indians decision was to be the very last opinion that Van Devanter would ever write, and he was undoubtedly pouring his best energies into it.

recess of the Court. He was a staunch States' rights Southerner, and the very thought of Social Security legislation being declared constitutional was almost beyond his comprehension and endurance. How could the country ever survive if Social Security became the law of the land in the manner provided for in this Act?

Eventually I dreaded having to report for work each morning while McReynolds was in such a cantankerous mood. Therefore, I managed to slip away now and then to spend a relaxing hour or two with friends.

The Clerk's office was constantly receiving new petitions for certiorari and by Monday, May 10, I was so far behind in typing summaries of them that I worked from 8:00 until 11:00 P.M. that evening reading petitions. This was done in my unused office at the Court as I did not wish to stay this late in the Justice's apartment. However, the cold and elegantly furnished office always repelled me, and I never used it unless necessary.

McReynolds finally worked himself into such a fret in trying to write his dissent in the Social Security case that on Thursday, May 13, he came down with an attack of the gout and could not even leave the apartment for his usual afternoon walk. This attack was painful and caused him to be even more temperamental. "Harry!" he would call, "Harry!" and poor Harry would be hurrying from one room to another trying to be of help and yet attend to his regular duties.

The sixteenth opinion day of the term took place on Monday, May 17, but I did not ask McReynolds if I could drive to Court with him [as his only opinion was in the *Old Colony* case].[12] I wished to remain in the apartment to continue my study for the bar examination. Nine decisions were to be announced that Monday—including the *Anniston* case and Justice Van Devanter's opinion concerned the Chippewa Indians. I would have made a special effort to attend Court had I known this was to be the very last decision Van Devanter would ever read.

After the reading of the nine opinions the Chief Justice declared another recess—until Monday, May 24. Those who attended Court on the seventeenth must have been considerably disappointed as no opinion concerning Social Security was handed down on that day. There was great interest throughout the country as to whether the Social Security Act of 1935 would or would not be declared constitutional. Another opinion day had now passed without any mention of Social Security, and therefore I anticipated a huge crowd in the Court building on the next opinion day.

12. See note 7 *supra*.

McReynolds drove home immediately after Court adjourned on the seventeenth, and he went directly to his study. He did not ask to dictate any letters, so I began reading another petition for certiorari. At 5:00 P.M. I heard the doorbell ring. Harry answered, and as I casually looked out from my little office to see who was calling I was surprised [that it was] Justice Van Devanter. He was greeted by Harry, who took his hat and then asked the Justice to follow him. Apparently Van Devanter had been expected, and he solemnly walked a few steps behind Harry down the long hall and into the living room. Both proceeded at a slow pace, but I did not catch the eye of either of them as they passed my office.

"Please be seated," Harry said, "and I'll tell the Justice you are here." Harry then walked into McReynolds' study, and in a few moments McReynolds joined Van Devanter in the living room. The two men greeted each other very cordially and began engaging in some small talk. I then decided to leave and did so within a few minutes. My withdrawal may have seemed to be a gesture of politeness so as not to overhear their conversation, but the real reason was that I wanted to eat an early dinner and attend the circus that night. Besides, I considered Van Devanter's call a mere routine visit. In any event I did not realize that an historic meeting was taking place between two of the arch conservative Justices of the Supreme Court of the United States—their last meeting prior to Van Devanter's resignation.

For months there had been rumors that one of the nine Justices would soon resign—either Brandeis or Sutherland or Van Devanter. However, I had always discounted such rumors as I felt that no Justice would leave the bench during the Court-packing struggle. It is true there had been no retirement from the Court in more than five years—not since Justice Holmes had resigned on January 12, 1932. This interval had been one of the longest periods in the history of the Court during which no change of membership had occurred. But I considered that a resignation during the heated debates on the President's proposed bill would resemble an ignominious retreat under fire. I therefore assured myself that there would be no resignation in the immediate future despite a recently enacted retirement law which had gone into effect on March 1, 1937.[13]

Early the next morning—Tuesday, May 18—Van Devanter telephoned to a newspaperman, whom he had known for years, and asked him to call at the

13. [Editors' note: See David J. Garrow, "Mental Decrepitude on the U.S. Supreme Court: The Historical Case for a 28th Amendment," 67 U. Chicago L. Rev. 995, 1021–22 (2000).]

Justice's apartment on his way to work. When the newspaperman arrived at 2101 Connecticut Avenue, N.W., Van Devanter gave him a copy of a letter of retirement which was not to be made public until after it had reached the White House. However, the original of the letter was at that moment on its way to the Executive Mansion in care of a messenger. When this messenger arrived at the front door of the White House at 9:45 A.M., President Roosevelt was sitting up in bed scanning the morning newspapers before arising. He was informed that a personal message had just arrived from one of the Justices of the Supreme Court, and upon hearing this news Roosevelt thrust the newspapers aside as he was handed [Justice Van Devanter's resignation, pursuant to the "Act of March 1, 1937" and effective "the second day of June, 1937, that being the day next following the adjournment of the present term of the Court"]. Upon reading this very unexpected message, Roosevelt wrote a hurried reply with a pencil. Later his reply was typed and sent at once to Van Devanter; [it said, in part, "May I as one who has had the privilege of knowing you for many years extend to you every good wish. Before you leave Washington for the summer it would give me great personal pleasure if you would come in to see me"].

As soon as Van Devanter's letter was received at the White House, the copy given the newspaperman was made public. The capital was taken by complete surprise—especially as Van Devanter was apparently in the best of health. Only the day before he had delivered an opinion in Court and had spoken in a strong and clear voice for more than half an hour.

On that same Tuesday the news of the Justice's retirement reached the eighteen members of the Senate Judiciary Committee just as they were preparing to enter the committee room to ballot on the President's program for the reorganization of the judiciary. Apparently the resignation did not alter any votes, but in any event seven Democrats joined with three Republican members of the Committee to send the President's proposed bill to the Senate calendar with an adverse report. The other seven Democrats and Senator Norris, Independent, voted for a favorable report on the measure. The decisive ballot was, therefore, ten to eight as had been generally forecast. The ten who had been victorious then set to work immediately to draw up their majority report to recommend that the bill [should not pass], and they promised that there would be as little delay as possible.

That afternoon the President also held a press conference. One of the newspapermen present mentioned Justice Van Devanter's sudden retirement and asked the President if there was any special significance in the fact that a band was at that moment playing on the White House lawn. Roosevelt laughed heartily and said he thought the point "was well taken," but he declined to comment further.

Harry told me the news of Van Devanter's retirement shortly before I went to lunch that day. I was thunderstruck. McReynolds was in the apartment at the time and had never even mentioned it. I could scarcely believe that the Nine Old Men would soon pass into history, and that one of them had resigned even before the end of the term. And I was even more surprised when I read in the evening papers of the 10-8 vote of the Senate Judiciary Committee. "The President's bill is doomed," I said to myself, "so why didn't Van Devanter hold out a little longer? Why did he have to go and resign now at just the wrong time? If only I had known what he had in mind, I would have asked to see him. Maybe I could have talked him out of it!" But, of course, this would not have been possible, and in any event it was now too late.[14]

Before going to bed that night I wrote the following comments in my diary.

> Justice Willis Van Devanter causes nationwide sensation by resigning from the Supreme Court of the United States. The Committee on the Judiciary of the Senate returns a vote of 10-8 against the President's proposal to pack the Court. A day of great judicial importance. . . .

> Tonight I declined to go to dinner at the Cosmos Club with Mrs. Savage and Mrs. Driggs.

14. [Editors' note: The day after the resignation was announced, Knox sent a handwritten note to Van Devanter—a curious mixture of genuine regret, gratitude, and self-absorption:

> Your decision to leave the Court causes me considerable regret. I thought possibly you were resigning when you asked Justice McReynolds for his autographed picture. I am very sorry to see you go, but in a situation like this you know best, of course. There were possibly circumstances leading you to your decision of which the public does not know.

> I shall always be much indebted to you for making it possible for me to come to Washington. Though I was hardly more successful in my Secretaryship than my predecessor, still the experience was most worthwhile. At first I was very lonesome in Washington, but after I moved away from 2400 16th Street I began making friends my own age and came to like Washington better. The sudden change from the many pleasant contacts at law school to living in a tiny room alone at 2400 for months on end and never seeing any young people contributed to my defeat more than anything else. I trust that my successor will not be required to live at 2400.

> You leave the Court with my very affectionate regards. No one in Washington has done more for me than you have. Your kind deed will ever be remembered. With great respect, John Knox.

Knox to Willis Van Devanter, May 19, 1937, Box 44, Van Devanter Papers, Manuscript Division, Library of Congress.]

The events of that Tuesday had been too much of a surprise to spend a quiet evening at the Cosmos Club. And McReynolds had remained a sphinx to the very end regarding Van Devanter's impending resignation and the breakup of the conservative Justices who had opposed the New Deal for so long. However, perhaps he did not have the heart to admit even to his secretary that defeat had finally arrived for the conservative wing of the Court. In any event, the resignation came at the worst possible time for McReynolds. He had not yet completed his dissent in the [*Steward Machine Company* case]. Less than a week remained before Justice Cardozo expected to deliver the majority opinion in the case. And to make matters worse there was a second Social Security decision concerning the scheme of Federal Old-Age Benefits set up by Title II of the Social Security Act. This was a 7-2 decision, and the majority opinion had also been written by Justice Cardozo.[15] Both opinions were to be announced on May 24—the following Monday—and in the second case only Justice Butler had dissented along with McReynolds. It had been the last opportunity for the conservative bloc to stand together as a unit, and it had failed to do so. Van Devanter and Sutherland had actually voted with Hughes, Brandeis, Stone, Roberts, and Cardozo to declare Title II constitutional!

It had, in short, been a year of disaster as far as McReynolds was concerned. During the entire 1936 term the Court had not ruled against a single New Deal statute. This incredible result had occurred only because of Justice Roberts' alignment with the four liberals. Therefore, the days immediately ahead were destined to be very trying for McReynolds, and the members of his household were to feel the full force of the strain under which he was laboring.

15. [Editors' note: *Helvering v. Davis*, 301 U.S. 619 (1937).]

13

THREE OPINIONS were to be read
on Monday, May 24, and they were destined to take their places among the
great decisions of the Court. The lives of Americans for generations to come
would be directly affected by the Court's interpretation on that day of the
"general welfare" clause of the Constitution. So important were the questions
involved that five different Justices expected to state their views. This would be
the first time in American history that the Court had applied the welfare
clause directly. It was also to be the last conflict of the term between the liberal
and conservative Justices. Cardozo and Stone were to speak for the majority
in favor of a liberal interpretation of the welfare clause. McReynolds, Sutherland, and Butler intended to deliver separate dissenting opinions expressing
their own individual conservative views. As yet, however, McReynolds had
not completed his dissent, and I knew that the next few days would be very
busy ones reminiscent of his last-minute attempts to finish his dissent in the
Labor cases.

The first federal Social Security Act became law on August 14, 1935, and at
that time it was greeted by its advocates as being a major extension of "the
frontiers of social progress." Now the law was also to be declared constitutional on May 24, 1937. Among other things this Act provided for a system of
unemployment insurance (approved by a 5-4 vote) and for old-age benefits
(upheld by a 7-2 vote). The Court had also given its approval to certain state
laws in another 5-4 ruling. Hence I looked forward with great anticipation to
attending the session of May 24, as it was evident that particular Monday

234

would be a landmark in American judicial history. It would also be Justice Cardozo's sixty-seventh birthday.[1]

The "general welfare" clause in the Constitution had remained unchanged since 1787, but the concept of general welfare had, of course, altered with the passage of time. Cardozo, for instance, had just sent McReynolds the final draft of an opinion which contained these words: "Nor is the concept of the general welfare static. Needs that were narrow or parochial a century ago may be interwoven in our day with the well being of the Nation. What is critical or urgent changes with the time."[2]

Cardozo took a broad view concerning the powers that Congress can exercise under the "welfare" clause. He was, in fact, asserting the doctrine of Alexander Hamilton as opposed to the views once expressed by Thomas Jefferson and James Madison. These philosophers of the Constitution had engaged in a great debate which turned primarily upon an interpretation of Article I, Section 8, Paragraph 1 of the Constitution: "The Congress shall have power to lay and collect taxes, duties, imposts and excises, to pay the debts and provide for the common defense and general welfare of the United States."

From the very foundation of the Republic sharp differences of opinion existed concerning the correct construction of these words. The controversy began because of the comma appearing after the word "excises." Should it be there or not? Jefferson and Madison insisted on interpreting the general welfare clause as if there were no comma at all after "excises." They read the whole clause in a single breath, so to speak, and alleged that the power of Congress was not to provide for the general welfare, but only to raise the wherewithal to pay for the general welfare after that welfare had been determined in other ways than by the sole judgment of Congress. In 1937, at the time Cardozo wrote his two opinions, this view was being sponsored by so-called Jeffersonians such as Alfred M. Landon and Ogden Mills—representing the conservative wing of the Republican Party.

Hamilton, on the other hand, took a broader view, which was later sponsored by Justice Story in his commentaries. The welfare clause, according to Hamilton, conferred on Congress a power separate and distinct from those powers later enumerated in Section 8. Hamilton insisted on stressing the comma after the word "excise." He read the clause as follows: "The Congress

1. [During my last meeting with Justice Cardozo, I congratulated him on his "busy birthday"—delivering the two Social Security decisions.] "Oh, yes," replied Cardozo with a smile. "I never expected to achieve such prominence on the day I was sixty-seven."

2. *Helvering, Commissioner of Internal Revenue, et al. v. Davis*, 301 U.S. 619 at 641 (May 24, 1937).

shall have power to lay and collect taxes, duties, imposts, and excises, [shall have power] to pay the debts and [shall have power to] provide for the common defense and general welfare of the United States." Under this view Congress has the power to do anything it finds necessary to do for the general welfare. This was the position upheld in 1937 by the liberal wing of the Democratic Party as represented by President Roosevelt, James A. Farley, and Senator Joseph Robinson. Since 1787 these two conflicting theories had had their champions, but in the end the Hamiltonian view finally prevailed.

On Wednesday, May 19, McReynolds began devoting every available minute to completing his dissent. He had Cardozo's two opinions before him as well as the draft of a third opinion by Justice Stone. The next few days, therefore, were extremely busy ones, and they were interspersed with a number of temperamental outbursts on the part of McReynolds due to the fact that he was once again working under pressure. Even though a large part of the dissent consisted merely of quotations, it was not until 4:00 P.M. on Saturday the twenty-second that I made my last trip to Mr. Bright's office for the final printed copies of the opinion. It was nearly six o'clock when I returned to 2400, and not only was I very tired but I am sure that McReynolds was, too. After making preparations for the dissent to be circulated to the other Justices, I was excused from further work for the day. I then left but took with me a number of petitions for certiorari which I had not yet had time to read and summarize.

On the morning of the next day, I spent two hours at the bar review course and then went to Court, where I remained until 9:00 P.M. There I read the petitions in Justice Stone's office.[3] When I had summarized the last "cert" I left the building, caught a streetcar uptown, and met a friend for dinner. [My friend handed me an article on McReynolds from that Sunday's edition of the *New York Times.* A] large and recent photograph of the Justice [appeared] on the first page of the write-up. He was shown strolling along a Washington street while carrying his cane, but there was an expression on his face which repelled me. He had apparently glanced up just as the camera was pointed at him, and he appeared very grim indeed—in fact almost Satanic.[4]

3. There was no typewriter available in McReynolds' chambers at the Court. Though I did not mention him in my diary, Stone's law clerk—Harold Leventhal—must have been working in the building that Sunday as I had no key to Stone's chambers.

4. [Delbert Clark, "Staunch States' Righter of Our High Court: McReynolds, Spokesman for Conservatives, Upholds the Constitution 'As It Is Written,'"] *New York Times Magazine,* Sunday, May 23, 1937, p. 7.

After reading this article my first thought was, "How in the world did a reporter ever get into his apartment to learn all this? He must have called some evening when Harry and I were gone!" The story was well written and true, and I found it of considerable interest. However, I never mentioned it to the Justice, though I should have, and he never spoke of it to me.

The next morning—Monday, May 24—McReynolds was amiable and even talkative, although he once more expected to represent the losing side in Court that day. [After agreeing to my accompanying him to Court, he] went to his study to reread the opinions of the other Justices which were to be announced that day. I did not disturb him at such a time, but unfortunately he lingered too long. It was 11:30 A.M. when we finally left 2400, and this proved to be an almost fatal error. Harry had long since departed for Court. McReynolds drove as fast as the law allowed [but] did not blame me for allowing him to start out late, and luckily there was no mishap on the way. By the time we entered the building, however, he had no more than five minutes to spare until he was due to ascend the bench with the other Justices promptly on the stroke of twelve. I suspect he was a bit out of breath by the time he reached the robing room.

When the Justices stepped from behind the great curtain in the back of the room to take their seats, McReynolds did not appear ruffled in the least. Nine decisions were to be announced that day, not counting dissenting opinions.

Throngs of people were still milling about before the door of the Courtroom itself, and of course every available seat in the room was taken. At least five Senators were in the audience that morning—Robinson, Borah, Connally, Steiwer, and Minton. The air was tense with expectancy, but even those present did not yet realize that this was to be one of the most historic sessions in the entire history of the Court. In fact, I later considered it the most memorable session I ever attended—the ultimate climax in the great struggle between the two opposing factions within the Court during the Court-packing controversy.

A few preliminary matters were disposed of, and then the Chief Justice nodded to Justice Cardozo, who had two decisions to announce. A rustle was heard in the Courtroom as soon as he began reading because those in the know instantly realized that the Court was now ready to announce its long-awaited ruling on Social Security. As I recall, Cardozo delivered his opinion in the *Davis* case first.[5] This was the 7-2 decision concerning old-age benefits and

5. *Helvering, Commissioner of Internal Revenue, et al. v. Davis*, 301 U.S. 619 (May 24, 1937).

the question of the constitutionality of Titles II and VIII of the Social Security Act. Those titles provided for the payment of such benefits and the levying of so-called old-age benefits taxes upon employers.

A stockholder in the Edison Electric Illuminating Company of Boston, by the name of George P. Davis, had challenged the old-age benefits provisions. He sought to prevent the Company from making the payments and deductions required by the Social Security Act. In upholding the Act, Cardozo gave special attention to conditions within the country.

Titles II and VIII of the Social Security Act were, therefore, declared constitutional. Justice McReynolds, however, had dictated the following short paragraph to me, which was to be printed in the Supreme Court reports immediately following Cardozo's opinion: "Mr. Justice McReynolds and Mr. Justice Butler are of opinion that the provisions of the Act here challenged are repugnant to the Tenth Amendment, and that the decree of the Circuit Court of Appeals should be affirmed." [6]

The second case of Cardozo's concerned the validity of Title IX of the Social Security Act and the tax imposed upon employers of eight or more persons. This was the *Steward Machine Company* decision in which the Court split 5 to 4 on the question of unemployment insurance.[7] A small Alabama concern—the Charles C. Steward Machine Company—employed about fifteen persons and was engaged chiefly in the manufacture of mining equipment. The company had paid $46.14 to the government under the provisions of the new Social Security Act, and it then brought suit to recover this amount on the ground that unemployment insurance was unconstitutional. As Cardozo read his opinion, however, it was evident that Title IX of the Act—a "Tax on Employers of Eight or More"—was indeed constitutional. The Justice was speaking in a calm voice, which could be heard distinctly throughout the room.

As soon as Cardozo had completed the reading of his two opinions, he glanced at the Chief Justice. Hughes then looked momentarily at McReynolds, and that Justice began delivering his dissent at once and without a moment's hesitation. He paid no attention to his written opinion, which was apparently in front of him on the dais. McReynolds soon plunged into a bitter denunciation of the Social Security Act. Once again he was speaking [extemporaneously] and with much feeling—the same as he had done when announcing

---

6. Ibid. at 646.

7. *Steward Machine Co. v. Davis, Collector of Internal Revenue*, 301 U.S. 548 (May 24, 1937).

his views in the Labor cases. This time he felt that the very existence of state sovereignty was jeopardized by the majority opinion which had just been announced. He enlarged considerably upon the views expressed in his written opinion, but no stenographic report, of course, was taken of his exact words. Nor was I in a position to take down any notes during the time he was speaking. All that is now available, therefore, is his written dissent.[8]

McReynolds [spoke] in a tone of voice which indicated both contempt and alarm, but Cardozo sat very quietly in his chair and looked straight ahead with an impassive expression on his face. I already knew—of course—that McReynolds disliked Cardozo personally, but I now realized that he evidently loathed every word Cardozo had ever written while a Justice.

As soon as McReynolds finished speaking he was followed by Justice Sutherland, who spoke at some length in his own quiet and detached way. Sutherland was then followed by Justice Butler, who appeared even more grim than usual when he read from his dissent.

It was now Justice Stone's turn to begin reading. He had three opinions to announce that day, but by far the most important of them concerned the Unemployment Compensation Act of Alabama.[9] This 5-4 decision upheld the Alabama law which had been enacted as a result of the federal Social Security Act. Alabama allowed employers a credit against their federal unemployment insurance tax for contributions made to a state unemployment fund. The Justice's opinion was lengthy—more than twenty-two pages—and he decided all questions in favor of the constitutionality of the Alabama law. He discussed it from many aspects, and he also dealt with the conditions of "social and economic wastage" which justify such a statute.

After Justice Stone finished reading the majority opinion, he was followed by Justice Sutherland, who read a short dissent in which Justices Van Devanter and Butler concurred. Sutherland ruled against the Alabama law, but he indicated that under certain conditions state unemployment insurance codes would meet with his approval. He admitted that the objective of unemployment relief was within the constitutional power of Alabama. This objective, however, must be attained without any violation of the due process and equal protection clauses of the Constitution. The Justice felt that both of the clauses had been violated by the Act in question. Alabama, for instance, had placed a

8. [Editors' note: See especially 301 U.S. at 598–599, 609.]

9. *Carmichael, Attorney General of Alabama, et al. v. Southern Coal & Coke Co.,* 301 U.S. 495 (May 24, 1937).

disproportionately heavy burden upon employers who contributed least to unemployment because they were "engaged in industries where the number of men employed remains stable, or fairly so."

Justice McReynolds, however, disagreed on all points involved in the majority opinion, but he filed no separate dissent on his own behalf. Therefore, Sutherland merely noted orally that Justice McReynolds thought the decree [of the lower court] should be affirmed.[10]

The audience was becoming weary by the time Justice Stone finished speaking, but the session continued on as six more opinions remained to be read. Two of these disclosed once again the wide cleavage existing between the liberal and conservative factions of the Court. In one case Justice Brandeis read the majority opinion in a 5-4 decision which involved two questions: (1) what constitutes a "labor dispute" within the meaning of the Wisconsin Labor Code, and (2) what acts done by a labor union are among those declared lawful by the Code.[11] The four conservatives thereupon dissented in an opinion read by Justice Butler. And in a second case McReynolds delivered the *majority* opinion in a unique 5-4 decision involving a statutory discrimination between mutual and stock insurance companies.[12] This was to be the very last case in which the four conservatives were joined by a fifth Justice—thus enabling them to be in the majority.[13]

The Chief Justice had only one opinion to read that day, and he spoke last. He then announced an adjournment until Tuesday, June 1. The next session would be the final one of the term, and though no mention was made of Justice Van Devanter, I knew that he would be making his last appearance on the bench at that time. After the June 1 date was announced, the Justices solemnly rose and left the room. One of the most important sessions in the entire history of the Court had come to an end, and the four conservative Justices had gone down to defeat for the very last time. They had, in effect, resisted social progress to the bitter end.

It had indeed been a memorable day at Court, but I did not know as yet that another significant event had just taken place on Capitol Hill. Not only

10. See 301 U.S. 495 at 527.

11. *Senn v. Tile Layers Protective Union et al.*, 301 U.S. 468 (May 24, 1937).

12. *Hartford Steam Boiler Inspection & Insurance Co. et al. v. Harrison, Insurance Commissioner,* 301 U.S. 459 (May 24, 1937).

13. Hughes had voted with Van Devanter, McReynolds, Sutherland, and Butler. Roberts then wrote a dissent in which he was joined by Brandeis, Stone, and Cardozo.

had the Justices met at noon, but also at the same hour and on the same day both houses of Congress were convened for important sessions. In both chambers a long-awaited message was read from the President of the United States. It concerned industrial wage-and-hour standards. "The time has come," Mr. Roosevelt announced, "to take further action to extend the frontiers of social progress. Our nation, so richly endowed with natural resources and with a capable and industrious population, should be able to devise ways and means of insuring to all our able-bodied working men and women a fair day's pay for a fair day's work." The President then recommended governmental control over maximum hours and minimum wages, over child labor, and [over] "the exploitation of unorganized labor." He admitted that his program was "rudimentary." He expected difficulties because of geographical and industrial differences and the fact that federal power could not reach intrastate business. However, he asked that administrative machinery be started to establish labor standards that "will permit the maximum but prudent employment of our human resources."

After the reading of the President's message, similar bills embodying his recommendations were then introduced in the Senate and in the House. The chief provisions of these bills were: (1) the creation of a board empowered to fix industrial wage-and-hour standards—but having due regard for sectional and economic conditions; (2) the outlawing of labor practices which were defined as "oppressive"; and (3) the exclusion from interstate commerce of goods produced by children under sixteen or in factories which violated certain standards to be set up by the proposed board.

The President was apparently hoping that in the future the Supreme Court would uphold any federal legislation that might be enacted in regard to hours and wages.[14] He mentioned the earlier attempt to exclude from interstate commerce the products of child labor, and that the Court had ruled against such a law.[15] He quoted from Justice Holmes' dissent on that particular occasion. Holmes had contended that Congress did have the power to regulate child labor; also that Congress can act in the national welfare. Mr. Roosevelt

---

14. With Van Devanter's resignation Roosevelt expected to fill the first vacancy that had occurred on the Court during his administration. By this time Roberts had also definitely aligned himself with the "liberals."

15. [Editors' note: *Hammer v. Dagenhart*, 247 U.S. 251 (1918). The Court held, 5-4, that Congress could not exclude the products of child labor from interstate commerce, because "manufacture" of the goods was not yet "interstate commerce." Justice Holmes wrote an uncharacteristically impassioned dissent.]

said, "Although Mr. Justice Holmes spoke for a *minority* of the Supreme Court, he spoke for a *majority* of the American people."

As soon as it became known in Congress that day that the Supreme Court had actually upheld the Social Security Act, plans were made almost immediately to extend the protection of that Act to persons not then covered by it. These included about 2,500,000 unemployed citizens, persons over sixty-five years of age, seamen, etc. About 27,500,000 were already covered by old-age benefits and another 18,600,000 by unemployment insurance.

It might also be noted that the President's proposed bill for the reorganization of the judiciary was weakened still further by the Court's opinion on Social Security. With such an important administration victory following closely upon the unexpected announcement of Justice Van Devanter's retirement, leaders on Capitol Hill now began hoping that some sort of compromise plan could be worked out which would be acceptable to all concerned. Strange to say, however, there was no sign from the White House indicating that Mr. Roosevelt would be agreeable to accepting any other plan than the one he had laid before Congress nearly five months before.

A minor crisis now arose at 2400. Beginning on Tuesday, May 25, it was apparent that I no longer had enough work to do to keep me busy the entire day. There were generally a few letters to type for the Justice and now and then some petitions for certiorari to read and summarize but otherwise the work of the term was finished. I therefore expected to be asked to leave immediately after the last session of Court on June 1, but for some reason McReynolds made no mention of my going. He simply remained in his apartment during the day, said little, and soon did not have enough to do to keep himself busy either. He then became very restless and began rearranging furniture and pictures—anything, in fact, to have something to occupy his time during the day. I kept wishing that he would just sit down and relax or else remain in his study and read a book. But now he seldom even went for a walk—apparently due to the warm weather which had come to Washington—and of course it was out of the question for me to study for the bar examination during office hours. So I just sat quietly in my office and answered an occasional phone call for the Justice. I did not even read any book myself for fear it might appear that I was merely wasting my time. On the other hand, I did not mention the bar examination to him either.

Finally McReynolds announced that he had decided to go to New York for two days (May 27 and 28) and then leave for a trip to Tennessee on June 1, following the last session of Court. He expected to be away from Washington until at least the middle of June, and shortly after his return he planned to sail for

Europe. This news pleased me very much. It would be a heaven-sent opportunity to study full time for the bar examination. With him out of the apartment during the day, I could cram for the three-day test, summarize any petitions for certiorari that might be received, handle incoming phone calls, and yet not be bothered with the Justice. I also hoped that he would remain away until after the examination, which was scheduled to take place on June 24, 25, and 26.

Unfortunately I allowed matters to drift and made no mention of leaving either on June 1 or on July 1. My main concern was to get the bar examination out of the way and remain a law clerk until after it was over. McReynolds, however, soon began to resent the fact that I was not kept busy all day long—especially since I was still being paid my salary. It never seemed to occur to him that he also had no more legal work to do at the moment and yet was collecting his salary. A Justice, however, was apparently one thing and a law clerk quite another. Even though he did not pay me out of his own pocket, and though my apartment rent and other living expenses still continued on, he became more and more disagreeable and began to remember that on certain occasions in the past I had not been very busy either. I then wanted to remind him of the overtime I had put in on the Labor Act and Social Security dissents, but I did not do so as I wished to remain on good terms with him until the end. However, when I turned to my diary in the evenings I began to write some very uncomplimentary things about James Clark McReynolds which need not be quoted here.[16]

McReynolds did spend two days in New York—going there with a friend—and he returned to Washington by train at 7:00 P.M. on Friday the twenty-eighth. When I arrived for work on Saturday, the Justice made no comment about his trip, but he was anxious to review everything once more before going to the conference, which would be convened promptly at noon. Once again he lingered in the apartment until 11:30 A.M. This time he expected to drive to Court alone, but he did not seem to care whether he would be late or not. I did, however, walk out to the car with him—carrying the big red book as well as various other papers and briefs. On the way to his Buick, I thought to myself, "This is the very last time we shall ever leave this building together, and I wish I had a picture of us now!"

I was still in the apartment that Saturday when he returned from the conference. Upon his arrival he announced that I could leave but that he would

16. [Editors' note: No such entries survive among the extremely incomplete remaining diary materials. See the foreword, note 23.]

expect me to work on the following Monday, even though it was Memorial Day. I then spent Sunday the thirtieth studying at the Court after attending another bar review class that morning. In the evening Richard Hogue, one of the Chief Justice's law clerks, stopped by for a long talk [about the term].

On Memorial Day, McReynolds kept me busy until 4:00 P.M. as he expected to leave for Tennessee the next day. That evening I had an appointment to call on Justice Cardozo, and after dinner I decided to walk to his address even though it was some distance away and the weather was very warm and uncomfortable.[17]

That evening I saw him for the last time as he stood framed in the open doorway when I took my final leave. His face shown like a cameo in the reflection of the light. "Thank you for everything you have done for me this year," I said quietly as we shook hands for the last time. Then I started to walk down the hall of the apartment house, but after a few short steps I turned half round and stopped. He had not moved and was still looking at me, so I raised one hand ever so slightly and waved a final farewell in silence.

To me he is still standing in that open doorway and all the faces that pass by in the steady stream of life cannot erase the memory of the great one whom I knew and loved in those far-off days.[18]

"I was secretary to the wrong Justice," I thought to myself as I walked back to 2400.

On Tuesday, June 1, the Justice made his usual preparations to drive to Court. This was to be the last session of the term and also the last time that Van Devanter would appear on the bench.[19] I was, of course, anxious to attend and asked McReynolds if I could drive with him. This request was a routine one which he had courteously granted numerous times before, but on this

17. [Knox later wrote that his final conversation with Cardozo was one of his most cherished memories of the year. "In my last evening spent with Justice Cardozo, he read *Goodbye, Mr. Chips* to me while he fed me with ice cream and cookies he had been saving for me." Knox to Monte J. Povda, Feb. 4, 1978, D'Angelo Law Library Collection, University of Chicago Law School.]

18. Before the end of that year Cardozo began to have sinking spells followed by a severe heart attack, and he could no longer attend sessions of the Court. On January 8, 1938, he suffered a stroke. He died on July 9, 1938. On Monday, October 3, 1938, the Chief Justice and six Associate Justices expressed in open court their profound sorrow at Cardozo's death. Justice McReynolds absented himself from Court that day.

19. Only two decisions were to be handed down, and both were relatively unimportant. *Great Lakes Transit Corp. v. Interstate Steamship Co. et al.*, 301 U.S. 646; *Thomas, Collector, v. Perkins et al.*, 301 U.S. 655.

particular Monday the Justice replied, "No, I want you to remain. Harry will be at Court to serve my lunch, and I may receive some phone calls here. I certainly don't trust Mary to get any message straight, and remember I am leaving for Tennessee at six o'clock."

McReynolds' decision that I should remain in the apartment was, of course, a very legitimate one. I therefore stayed until Harry returned, but no one had telephoned in the meantime. Not until then did I go to lunch, and by the time I walked back to the apartment McReynolds had also returned. The session was over, Court was adjourned for the summer, and he was busily preparing to leave town. When his luggage was finally packed to his satisfaction and he had eaten an early dinner, he asked Harry to drive him to the Union Station. When the two of them finally left I bade the Justice a cordial goodbye, but I was surprised that he had said nothing all afternoon about how I was to conduct myself in his absence. I still had not mentioned the bar examination, and it was obvious that I would not have enough Court work to do to keep myself busy while he was out of town. In fact, he had not even referred to my leaving on July 1, and I thought this most strange. However, I was glad to delay any mention of my departure until after the bar examination had taken place. Perhaps he had decided that I should stay until it was time for him to leave for Europe, but as yet I did not even know when this might be. According to newspaper reports the Justice also expected to address the commencement exercise at Vanderbilt University, where he had graduated in 1882. McReynolds had not, however, made any mention of such a speech to me, and he had not dictated any prepared statement for me to type.

That evening I spent two hours at the review class. I was by now very far behind in the course, and to make matters more difficult the weather had become extremely sultry and uncomfortable. The next morning—Wednesday, June 2—I appeared for work on time just as if McReynolds were still in town. In fact, I thought he might be, but Harry said the Justice had actually gotten on the train and that I could now devote all of my energies to studying for the examination. After some discussion we decided that I should move into McReynolds' air-conditioned office at the Court instead of trying to study in his overheated apartment. Harry would be on hand each day to answer the telephone, and it was doubtful that the Justice would spend the money to telephone all the way from Tennessee to check on my whereabouts. So on Thursday, June 3, I took all of my books, papers, and notes and moved to Court to spend as much time as possible in concentrated study. Upon my arrival I borrowed a typewriter from one of the other offices, closed the door of McReynolds' suite, took off my coat, sat down, and prepared to tackle the most difficult examination of my life. First, however, I wrote a few words in my diary:

> Brandeis' secretary [Willard Hurst] is leaving, but where he is going I don't know. I have only seen him twice since I came to the Court and have not talked with him for more than four minutes in the entire year.
>
> . . . McReynolds spent most of the day yesterday cussing out his messenger who was packing suitcases for him. Not even on the last day could he say a kind word to Harry. Harry has worked like a slave all year and he told the Justice he was tired out, and the J. said, "What have you done to get tired?" Harry asked for 30 days vacation this summer like all the other messenger always get, and McR. said he could only have 15.
>
> . . . McR. is mad at the C. J. and mad at everybody. He is, all in all, the most contemptible and mediocre old man I ever came in contact with. His selfishness and vindictiveness are unbelievable.
>
> McR. is unbelievably stingy. He won't buy anything if he can help it— not even a ten cents soap dish. He tells his friends that he is poor man (untrue, as I know his bank balance). Last month he asked ———— ———— if she would give him an Oriental rug out of her living room. She was quite shocked, as the thing must be worth $1,000. She told me she was not going to do it. In some ways he is gravely unbalanced.
>
> . . . I shall buy two wooden boxes but not start to pack until after the exam. I have no idea as yet whether I can pass it.[20]

McReynolds had by now reached Elkton, Kentucky, to visit friends and relatives, and two other Justices had also left Washington to begin their summer vacations. Van Devanter was already at his farm near Ellicott City, Maryland, and on Wednesday, June 2, Chief Justice Hughes departed by auto for a trip to New England. Stone was preparing to journey to Mexico and then go to Isle au Haut off the coast of Maine where he had a summer home. Roberts expected to spend the summer at Bryn Coed, his place in Chester County, Pennsylvania. Cardozo was going as usual to Rye, New York, to be near old friends. Brandeis had a summer home at Chatham, Massachusetts, on Cape

20. Even after the lapse of a quarter of a century I can hardly bring myself to reread once again the comments made in my diary during the months of May and June 1937. I also hesitate to make direct quotations from these entries as some of them were, of course, written under considerable emotional stress when I was trying to prepare for a difficult three-day bar examination. All of the comments are, of course, true, but eventually the diary will be destroyed. As I read it over once again, however, Harry grows in stature with each passing day. [Editors' note: See note 16, *supra.*]

Cod and would spend his vacation there. Sutherland planned to spend the summer driving through England, Scotland, and the Continent. He also expected to visit his birthplace at Buckinghamshire, England. And lastly Butler was to spend his vacation at Blue Ridge Summit, Pennsylvania, which was situated in a cool mountain altitude near the Maryland-Pennsylvania line. Here he could play golf and rest in a community only seventy miles from Washington. Thus did the Nine Old Men disperse for the summer of 1937.

One of the most remarkable sessions in the entire history of the Supreme Court had now come to an end, and not once during the term had there been a ruling against any important New Deal legislation. Since October the sentiment of the Justices had been tested seventeen times, and in all seventeen instances New Deal laws had been upheld. In previous terms eleven vital cases had been decided against the administration and only two in its favor. As a result some observers now thought that the pressure which had been exerted by the President for remaking the Court had had considerable influence on the Justices' decisions. Other observers, however, denied that the Justices had ever reacted under pressure.

Some of the government's outstanding success during the 1936–37 term had undoubtedly been due to more carefully drafted laws, more efficient preparation of cases, and better arguments by attorneys who had appeared before the Court. And then there was the part played by Chief Justice Hughes and by Justice Roberts in this historic term. Both men, for example, had previously voted against the government on the agricultural control issue. Both, however, had later voted for the Wagner and Social Security Acts. In fact, Justice Roberts had made the most remarkable shift of any of the nine members of the Court—from the conservative to the liberal wing. He, more than any other Justice, was responsible for the change in the trend of the Court's decisions. And because of Roberts, the majority which had controlled decisions in the past had been cut down to a minority of four Justices—the famous quartet of conservatives. By June 1937, this once solid phalanx of four was still ultra-conservative, but it had just been broken by the retirement of Justice Van Devanter. And despite the Presidential election of 1936, Mr. Roosevelt's attack upon the Court, the long-continued depression, changing social and economic conditions, and the pressing need for minimum wage legislation, etc., Justices Van Devanter, McReynolds, Sutherland, and Butler had remained implacable foes of the New Deal and even of twentieth-century progress. I think it can be said honestly and impartially that *these four conservative Justices would have permanently wrecked the Supreme Court as it was then constituted had not Justice Roberts forsaken them and allied himself with Hughes, Brandeis, Stone, and Cardozo.* The Court could not have withstood the stresses and storms of the 1936–37 term had the four conservatives been in control.

And what of that bill? By the close of the term on June 2, 1937, the President's chances of driving through his legislation were declining by the hour if not by the minute. Since Mr. Roosevelt still refused to alter his original demands, he was proving as stubborn in maintaining his position as the four conservative Justices had been in standing firm in their beliefs. Both sides had long since drawn their battle lines and were determined not to yield an inch, and in the end both went down to defeat. By June 2 Mr. Roosevelt's defeat was fast approaching.

During the time Justice McReynolds was out of town and I was busy studying for the bar examination, I arrived at his apartment every morning at nine o'clock as usual. After sorting through the mail, I answered any letters that needed to be attended to and then Harry drove me to Court in McReynolds' car. "There's no use letting it sit in the garage and just let the battery get low," was Harry's justification for our daily excursions. We were generally on our way not later than noon, but I kept wondering if the Justice would examine the [odometer] upon his return.

On Monday, June 7, I worked at McReynolds' apartment until noon and then was driven to Court again. On Tuesday, Harry drove me to Harlan F. Stone's residence, where I had a noon appointment to see the Justice. We talked for a full hour in the beautiful library of his home. Stone was extremely outspoken in discussing some of the members of the Court and in summarizing the work of the term. He was also interested to learn how I had fared with Justice McReynolds. I told him that I had managed to last through the term tolerably well and that everything was on an even keel—at least as far as I knew. I also mentioned that I was busy studying for the bar examination while McReynolds was out of town. Stone wished me well and said he hoped to see me again whenever I returned to Washington for a visit.[21]

---

21. By now the approaching bar examination seemed to be coming toward me with the speed of an express train, so when I arrived home that evening I decided not to take time to summarize Stone's conversation in detail. It was then so clear in my mind I thought that I could remember it forever, but after the lapse of a quarter of a century I cannot now recreate it in sufficient detail to describe here. Stone always impressed me as a highly intelligent but matter-of-fact businessman. There was no show or pretense about him, and I always felt completely at ease in his presence. On subsequent trips to Washington I saw him several more times. Whenever I talked with him in private his pent-up feeling about McReynolds and the quartet of conservatives seemed to burst forth. The Justice told me he could be earning ten times his judicial salary if he resigned from the bench and returned to the Wall Street law firm where he had formerly practiced. However, Stone said that he preferred to remain in government service to do what he could in the shaping of the law. He was, of course, serving as Chief Justice at the time of his sudden death in 1946.

My hours of study at the Court building were interrupted by unexpected callers during the next two days, and this hampered my last-minute preparations for the bar examination. On June 9, for instance, two friends from Chicago arrived, and I spent considerable time showing them through the building. On June 10 the Marshal's office informed me that three more had come—two were from Iowa and one from Washington. I took these three to a late lunch at the Methodist Building near the Court, and I also spent the remainder of the afternoon with them. Fortunately I had no callers on Friday, the eleventh. On Saturday, I declined a dinner invitation for that evening in Georgetown. The thirteenth was spent in another dismal day of Sunday study in the deserted Court building. I was also at Court [all day Monday].

On Tuesday the fifteenth I was again at Court. The big and important news of that day concerned the long-awaited report of the Judiciary Committee, which had reached the Senate. The report denounced the President's proposed bill to reorganize the courts as "a needless, futile, and utterly dangerous abandonment of constitutional principle." There was a recommendation that the bill be rejected. This report, which represented the views of ten of the eighteen members of the Judiciary Committee, declared that the bill was "a proposal that violates every sacred tradition of American democracy," and it called upon the Senate to reject the proposal so emphatically "that its parallel will never again be presented to the free representatives of the free people of America." The report also stated that the bill was a proposal without precedent or justification, and that it was an attempt to subjugate the courts to the will of Congress and the President and thereby destroy the independence of the judiciary.

It was now certain that it would be almost impossible for the President to salvage any part of his court-enlargement plan. There seemed to be no other topic of conversation at the Court that day except the Committee's report. "The bill has been defeated," I said to an attendant from the Marshal's office, "but at least Roosevelt can appoint some brilliant and outstanding young jurist to take Van Devanter's place on the Court." It was widely rumored that the President would give the post to a prominent Senator [Joseph T. Robinson, D-Ark.] who had been exerting every effort to get the proposed bill enacted.

On Wednesday, June 16, I went to Court as usual and remained there all day. It was a fateful date, and for years thereafter it stood forth in my memory in painful recollection. Before McReynolds left town he had told me he expected to be away from Washington until "at least the middle of June." It was now one day past the middle of the month, but we had not heard any news about his returning to town. I was also so immersed in study that I led myself to believe he probably would remain in Kentucky until June 26 at least—the last day of the bar examination. But alas! On the morning of the sixteenth, McReynolds unexpectedly returned to Washington. Harry had just arrived at the apartment after driving me to Court, and luckily he and Mary were there when the front door opened and the Justice walked in. McReynolds was undoubtedly carrying just a suitcase and had probably hailed a taxi upon arriving at the Union Station. In any event there was no chance for Harry to telephone and ask me to return to 2400 at once. For the first time since I had assumed my duties as a law clerk, I was not on hand when the Justice returned to his apartment. I was not just "out to lunch"—I was, in fact, not there at all. Nor was I expected back at any time that afternoon, and Harry explained that I was probably in the library at Court studying for the bar examination. He was also not able to reach me that evening, for I attended another bar review class until 10:30 P.M.

At nine o'clock on Thursday, June 17, I appeared as usual at McReynolds' apartment to pick up the morning mail and answer any letters that needed to be attended to. I was, of course, astounded to find that McReynolds was there and that he had just finished his breakfast. And yet I should not have been surprised at all: he had returned at exactly the time he said he would, for it was now past the middle of the month. I managed to greet the Justice as nonchalantly as possible, but at ten o'clock he rang for me to come to his study. I can still remember the awful sound of the buzzer on my desk as it began to hiss almost like a rattlesnake.

What had I been doing away from his apartment at a time when he was out of town?

Wasn't I hired as his clerk and secretary to remain in the apartment to attend to whatever duties there might be at such a time?

What was all this about spending my time at Court studying for a bar examination?

Who gave me permission to devote my time to such an undertaking?

Yes, I explained, I had decided to write the three-day bar examination which was scheduled for the following week, and I thought he would not mind since he had been out of town and the work of the term was over. Besides, I had taken care of the daily mail and even summarized a few petitions for certiorari that had been received during his absence.

"You are being paid to be my law clerk and not to spend your time writing a bar examination," McReynolds replied as his eyes narrowed. "If you persist in your plans I shall telephone the Clerk of the Court and order your salary stopped at once."

I turned and looked at McReynolds with what must have been an expression of both helplessness and sadness on my face, and for a few moments I could say nothing. A Justice of the Supreme Court of the United States was impatiently awaiting my answer, but the words would not come and my throat seemed to choke up. Should I give in to him and promise not to take the examination? Or should I disagree with him, lose my job and my salary, and perhaps even fail the examination, too?

I realized it was little short of a disaster to have any misunderstanding so late in the year, when all the hard work of the term was over and the summer vacation had at last arrived. It was true that the Justice had a perfect right to insist that his law clerk remain in the apartment at all times and not devote any attention to outside interests during office hours. But it was also true that in a few weeks McReynolds would be leisurely touring Europe and yet collecting his salary at the same time. Besides I could not practice law unless I became a member of the bar of some state or of the District of Columbia. I knew, therefore, what my answer must be, and finally I began to speak.

14

"THE BAR EXAMINATION is only a week away," I replied, "and unless I pass it I cannot practice law anywhere. I've also paid twenty-five dollars and been assigned a seat number. I *must*, therefore, write this examination."

A few moments of silence followed, and then Justice McReynolds shrugged his shoulders in a gesture of indifference. "Very well," he said, "your salary will stop at once, and your job is over." In making this pronouncement, McReynolds was as impersonal as if he were merely ordering a second cup of coffee for breakfast. From the tone of his voice one could never have guessed that he was summarily dismissing the law clerk and secretary who had worked in intimate contact with him six days a week for months during a time of crisis such as the Supreme Court had never before experienced.

I was so taken aback that I did not know what else to say. There was, in fact, nothing more to be said. I had made my decision, and he had made his. After a few moments of silence, therefore, I merely mentioned that I would leave at once. To this statement he made no reply, and there was no expression of "I wish you luck with the examination" or even a "Goodbye." I then walked out of the room without making any further comment, and I soon began to clear out my desk. At this moment Harry walked to the door of my office, and as I turned and looked up at him I noticed that he held in his hand a group photograph of all of the nine Justices. The picture was a well-known likeness of the Nine Old Men which had been taken several years before by Harris & Ewing of Washington. I also noticed that eight members of the Court had already autographed the picture in ink at the bottom of the photograph. Only the signature of Justice McReynolds was missing.

"Mr. Knox," Harry said, "Justice Cardozo just sent this picture over for

Justice McReynolds to sign. As soon as he writes his name on it I'll send it back."[1]

I stopped cleaning out the right top drawer of my desk long enough to look closely at Harry. My first thought was, "He'll never autograph any picture now—not after what's happened!" Then a moment later I said to myself, "Well, he might sign his name if he doesn't know who sent the picture. So I won't mention that it is from Cardozo." I then told Harry that I would take care of the matter at once. He said nothing more but merely turned around and sauntered down the hall to the kitchen—still not knowing that I had just been dismissed. As soon as Harry had left, I walked into McReynolds' study for the very last time during that term of Court. I held the photograph in my right hand but made no comment except to say that Harry wanted it signed. The Justice was sitting at his desk writing a personal letter, and I fully expected him to balk or to be in a bad mood because of the interruption. To my surprise, however, he merely glanced up, reached for the picture, and autographed it at once. He was as impersonal about the matter as if I had never even been in his office that morning.

I walked down the hall to the kitchen with the picture. As soon as the folding door closed behind me I said to Harry, "Here it is. He didn't object to signing his name."

Harry happened to be at the sink running the water over some vegetables he was preparing for the Justice's lunch. Looking around at me after shutting off the water he said, "Well, why should he? Pussywillow's been signing pictures for years. But this one wasn't sent over here until the rest of them signed first."

"Everyone has written on the picture now," I replied, "all nine of them. They know that McReynolds is so temperamental he might have refused to sign unless the other eight did so first." I then hesitated for a few moments before saying, "And I have something else to tell you. Getting this picture autographed is my last duty as a law clerk. I won't be staying around until July 1 after all. I've just been fired—and only thirteen days before the time I expected to leave!"

Upon hearing these words, both Harry and Mary immediately stopped what they were doing, gasped under their breath, and said almost simultaneously, "Fired? You mean fired?"

---

1. Since Harry was standing just a few feet from McReynolds' office, his conversation was formal. He did not, for instance, refer to the Justice as "Pussywillow." Nor did he address me as

"Yes, fired!" I replied grimly. "He says he's going to stop my salary, too. He doesn't want me to take the bar examination next week, but I told him I had to. And when you brought in the picture I was just beginning to clean out my desk. I'll be ready to leave in about half an hour."

The announcement of my imminent departure—even before lunchtime—was received with considerable regret. After his initial surprise, however, the news did not seem unusual as far as Harry was concerned. He had, in fact, warned me many times that I would be dismissed if I should ever be away from the apartment without an adequate excuse when the Justice returned. Even though Court was adjourned and there was virtually no legal work to keep me busy during the day, nevertheless McReynolds had come back to town after a lengthy absence and found me gone. I was not just "out to lunch"—I was five miles away and did not put in an appearance for the rest of that day.

"Well, I sure hate to see you leave," were Harry's next words. "It was nice having you around this year."

"It's too bad," Mary said, "but you would [have] stayed only a few days more anyhow. But where you going after you walk out of here today?"

"I just don't know," I replied, "but I'll be back and see both of you before I leave Washington."

I then returned to my office without tarrying any longer in the kitchen— just in case the Justice might walk in and find the three of us talking. And as I finished cleaning out my desk I thought to myself, "All these months Harry, Mary, and I have been afraid to speak to each other while McReynolds was in the apartment. We have lived in fear, but now that has ended—at least for me. When I get out of here today it will seem like walking into fresh air again!"

In a few minutes I left my offices, taking several possessions with me. These consisted chiefly of shorthand notebooks. For weeks I had expected the Justice to ask that they all be delivered to him—to be destroyed—but he had never mentioned them at all. I then returned to the kitchen to say goodbye to Harry and Mary. Mary was wearing an apron, and after hastily wiping her hands on it she extended her right hand for me to shake. "I never would have believed it," she said, "that you would up and leave like this after getting along so well all this time. But don't be upset one bit. You know how he is."

Harry then turned to me, solemnly shook hands, and said, "Remember I

"Shoefenicks." However, his conversation could not have been heard by the Justice, who was sitting in his office and not walking in the hall.

kept telling you about Pussywillow, and everything would have come out all right if you hadn't been at Court yesterday when he came back here."

"I doubt it," I replied. "I still would have had to ask for three days off next week to write the exam, and he probably would have fired me when he heard that."

"Maybe so, maybe so," commented Harry thoughtfully. "One never can tell about Pussywillow!"

I did not return to McReynolds' study to say goodbye or to mention that I had enjoyed my year in Washington. The truth was that I had enjoyed it very much. I had lived in close proximity to the highest court in the land during its most difficult year. I had also met many interesting people, and all in all it had been a rich and rewarding experience. It had been, that is, with one exception. That exception, of course, was James Clark McReynolds' personality.

I then waved farewell to Harry and Mary, and with my possessions under one arm I left the Justice's apartment by the kitchen door. As soon as I reached my room at 2700 Connecticut Avenue, N.W., I put the shorthand notebooks on my dresser and decided on the spur of the moment to take a taxi to the Court and see the Clerk—Charles Elmore Cropley. When I made this decision, however, I did not know that Justice McReynolds had already telephoned Mr. Cropley—requesting that my salary be stopped at once. This phone call was evidently made while I was in the kitchen returning the autographed picture to Harry.

Poor Mr. Cropley! He had long considered me as a fair-haired boy who had somehow managed to survive the entire term with Justice McReynolds without any seeming difficulty at all. Each time I had seen Mr. Cropley at Court during the year, he had always been flattering in his comments regarding my supposed progress. And now to have everything end like this!

I arrived at Court just as Mr. Cropley was preparing to go to lunch. As soon as I reached his office, however, he asked me to sit down and tell him what had happened. He had such a puzzled expression on his face that I smiled and said, "Nothing serious happened. I didn't murder Harry or anything like that! Remember I have been studying here at Court for the bar examination— in order to take advantage of the air conditioning—and yesterday I was not in the Justice's apartment when he returned from his trip to Kentucky. Nor did I show up there until this morning—so he fired me."

Some moments passed before Mr. Cropley made any reply, and then he said with great seriousness, "Of course, Justice McReynolds can stop your salary as of today if he wants to, but I feel that he should never again be assigned a secretary who is not at least forty years old. It is too rigorous a job for a young man just out of law school." He then mentioned that my successor was apparently past forty. This was J. T. McHale, who had been Justice Van Devanter's long-time secretary and law clerk.

"I also feel," Mr. Cropley continued, "that Justice McReynolds' clerk should be paid as much as some of the other clerks are receiving. This is something I shall discuss with the Chief Justice when he returns to town. Let's see, your annual salary was $2,750.00, and it should have been at least $3,000.00. You were also confined in his apartment instead of working here at Court."

"I certainly regret that this had to happen," I said. "There would have been no difficulty if I had not wanted to take the bar examination next week. He just doesn't believe that I should be paid while studying for the exam."

"Well, that's one way of looking at it," Mr. Cropley replied, "but his phone call was certainly a surprise."

It was then decided that I should continue my studies at the Court—in order to take advantage of the air conditioning. In fact, I would have more time to prepare for the bar examination now that I had no further duties as a law clerk. I thanked Mr. Cropley and then walked to Justice McReynolds' suite of offices—which he had never used. I sat down at a typewriter I had borrowed from another office and wrote a letter to Justice Van Devanter telling him that I had been dismissed and just what had happened. Unfortunately I could not find any carbon paper in McReynolds' office, so I did not make a carbon copy of this letter. It was, in fact, the only letter which I wrote during the entire time I was in Washington of which I do not have a carbon copy. All that I can remember of its contents is that I made some very barbed comments about McReynolds—though at the same time telling Van Devanter once more that I very much appreciated his having selected me for the position of law clerk during what proved to be a most eventful term of Court.[2]

That evening I also wrote a letter to my parents and told them what had happened. After completing the letter I checked my bank balance and then typed a postscript on a separate sheet of paper. I still have this postscript, which reads as follows: "I have $67.89 in the bank. This constitutes my entire fortune. I was banking a great deal on being paid for this month."

By that time I had become so angry with Justice McReynolds that I did not notice I used the word "bank" in two different meanings instead of writing, "I was relying a great deal on being paid for this month." In any event I was

---

2. [Editors' note: The letter does not survive in the Van Devanter Papers held in the Manuscript Division, Library of Congress.]

"broke" as my monthly salary calculated on a yearly stipend of $2,750.00 had all been spent in what at that time seemed to be the "high cost of living in Washington."

My parents must have been enormously disappointed upon receiving the letter I had typed in such anger. In reality there was no need that I ever tell them what had happened. They expected to arrive in Washington on July 3 and then drive me to Richmond to visit some Confederate historical sites. I could have remained quiet, and they would always have assumed that my year with McReynolds had ended as a splendid success. Even Harry would have covered up for me on that score—I expected to introduce him to my father and mother—but by now I was so angry that I spared no punches in the letter to my parents. After working all year for McReynolds under strict conditions that left much to be desired, it was hard to realize that I had been dismissed for merely trying to become a member of the bar. Granted that I had not been hired to take a bar examination, still I could not forget that McReynolds would be collecting his salary as usual while leisurely touring Europe during the summer. After all, didn't he want to extend a helping hand even to his own law clerk?

After mailing the letter to my parents, I went to bed. When I awoke the next morning, however, my anger was all gone. By then I felt that I was moving along irresistibly toward the last act of some classic Greek tragedy. It was Friday, June 18, and for the first time since my arrival in Washington I had no job to go to. Nor was any more salary to be paid me. The weather had also become unbearably hot—making if difficult to sleep—and I was no longer in the mood to do any studying, let alone write a difficult three-day bar examination. I remembered that it was exactly one year since I had graduated from Harvard at the famous Tercentenary Commencement. On June 18, 1936, the letter from Justice McReynolds has also arrived just as I was preparing to walk over to the Yard and receive my degree. A year had passed, and what a year!

I spent all day Saturday and Sunday, June 19 and 20, studying at Court. Once again the deserted building seemed like a vast and forbidding tomb of the ancient pharaohs. Then on Monday afternoon, the twenty-first, Mr. Cropley asked if I would do him the favor of moving from Justice McReynolds' suite to the unused office which had been assigned to Justice Brandeis. The Clerk of the Court said that he feared Justice McReynolds would make a special trip to the building to see whether I was using his offices; also that McReynolds was in a bad mood after I had crossed him by insisting on taking the bar examination. Mr. Cropley wished to avoid the possibility of any further conflict, and he also said, "Surely Justice Brandeis would not object if he knew you were studying in his offices! If you are there Justice McReynolds will have nothing more to complain about." So on Tuesday, I moved to the Brandeis suite and turned on the air conditioning there. I studied at Court until 10:30 P.M. that day—having decided not to attend the bar review class.

The last day before the examination was Wednesday, June 23. Once again I studied at Court all that day, and in the evening I attended the final session of the bar review course. The next morning bright and early I presented myself along with more than eight hundred other hopeful candidates at the Georgetown Law School, 506 E Street, N.W. From 9:00 until 12:00 that morning the examination covered the subjects of Bailments and Carriers, Contracts, Bills and Notes, and Agency. This was followed by a hasty lunch, and from 1:00 until 4:00 I answered questions in the fields of Equity Jurisprudence, Corporations, and Bankruptcy. That evening after dinner I studied at the Court until 10:30 P.M.

The second day of the examination was Friday, June 25. From 9:00 until 12:00 the questions concerned Wills and Administration of Estates, Domestic Relations, and Personal Property. In the afternoon from 1:00 until 4:00 the subjects covered were Evidence, Torts, and Partnerships. And again that evening I studied at the Court—not leaving the building until 11:00 P.M.

The third and final day of the examination was Saturday, June 26. From 9:00 until 12:00 I wrote answers to questions concerning Real Property, Eminent Domain, Common Law Pleading, and Equity Pleading. Then the final afternoon was spent from 1:00 until 4:00 on Criminal Law, Criminal Procedure, Constitutional Law, Extraordinary Legal Remedies, and Legal Ethics. As soon as the examination was over I returned to my room, and by pre-arrangement my landlady took me to dinner with two of her friends—to celebrate my "passing the bar." I was so tired, however, that I felt as if I had "crossed the bar" instead. The next day I slept until noon. When I awoke, however, I felt that I had at least a 50-50 chance to pass the examination. In fact, I became quite hopeful that I would soon be a member of the bar instead of just a law school graduate.

I spent Monday, June 28, packing my trunk, typewriter, three boxes, etc. and later doing some sightseeing around Washington. While I was in my room, Mr. McHale unexpectedly telephoned to ask if I would meet him at Court the next day to show him the ropes. I thought that I had seen the last of the Court building for a while, but I did agree to meet my successor there at 10:00 A.M. on Tuesday. In fact, I worked at the Court until 9:30 P.M. that day— not only instructing Mr. McHale how to avoid various pitfalls during the coming year but also bringing all of McReynolds' accounts for May up to date.

I wanted to do everything possible to make the following term of Court a successful one for Mr. McHale as I knew the change from Justice Van Devanter to Justice McReynolds would be a very difficult one for him to make.

My parents arrived on schedule along with several other relatives, and on Saturday, July 3, I took them on a tour of the Supreme Court building. Harry was not there at the time, but we did meet him later in the day. He was on an errand uptown, and I remember him talking briefly with my relatives as they sat in their car ready to leave Washington. This was to be my last glimpse of Harry for another year. As soon as we said goodbye to him, we left at once for Richmond to begin an extensive tour of Civil War landmarks. A few days later we visited the graves of certain prominent Confederates, and I was photographed standing in front of a monument of Jefferson Davis. "I want to have my picture taken with him," I said, "because we were both involved in lost causes. And neither of us had sense enough to know it at the time—until it was too late."

It was not until Sunday evening, July 11, that I finally reached my home in a suburb of Chicago. And on July 14 I made the following entry in my diary: "Senator Joseph T. Robinson of Arkansas died last night of an unexpected heart attack on the eve of his appointment to the U.S. Supreme Court." The senator's sudden death left President Roosevelt free to name whomever he wished to fill the vacancy caused by Justice Van Devanter's retirement. The White House had been under obligation to Robinson because of the Senator's valiant but futile efforts to secure passage of the President's proposed judiciary bill.

On Friday, July 23, I wrote: "The Senate has finally killed President Roosevelt's attempt to 'pack' the Supreme Court of the United States." Thus the long battle had finally ended in defeat for F.D.R. However, one vacancy had already occurred on the Court, and it was evident that several other Justices could not remain active much longer. Yet Justice McReynolds was not one of them, and he still appeared to be in the best of health and gave no indication of resigning despite his seventy-five years.

Eventually a letter arrived from a friend in Washington, and I was informed that the names of those candidates who had successfully passed the June 1937 bar examination in the District of Columbia had just been made public. My name, however, was not on the list. *I had failed the bar examination.* I would now have to begin all over again to attend another bar review course. But everything would be more difficult than before as I was no longer in the District of Columbia, but in the State of Illinois, and various new and different rules and regulations would have to be learned.

The day after receiving the news from Washington I wrote to Mr. Cropley and told him. He replied at once saying that everything was bound to work out all right in the end and that I should not be discouraged. Ultimately, however, I had to spend many a weary hour of study before becoming a member of the Illinois and New York bars. As soon as I was qualified to practice in Illinois I wrote to Mr. Cropley again and told him of my belated success. However, I did not inform Justice McReynolds that I had at last become a duly licensed attorney-at-law.

In July 1938, I was again in Washington, and shortly after I arrived I called on Justice Van Devanter.[3] The Justice was very cordial and spent a half-hour talking with me, but there was no mention by either of us of Justice McReynolds. I then drove to 2400 to call on Harry and Mary. A year had passed since I had last seen them, and so we discussed many things as I sat once more in the kitchen of McReynolds' apartment. However, I did not even inquire about the Justice, and since it was July I assumed that he was out of town. To my surprise, however, Harry finally mentioned him and said that he was in the apartment at the time. "In fact," said Harry, "I think it would be nice if you walked in to his office and said hello."

To this suggestion I replied with surprise, "Harry! You can't mean it! Not after the way he acted when I wanted to take the bar examination!"

"Yes, I do mean it," Harry said solemnly. "I think you two should make up. You were real mad at him when you left a year ago, but now both of you should be friends again."

"But he wouldn't want to see me even if I wanted to see him—which I don't!" I protested.

"Oh, yes he would," Harry insisted. And then after a moment or two of silence he continued, "Pussywillow gets real lonely now and then—I'm sure of that—so I'll go in now and tell him you're here."

"Harry, this is crazy," I insisted. "You know it is!" And then I said, "I'm going to leave right away! Why didn't you tell me he was here. I wouldn't have stayed so long!"

Mary then began to laugh as Harry opened the folding door to the dining room and started to walk toward the Justice's study. In a few minutes he returned and said that everything was now ready for me to walk in and see

---

3. I had just driven in from Gettysburg, where I attended the celebration by Union and Confederate veterans of the seventy-fifth anniversary of the battle. This was the last time I saw Justice Van Devanter. I continued to correspond with him from time to time until shortly before his sudden death on February 8, 1941.

McReynolds. I gave Harry and Mary a long and searching look, slowly opened the door, walked alone through the familiar dining room and hall, and in a few moments I was standing once again at the threshold of the Justice's study. And then a strange thing happened. He looked up from his desk as if he had never seen me before in all his life, and that I was someone who was calling for the first time. "Oh, do sit down," he said in a very cordial tone of voice. This I did with some misgivings, and for about ten minutes he discussed various topics of the day with a cool and detached formality that almost made me believe that I had never even seen him before. And then of a sudden it dawned upon me that I was witnessing a repetition of the interview he had had in September 1936 with one of his former secretaries. The wheel of fate had now come full circle, and I, too, was returning to 2400 as a former secretary who was being talked down to in the same cordial but distant manner. McReynolds, in fact, seemed to be attempting to break through some invisible wall that surrounded him, and to communicate with me somehow, but this attempt was doomed to failure—even with a former secretary. How strange it all seemed!

I soon made my way back to the kitchen—feeling a bit chilled despite the warm weather—but at least Harry was pleased to know that Pussywillow and I had finally "made up again." As for me, I did not comment further about the matter, and I soon left and walked one flight upstairs to call on Mrs. Savage. It was good to see her again.

McReynolds' seventy-ninth birthday occurred on February 3, 1941. That day was a Monday, and the Justices reconvened after a recess but McReynolds did not appear as usual to take his seat upon the bench. After the opening of Court Chief Justice Hughes then announced:

> On February 1, 1941, Mr. Justice James Clark McReynolds retired from active service as Associate Justice of this Court. Forthright, independent, maintaining with strength and tenacity of conviction his conceptions of constitutional right, he has served with distinction upon this bench for upwards of twenty-six years and has left a deep impress upon the jurisprudence of the Court. It is hoped that, relieved of the burden of active service, he will long enjoy his accustomed vigor of body and mind.

When contacted by reporters McReynolds said, "I have no plans and there will be no interviews." He merely told friends that he thought it best to retire while "in full possession of my faculties and health." It is interesting to note, however, that *the other eight Justices did not send him a letter of appreciation upon his retirement*—such as had been done upon the retirement of Justice Van Devanter and numerous other Justices.

At the opening of Court on Monday, February 10, 1941—just a week after the announcement of McReynolds' resignation—Chief Justice Hughes [announced the death of Justice Van Devanter]. A few months later—on June 2, 1941—Chief Justice Hughes also retired and was succeeded by Harlan F. Stone. By then only Chief Justice Stone and Justice Roberts remained of the original Nine Old Men.

In July 1941, in the midst of the European war, the newspapers announced that McReynolds had "adopted" some thirty-three British children who were victims of the blitzkrieg on Great Britain. It was said that he was supporting the children and personally corresponding with every one of them. Some cartoons in the press depicted a crusty old bachelor who resembled the "old woman who lived in a shoe." It was also reported that he had offered to contribute the first ten thousand dollars to a ten-million-dollar Save the Children Fund.

In December 1942, while I was on a trip to Washington for the War Production Board, Travis Brown—then a Lieutenant in the Navy—moved my admission as a member of the bar of the Supreme Court of the United States. As I stood briefly before the nine Justices I noticed, of course, that it was an entirely new Court with the exception of Chief Justice Stone and Justice Roberts. How odd it seemed to glance up and see someone other than Charles Evans Hughes sitting in the chair of the Chief Justice! I also instinctively looked at the far chair on my right—Cardozo's old place—but, of course, he was not there.

On Monday, April 22, 1946, Chief Justice Stone died very unexpectedly a few hours after suffering a stroke while presiding at a Monday session of the Court. His funeral was held in the Washington Cathedral on Thursday, the twenty-fifth, and it was attended by both the active and the retired Justices. At this funeral McReynolds made what was to be his last public appearance, and the newspapers noted that "he stuck by the side of Justice Burton, the lone Republican on the Court." A picture of the Justices who attended the funeral appeared in a contemporary issue of *Life* magazine, and in this photograph Chief Justice Hughes and Justice McReynolds are clearly visible. They had been retired for some three years, and both were then in their eighty-fifth year. I noticed that McReynolds was impeccably dressed as usual. Both also appeared to be in excellent health, but I did not know that at the time this photograph was taken McReynolds was already stricken with a slow-growing cancer.

Soon Mrs. Savage began writing from Washington that the Justice's health was failing at last. I was then living in New York City, and in August 1946, she replied to a letter of mine as follows:

Yesterday I went to Walter Reed Hospital by appointment. The Justice is now so ill that he cannot see anyone for more than a few minutes. It is difficult for him to talk as it takes his strength. Moreover he has hiccoughs all the time and that makes trying to talk more difficult and increases the intensity of hiccoughing. The nurse said that when the disease reaches a certain stage the end will come rapidly. He has not reached that stage and may not for sometime.

Yesterday he remarked that he was a very sick man.

On the 8th of June I began going out with the Justice to Walter Reed where the doctors would see him for half an hour and sometimes much longer. In the evenings he would ask me to play Chinese checkers, just to divert his thoughts and not be alone.

The Justice had cancer of the stomach and knew it. . . .

The Justice suggested my going again tomorrow—evidently did not want me today. I know of only two of his friends who see him. In fact nearly everyone is away.

Really there seems to be nothing that anyone can do.

Either Mrs. Savage or Harry then wrote a few days later saying that the Justice's condition had become worse and asking if I cared to see him before it was "too late." This request caused me considerable soul-searching to say the least. At first I decided to take a Saturday train from New York to Washington and spend a few minutes with McReynolds at Walter Reed Hospital. "How lonely he must be!" I thought. "Harry is now messenger to another Justice. . . . Who is now doing all the things for him that Harry used to take care of so faithfully?" There was never any indication, of course, that the Justice requested I come to see him. If there had been I undoubtedly would have gone, but to call on him unannounced and without any invitation was something I just did not care to do.

In subsequent correspondence with Mrs. Savage and with Harry, I was able to follow the Justice's rapid decline. There was now a placard on the door of his room reading, "No Admittance," but he had written the following on a card: "Please allow Mrs. Savage to come any time that she is willing to do so." When Mrs. Savage did visit the Justice, she never inquired about his condition or asked how he felt. She wrote that he seemed to appreciate her doing this.

Apparently his nephews did not journey from Los Angeles, but his brother arrived from that city before the end. This was Dr. John P. McReynolds, whom I had met in the fall of 1936.

In 1953 Mrs. Savage wrote, "I think it was about 3 days or less before he died that some officious person telegraphed his brother to come. This I knew would displease him." I was then certain that I had made the correct decision in not going to Washington myself. If McReynolds would be displeased in seeing his own brother, then he couldn't have [wanted me to arrive] on the scene unannounced.

Dr. McReynolds left Washington to return to Los Angeles on Friday, August 23, in the apparent belief—so the newspapers said—that the patient was improving. He was scarcely on the train, however, before the Justice developed signs of broncho-pneumonia and a failing heart which did not respond to treatment. The doctor was intercepted when he reached Chicago, and he returned east again but apparently by train and not by air. The Justice sank rapidly, and he died at 9:05 P.M. on Saturday, August 24. *Only physicians and hospital attendants were at his bedside at the time, and not a single relative or old friend was present.* The Justice, therefore, died as he had lived—aloof and alone—but perhaps he preferred it that way. His brother did not reach Washington again until Sunday morning, August 25.

McReynolds' will requested that he be buried in Elkton, Kentucky, a town of twelve hundred persons in the southwestern part of the state, near the Tennessee border. It was there that the funeral was held. The Supreme Court appointed an official representative to accompany the body to Elkton along with Dr. McReynolds. This was Mr. Thomas E. Waggaman, the Marshal of the Court.

Six Elkton businessmen, all friends of the Justice, bore the casket to the little Christian Church of Elkton, where services were held at 2:00 P.M. on Thursday the twenty-ninth. A brief scripture was read and then a prayer was offered. The entire services lasted less than five minutes. The casket was then taken to Glenwood Cemetery, where McReynolds was buried in the family plot beside his parents.

Thus passed James Clark McReynolds, an Associate Justice of the Supreme Court of the United States for over twenty-six years. The press commented that he once served as Secretary to United States Senator Howell E. Jackson, who later became a Supreme Court Justice.[4] In 1913 President Wilson

---

4. McReynolds never mentioned this fact to me. I have since wondered why he, having once been a secretary himself, was not more responsive to the needs of Harry, Mary, and myself.

appointed McReynolds to a cabinet position—that of Attorney General—but McReynolds' career in that capacity soon became stormy and controversial. Once in Washington he was not able to remain on friendly terms with a number of prominent men in the government, [including the Secretary of the Treasury]. "Thereafter negotiations between the two departments were carried on through the President," the press commented in one news item, and before long Wilson solved the difficulty by appointing McReynolds to the Supreme Court in August 1914 to succeed Justice Horace Harmon Lurton, who had died on July 12, 1914. *This appointment would surely rank as one of the greatest mistakes of Wilson's career.* McReynolds was then confirmed by the Senate on August 29, 1914, and he took the oath of office on September 5, 1914.[5] His first opinion was handed down on November 30, 1914, and his last one on January 20, 1941—twenty-six years and almost two months later.

On August 27, 1946—three days after Justice McReynolds' death—his will was filed with the Register of Wills in the District of Columbia. In his will the Justice's language is direct, to the point, and somewhat disjointed. (This was characteristic of his judicial opinions.) Harry received five thousand dollars and Mary's bequest totaled fifteen hundred dollars. I do not know how long Mary worked for the Justice, but I was glad to learn that she and Harry had at least been remembered. I then recalled how they used to sit in the kitchen of the Justice's apartment and talk in subdued tones about the possibility of being remembered in McReynolds' will. If they worked long and faithfully, perhaps he—a bachelor—would help free them from financial worry in their old age.

Harry served as messenger for the Justice from 1914 until 1941—a total of more than twenty-six years.[6] Therefore, the Justice's bequest of five thousand dollars to him amounted to a little less than twenty dollars a year for the twenty-six years. There were many provisions in the will, but no person, charity, or institution received more than ten thousand dollars. *Cash bequests to relatives, friends, and charities totaled $190,350.00.*

---

5. Harry Parker then began his long service as the Justice's messenger. I remember Harry saying that horses and buggies were still being used in Washington at that time. (In fact, Justice Brandeis was photographed driving his horse as late as 1919.) McReynolds also drove, or perhaps Harry did, but Harry said that the new Justice proved difficult from the very beginning—even complaining about the way Harry placed the blanket in the carriage.

6. [Editors' note: Obituaries reported that Parker began working for McReynolds in 1919, not 1914, as Knox believed. See, e.g., "Parker Rites Will Be Held on Thursday," *Washington Post*, Nov. 4, 1953, p. 22; "Warren, 5 Associates at Court Aide's Rites," *New York Times*, Nov. 6, 1953, p. 27.]

Two memorial services were held in Washington in memory of the Justice, [the traditional meeting of the Bar of the Supreme Court and the Officers of the Court on November 12, 1947, and the traditional presentation of "Resolutions" of the bar to the Court on March 31, 1948.[7]] Later on a sixty-three-page pamphlet—which also contained the Justice's picture—was printed and distributed to all interested parties. I requested a copy of this pamphlet since I had not been able to be present at either of the memorial proceedings.

As the years passed by I kept in touch with Harry, and he often ended his letters by writing, "Mary sends her regards and hopes you are fine." In the spring of 1953, however, Harry contracted pneumonia. He made a partial recovery but soon his health began failing, and he passed away on Monday, November 2, in that year. Harry's funeral was held on the following Thursday [and was attended by Chief Justice Earl Warren and Justices Robert H. Jackson, Felix Frankfurter, Tom C. Clark, Sherman Minton, and Harold H. Burton, according to the *New York Times* obituary[8]].

The last time I was in Washington [was 1954, and after visiting the Mellon Art Gallery,[9] I seized the impulse to hail a taxi.] "Take me to 2400 Sixteenth Street, Northwest," I told the driver. "It is the big apartment house on Sixteenth Street across from Meridian Park."

"I know which one it is," he replied. "Nobody could miss that address!" And as I settled back in the cab I had a strange feeling that it was June 1936 again, and that I was going to 2400 for the very first time. When we finally reached our destination, everything seemed about the same. As I entered the great apartment building, I walked through the familiar lobby as I had done so often in the old days, and I instinctively felt that I should stop at the desk and pick up the Justice's afternoon mail. And when I stepped into the elevator, I realized with surprise that the negro woman who was operating it was the same one who had worked in the building when I lived there. When we arrived at the fifth floor I left the elevator, and as the door closed behind me I found myself standing alone in the hall I remembered so well. I turned and walked quietly down the long corridor to the entrance of apartment 507.

As I stood before that door I had a strange feeling that if I would just press the bell the door would be opened once again by Harry, and that the Justice

7. See 334 U.S. v (1948).

8. [Editors' note: *New York Times,* note 6 *supra.*]

9. [Editors' note: Now the National Gallery of Art.]

would soon appear and announce that he was ready to drive to Court again after inquiring whether I had all the necessary briefs and papers with me. The same numbers, "5 0 7," were still on the door—those large and silvery figures which I had seen for the first time in June 1936. Even the heavy carpeting on the fifth floor seemed exactly the same as I had known it.

For several minutes I stood alone in the deserted hall and thought to myself, "Where are you now? Where have you gone? I have come back, back here, and don't you know I have returned?"

Afterword

THE PERSONAL drama of the 1936–37 Supreme Court term which John Knox so richly detailed had political and constitutional consequences that stretched far beyond his account. The bitter political debate over the Court-packing plan split the New Deal coalition and severely damaged Roosevelt's presidency.[1] When the Court appeared to capitulate to Roosevelt in the spring of 1937, both on state regulatory power[2] and the scope of federal power over interstate commerce,[3] the reason for the president's plan was deflated. Justice Willis Van Devanter's resignation near the end of the term symbolized the defeat of the old constitutional guard and made continued pressure on the Court, to use Justice McReynolds' ill-chosen allusion, seem like bad sportsmanship.[4] The president's bill died in committee over the summer, but the doctrinal ramifications of what wags called the "switch in time that saved nine"[5] did not begin to become clear until late in the following term. Tucked away in the fourth footnote to an otherwise dull

---

1. See generally, William E. Leuchtenburg, *The Supreme Court Reborn* (New York: Oxford University Press, 1995), chapter 5.

2. *West Coast Hotel Co. v. Parrish*, 300 U.S. 379 (1937).

3. *National Labor Relations Board (NLRB) v. Jones & Laughlin Steel Corp.*, 301 U.S. 1 (1937) and related cases.

4. See chapter 10.

5. Edward S. Corwin to Homer Cummings, May 19, 1937, Corwin Papers, Princeton University, quoted in Leuchtenburg, "Comment: FDR's Court-Packing Plan: A Second Life, a Second Death," 1985 Duke L. J. 673 n. 2.

opinion, the Court announced, for all intents and purposes, the new metes and bounds of judicial review. Written by Justice Harlan Fiske Stone, the footnote declared that different types of legislation demanded different degrees of judicial superintendence: economic regulation, which the Four Horseman had often invalidated on various grounds, would now enjoy deferential treatment, but laws appearing to infringe the Bill of Rights or the Due Process and Equal Protection Clauses of the Fourteenth Amendment would be "subjected to more exacting judicial scrutiny."[6] In other words, the Court would by and large leave the control of the economy to the states and to Congress, but would use its power to protect those rights and groups—religion, speech, and "discrete and insular minorities"[7]—that by definition were less likely than economic interests to be vindicated in the political process. The two-tiered approach became, despite its modest origin in the margin of a now-forgotten case, the theoretical axis of modern judicial review. Taken together, the decisions in the springs of 1937 and 1938 constituted what would later be called the Constitutional Revolution of 1937,[8] a fundamental redefinition of the Supreme Court's role.

By the time the "footnote 4" theory was announced, Justice Sutherland had joined Van Devanter in retirement. Justice Butler wrote a separate opinion concurring in the decision; only Justice McReynolds dissented. Although McReynolds remained on the Court for almost three more years, he was a man shaken in spirit and increasingly broken in health. He dissented more than ever, although much of the fire had flamed out of his rhetoric. On a personal level, the hidden tenderness that Justice Holmes had detected earlier in his career began to materialize publicly during World War II, as Knox notes in chapter 14; his adoption of thirty-three English children victimized by the blitzkrieg and his generous contribution to the Save the Children Fund were warmly admired, as were the numerous charitable gifts under his will. Knox criticized McReynolds for giving so little to Harry Parker, but he neglected to

---

6. *United States v. Carolene Products Co.*, 304 U.S. 144, 152–153 n. 4 (1938).

7. Ibid.

8. See generally, Leuchtenburg, note 1 *supra*, at chapter 8. Leuchtenburg provides the classic account of the Court's volte-face. For a different view—that the Court had already started to change direction in 1934 with *Nebbia v. New York*, 291 U.S. 502 (1934)—see Barry Cushman, *Rethinking the New Deal Court: The Structure of a Constitutional Revolution* (New York: Oxford, 1998). The debate is considered in several essays commissioned by the *Yale Law Journal* and published in vol. 108, no. 8 (June 1999). See also G. Edward White, *The Constitution and the New Deal* (Cambridge, Mass.: Harvard University Press, 2000).

consider that Parker remained on the payroll of the Supreme Court (he served as Justice Robert H. Jackson's messenger until his death in 1953 at age seventy-four) and that McReynolds probably assumed he was less in need of a bene-faction than Mary Diggs, who was not a Court employee. In fact, Mrs. Diggs' legacy of fifteen hundred dollars was one thousand dollars more than McReynolds initially planned and was prompted by her unstinting service during his final illness.

Over time, McReynolds faded as a figure in the history of the Supreme Court. He was best remembered for his thundering extemporaneous dissent-ing statement in the Gold Clause Cases,[9] which Knox discusses in chapter 5, and for his widely publicized bigotry. His opinions were too few and too brisk to produce any doctrinal ferment, and, with two exceptions, too dated in out-look to have any enduring influence. The two exceptions were a pair of deci-sions in the 1920s in which McReynolds found that the Due Process clause of the Fourteenth Amendment protected parents who wanted their children to learn German in public schools[10] and parents who wanted to comply with compulsory schooling laws by sending their children to sectarian schools.[11] The decisions were products of the free-wheeling days when the Court dis-covered "fundamental rights" in the Due Process clauses, but, with an irony that would have infuriated McReynolds, they were revived a generation later to help buttress first the Court's announcement of a constitutional right to privacy in *Griswold v. Connecticut*[12] and then Justice Harry A. Blackmun's opinion for the Court in *Roe v. Wade*,[13] upholding a pregnant woman's consti-tutional right to choose between abortion and carrying a pregnancy to term.

Notwithstanding the circumstances of his separation from the Supreme Court, John Knox kept up his correspondence with many who continued to

---

9. *Norman v. Baltimore & Ohio Railroad Co.*, 294 U.S. 240 (1935); *Nortz v. United States*, 294 U.S. 317 (1935); *Perry v. United States*, 294 U.S. 330 (1935).

10. *Meyer v. Nebraska*, 262 U.S. 390 (1923). McReynolds wrote that the "liberty" of the due process clause includes an individual's right "to contract, to engage in any of the common occupations of life, to acquire useful knowledge, to marry, to establish a home and bring up children, to worship God according to the dictates of his conscience, and generally to enjoy privileges, essential to the orderly pursuit of happiness by free men." Id. at 399.

11. *Pierce v. Society of Sisters*, 268 U.S. 510 (1925).

12. 381 U.S. 479 (1965).

13. 410 U.S. 113, 152 (1973). See also David J. Garrow, *Liberty and Sexuality: The Right to Privacy and the Making of Roe v. Wade*, rev. ed. (Berkeley: University of California Press, 1998).

work in the building after he returned to Chicago after sitting for the D.C. bar examination. He dropped notes periodically to Justice Van Devanter and to Mrs. Savage, exchanged gossipy letters with Gertrude Jenkins, Justice Stone's (and later Justice Felix Frankfurter's) secretary, and, of course, with Harry Parker. Knox and Parker had little to share other than bittersweet memories, and Knox's letters soon became requests for autographs of newly appointed justices or for official photographs of the Court signed by all nine members. As hostilities in Europe seemed more imminent, Knox became more and more preoccupied with the costs of war and began focusing his avocational energies on isolationist tracts, one of which made its way into the *Congressional Record*.[14] After the war, personal issues overtook Knox, and correspondence with his extended Supreme Court family—or what was left of it following the deaths of McReynolds and Van Devanter—went into eclipse.

John Knox's experiences as a law clerk could never be far from his active memory, however. In 1962, twenty-five years after ignominiously completing his clerkship with Justice McReynolds, Knox looked back on his career and concluded that "[i]n many ways I am a pathetic failure."[15] Comparing himself to his peers—he was then fifty-five—he had "no money, am thousands of dollars in debt and just hanging on to the status quo by a thread."[16] The sleek young man about Washington of October term 1936 had become a pudgy, sour, and chronically ill middle-aged man with no career accomplishments and bitter recriminations, mostly directed at himself. He tried to diagnose his failed promise in a series of diary entries during June of 1963, two months after he finished the first draft of his memoir. The downfall began, of course, with McReynolds: "June, 1937. In this month my decline began. Justice McReynolds 'fired' me thirteen days before the end of my year's term and I wished to take the District of Columbia bar examination. I did write it— three days of hell—and failed the exam."[17]

Knox returned to Chicago and to the rambling six-bedroom house in Oak Park which his father had purchased in 1923 when the family relocated for the third time since Knox's birth. The elder Knox ran a mail-order business sell-

14. John Knox, "British War Aims," Aug. 4, 1941 (extension of remarks by Sen. Gerald P. Nye of North Dakota), 87 Cong. Rec. A3722, 77th Congress, 1st Session).

15. Knox diary, December 28, 1962, Knox Papers, Box 20, Georgetown University Library (cited hereafter as "Georgetown Collection").

16. Knox diary, June 18, 1963, Box 20, Georgetown Collection.

17. Ibid.

ing "how-to" books for salesmen which he wrote himself, eight in all: *Personality in Action, Salesmanship and Business Efficiency* and *A Modern Course in Salesmanship* were the top sellers, usually to high schools and business colleges. Before the news of his bar failure reached Chicago, John Knox had landed an enviable position with a large (forty lawyers) and prosperous Chicago law firm, then called Mayer, Meyer, Austrian, and Platt. He quickly disliked the work ("writing memoranda of law and sitting in a huge library without even a desk to call my own"[18]) and felt he did not "fit in with the Jewish-Gentile combination of a high-powered and extremely successful Chicago law firm."[19] His failure of the D.C. bar blotted his copy-book with the firm, and when he failed the Illinois bar in March of 1938, he was fired.[20] "They were as glad to get rid of me as I was of them," he later confided to his diary.[21]

Knox then cashed in on a family friendship that he had cultivated throughout law school and during his tenure in Washington with Frank J. Loesch, the aging senior partner (he was then eighty-six) of Loesch, Scofield, Loesch, and Burke and recently retired chairman of the Chicago Crime Commission. The atmosphere at the new firm was more to Knox's taste, the workload was lighter, and the client list was suitably impressive—the Pennsylvania Railroad, the American Medical Association, Holland-America Lines, and RCA, among others. All went well until September of 1938 when Knox failed the Illinois bar for the second time in six months. He did not successfully negotiate the bar examination until March of the following year. He wrote several friends that he enjoyed his new firm, even though he was only paid one hundred dollars a month: "In Washington I was unhappy with McReynolds on $230 a month. Here, I am happy on $100."[22] Just when his professional world finally seemed to be in order, the "firm began falling apart."[23] Men left for the

18. Knox to James Gordon, June 8, 1938, Knox Papers, D'Angelo Law Library, University of Chicago Law School (cited hereafter as "Chicago Collection").

19. Knox diary, June 18, 1963, Box 20, Georgetown Collection.

20. He scored 340 with passing set at 350; a perfect score was 500. He tried to mitigate his failure in a letter to family friends in Chicago by pointing out how close he came to passing, but he added: "Since I had failed all the Practice Act questions, it was finally decided to fail me on the bar examination notwithstanding my Harvard and Supreme Court experience." Knox to Mr. and Mrs. Frank J. Loesch, May 29, 1938, Chicago Collection.

21. Diary fragment, n.d. (probably summer 1938), Chicago Collection.

22. Knox to James Gordon, n.d. (probably May or June 1939), Chicago Collection.

23. Ibid.

armed services, business fell off, and Knox decided to cut his losses by going to work for the War Production Board in November of 1942.

He spent most of the war as assistant regional counsel, War Production Board, Region VI—initially an eleven-state and later a four-state area covering the Midwest. A change in regional counsel put him out of a job, so in December of 1944 Knox moved to New York, where he secured a position—"for the duration" only, he was told—with the Wall Street firm of Cravath, Swaine, & Moore. In hindsight, he concluded that he had "made a bad mistake in not trying to secure a job in Chicago. . . . To accept a job only for the duration of the conflict was a fatal error on my part." He worked at Cravath, largely on contract business for Westinghouse, until January of 1947, when he was "asked to go": "I was now 39 years old and completely out of a job. The men were coming back from the war and the labor market for lawyers was glutted all of a sudden." While he was with Cravath, his father, who had been combating leukemia since 1942, died, and the wound must have cut deeper because Knox arrived back in Chicago after an all-night train trip "an hour after he died."[24]

From January to November of 1947, John Knox engaged in his most successful and most lucrative ($124 per week in take-home pay) legal work yet. He worked alone drafting and negotiating theatrical contracts for the Marquis George de Cuevas, the grandson-in-law to John D. Rockefeller, Sr. Knox worked with actors and ballet dancers, and he formed lasting friendships with several performers, notably Oleg Tupine, Andre Eglevsky, and Fernando Alonso—all major ballet figures of the period. Again, as soon as fortune smiled on Knox, his luck turned. The Rockefeller money was suddenly turned off, and Knox was out of a job.

With his father dead and his mother struggling to keep the book company afloat, Knox decided to return to Chicago and take over the family business. The books were outdated, in both tone and strategy, and Knox set about rewriting three of them—one a year—between 1948 and 1950. With little income to the company, he was forced to borrow on his life insurance policy and to cash in series "E" government bonds to finance reprinting of the three new editions. Orders initially picked up, but the business soon fell into a steady decline. From a gross income of ten to twelve thousand dollars per year in the late 1940s, revenues dropped 50 percent and never exceeded five thousand dollars annually for the next decade. By the spring of 1956, Knox felt he was "at the end of my financial rope—to say the least," so he answered a

24. All quotations in the paragraph are from Knox diary, June 18, 1963, Box 20, Georgetown Collection.

newspaper advertisement for a job—a "blind ad," he called it in his diary, suggesting a source of employment beneath his station. The position was as an adjuster for the Allstate Insurance Company, for whom he henceforth labored locally in Oak Park for three and one-half years before receiving a promotion to the Allstate Claim Office in downtown Chicago. Having previously been passed over several times for promotion, and growing weary of field work, the new position "'saved' me at the eleventh hour." [25]

Knox finally had a job that suited him, in part because he felt he was "dazzling successful from the beginning." [26] He was also out of the field—the "negro area" and "white hill-billy area" which his service territory covered and which in time he found to be a "ghastly nightmare." [27] The new duties were light and well-suited to his meticulous passion for organization. There was plenty of time for lunches away from the office, early departures for the symphony or opera, and plenty of odd snatches of time to work on his memoir. His only remaining disappointment was his failure to attract a publisher for the memoir. After reviewing outlines and sample chapters over a period of several years, Simon & Schuster rejected the project in 1964. Knox tried to find an agent to push the manuscript, but he was unwilling to release more than two sample chapters, and the effort was half-hearted at most.

In 1973 John Knox retired from Allstate, which was a subsidiary of Sears. The family business was defunct, and he was living alone in the rambling, and now under-maintained, old house in Oak Park, pondering his future. His retirement finances were based on Sears stock acquired through profit-sharing plans, and the stock was trading at $123 when he left the company. Believing that the stock would rise and split, he held his shares even as the price began to fall steadily; by 1979, the price had dropped to $20 and Knox was again living on a financial knife-edge. He kept his thermostat set at 55 degrees during the winter, sold some family heirlooms, and pinched pennies for the rest of his life. He even abandoned a long-standing hobby—keeping birds (he was sometime recording secretary for the Illinois Budgerigar Society).

But he continued to work on his memoir, making small changes here and there but not fundamentally changing the manuscript that had become an obsession of nearly three decades. Unable to find a publisher for the massive and quirky work, Knox returned to a format and to forums he had first explored

25. Ibid.

26. Ibid.

27. Ibid.

shortly after his clerkship—short biographical sketches in professional journals.[28] In 1974 he published a note recounting his associations with John
Henry Wigmore, whom he had known while a student at Northwestern,[29] and
in 1975 he recounted his luncheon with Justice Holmes in 1930.[30] He wrote up
a number of other brief historical sketches on various topics,[31] but none was
published until 1983 when the quarterly newsletter of the Supreme Court Historical Society printed an unsigned account of Justice McReynolds' career,
which was accompanied by several photographs, including one taken by Knox
in 1936.[32] Then, in 1984, the Supreme Court Historical Society published in its
Yearbook what was in effect a lengthy précis of Knox's monograph in the form
of a recollection of Chief Justice Charles Evans Hughes, focusing on the tumultuous 1936–37 term.[33]

John Knox was seventy-seven years old—two years older than McReynolds was in the year of the clerkship—when his reminiscences, even in highly
abbreviated form, finally were in print. What he hoped would be the first of
many publications turned out to be the last. And shortly after the *Yearbook*
came out, bad luck struck again. In January of 1985, Knox was diagnosed with
prostate cancer, and he began an agonizing decade of doctors and medica-

28. "Recollections of Justice Cardozo," 21 Chi. Bar Rec. 9 (Oct. 1939); "Some Correspondence with
Holmes and Pollock," 21 Chi. Bar Rec. 219 (March 1940); "Justice George Sutherland," 24 Chi. Bar
Rec. 16 (Oct. 1942).

29. "John Henry Wigmore, 1863–1943," 70 *The Brief: Phi Delta Phi Quarterly* 88 (Winter 1974–75).

30. "A Luncheon with Justice Oliver Wendell Holmes, Jr., and Alger Hiss," 71 *The Brief: Phi Delta
Phi Quarterly* 96 (Winter 1975–76). Knox later wrote that the visit was an "enormous disappointment," because Holmes was the only Civil War veteran he interviewed who "clammed up"
and refused to discuss his battle experiences in detail, "and I still feel this disappointment more
than a half-century later." Memorandum, Sept. 29, 1981, Chicago Collection. See also Knox Papers, Box 2, folder 14, Harvard Law School Library (cited hereafter as "Harvard Collection").

31. For example, "Unpublished Eyewitness Accounts by American Civil War Veterans," read to
the Chicago Literary Club (more commonly known as the "Cliff Dwellers") Oct. 24, 1977; "Unpublished Eyewitness Accounts by British Aviators in World War I (all shot down by Baron Man-
fred von Richthofen)," read to the Cliff Dwellers, March 26, 1979. These and other fragmentary
manuscripts are collected in Box 2, Harvard Collection. Knox also read excerpts from his memoir to the Cliff Dwellers in 1954. See the foreword, note 1.

32. "James C. McReynolds: Last of the Old Guard," 5 *Quarterly: The Supreme Court Historical Society* 4 (Winter 1983). Knox obviously contributed both information and language to the sketch,
although he does not receive writing credit.

33. "Some Comments on Chief Justice Hughes," *1984 Yearbook: Supreme Court Historical Society* 34.

tions. His home was burglarized and many of his prized photographs were stolen. Friends, and even strangers—who wrote him out of the blue just as he had written celebrities as a youth—indulged his generosity and carted away autographed letters and pictures, sometimes literally by the bag-full. The collection of papers that he sold to the Georgetown University Library in 1992 contains only a fraction of the photos and autographed memorabilia he had collected.[34] Slowly stripped of his treasured artifacts, Knox was left only with his lifelong passion for the past and what even he recognized as a tendency to self-pity. He never married and his last years were visited constantly by what he once referred to in his diary as the "dragon of loneliness."[35] By his ninetieth year, he was painfully infirm and prepared, almost eager, for death; it came on February 27, 1997. After his passing, two of his final requests were honored: his obituary noted his memberships in lineage societies (the Society of Mayflower Descendants, the Society of Colonial Wars, the Sons of the American Revolution, and the Society of the War of 1812),[36] and at his funeral service his casket was draped in a Confederate flag.

34. The collection has not been completely processed, although a preliminary inventory has been prepared.

35. Knox diary, Nov. 25, 1936, Chicago Collection.

36. "John Knox," *Chicago Tribune*, March 3, 1997, p. M5.

Index